The Global Testing Culture:
shaping education policy, perceptions, and practice

The Global Testing Culture:
shaping education policy,
perceptions, and practice

Edited by
William C. Smith

Oxford Studies in Comparative Education
Series Editor: David Phillips

SYMPOSIUM
BOOKS

Symposium Books
PO Box 204, Didcot, Oxford OX11 9ZQ, United Kingdom
www.symposium-books.co.uk

Published in the United Kingdom, 2016

ISBN 978-1-873927-72-4

This publication is also available on a subscription basis
as Volume 25 Number 1 of *Oxford Studies in Comparative Education*
(ISSN 0961-2149)

© Symposium Books Ltd, 2016

All rights reserved. No part of this publication may be reproduced,
stored in a retrieval system or transmitted in any form or by any means,
electronic, mechanical, photocopying, recording or otherwise, without
the prior permission of the publisher.

Printed and bound in the United Kingdom by Hobbs the Printers, Southampton
www.hobbs.uk.com

Contents

Chapter 1. **William C. Smith**. An Introduction to the Global Testing Culture, 7

SECTION 1: THE GLOBAL TESTING CULTURE AND THE INTERNATIONAL EDUCATION AGENDA
Chapter 2. **D. Brent Edwards Jr**. A Perfect Storm: the political economy of community-based management, teacher accountability, and impact evaluations in El Salvador and the global reform agenda, 25

Chapter 3. **Rie Kijima & Jane Leer**. Legitimacy, State-Building, and Contestation in Education Policy Development: Chile's involvement in cross-national assessments, 43

Chapter 4. **Hilla Aurén & Devin Joshi**. Teaching the World that Less is More: global education testing and the Finnish national brand, 63

Chapter 5. **Ji Liu**. Student Achievement and PISA Rankings: policy effects or cultural explanations?, 85

Chapter 6. **Angeline M. Barrett**. Measuring Learning Outcomes and Education for Sustainable Development: the new education developmental goal, 101

Chapter 7. **Karen E. Andreasen & Christian Ydesen**. The International Space of the Danish Testing Community in the Post-war Years, 115

SECTION 2: THE ABSENCE OF FORMATIVE TESTING AND THE POLITICS OF ACCOUNTABILITY
Chapter 8. **Sumera Ahsan & William C. Smith**. Facilitating Student Learning: a comparison of classroom and accountability assessment, 131

Chapter 9. **Renáta Tichá & Brian Abery**. Beyond the Large-Scale Testing of Basic Skills: using formative assessment to facilitate learning, 153

Chapter 10. **Anthony Somerset**. Questioning across the Spectrum: pedagogy, selection examinations, and assessment systems in low-income countries, 171

Chapter 11. **Sean W. Mulvenon & Sandra G. Bowman**. An Evaluation of how the 'Politics of K-12 Testing' Impact the Effectiveness of Global Testing Programs, 193

Chapter 12. **Mariam Orkodashvili**. How Much Stakes for Tests? Public Schooling, Private Tutoring, and Equilibrium, 213

SECTION 3: THE GLOBAL TESTING CULTURE IN NATIONAL CONTEXT

Chapter 13. **Kristine Kousholt & Bjørn Hamre**. Testing and School Reform in Danish Education: an analysis informed by the use of the 'dispositive', 231

Chapter 14. **Pearl J. Chung & Hyeonwoo Chea**. South Korea's Accountability Policy System and National Achievement Test, 249

Chapter 15. **David Balwanz**. The Discursive Hold of the Matric: is there space for a new vision for secondary education in South Africa?, 261

Chapter 16. **Tracey Burns, Patrick Blanchenay, & Florian Koester**. Horizontal Accountability, Municipal Capacity, and the use of Data: a case study of Sweden, 279

Notes on Contributors, 297

CHAPTER 1

An Introduction to the Global Testing Culture

WILLIAM C. SMITH

ABSTRACT The global testing culture permeates all areas of education, reconceptualizing the role of educational actors, the aims of education, and the accepted practices of education, as well as the general position of education in society. Characterized by census-based standardized testing with links to high-stakes outcomes, the global testing culture can be seen in the expansion of testing and accountability systems around the world and the increasingly 'common-sense' notion that testing is synonymous with accountability, which is synonymous with education quality. This chapter describes the foundational attributes, including the core assumptions, values, and cultural models, that define the normative expectations of actors in the global testing culture. The final section introduces the rest of the volume, which seeks to explore how the global testing culture is embedded in and reinforced by policy and practices of stakeholders at all levels, and to provide case studies exploring the incorporation of testing in national contexts.

Introduction

The past thirty years have seen a rapid expansion of testing, exposing students worldwide to tests that are now, more than ever, standardized and linked to high-stakes outcomes. The use of testing as a policy tool has been legitimized within international educational development to measure education quality in the vast majority of countries worldwide. The assumed, taken-for-granted, nature of testing can be described as the global testing culture and permeates all aspects of education, from financing, to parental involvement, to teacher and student beliefs and practices. The reinforcing nature of the global testing culture leads to an environment where testing becomes synonymous with accountability, which becomes synonymous with education quality.

William C. Smith

    The global testing culture has yet to be acknowledged and clearly described. In the United States, Moses and Nanna (2007) have identified a national testing culture where the practice is so common that no one questions the legitimacy of standardized tests. Following the massive expansion of testing after the passage of No Child Left Behind in the USA which mandated annual testing between grades 3 and 8 as well as once between grades 10 and 12, popular media cautioned the public that students were being over-tested and school time was being reallocated to test taking. Scherer (2009) reported that one teacher spent up to 40 school days a year administering standardized tests, and this did not take into account the time in test preparation or review. In 2006, Valerie Strauss of the *Washington Post* completed a series on testing. The series' first installment, 'The Rise of the Testing Culture', describes the process some pre-schools go through to ensure their students are ready for testing, which can start as early as age six. Although present within a national context, a global culture which goes beyond national boundaries has not yet been clearly articulated.

    This chapter fills this void by describing the foundational attributes of the global testing culture. The first section provides a brief review of the expansion of testing worldwide and the reduction of assessment diversity. The second section explores alternative global movements or phenomena that hint at but do not concretely articulate a global testing culture – including the 'global education compact', 'global education reform movement', and 'age of accountability' – before using World Culture theory (Ramirez, 2003; Boli, 2005) to define the global testing culture. The subsequent section uses Groeschl and Doherty's (2000) metaphor of culture as concentric rings to describe the core assumptions, values, and cultural models of the global testing culture. The final section introduces the other contributions in this volume and highlights how they contribute to the dialogue around the global testing culture.

A Swell in Testing

The expansion of testing can be captured through the increased number of countries participating in international assessments and conducting national assessments, as well as the overall rise in the number of standardized tests that schools administer. International or cross-national assessments were first initiated in the 1960s. However, it was the creation of the Programme for International Student Assessment (PISA) and the Progress in International Reading Literacy Study (PIRLS) at the turn of the twenty-first century that led to a substantial shift in the number of countries participating in the three largest international assessments – PISA, PIRLS, and the Trends in International Mathematics and Science Study (TIMSS) – increasing participation by approximately 50% between 1999 and 2012 (Smith, 2014). Additionally, early grade reading assessments (ERGA) – oral assessments established in 2006 by RTI International (Gove & Wetterberg, 2011) – have been administered in over 60 countries in its first eight years of existence (UNESCO, 2015).

The growth of national assessments has been well documented, with Phelps (2000) at the end of the twenty-first century concluding, somewhat prophetically, that there is a 'clear trend towards adding, not dropping testing programs' (p. 19). Between 1995 and 2006 the number of countries that conducted a national assessment more than doubled, increasing from 28 to 67 (Benavot & Tanner, 2007), and from 2000 to 2013 over 1100 national assessments were conducted globally, spanning both the developed and developing world (UNESCO, 2015). At the same time, and largely as a consequence of these international and national assessments, more and more standardized tests are being administered in classrooms. Tracking prevalence using PISA questionnaires, the number of schools globally that conducted two or more standardized external exams annually increased from approximately one in eight schools in 2000 to nearly one in three schools in 2009 (Smith, 2014).

The growth of testing was accompanied by a change in aims and characteristics. Most noticeably, tests are increasingly standardized and linked to high-stakes outcomes. Tests are considered high-stakes if they have 'real or perceived consequences for students, staff, or schools' (Chapman & Snyder, 2000, p. 458). Following conservative party control in the USA and UK during the 1980s, the high stakes of testing has transitioned from its traditional focus, students, to a more central focus on teachers and administrators (Smith, 2014). With multiple actors held to high stakes at different times and to different levels, accountability becomes an entrenched feature in education. The emphasis on accountability reduces the diversity in types of testing (Tichá & Abery, 2016), making it difficult to distinguish between examinations – where high stakes are attached to student achievement scores – and assessments – which are designed to inform and improve instruction (Organization for Economic Co-operation and Development [OECD], 2011) – as both are co-opted under the umbrella of high-stakes standardized testing. These high-stakes standardized tests, administered to all students in a target grade or age, form that foundation of the global testing culture.

A Global Testing Culture?

The presence of a testing culture in the global arena has been hinted at through other global education policy trends. The establishment of global education goals, such as those found in Education for All, the Millennium Development Goals, and the soon to be adopted Sustainable Development Goals, is due, in part, to a convergence of agendas between the traditionally neo-liberal-leaning institutions (i.e. World Bank and International Monetary Foundation) and human rights focused institutions (i.e. United Nations). Mundy (2006) and others (see Prichett, 2004; Sperling & Belu, 2005; Daun

& Mundy, 2011) have identified a series of contested reforms that are supported through this 'global education compact', including 'reducing unit costs of primary education, making good use of the private sector, introducing standardized testing regimes and decentralizing control' (Mundy, 2006, p. 33). Similarly, Sahlberg (2010), in his description of the 'global education reform movement', focuses on the narrowing of curriculum to core subjects, increased between-school competition, and measurable results linked to teacher and school accountability. Additionally, the recent movement towards increased accountability in areas such as security, health, and education led Hopmann (2008) to deem the present era the 'age of accountability'. The rapid rise in accountability in the public sector can lead to a rethinking of how societies deal with themselves and the individuals that live within them. The permeation of these practices can lead to what Dubnick (2005) calls fourth-order accountability where 'the ones held accountable internalize the norms, values, and expectations of the stakeholders' (Hopmann, 2008, p. 422).

Adopting a World Culture theoretical perspective, the *global testing culture* is defined as a culture in which high-stakes standardized testing is accepted as a foundational practice in education and shapes how education is understood in society and used by its stakeholders. The global testing culture is part of an overarching world culture and is self-reinforcing. World Culture theory is a useful lens in describing the global testing culture as it 'focuses not on the power of the actors but on the power of the culture itself' (Ramirez, 2003, p. 252). World Culture theorists are interested in identifying similarities across heterogeneous environments (Boli, 2005). The similar structure and policy in educational systems across the globe (Macnab, 2004), therefore, can be seen as the 'result of shared meanings and values that identify appropriate rules and routines' (Smith, 2014, p. 12; see also Meyer, 1977). Common practices and policies across societies outline the normative scripts or cultural models that legitimate behavior (Meyer et al, 1997; Schofer et al, 2012). Notably, in education, this includes the social construction of norms for students, teachers, parents, administrators, schools, and education systems (Jepperson, 2002). For example, there is a growing international consensus that participation in international testing and the use of a national assessment system are essential in a legitimate education system (Kamens & McNeely, 2010; Meyer & Benavot, 2014). This is due in part to the loan conditionalities set by international finance institutions where 'an expanding number of donor agencies and multilateral organizations are mandating some form of learning assessment to accompany their loans and other aid support' (Kamens & McNeely, 2010, p. 6). Lending practices have been reinforced by rhetoric in the World Bank's Education Sector Strategy 2020 where testing, results, and accountability play a large role (Joshi & Smith, 2012), as well as the voluntary but normative ability of the World Bank's Systems Approach for Better Education Results (SABER) to increase participation in national and international assessments (Smith,

2014). As a result, 'both assessment and testing are likely to increase as more countries become fully integrated in the world polity' (Kamens & McNeely, 2010, p. 22). As the global testing culture spreads, cultural models are internalized by actors and the underlying assumptions and values are no longer questioned (Wiseman et al, 2010). This can lead to a society where test scores become an end in themselves (Froese-Germain, 2001; Booher-Jennings, 2005), the practice of testing becomes synonymous with education quality (Balwanz, 2016), and testing is equated with accountability as testing is seen as 'both a treatment and a monitoring system' (Supovitz, 2009, p. 222).

Describing the Global Testing Culture

Essential to the understanding of any culture is the recognition that culture is socially constructed and provides a template for society across generations (Hoppers, 2009). Figure 1 uses Groeschl and Doherty's (2000) metaphor of culture as concentric rings to illustrate how culture builds from core assumptions to individual behavior. Underlying every culture are basic assumptions about human nature and how the world works. Values then manifest from these assumptions and form the basis for the community's norms (Henslin, 1998) or cultural models (Meyer et al, 1997). Cultural models identify scripts, or appropriate, expected behavior for each role in society. Individuals then act in an environment that is formally and informally regulated and their individual behavior is evaluated against the normative standard and judged as legitimate or deviant (Smith, 2014).

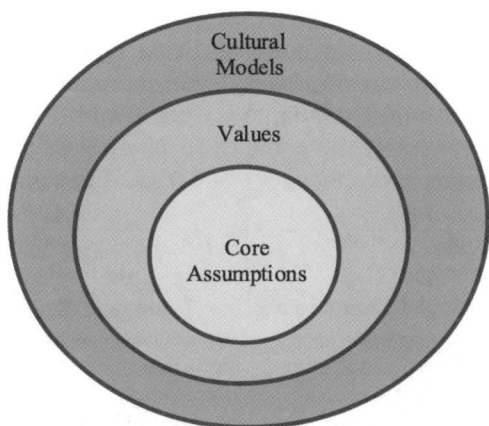

Figure 1. Elements of culture.

Core Assumptions

Core assumptions provide the foundation for the global testing culture. At least two core assumptions can be seen underlying all aspects of the global testing culture: positivism and individualism. *Positivism* assumes that reality can be observed and objectively measured (Abraham, 1994). Comte (1975), an early advocate of positivism, hoped that 'all ideas of quality are reducible to ideas of quantity' (p. 109). Exploring further, however, Comte limited this insight to physical sciences, believing that social phenomena were too complex to be quantified. Although numerous iterations of positivism exist, the one most closely associated with the global testing culture is instrumental positivism as outlined by Gartrell and Gartrell (1996). Central to this form of positivism is the development of hypotheses that can be empirically evaluated through quantitative statistical techniques to form law-like statements.

Individualism can be understood as the belief that when individuals are given freedom to choose, they will act in their own self-interest. Individuals are independent and endowed with rights and freedom (de Tocqueville, 1969). As independent actors, an individual's self-worth is often tied to their personal accomplishments (Hofstede, 1980). Self-interest is situated within the 'constitutional limitation of man's knowledge and interest' (Hayek, 1952, p. 14) where individual actions are motivated by an understanding of the immediate consequences, subject to their known environment. Essential to the individualism at the center of the global testing culture is a belief that people are fully aware of and able to comprehend the information necessary to successfully maneuver within their particular environment.

Values

Values stem from the core assumptions of a culture. Table I presents an important, but not exhaustive, breakdown of some of the dominant values associated with the global testing culture (adapted from Smith, 2014). Although part of the overall world culture, these values speak directly to the global acceptance and encouragement of high-stakes standardized testing.

Values	Description	Relationship to the global testing culture
Education as a human right	Emphasizes education as a human right available to all and important for later life outcomes. Its position as a key factor in both individual and societal development lead to mandatory policies that require all children attend.	To ensure that all students have access to high-quality education, standardized measures and the corresponding accountability is applied.

Academic intelligence	Cognitive and scientific dimensions of intelligence are valued. An emphasis is placed on subjects that emphasize this type of knowledge, namely mathematics and science.	Time spent in less academic subjects, such as visual arts, has diminished. Mathematics and science are two of the three most commonly tested subjects globally (reading is the third).
Faith in science	Scientific findings are recognized as the objective arbiter of truth. Increasingly, quantitative statistics are publicly viewed as synonymous with science.	Faith in science leads to the belief that test scores can accurately capture measures of academic intelligence.
Decentralization	Globally more nations are decentralizing their education system, placing more authority and autonomy at the local level. Decentralization leads to more variant education practices.	External exams are put in place to ensure that education quality is equivalent across heterogeneous communities.
Neoliberalism	Neoliberalism, as an economic system, has been adopted by the majority of countries. It emphasizes open markets, consumer choice, and greater efficiency through decreased government involvement.	Test results provide information to improve consumer choice and overcome the principal–agent problem. Accountability measures are used to measure the efficiency of government education investments.

Table I. Select values of the global testing culture.

Recognizing that education is a human right, available to all regardless of individual capacity, is an important value of the global testing culture (Kamens & McNeely, 2010; Baker, 2014). It speaks too much of the rhetoric surrounding standardized assessments as a great equalizer, able to identify and remedy equity gaps in society (Lemann, 1999). As all individuals have the right to a quality education, test scores and the associated accountability mechanisms are celebrated as an avenue to ensure individual rights are being fulfilled.

Throughout the twentieth century the increasing cognitive intensity of education (Baker et al, 2015) has highlighted academic knowledge as legitimate knowledge (Baker, 2014). Academic knowledge emphasizes metacognition and encourages individuals and institutions to focus on subjects that elicit such knowledge, namely science and mathematics (Wiseman, 2010). Aligned with the Western model of education, the belief that education should be universal expands the traditional restrictions to academic knowledge beyond the elite, claiming that all students can be an engineer or a mathematician (Kamens et al, 1996).

Faith in science draws directly from positivism. The continued emphasis on science as the 'objective arbiter of truth' (Smith, 2014, p. 13) can be seen in the increased number of scientific publications, scientific training courses and programs, and national science programs worldwide (Baker, 2014). An unflinching faith in science suggests that student test scores are able to accurately and objectively measure student achievement and are, therefore, perhaps the only acceptable way to evaluate students, schools, and educators.

Global shifts towards more decentralized education systems (Astiz et al, 2002) left policy makers looking for practices that could sustain quality across diverse communities. Standardized tests were often adopted to compare schools and communities as they adapted national policy to local preferences. Holding educators and schools responsible for student test scores was then seen as 'one way to resolve the dilemma between granting autonomy and authority to educators and keeping them under some political control' (Dorn, 2007, p. 13).

As the last value discussed here, neo-liberalism fuels between-school competition in the hope that competition fuels greater efficiency and quality (Harvey, 2005). Test results provide the information consumers (parents) need to make informed decisions. The choice, or fear of choice, by parents creates market pressure that can shape educator behavior as schools work to ensure adequate student enrolment (Ball, 1993). Additionally, accountability follows a neo-liberal investment model where all investments must be justified and returns recorded (Supovitz, 2009; Smeed & Victory, 2010).

Cultural Models

Values within the global testing culture prescribe the behavioral guidelines for individuals. These guidelines or cultural models affect all actors associated with education, including both direct actors – students, teachers, parents, and government – and indirect actors – businesses, investors, and the larger community. For all actors cultural models outline legitimate behavior specific to their social role. Individual behavior that fails to align with the cultural model provided is considered deviant and formally or informally sanctioned.

Although too numerous to explore in this chapter, two cultural models are included here as examples. First, the labeling of parents as consumers in a neo-liberal market, with access to high-quality, objective information, dictates that parents, as informed consumers acting in the best interest of their family, will evaluate the information and come to an appropriate decision. This decision should be based on the achievement or perceived academic quality of the school, not by such factors as distance or friendliness of staff. Parents that fail to take an active role in the school choice process will be shunned by society (Ball, 1993). Academic literature has already started to chastise parents that are unable or unwilling use test scores when considering their child's schooling, suggesting that their behavior reflects 'how strongly parents care for their children's progress' (Woessman, 2004, p. 4).

In the global testing culture teachers are in a precarious position as they recognize that all students have a right to learn but also follow their own self-interest in a system that links their professional livelihood to student test scores. The result is an expectation that teachers do everything they can to adequately prepare students and help them achieve on tests. Teachers who fail to prepare students for tests are often branded 'bad teachers'. Peers in this situation may 'doubt their colleagues' competence', including questioning their integrity, and the 'colleagues' allegiance to the school's mission to improve test scores' (Booher-Jennings, 2005, p. 254). In addition to being blamed by peers, teachers in schools that have educator performance linked to student test scores also increasingly question their own practice, leading to intense feelings of anxiety and shame (Certo, 2006; Jones & Egley, 2006).

Global Testing Culture Shaping Education: the organization of this book

The chapters collected in this volume further explore how the global testing culture shapes education policy, perceptions, and practice. Divided into three sections, this volume aims to describe the global testing culture, how it is embedded in and reinforced by policy and practices of stakeholders at all levels, and to provide case studies exploring the incorporation of testing into national contexts.

Section 1: The Global Testing Culture and the International Education Agenda

In this section authors explore how national and international level practices help shape the global testing culture, which in turn legitimates and perpetuates state behavior. For example, the World Bank, a critical figure in shaping education policy in the developing world, used El Salvador as a showcase to produce favorable research that promotes community-based accountability of teachers. Brent Edwards examines the political economy surrounding the rise of EDUCO as a model program in El Salvador. EDUCO's rise to prominence can be largely attributed to the growing neo-liberal influence of the United States during the country's civil war. The US establishment of think tanks during the late 1980s, combined with their support of right-wing candidate Alfredo Cristiani for president, put leaders in place who would use largely market-based mechanisms in the country's post-war transition. In the EDUCO program – primarily rural community based initiatives inspired by the self-organization observed in opposition-controlled areas during the civil war – the Ministry of Education and World Bank found a compelling common ground. Through the EDUCO program, the government would diminish the influence of their opposition while providing the World Bank with an opportunity to demonstrate the power of decentralizing responsibility to the community. Edwards goes on to explain how World Bank impact evaluations, through a selective interpretation of results, began to promote EDUCO as the model program. Quickly, other organizations, such as UNESCO, the Brookings Institution, and Save the Children, promoted the benefits of EDUCO, as cited in the World Bank research, further encouraging local accountability measures that link student outcomes to teacher livelihoods.

The global testing culture provides cultural models for all actors involved in education. For states this includes the incorporation of high-stakes standardized testing into their education system and participation in international assessments. Rie Kijima and Jane Leer demonstrate how the choice of Chilean officials to participate in a large number of international assessments was largely an attempt to prove to their citizens that they were an effective and legitimate government after years of dictatorship. Using Weiler's concept of compensatory legitimization, Kijima and Leer find that state officials use their participation in international assessments to strengthen and signal their capacity to effectively govern and encourage public participation.

Finland, largely through the legitimating power of international assessments, has been highlighted as a global education leader. Hilla Aurén and Devin Joshi illustrate how leaders in Finland have recognized this area of strength and used their prominence in education to spur their economy. Exporting curriculum, contract-based degrees, and other educational programming has been reinforced by large contingents of education experts from other countries visiting Finland to research the pathways to their success. Aurén and Joshi end with a word of caution, noting that the entire Finnish education model may not be exportable to other contexts and instead it is the core of respecting teachers as educators, valuing education, and ironically limiting national tests, that must be assimilated into national communities before exports will be effective. Interestingly, Ji Liu, in his study on the connection between education reform and PISA scores, calls into question whether PISA results reflect effective educational programming or underlying cultural influences. His results suggest that caution should be taken when attributing changes in PISA scores to national-level education policy.

Angeline Barrett problematizes the narrow definition of learning emerging in the post-2015 education agenda. Recognizing the global shift in attention from access to outcomes, Barrett uses a social justice perspective to identify the tension between individual achievement, as the sole measure of learning, and sustainable development. Specifically, she suggests that the emerging Sustainable Development Goals focus disproportionately on the instrumental benefits of education to the detriment of the process-oriented social learning necessary for sustainable development.

Finally, Karen Andreasen and Christian Ydesen use the analytic lens of 'the spatial turn' to describe the entrenchment of the Danish testing community, using a historical analysis of three key institutions. Andreasen and Ydesen make it clear that testing in Denmark was largely influenced by many of their European neighbors, as well as the United States. These international collaborations strengthened the position of science in measuring education quality and commercialized standardized tests which, when used by educators, were then able to legitimize their teaching practices.

Section 2: The Absence of Formative Testing and the Politics of Accountability

The global testing culture is marked by large-scale standardized tests. Other types of testing have increasingly disappeared as standardized tests are promoted for their objective and fair character. However, the presence of standardized testing alone is not enough to reinforce the global testing culture; high stakes must be attached to testing, thus creating the motivation that drives behavior change. High stakes can be placed on actors at all levels of education, alternatively holding some actors accountable for education over others. This section highlights the erosion of formative testing and the politics around placing high stakes on tests and communicating outcomes of high-stakes testing with interested parties.

In their comparison of classroom assessments and accountability assessment, Sumera Ahsan and William Smith use social constructivist learning theory and the work of Vygotsky to examine which approach to testing is more likely to facilitate student learning. They conclude that teacher created and administered classroom assessments provide the flexibility and immediate feedback necessary to account for student differences through scaffolding and help individual students progress through their zone of proximal development. Renáta Tichá and Brian Abery remind us that both formative and summative testing serve a purpose in education by addressing different goals. They highlight, however, the misalignment between a test's initial intention and actual use. Using examples of Curriculum-Based Measurements, they describe how the misuse of tests diminishes their potential utility in improving teacher instruction and student learning.

With emphasis placed on large-scale standardized tests that are summative in nature, it is not surprising that teacher practices mirror these testing parameters. Anthony Somerset explores the classroom pedagogical activities used by teachers in low-income countries. He describes a troublesome pattern of teacher-centered, one-way pedagogy that fosters rote memorization and fails to engage higher-level cognitive skills. These basic pedagogical practices, including direct lectures and student-chanted responses, were more common in years directly preceding standardized national exams. Somerset concludes that low-quality standardized tests promote low-quality teacher practices that do not contribute to effective student learning.

The pedagogical practices illustrated by Somerset are likely to be more pronounced in high-stakes environments where the presence of high stakes, regardless of where they are placed, may be enough to corrupt the goals of education and lead to some of the negative outcomes associated with the global testing culture. Sean Mulvenon and Sandra Bowman suggest that these negative outcomes are not a result of tests themselves, or even the high stakes associated with them, but instead are a by-product of simplistic policies that reduce the face validity of the test and muddle its interpretation by the public. Accountability systems that produce overall school grades or cluster schools in large, ill-defined categories fail to provide the information necessary for parents to understand the context of testing or the specific strengths and weaknesses of a school or their child. This can lead to frustration when 'proficient' students are told in higher education that they lack certain fundamental skills and must retake a course.

Mariam Orkodashvili refers to the connection between high-stakes testing and after-school tutoring. She finds that when the high stakes of testing are placed on students, students are more likely to participate in after-school tutoring. Furthermore, the amount of time students are engaged in tutoring may influence their achievement scores, as demonstrated by scores on PIRLS and TIMMS.

Section 3: The Global Testing Culture in National Context

National case studies are included in the final section, illustrating how testing is incorporated into national education systems and understood by the surrounding society. Following a 2004 OECD report that suggested a weak assessment system was partially responsible for Denmark's underperformance in international assessment, Danish officials began to explore testing practices that would better prepare students and increase their international competitiveness. Kristine Kousholt and Bjorn Hamre describe the 2014 Danish school reform which used computer adaptive tests and combined the traditional role of testing with a new construction making the pupil responsible for their own potentiality and future. The authors use Foucault's concept of the dispositive to demonstrate how the dispositives of discipline, security, and optimization emphasize and problematize different aspects of testing, and they argue that the seemingly progressive ways of testing, outlined in the 2014 reform, call for a substantial new critic.

South Korea has traditionally been one of the highest-performing countries on international assessments. The country's history of achievement made the dramatic shift toward educator-based accountability in 2008 surprising. Pearl Chung and Hyeonwoo Chea describe the decision-making process used by the Lee Myung-Bak administration in its implementation of public school report cards and movement towards a punitive model of accountability. Strong resistance by parent and teacher groups led to modifications of the reform in 2013 when the Park Geun-Hye administration came to power. The core of census-based assessments that linked student test scores to educator performance, however, remained the same, creating a competitive, high-pressure environment that reduced the professionalism of teachers.

David Balwanz, drawing on field research conducted in two small districts in South Africa, explains how the South African secondary leaving examination, commonly known as the matric, has become the sole goal of upper secondary education. Education quality in South Africa is equated with matric pass rates and the entire final year of upper secondary education is considered a student's matric year, entirely devoted to the test. As a result, other potential purposes of education are crowded out and South African education inadequately engages with the social justice and transformation agenda laid out after apartheid.

In the final chapter, Tracey Burns, Patrick Blanchenay, and Florian Koester explore Swedish education reform in the 1990s. Since this time the combination of decentralization and liberalization through school choice has led to an educator-based accountability system where competition is created between schools as they fight for consumers. Essential to the school choice movement is the Swedish Association of Local Authorities and Regions, which provides publicly available success indicators and rankings based on school aggregated test scores. These simple, media-friendly rankings are often trumpeted by policy makers, leading to an emphasis on data that does not provide the depth needed to inform long-term development decisions. This misuse of data is exasperated by decentralization practices that do not include local capacity building and fail to clearly delineate roles.

Challenging the Global Testing Culture

The embedded nature of the global testing culture shapes the actors of education and reconstitutes the preferred aims and outcomes. The pervasiveness of high-stakes standardized testing speaks to the common-sense notion that such tests are effective and legitimate education practices. This volume hopes to problematize this culture. Challenging internalized constitutional mindsets is always difficult, and while this is the case in the global testing culture, the critical dialogues presented here and elsewhere provide a gleam of optimism in prompting future discussions.

References

Abraham, J. (1994) Positivism, Structurationism and the Differentiation-polarisation Theory: a reconsideration of Shilling's novelty and primacy thesis, *British Journal of Sociology of Education*, 15, 231-241.

Astiz, M.F., Wiseman, A.W. & Baker, D.P. (2002) Slouching towards Decentralization: consequences of globalization for curricular control in national education systems, *Comparative Education Review*, 46(1), 66-88. http://dx.doi.org/10.1086/324050

Baker, D.P. (2014) *The Schooled Society: the educational transformation of global culture.* Stanford, CA: Stanford University Press.

Baker, D.P., Eslinger, P.J., Benavides, M., et al (2015) The Cognitive Impact of the Education Revolution: a possible cause of the Flynn Effect on population IQ, *Intelligence*, 49, 144-158. http://dx.doi.org/10.1016/j.intell.2015.01.003

Ball, S.J. (1993) Education Markets, Choice and Social Class: the markets as a class strategy in the UK and the USA, *British Journal of Sociology of Education*, 14(1), 3-18. http://dx.doi.org/10.1080/0142569930140101

Balwanz, D. (2016, this volume) The Discursive Hold of the Matric: is there space for a new vision for secondary education in South Africa?, in W.C. Smith (Ed.) *The Global Testing Culture: shaping education policy, perceptions, and practice.* Oxford: Symposium Books.

Benavot, A. & Tanner, E. (2007) The Growth of National Learning Assessments in the World: 1995-2006. Background paper for the Education for All Global Monitoring Report 2008: Education for All by 2015: will we make it. http://unesdoc.unesco.org/images/0015/001555/155507e.pdf

Boli, J. (2005) Contemporary Developments in World Culture, *International Journal of Comparative Sociology*, 46(5), 383-404.

Booher-Jennings, J. (2005) Below the Bubble: 'educational triage' and the Texas accountability system, *American Education Research Journal*, 42(2), 231-268. http://dx.doi.org/10.3102/00028312042002231

Certo, J. (2006) Beginning Teacher Concerns in an Accountability-based Testing Environment, *Journal of Research in Childhood Education*, 20(4), 331-349. http://dx.doi.org/10.1080/02568540609594571

Chapman, D. & Snyder, C. (2000) Can High Stakes National Testing Improve Instruction: re-examining conventional wisdom, *International Journal of Educational Development*, 20, 457-474. http://dx.doi.org/10.1016/S0738-0593(00)00020-1

Comte, A. (1975) *Auguste Comte and Positivism: the essential writings*, ed. G. Lenzzer. Chicago, IL: University of Chicago Press.

Daun, H. & Mundy, K. (2011) *Education Governance and Participation with Focus on Developing Countries.* Stockholm: Stockholm University, Institute of International Education.

de Tocqueville, A. (1969) *Democracy in America*. Garden City, NY: Anchor Press. (Original work published 1835.)

Dorn, S. (2007) *Accountability Frankenstein: understanding and taming the monster*. Charlotte, NC: Information Age.

Dubnick, M.J. (2005) Accountability and the Promise of Performance: In search of the mechanisms, *Public Performance and Management Review*, 28(3), 376-417.

Froese-Germain, B. (2001) Standardized Testing + High-stakes Decisions = educational inequity, *Interchange*, 32(2), 111-130. http://dx.doi.org/10.1023/A:1011985405392

Gartrell, C.D. & Gartrell, J.W. (1996) Positivism in Sociological Practice: 1967-1990, *Canadian Review of Sociology*, 33(2), 143-158. http://dx.doi.org/10.1111/j.1755-618X.1996.tb00192.x

Gove, A. & Wetterberg, A. (2011) The Early Grade Reading Assessment: an introduction, in A. Gove & A. Wetterberg (Eds) *The Early Grade Reading Assessment: applications and interventions to improve basic literacy*, pp. 1-38. Research Triangle, NC: RTI Press.

Groeschl, S. & Doherty, L. (2000) Conceptualizing Culture, *Cross Cultural Management*, 7(4), 12-17. http://dx.doi.org/10.1108/13527600010797138

Harvey, D. (2005) *A Brief History of Neoliberalism*. New York: Oxford University Press.

Hayek, F.A. (1952) *Individualism and Economic Order*. London: Routledge & Kegan Paul.

Henslin, J. (1998) *Essentials of Sociology*. Boston, MA: Allyn & Bacon.

Hofstede, G. (1980) *Culture's Consequences*. Beverly Hills, CA: Sage.

Hopmann, S.T. (2008) No Child, No School, No State Left behind: schooling in the age of accountability, *Journal of Curriculum Studies*, 40(4), 417-456. http://dx.doi.org/10.1080/00220270801989818

Hoppers, C. (2009) Education, Culture and Society in a Globalizing World: implications for comparative and international education, *Compare*, 39(5), 601-614. http://dx.doi.org/10.1080/03057920903125628

Jepperson, R.L. (2002) The Development and Application of Sociological Neoinstitutionalism, in J. Berger & M. Zelditch, Jr (Eds) *New Directions in Contemporary Sociological Theory*, 229-266. Lanham, MD: Rowman & Littlefield.

Jones, B. & Egley, R. (2006) Looking through Different Lenses: teachers' and administrators' views of accountability, *Phi Delta Kappan*, 87(10), 767-771. http://dx.doi.org/10.1177/003172170608701012

Joshi, D. & Smith, W. (2012) Education and Inequality: implications of the World Bank's Education Strategy 2020, in A. Wiseman & C. Collins (Eds) *Education Strategy in the Developing World: revising the World Bank's education policy*, pp. 173-202. Bingley: Emerald Publishing.

Kamens, D.H. & McNeely, C.L. (2010) Globalization and the Growth of International Educational Testing and National Assessment, *Comparative Education Review*, 54(1), 5-25. http://dx.doi.org/10.1086/648471

Kamens, D.H., Meyer, J.W. & Benavot, A. (1996) Worldwide Patterns in Academic Secondary Education Curricula, *Comparative Education Review*, 40(2), 116-138. http://dx.doi.org/10.1086/447368

Lemann, N. (1999) *The Big Test: the secret history of the American meritocracy*. New York: Farrar, Straus & Giroux.

Macnab, D. (2004) Hearts, Minds, and External Supervision of Schools: direction and development, *Educational Review*, 56(1), 53-64. http://dx.doi.org/10.1080/0013191032000152273

Meyer, H.D. & Benavot, A. (2014) PISA and the Globalization of Education Governance: some puzzles and problems, in H.D. Meyer & A. Benavot, *Pisa, Power, and Policy: the emergence of global education governance*, pp. 9-26. Oxford: Symposium Books.

Meyer, J.W. (1977) The Effects of Education as an Institution, *American Journal of Sociology*, 83, 55-77. http://dx.doi.org/10.1086/226506

Meyer, J., Boli, J., Thomas, G.M. & Ramirez, F. (1997) World Society and the Nation-state, *American Journal of Sociology*, 103(1), 144-181. http://dx.doi.org/10.1086/231174

Moses, M.S. & Nanna, M.J. (2007) The Testing Culture and the Persistence of High Stakes Testing Reforms, *Education and Culture*, 23(1), 55-72. http://dx.doi.org/10.1353/eac.2007.0010

Mundy, K. (2006) Education for All and the New Development Compact, *Review of Education*, 52, 23-48. http://dx.doi.org/10.1007/1-4020-4722-3_2

Organization for Economic Co-operation and Development (OECD) (2011) How are Schools Held Accountable?, in *Education at a Glance 2011: highlights*. Paris: OECD Publishing.

Phelps, R.P. (2000) Trends in Large-scale Testing outside the United States, *Educational Measurement: Issues and Practice*, 19(1), 11-21. http://dx.doi.org/10.1111/j.1745-3992.2000.tb00018.x

Prichett, L. (2004) *Towards a New Consensus for Addressing the Global Challenge of the Lack of Education*. http://www.hks.harvard.edu/fs/lpritch/Education%20-%20docs/ED%20-%20Systems/challenge_education_cup.pdf

Ramirez, F. (2003) The Global Model and National Legacies, in K. Anderson-Levitt (Ed.) *Local Meanings, Global Schooling: anthropology and world culture theory*, pp. 239-254. New York: Palgrave Macmillan.

Sahlberg, P. (2010) Rethinking Accountability in a Knowledge Society, *Journal of Educational Change*, 11, 45-61. http://dx.doi.org/10.1007/s10833-008-9098-2

Scherer, M. (2009) The Tests That Won't Go Away, *Educational Leadership*, 67(3), 5.

Schofer, E., Hironaka, A., Frank, D.J. & Longhofer, W. (2012) Sociological Institutionalism and World Society, in E. Amenta, K. Nash & A. Scott (Eds) *The Wiley-Blackwell Companion to Political Sociology*, pp. 57-68. Oxford: Blackwell.

Smeed, J. & Victory, M. (2010) Testing for Accountability, *TLN Journal*, 17(3), 28-29.

Smith, W.C. (2014) The Global Transformation toward Testing for Accountability, *Education Policy Analysis Archives*, 22(116).

http://dx.doi.org/10.14507/epaa.v22.1571http://dx.doi.org/10.14507/epaa.v22.1571

Sperling, G. & Belu, R. (2005) Designing a Global Compact in Education, *Finance and Development*, 42(2), 38-41.

Strauss, V. (2006) The Rise of the Testing Culture, *Washington Post*. http://www.washingtonpost.com/wp-dyn/content/article/2006/10/09/AR2006100900925.html

Supovitz, J. (2009) Can High Stakes Testing Leverage Educational Improvement? Prospects from the Last Decade of Testing and Accountability Reform, *Journal of Educational Change*, 10, 211-227. http://dx.doi.org/10.1007/s10833-009-9105-2

Tichá, R. & Abery, B. (2016, this volume) Beyond the Large-scale Testing of Basic Skills: using formative assessment to facilitate learning, in W.C. Smith (Ed.) *The Global Testing Culture: shaping education policy, perceptions, and practice*. Oxford: Symposium Books.

UNESCO (2015) *EFA Global Monitoring Report. Education for All 2000-2015: achievements and challenges*. http://unesdoc.unesco.org/images/0023/002322/232205e.pdf

Wiseman, A. (2010) The Uses of Evidence for Educational Policymaking: global contexts and international trends, *Review of Research in Education*, 34, 1-24. http://dx.doi.org/10.3102/0091732X09350472

Wiseman, A., Pilton, J. & Lowe, J.C. (2010) International Educational Governance Models and National Policy Convergence, *International Perspectives on Education and Society*, 12, 3-18. http://dx.doi.org/10.1108/S1479-3679(2010)0000012004

Woessman, L. (2004) The Effect Heterogeneity of Central Exams: evidence from TIMSS, TIMSS-repeat and PISA, *CESifo Working Paper No. 1330*.

CHAPTER 2

A Perfect Storm: the political economy of community-based management, teacher accountability and impact evaluations in El Salvador and the global reform agenda

D. BRENT EDWARDS JR

ABSTRACT During the 1990s and 2000s, a policy known as Education with Community Participation (EDUCO) not only became the cornerstone of education reform in El Salvador but also became a global education policy, one which is known for instituting teacher accountability by decentralizing to rural families the responsibility for hiring and firing them. As is shown in this chapter, the rise to fame of EDUCO was not only a product of the particular political-economic context in which it was born, but was also a product of the (erroneous) impact evaluations produced by the World Bank, which served as the evidence base through which this and other international institutions could legitimately promote the EDUCO model, a model which has helped to extend outcomes-based accountability for teachers.

Introduction

A major focus of this book is the way that outcomes-based accountability has come to characterize the work of teachers. To that end, the present chapter makes a valuable contribution by critically unpacking the trajectory of a well-known policy which has fed into and reinforced the idea that teachers can and should be held accountable based on such indicators as test scores and student retention rates. More specifically, this chapter examines the history of a policy known as EDUCO (Education with Community Participation), which gave the legal responsibility for hiring, firing and supervising teachers to a council of parents, mostly in rural areas. In looking at this policy, I show how it first emerged from the context of El Salvador in the early 1990s and then subsequently entered the global reform agenda by the late 1990s, thereafter continuing to be promoted during the 2000s – with the high point of this policy's trajectory being its inclusion in the World Bank's 2004 World Development Report as *the* policy to emulate in order to introduce accountability into the provision of education services. Put differently, this chapter explicates one of the most popular education reforms of the past 20 years and, in so doing, provides insight into the evolution of the current thinking around teacher accountability. A particular focus of the chapter is impact evaluations – both how they help to legitimate questionable policies as well as the need to problematize them, as well as the way they tend to sit at the nexus of financial, political and ideological interests. That is, in showing the relationship of EDUCO to these developments, I highlight and attempt to problematize the political economy of both education reform and the creation of the legitimate knowledge that is leveraged to influence the global education agenda.

Theoretical Orientation

This chapter comes from and contributes to a larger project that seeks to understand the emergence and life cycle of policies that go global. In examining this phenomenon, a number of issues are central – those issues being vertical and horizontal, structural and processual, and semiotic and material. Put differently, both theoretically and for the purpose of analysis, this research takes numerous aspects into account, including: (a) the geopolitical context within which El Salvador found itself in the late 1980s and 1990s; (b) the involvement of a range of international organizations; (c) the processes through which national and international actors negotiated the reform agenda in El Salvador during this time; and (d) not only the mechanisms by which key international organizations influenced the direction and content of that reform agenda, but also the mechanisms by which those organizations legitimated and disseminated the policy model globally. As can be seen, then, this research understands the origins of global education policies as a result of the dynamic interaction of multiple organizational actors in key policy-making spaces, with those policy-making spaces being constrained and facilitated by the political-economic characteristics of the local, national and international contexts of the time. Following on from this, the subsequent evolution and global promotion of such policies is understood to result not simply from the material resources of policy proponents but also from the ability of those proponents to produce and to strategically employ a legitimate evidence base that resonates with the overarching ideational currents of the time. Elsewhere, this approach has been labelled Critical International Political Economy (Edwards, 2015).

Methods

The findings discussed here have resulted from ongoing research that began in 2009, with the most recent period of data collection occurring in January 2015 (see e.g. Edwards, 2012a, 2013a, b, 2015; Edwards & Klees, 2012; Edwards & DeMatthews, 2014; Edwards et al, 2015). Multiple data sources have been consulted. These include, first, over 100 interviews with key actors from national and international organizations, including governmental ministries, which have been directly or indirectly involved in the origins, implementation and/or the promotion of EDUCO. Among these organizations were the Ministry of Education in El Salvador (MINED); the United States Agency for International Development (USAID); the World Bank; the United Nations Education, Science, and Culture Organization (UNESCO); and the Central American University, not to mention think tanks within and outside El Salvador as well as national and international non-governmental organizations. The archival collections of these organizations were also reviewed, with a focus on the years from the 1970s to 2012. These actions were complemented by – and benefited from – an extensive review of the academic and non-academic literature that is available on EDUCO. Ten months of full-time fieldwork in El Salvador during 2012-13 through a Fulbright Research Grant helped to ensure that data collection for this study was both broad and deep.

Analytically, the literature, archives and interviews conducted and collected were examined in accordance with Edwards (2012b). This meant extensively reviewing these sources in order (a) to establish the larger geopolitical context in which El Salvador was mired in the 1980s and 1990s and how that context affected the political landscape of the country during this time; (b) to identify and then trace the actions of the key actors from the local, national and international levels who were involved in education reform and who influenced the priorities for the education reform agenda; (c) to understand the process of EDUCO's implementation; and (d) to document the promotion of EDUCO within and outside El Salvador. The creation of critical-event timelines, actor-influence matrices, logic models and causal diagrams – in addition to the use of process-tracing methods and counter-factual analysis – helped to array and interpret the information collected.

Context: conflict, structural transformation and international reform trends

Because the background to EDUCO's emergence has been extensively documented in other publications (see e.g. Edwards, 2015, forthcoming; Edwards et al, 2015), only the essential characteristics of the political-economic context will be reviewed here. To that end, there are three features that need to be acknowledged. The first is the fact of civil war (1980-1992) and the effect this had on the country's politics. Specifically, not only was the

Salvadoran government caught in an ongoing war with the Farabundo Martí National Liberation Front (FMLN) – a coalition of five rebel groups fighting for socialist reform of the land, economy and social services (LeoGrande, 1998) – but this conflict triggered the involvement of the United States, which was operating from a Cold War mindset. In all, during the civil war, the United States channeled $6 billion in military, economic and social aid to El Salvador (Robinson, 2003), with $533 million in military aid arriving in 1985 alone (Booth et al, 2006). The United States thus held significant influence in Salvadoran politics, particularly as a result of the military and economic aid, without which it is doubtful the government would have been able to remain in power or prevent the economy from collapsing (Montgomery, 1995).

Dovetailing with the first issue was the second: that is, the international promotion of neoliberal ideology and reform by the Reagan administration, notably through USAID (Harvey, 2005; Klein, 2007). This organization, as a major player in El Salvador during the 1980s, funded the establishment and rise of Salvadoran think tanks that supported the foreign policy preferences of the United States – a strategy, it should be noted, that has been employed elsewhere (Rappleye, 2011). These think tanks then lent credibility to neoliberal reform principles (e.g. market deregulation, privatization of state agencies, austerity measures, shrinking of governmental agencies, elimination of state planning, etc.) by hosting famous economists (including the 'Chicago Boys') in addition to helping elevate the profiles of Salvadoran economists and businessmen, who then promoted and employed the technocratic approaches to policy that resonated with USAID. In these ways, USAID was instrumental in transforming the national political context of El Salvador during the 1980s.

The third and final aspect of relevance here relates to the election in 1989 of the right-wing candidate for president, Alfredo Cristiani. Beyond having his campaign supported by USAID, he came from one of the think tanks that had been funded by this same organization. Moreover, when he transitioned to the presidency, he brought with him 'at least 17 business leaders and persons linked with [the USAID-funded think tank]' (Segovia, 1996, p. 55). As the culminating political development of the 1980s, Cristiani's election has serious implications for the subsequent period of governmental reform. In particular, under the label of modernization, his election signaled that all governmental action would have to accord with the market-based principles of accountability, efficiency and effectiveness. This state of affairs was a far cry from the agrarian reform and social welfare programs that had been pledged by José Napoleón Duarte, president during 1984-89 and who represented the Christian Democrat party (LeoGrande, 1998).

EDUCO's Rise: constrained political space and key actor interests

In 1990, after 10 years of war, 37% of children aged 7-14 were out of school, and statistics were much worse in rural areas where government-provided services were often unavailable (MINED, 1990). While responding to this situation was one of the first priorities of the Cristiani administration, it is important to note that there were multiple actors vying for influence at this point in time. Moreover, it is essential to highlight that the MINED did not have control of large portions of the country, particularly in the northern regions along the Honduran border, where the FMLN and affiliated rural communities were following an approach to education – known as 'popular education' – that had its roots in liberation theology and which reflected the educational philosophy of Paulo Freire in that it taught students to identify the political-economic structures that contributed to their oppression and to mobilize against them (Hammond, 1998). Importantly, though, beyond the critical nature of this educational approach, the informal schools in these areas (and even beyond) were staffed by parents who worked in exchange for donations from the communities. These schools, thus, by default, were community controlled, managed, staffed and financed. Furthermore, in that they represented a challenge to the authority of the MINED, the new Minister of Education as of 1990 saw it as one of her goals to incorporate these communities into the official education system going forward.

With the above characteristics in mind, consider the following inter-institutional dynamics. First, after conducting a needs assessment mid-year 1990, a key consultant from UNESCO, who had previously worked on indigenous rights in Bolivia, recommended to the Minister of Education that the government build on the community-based model she had observed while collecting data for her study. For the Minister of Education, however, this was initially seen as an untenable suggestion because it implied building on the educational model of the FMLN. Additionally, the idea that rural parents could manage schools was seen as unrealistic.

The World Bank was equally skeptical of this suggestion at first. This is important to note because the World Bank – which had recently, in 1989, begun to work in El Salvador again – was at the center of many of the reforms being considered once Cristiani entered office, both within and outside education. Indeed, the World Bank was in the midst of negotiating a structural adjustment loan at the same time that the Minister of Education was exploring options for funding education reform. The implication is that serious education reform could not be pursued without buy-in from the World Bank, since this institution would be the one to fund it (note that USAID was funding education reform, too, but its involvement was not focused on the reform of system governance).

Although initially favoring a reform model based on the voucher system in Chile, the representatives of the World Bank working in El Salvador began to see the opportunity that community management offered. This change of heart was prompted by two developments. First, the UNESCO consultant showed, through the implementation of a pilot program in early 1991, that rural, uneducated parents could, in fact, be trained to hire and pay teachers.

Second, the World Bank staff in El Salvador recognized that a model of educational management based at the community level would represent an extreme form of decentralization. The second realization was crucial for them because, throughout the 1980s, decentralization was a key theme in international development (Conyers, 1983; Edwards, 2012b; Edwards & DeMatthews, 2014). Yet, to that point, the decentralization of state functions had only been envisioned at the state or district level (Winkler, 1989). One reason for decentralization's popularity was because – as conceived in the dominant, neoliberal discourse – it was portrayed as a way to make the management and provision of government services more efficient and responsive to the demands of citizens because those citizens would themselves be able to participate in those services and influence (if only by voting with their feet) the way local governments provided them. Thus, by extending the idea of decentralization to the community level – and here is a critical point – the World Bank would be able, if successful in El Salvador, to promote and sell a model where the community was thought to hold the teacher accountable, and in a way that was seen as novel since the community would be formally responsible for hiring and firing the teacher (who worked on a one-year contract renewable at the discretion of the school council, itself made up of five parents elected from the surrounding community). Ultimately, then, this idea took the principles of accountability, efficiency and effectiveness and extended them in a way that generated significant excitement on the part of the World Bank.

Once the World Bank saw the potential of the community-based model, it put significant financial and technical resources behind the program – initially $10.3 million and $69.3 million overall in conjunction with the Inter-American Development Bank (Edwards, 2013b). The World Bank also began to promote the program in terms of neoliberal principles, sanitizing its critical origins. The Minister of Education, for her part, went with this idea because it met the conditions that constrained her: that is, (a) it expanded educational access, (b) it aligned with the neoliberal principles that were to guide all reform in El Salvador at that time, (c) it had the blessing of the World Bank, and (d) it incorporated and undermined the FMLN communities (because these communities, which suffered from insufficient resources, were not only required to join the EDUCO program if they wanted government funding, but they were also required to hire qualified teachers, which necessarily precluded them from hiring their own popular education teachers, who did not have the proper certifications).

To be clear, the EDUCO program was theorized to function in the following way and to have the following impact. First, the education system would be more efficient if the central MINED transferred to the community level the responsibility for managing the hiring and firing of teachers; the latter would work on one-year contracts that were renewable at the discretion of the school council (of five elected, volunteer parents from the community) that hired them (note that these tended to be small schools without principals, though one of the teachers would by default assume some of the administrative duties typically associated with the principalship). Not only was this community arrangement seen as inherently more efficient on a system-wide basis (perhaps unofficially because parents helped to build and maintain the school without compensation), but, in addition, this arrangement was seen as more efficient because the school councils would manage the school's budget and would, as such, be responsible for purchasing only the educational materials that the school needed, thereby eliminating waste in purchasing. Moreover, it was thought that this arrangement would promote effectiveness because it would lead to more consistent teacher attendance and improved student test scores, a consequence of the fact that teachers were under the scrutiny of community actors to perform well or lose their job.[1]

Clearly, then, and with relevance for this chapter, the idea of teacher accountability was central. By turning the local community into an accountability lever, the MINED could affect improved outcomes. The community model of FMLN – imbued as it was with notions of solidarity and critical consciousness – had thus been transformed into a neoliberal experiment inscribed with mechanistic notions of teacher monitoring and punishment.

Before proceeding, it should be noted that the implementation of this policy was not in doubt. All the dominant organizational and political actors agreed on this policy choice, and so it was only a matter of time and effort. Going forward from 1991, when the first education loan was approved, the World Bank provided close monitoring of the program as well as guidance at each step in the process. By 1994, thousands of communities had been integrated into the EDUCO program. Concretely, while the program began in 1991 with six communities, 3 years later it had 2316 teachers and served 74,112 students (Cuéllar-Marchelli, 2003). Ten years later, in 2004, these figures had risen to 7381 and 378,208, respectively.[2] Approximately 55% of rural public schools, which make up two-thirds of all schools in El Salvador, would operate under the EDUCO program (Gillies et al, 2010).

**Mobilizing Legitimate Knowledge:
producing and leveraging rigorous research**

Whereas other publications have focused on the emergence of the EDUCO program (Edwards, 2015), the present chapter makes an important contribution by extending the analysis to include a focus on the role of EDUCO's evidence base and the way that this evidence was used to promote EDUCO internationally. Furthermore, although other mechanisms have been integral in extending the reach of the EDUCO example (Edwards, forthcoming), the model would not have received the level of attention it has without the research base that was produced by the World Bank. That is, while the World Bank promoted EDUCO internally, in Central America, and in regional conferences during the mid-1990s, it was not until the late 1990s and 2000s, after a few studies with positive findings began to emerge, that EDUCO began to be promoted with more vigor and started to take on a life of its own. To that end, what follows below is a list of examples that show the reach of the EDUCO program in the spaces and publications where global education policies tend to circulate.[3] Subsequently, a discussion will be presented of the problematic nature of these studies specifically and of impact evaluations generally.

- *Brookings Institution, 2008*: A report on improving development effectiveness spotlights EDUCO and the fact that the school council 'hires, monitors, retains or dismisses teachers' (Hartmann & Linn, 2008, p. 47).
- *World Bank, 2009*: A World Bank review of school-based management highlighted and classified the EDUCO program as one of the stronger models because community members are responsible for 'hiring, firing and monitoring teachers' (Barrera-Osorio et al, 2009, p. 7).
- *Global Partnership for Education, 2009*: The Global Partnership for Education (2009) focused on EDUCO as a 'way to ensure that the community contributes to improved educational outcomes' (p. 96).
- *UNESCO, 2009*: In the Global Monitoring Report, UNESCO underscored that EDUCO is a model that increases client 'voice', meaning that it entails mechanisms through which community members have recourse if teachers do not meet their expectations (UNESCO, 2008).
- *World Bank, 2011*: In a review of evidence on accountability mechanisms in education, the World Bank again focused on the EDUCO program as one of the 'stronger' examples (Bruns et al, 2011).
- *Save the Children, 2013*: In a report on community participation, EDUCO is cited in relation to what mothers can do to enhance student outcomes (Save the Children, 2013).

Of course, each of the examples in the list above came out after the publication of the World Bank's 2004 World Development Report (WDR). While the WDR is the flagship publication of the World Bank, the WDR 2004 has been recognized as perhaps the most influential WDR to date. For example, per the World Bank's own admission (World Bank, 2011), this report has been tremendously impactful in that its regional strategies and programmatic activities at the country level were realigned in terms of WDR 2004's accountability framework; and, internationally, the WDR 2004 has influenced the priorities of the Department of International Development of the United Kingdom. This is of significance here because the theme of 2014 – making services work for poor people – squarely focused on the notion of a 'short-route' to accountability, whereby local service providers must be monitored by and responsive to their clients. Moreover, when it came to education sector, EDUCO was presented as *the* model to emulate. The authors of this WDR have acknowledged that EDUCO never would have emerged as the exemplar of interest were it not for the ostensibly rigorous evidentiary foundation that existed when they set out to identify successful accountability-based reforms.

All of this – that is, EDUCO's success, but also the admission of the importance of EDUCO's studies – calls for a closer look at the studies themselves. That is to say, while EDUCO has clearly fed into a number of high-profile publications and organizations due to the connection that it makes between community management and teacher accountability, one is left to wonder: what do the underlying studies conclude, and on what basis? Moreover, and perhaps more importantly, are these conclusions defensible? On these questions, the findings discussed below are restricted, for the purpose of brevity, to two of the six studies produced by the World Bank.[4] Nevertheless, the critiques and conclusions presented here are relevant to the other studies, as well. A more detailed discussion of all six studies can be found in Edwards (2014).

The first study of interest here is Umanzor et al (1997). In this study, World Bank researchers, along with counterparts from the MINED, ran a series of *ex-post* matched comparisons between the EDUCO schools and the traditional public schools on a number of characteristics of interest. There were other findings but, with regard to the variables that have received the most attention, there were differences in neither student absenteeism, dropout, grade repetition nor student achievement on either the math or language tests (Umanzor et al, 1997). Although the comparison of the treatment and control group in this study did not show that EDUCO students had significantly better achievement than students in rural traditional public schools, these students also did not score significantly worse than their counterparts in public schools. Umanzor et al (1997) took this as a positive sign, given the relatively worse economic conditions of EDUCO students, located as they were primarily in rural and marginalized areas, and thus concluded that EDUCO students exhibit 'better than expected academic performance' (p. 26). However, it may be that the positive (or non-negative) results observed were not the result of the EDUCO program, per se, but rather a result of the pre-existing social capital that had accumulated during the civil war in the EDUCO communities (many of which were FMLN communities, at that time), when they were forced by their circumstances to work together to provide basic services, such as education.

The second study was by Jimenez and Sawada (1999) and emerged two years later in the *World Bank Economic Review*, 'the most widely read scholarly economic journal in the world' (Research Gate, n.d.). Here, Jimenez and Sawada (1999) employed more advanced econometric techniques to assess whether EDUCO had an effect on either student achievement or student absences. In order to answer these questions, they used the same 1996 data as Umanzor et al (1997) and applied regression analyses along with the Heckman two-step correction (Heckman, 1979) in order to attempt to correct for the sample selection bias inherent in the EDUCO treatment group, a by-product of the fact that the government targeted the most disadvantaged communities for participation in the program. The point here is that, as a result of the selection criteria, EDUCO communities tended to systematically differ from comparison group communities along certain characteristics. In their study, Jimenez and Sawada (1999) successively added controls for student, family, teacher, classroom, school and community participation characteristics. The comparison group was traditional rural schools.

In their discussion of student achievement, the authors state: 'EDUCO's ... effect on language test scores is positive and significant, while its effect on math performance is positive and not significant' (Jimenez & Sawada, 1999, p. 428). Yet, this statement is quickly followed by a concession: 'Our measure of EDUCO's advantage in language may be imprecise. The estimate of the EDUCO coefficient is sensitive to the specification of the participation equation' (p. 428). What they allude to is that their more completely specified models clearly show that the results for both language and math achievement are not significant. Nevertheless, the authors make inferences in the concluding section to their article from models missing controls for school inputs or community participation. They state: '[EDUCO] has improved language scores' (p. 440). The gravity of this short sentence should not be understated. Indeed, this finding is the cornerstone of much of the attention that EDUCO has received internationally. It is this study and this conclusion which has been picked up and extensively cited.

To continue, in addition to the specification issue, there is the matter of endogeneity stemming from sample selection bias. That is, the results provided by Jimenez and Sawada (1999) are confounded by the fact that the students who attended EDUCO schools also possessed unobserved characteristics that correlated with student achievement outcomes. Jimenez and Sawada (1999) recognize this when they write, 'The error terms of the participation and achievement equations are negatively correlated. This means that EDUCO students have unobserved characteristics that are negatively correlated with achievement test scores' (p. 428). Under conditions of endogeneity, one cannot truly parse out the impact of the intervention on student achievement because the participation of the student in the intervention is correlated with other factors which are also correlated with student achievement.

The second question posed by Jimenez and Sawada (1999) is whether there is an EDUCO effect on student attendance. They use the same data and controls as with their models for student achievement, changing only the dependent variable to indicate the number of days the student was absent in the month prior to the survey. Here, they find that EDUCO significantly reduces the number of days a student was absent. They thus conclude that the accountability relationships instituted between parents and teachers in EDUCO are responsible for reducing student absences.

However, if we decompose the effect of the EDUCO variable according to when the EDUCO schools were built, the picture changes (Jimenez & Sawada, 1999). If the EDUCO school was built between 1991 and 1995, there was no effect; however, if the school was built in 1996, it significantly decreased student absences. As opposed to attributing the effect to relationships of accountability, the result could simply be due to the fact that students received a new school in the same year that the survey was administered. The presence of a new school – where there had not been one previously – could significantly increase student attendance.

Nevertheless, the authors chose to highlight a particular conclusion, one that resonated with the theory of community-level accountability relationships and their ability to lead students and teachers to perform better (Jimenez & Sawada, 1999). These conclusions are powerful, particularly given the fact that they are offered by the World Bank and the fact that they were derived from methods that are widely seen as rigorous and objective (Verger et al, 2014). To that end, the literature shows that other authors have repeated these conclusions, as did Barrera-Osorio et al (2009) and Bruns et al (2011) in their reviews of the effectiveness of school-based management in developing countries. In this way, over time, conjecture can contribute to consensus around the idea that community-level decentralization can lead to fewer student absences through a certain model of teacher accountability.

In retrospect, then, the same studies which have supposedly shown the benefits of the EDUCO program – and which have been picked up and used to spread this idea – can be interpreted differently to offer alternative conclusions. These alternative conclusions clearly cast doubt on the advisability of EDUCO as a public policy and on the supposed benefits of the teacher accountability mechanism at the heart of the EDUCO model. Furthermore, by placing the above review of EDUCO studies in the political economic context of the 1990s, it is suggested that the alternative interpretations offered here indicate that EDUCO, on the whole, (a) was a program which didn't improve key indicators of quality, (b) imposed costs on the rural parents (who volunteered their time on the Community Education Associations and who helped to build and repair the schools in their communities), (c) sought to weaken the teachers' unions (by instituting one-year contracts for EDUCO teachers and precluding teachers from belonging to unions if they worked in an EDUCO school), and (d) was directed at undermining FMLN communities and incorporating them into the official education system (by replacing their popular education teachers and schools with the EDUCO program and with teachers from outside their communities). Of course, this alternative interpretation highlights the political motivations behind EDUCO. But it needs to be remembered that EDUCO was always a political decision, and that it has continued to have political consequences for the global education agenda in that it influenced the priorities of international organizations and other countries when it came to policy options.

Discussion and Conclusion: a perfect storm in need of problematizing

As a global education policy, the context and events that engulfed the EDUCO program can be considered a perfect storm. Recall, first, that the national political context was transformed over the course of the 1980s, such that, by the end of this decade, the 'context of reception' – to use Dale's (2013) phrase – was aligned with the policy preferences of the dominant geopolitical interests and international organizations working in the country at the time – namely, the United States and the World Bank. Second, recall that during 1990-91, before the end of the civil war in January 1992, and before the country had a chance to engage in democratic dialogue about the direction of reform, the Minister of Education was forced by her constraints (i.e. by political necessity) to pursue a particular version of community-based management grounded in notions of efficiency, effectiveness and mechanistic teacher accountability based on student outcomes. Third, and given this commitment from the MINED, funding, technical assistance and close monitoring from the World Bank ensured that the program would be scaled up. Fourth, the World Bank began a series of evaluations, once the program had been implemented in all 14 political departments of the country in 1994. Fifth, and finally, these studies were then promoted widely and picked up by other organizations, thereby extending the reach of EDUCO as a credible and successful model of teacher accountability, among other things.

Seen in long-term perspective, then, the evolution of the EDUCO program reflects an uncanny set of circumstances and events, with each development in its trajectory building on the last such that the program only continued to gain in momentum from the early 1990s through the 2000s. First and foremost, the history of this program sheds light on the dramatic effects that foreign powers and international organizations can have – in the right circumstances – on the structural transformation of a country's political-economic structures as well as on the reform of education policy specifically. However, an important corollary to this finding is that, once a policy is implemented, its purchase internationally depends on the whether or not a policy's proponents can produce an evidence base that will be seen as rigorous by researchers, education specialists and policymakers.[5]

In the current context of research politics, producing rigorous research means designing econometric studies that use experimental or quasi-experimental methods (Dumas & Anderson, 2014), with randomized control trials being the 'gold standard' (Castillo & Wagner, 2014). Although the specifics of two EDUCO studies were already problematized, the nature and production of this research needs to be further critiqued precisely because it is at the heart of how and why certain policies are often perceived as the best path for reform. And, as can been seen from the neoliberal reform trends of the past 15-20 years, the production of these studies is often in the service of policies and rhetoric that justify and extend narrow conceptions of accountability, competition, efficiency, etc.

For our purposes, there are two relevant issues, and these issues go beyond the methodological shortcomings of econometric studies, which are erroneously considered to produce – or at least to approximate – unbiased estimates of the effects of a program's impact.[6] As for the first issue, one must note that econometric methods, while useful for indicating the general nature of relationships or correlations among variables, cannot by their nature offer causal explanations. On one hand, this is because data do not speak for themselves, and so researchers and practitioners must interpret the relationships among variables based on their guiding frameworks, whether they be implicit or explicit (Kvernbekk, 2013). On the other hand, this is because econometric studies look at inputs and outputs without being able to unpack the 'black box' of how a policy works (Pawson, 2006). That is to say, econometric methods are limited in their ability to explain *how and why* each sub-component of a program – such as EDUCO, for example – works or does not work in practice. These methods restrict their focus to what goes in and what comes out, thereby failing to account for both the inner workings of a program as well as the many layers of context that impinge on how the program operates in implementation (Pawson, 2006). In the words of Dumas and Anderson (2014), 'Achieving high levels of rigor in quantitative studies involves limitations that include social and cultural decontextualization, ahistoricity, [and] the creation of randomization that is seldom generalizable to real life settings' (p. 5). Although contrary to how quantitative research is typically advertised, econometric studies are, just like other studies, subject to interpretations that are necessarily bound up in the worldviews and theories of their authors, particularly when those authors move from describing results to explaining the causes of the relationships among variables.

Relating to the first issue is the second: influential international organizations frequently operate in relation to a set of intersecting – and often conflicting – interests. As Samoff (1993) has written, these interests are financial-political-intellectual in nature. In short, and as shown in the case of EDUCO, certain international organizations (but particularly development banks) not only produce and disseminate policy-relevant knowledge (often by performing econometric studies) but also participate either directly or indirectly in the spaces and in the conversations where policy decisions are made, with the implication being that these organizations – beyond generating knowledge – have the opportunity to employ that knowledge to create or to sustain opportunities for financial benefit or financial influence, since these organizations often provide the funding for reform as well. Thus, in the political economy of education reform, it needs to be acknowledged, first, that econometric studies cannot claim the high ground in terms of objectivity, and, second, that many international organizations act within a set of dynamics that actually encourages them to produce findings that serve their own institutional interests.

Bringing the above discussion back to EDUCO and to the theme of this book, there are a number of points and suggestions to keep in mind going forward. First, future research on education reform in developing countries needs to be attentive to the intervention of foreign powers and to the involvement of international organizations, and from a long-term perspective that takes into account (a) shifting geopolitical dynamics, (b) processes of engagement between these external actors and their national counterparts, and (c) the role and limitations of the production of 'rigorous' research. Second, and relatedly, when it comes to the promotion and invocation of studies that support global education policies or the ideas they represent (such as outcomes-based teacher accountability), one must take care to review the claims made in light of the methods employed and the alternative possible explanations. Third, and more broadly, if the present case of EDUCO is any indication, we are encouraged not only to discard the lessons that proponents of this program have offered but also to seek out: (a) alternative (i.e. more equitable, more participatory and more socially just) institutional relationships in the process of education reform; (b) new methods for understanding the effects of EDUCO and other global education policies; (c) reconceived notions of accountability that go beyond narrow conceptions of the community serving as a lever for punishing the teacher; and, perhaps most importantly, (d) opportunities to contribute to the development of partnerships, collaborations and social movements that can help to mitigate against the tide of neoliberal rhetoric and neoliberal policy principles that is currently inundating education systems around the world – and often as a result of the kinds of studies reviewed here.

Notes

[1] For more on the experience of teachers, parents and students in EDUCO communities and schools, see Lindo Fuentes (1998); SIMEDUCO (2011); Srygley (2013); Edwards (forthcoming).

[2] While the EDUCO program was initially only intended as a strategy to provide education at the preschool level and in grades 1-3, it was subsequently expanded in 1994 to cover through grade 6 and then again in 1997 to cover through grade 9 (Meza et al, 2004). After 2005, even some high schools became EDUCO schools (Gillies et al, 2010).

[3] Note that the examples included here are restricted to those that emphasize accountability in relation to EDUCO. Elsewhere, other aspects of EDUCO have been promoted (Edwards, 2013b).

[4] Note that all impact evaluations of EDUCO were produced by the World Bank and its consultants.

[5] The EDUCO program remained a key and unaffected feature of education governance in El Salvador through 2009, at which point Mauricio Funes became the first FMLN candidate in the post-war period to be elected president. In this role, Funes began, in 2011, to dismantle EDUCO by removing the ability of parents to hire and fire teachers. Subsequent actions by the national government have continued to transition EDUCO schools to the same management systems to which regular public schools are subjected, wherein teachers experience much more stability (Edwards, forthcoming).

[6] See Lubienski et al (2009) and Klees & Edwards (2014) for further discussion of the methodological shortcomings of quantitative methods generally and randomized control trials specifically.

References

Barrera-Osorio, F., Fasih, T., Patrinos, H. & Santibánez, L. (2009) *Decentralized Decision-making in Schools: the theory and evidence on school-based management.* Washington, DC: World Bank.

Booth, J., Wade, C. & Walker, T. (2006) *Understanding Central America.* Boulder, CO: Westview Press.

Bruns, B., Filmer, D. & Patrinos, H.A. (2011) *Making Schools Work: new evidence on accountability reforms.* Washington, DC: World Bank. http://dx.doi.org/10.1596/978-0-8213-8679-8

Castillo, N. & Wagner, D. (2014) Gold Standard? The Use of Randomized Controlled Trials for International Education Policy, *Comparative Education Review*, 58(1), 166-173. http://dx.doi.org/10.1086/674168

Conyers, D. (1983) Decentralization: the latest fashion in development administration? *Public Administration and Development*, 3, 97-109. http://dx.doi.org/10.1002/pad.4230030202

Cuéllar-Marchelli, H. (2003) Decentralization and Privatization of Education in El Salvador: assessing the experience, *International Journal of Educational Development*, 23(2), 45-166.

Dale, R. (2013) Revisiting the Mechanisms of Globalization in Education. Paper presented at the conference of the Comparative and International Education Society, 10-15 March, New Orleans, LA.

Dumas, M. & Anderson, G. (2014) Qualitative Research as Policy Knowledge: framing policy problems and transforming education from the ground up, *Education Policy Analysis Archives*, 22(11), 1-24. http://dx.doi.org/10.14507/epaa.v22n11.2014

Edwards Jr., D.B. (2012a) The Approach of the World Bank to Participation in Development and Education Governance: trajectories, frameworks, results, in C. Collins & A. Wiseman (Eds) *Education Strategy in the Developing World: revising the World Bank's education policy*, pp. 249-273. Bingley: Emerald.

Edwards Jr., D.B. (2012b) Researching International Processes of Education Policy Formation: conceptual and methodological consideration, *Research in Comparative and International Education*, 7(2), 127-145. http://dx.doi.org/10.2304/rcie.2012.7.2.127

Edwards Jr., D.B. (2013a) The Development of Global Education Policy: a case study of the origins and evolution of El Salvador's EDUCO program. Unpublished diss., University of Maryland.

Edwards Jr., D.B. (2013b) International Processes of Education Policy Formation: an analytic framework and the case of Plan 2021 in El Salvador, *Comparative Education Review*, 57(1), 22-53. http://dx.doi.org/10.1086/668481

Edwards Jr., D.B. (2014) A Critical Analysis of Impact Evaluations within the Political Economy of Education Reform: the case of a global education policy from El Salvador. San Salvador, El Salvador: Universidad Centroamericana, José Simeón Cañas.

Edwards Jr., D.B. (2015) Rising from the Ashes: how the global education policy of community-based management was born from El Salvador's civil war, *Globalisation, Societies and Education*, 13(3), 411-432. http://dx.doi.org/10.1080/14767724.2014.980225

Edwards Jr., D.B. (forthcoming) *International Education Policy and the Global Reform Agenda: education with community participation in El Salvador*. New York: Palgrave Macmillan.

Edwards Jr., D.B. & DeMatthews, D. (2014) Historical Trends in Educational Decentralization in the United States and Developing Countries: a periodization and comparison in the post-WWII context, *Education Policy Analysis Archives*, 22(40), 1-36. http://dx.doi.org/10.14507/epaa.v22n40.2014

Edwards Jr., D.B. & Klees, S. (2012) Participation in International Development and Education Governance, in A. Verger, M. Novelli & H. Kosar-Altinyelken (Eds) *Global Education Policy and International Development: new agendas, issues and programmes*, pp. 55-78. New York: Continuum.

Edwards Jr., D.B., Victoria, J.A. & Martin, P. (2015) The Geometry of Policy Implementation: lessons from the political economy of three education reforms in El Salvador during 1990-2005, *International Journal of Educational Development*, 44, 28-41. http://dx.doi.org/10.1016/j.ijedudev.2015.05.001

Gillies, J., Crouch, L. & Flórez, A. (2010) Revisión estratégica del programa EDUCO. USAID. http://www.equip123.net/docs/E2_REVISION_DEL_PROGRAMA_EDUCO.pdf

Global Partnership for Education (2009) *Six Steps for Abolishing Primary School Fees: operational guide*. Washington, DC: World Bank.

Hammond, J. (1998) *Fighting to Learn: popular education and guerrilla war in El Salvador*. New Brunswick, NJ: Rutgers University Press.

Hartmann, A. & Linn, J. (2008) Scaling Up: a framework and lessons for development effectiveness from literature and practice. Brookings Global Economy and Development Working Paper Series. http://www.brookings.edu/research/papers/2008/10/scaling-up-aid-linn

Harvey, D. (2005) *A Brief History of Neoliberalism*. New York: Oxford University Press.

Heckman, J. (1979) Sample Selection Bias as a Specification Error, *Econometrica*, 47(1), 153-161. http://dx.doi.org/10.2307/1912352

Jimenez, E. & Sawada, Y. (1999) Do Community-managed Schools Work? An Evaluation of El Salvador's EDUCO Program. *World Bank Economic Review*, 13(3), 415-441. http://dx.doi.org/10.1093/wber/13.3.415

Klees, S. & Edwards Jr., D.B. (2014) Knowledge Production and Technologies of Governance, in T. Fenwick, E. Mangez & J. Ozga (Eds) *World Yearbook of Education 2014. Governing Knowledge: comparison, knowledge-based technologies and expertise in the regulation of education*, pp. 31-43. New York: Routledge.

Klein, N. (2007) *The Shock Doctrine: the rise of disaster capitalism*. New York: Picador.

Kvernbekk, T. (2013) Evidence-based Practice: on the function of evidence in practical reasoning, *Studier i Pedagogisk Filosofi*, 2(2), 19-33.

LeoGrande, W. (1998) *Our Own Backyard: the United States and Central America, 1977-1992*. Chapel Hill: University of North Carolina.

Lindo Fuentes, H. (1998) *Comunidad, Participación y Escuelas: EDUCO en El Salvador*. Washington, DC: World Bank.

Lubienski, C., Weitzel, P. & Lubienski, S. (2009) Is there a 'Consensus' on School Choice and Achievement? Advocacy Research and the Emerging Political Economy of Knowledge Production, *Educational Policy*, 23(1), 161-193. http://dx.doi.org/10.1177/0895904808328532

Meza, D., Guzmán, J. & de Varela, L. (2004) EDUCO: a community-managed education program in rural areas of El Salvador. Paper presented at Scaling Up Poverty Reduction: a global learning process and conference, 25-27 May, Shanghai.

MINED (1990) *Servicios educativos a niños pobres Salvadoreños de 0 a 14 años*. San Salvador: MINED.

Montgomery, T. (1995) *Revolution in El Salvador: from civil strife to civil peace*, 2nd edn. Boulder, CO: Westview Press.

Pawson, R. (2006) *Evidence-based Policy: a realist perspective*. London: SAGE.

Rappleye, J. (2011) Catalysing Educational Development or Institutionalising External Influence? Donors, Civil Society and Educational Policy Formation in Nepal, *Globalisation, Societies and Education*, 9(1), 27-49.

Research Gate (n.d.) The World Bank Economic Review. http://www.researchgate.net/journal/1564-698X_The_World_Bank_Economic_Review

Robinson, W. (2003) *Transnational Conflicts: Central America, social change, and globalization*. New York: Verso.

Samoff, J. (1993) The Reconstruction of Schooling in Africa, *Comparative Education Review*, 37(2), 181-222. http://dx.doi.org/10.1086/447181

Save the Children (2013) *The Right to Learn: community participation improving learning*. Westport, CT: Save the Children.

Segovia, A. (1996) Macroeconomic Performance and Policies since 1989, in J.K. Boyce (Ed.) *Economic Policy for Building Peace: the lessons of El Salvador*, pp. 51-72. Boulder, CO: Lynne Rienner.

SIMEDUCO (2011) *Ya no estamos dormidos*. San Salvador: Instituto de Derechos Humanos de la Universidad 'José Simeón Cañas'.

Srygley, M. (2013) Education in Rural El Salvador: a case study on value, quality, and accountability. Unpublished thesis, University of Maryland.

Umanzor, S., Soriano, I., Vega, M., Jimenez, E., Rawlings, L. & Steele, D. (1997) El Salvador's EDUCO Program: a first report on parents' participation in school-based management. Working Paper Series on Impact Evaluation of Education Reforms, No. 4, World Bank.

UNESCO (2008) *EFA Global Monitoring Report 2009. Overcoming Inequality: why governance matters*. Oxford: Oxford University Press.

Verger, A., Edwards Jr., D.B. & Kosar-Altinyelken, H. (2014) Learning from All? The World Bank, Aid Agencies and the Construction of Hegemony in Education for Development, *Comparative Education*, 50(4), 1-19. http://dx.doi.org/10.1080/03050068.2014.918713

Winkler, D. (1989) *Decentralization in Education: an economic perspective*. Washington, DC: World Bank.

World Bank (2011) Synopsis of WDRs (1995-2005). http://web.worldbank.org/WBSITE/EXTERNAL/EXTDEC/EXTRESEARCH/EXTWDRS/0,,contentMDK:20313941~isCURL:Y~pagePK:478093~piPK:477627~theSitePK:477624,00.html

CHAPTER 3

Legitimacy, State-building and Contestation in Education Policy Development: Chile's involvement in cross-national assessments

RIE KIJIMA & JANE LEER

ABSTRACT Participation in cross-national assessments (CNAs) has grown exponentially over the last 50 years. This chapter provides an in-depth analysis of one country's participation in CNAs: Chile, one of the first non-OECD countries to participate in CNAs. Through interviews with Chilean education policy officials, the authors explore the global and domestic factors influencing the Chilean government's decision to participate in CNAs. They find that Chile participates in CNAs in order to compare the country's education performance with other countries, build institutional capacity, align the curriculum with international standards and improve public accountability. They argue that these findings are best explained by compensatory legitimization theory, whereby the State participates in CNAs in order to improve state legitimacy. By analyzing Chile's involvement in CNAs, these findings contribute to an understanding of the historical, political, socioeconomic and educational contexts that influence a country's decision to participate in CNAs – above and beyond simply measuring the quality of education.

Introduction

The country is obsessed with evaluation, obsessed with competition, and maybe constantly hungry about these instruments' results. (Chilean government official)

The number of countries participating in cross-national assessments (CNAs) has grown exponentially over the last 50 years. Today, over 70 countries and economies participate in international or regional assessments.[1] While the increasing popularity of CNAs has been widely recognized, little is known about the motivations that drive individual countries to participate in CNAs. In this chapter, we analyze this global phenomenon and the factors associated with countries' decision to participate in CNAs through a case study of Chile. Chile makes for an interesting case study given the country's long-term involvement in CNAs, having been one of the first non-OECD (Organisation for Economic Co-operation and Development) countries to participate in the Six Subject Study and the First International Math and Science study (IEA, 2011a, b). Since then, Chile has participated in a number of international assessments, and is actively involved in Latin American regional assessments. The country also has a robust national assessment system, which signifies a strong early commitment to education quality and public accountability.

Specifically, we explore the following research question: *What are the domestic and international factors that influence Chile's participation in CNAs?* Through semi-structured interviews with key policy-makers, we find that the Chilean government's decision to participate in CNAs is motivated by a need to demonstrate the State's commitment to education, a need which was made all the more acute in the context of the return to democracy following the authoritarian military regime. We also find that participation in CNAs is further legitimized and even *demanded* by citizens, who use the results of CNAs to challenge the State's education policies. These findings support compensatory legitimization theory, in which educational planning and expertise are used to foster state legitimacy (Weiler, 1983).

Context

Chilean Educational Reform

The past twenty years have been marked by major transitions in Chile, from military dictatorship to democracy, from a socialist economy to capitalism, and in the education sector, from a centralized, mostly public system, to a highly decentralized system dominated by state-subsidized private schools. The most radical changes to the education system occurred under the authoritarian military regime of Augusto Pinochet (1973-1990) (Cox, 2006). These reforms were guided by the market-based 'Chicago Boys' policy agenda, which sought to increase school efficiency through devolving administrative authority to local levels, deregulating teacher labor markets, and promoting school competition.

From 1980 to 1990 the administration of primary and secondary schools was transferred to the municipal level, teachers were stripped of their civil servant status and incorporated into the private labor sector, and private schools were encouraged to compete with public schools through the distribution of 'capitation grants' (vouchers) paid to public and private schools on a per-student basis (Delannoy, 2000; Cox, 2006). As a result, state education spending declined by 27%, teachers' salaries were reduced by as much as 40%, and private (state-subsidized) enrollment grew by 93% between 1980 and 1998 (Delannoy, 2000). While Pinochet's privatized educational expansion can be credited with contributing to the achievement of near-universal secondary school enrollment, these reforms left teachers severely demoralized and exacerbated existing achievement disparities between socioeconomic groups (McEwan & Carnoy, 2000).

After the fall of Pinochet in 1990, the new coalition government prioritized education in its commitment to restoring democracy and promoting social integration (Cox, 2006). However, rather than reversing the reforms established under Pinochet, the transition government sought to improve educational quality and equity within the existing system. Reforms in the early 1990s, therefore, included the New Teachers' Statute, which provides for teacher tenure and centrally negotiated wages, the 'P-900' Program, which targeted state resources towards low-income and rural schools, and the Full School Day reform, which extended the school week from 30 to 38 hours and set the groundwork for the development of a new national curriculum (Delannoy, 2000).

These reforms were supported by increased state and private investments in education. Public expenditure grew from 2.4% of gross domestic product (GDP) to 4.4% between 1990 and 2001, while private expenditure grew from 1.4% to 3.3% during the same period (Matear, 2007). However, despite the democratic government's focus on equity, the class-based educational divisions triggered by the 1980s reforms continued through the 1990s and 2000s. To this day, low-income students remain disproportionately segregated in low-resource, low-performing public schools, while the majority of middle and upper-income students attend well-resourced, better-performing private and private-subsidized schools (McEwan & Carnoy, 2000; Matear, 2007; Valenzuela et al, 2014).

As such, the educational reforms of the 1990s and 2000s did little to assuage the growing discontent among citizens fed up with what they perceive as 'more of the same' policies that help the 'rich get richer' but do little to improve the quality of life and living conditions of average citizens (Donoso, 2013; Bellei et al, 2014). These grievances erupted in two major student protests. The first of these was the *Pingüino* movement in 2006, which called for the defense of public education and the elimination of for-profit educational providers. The more recent student movement in 2011 focused mainly on higher education, demanding egalitarian access to higher education and increased state involvement in education regulation. This movement culminated in the largest public protest since the return to democracy. On 16 June 2011, more than 100,000 people took to the streets of the capital, Santiago, demanding an end to class-based educational segregation (Bellei et al, 2014).

Rie Kijima & Jane Leer

National Assessments in Chile

Central to Chile's market-based educational expansion is the role of choice and competition in improving school quality. In this context, assessments are meant to provide citizens with the information necessary to make informed schooling decisions. In turn, given that schools receive funding on a per-student basis, schools have an incentive to ensure their students perform well on assessments in order to attract students. Thus, the development of national assessments has been a key facet of Chile's educational reforms since the 1980s (Cariola et al, 2008).

The first national assessment scheme, the *Programa de Evaluación del Rendimiento* (PER), was introduced in 1981, but was suspended after only three years in response to cost concerns and disagreements regarding test administration responsibility (Cox, 2006). The *Sistema de Medición de la Calidad* (SIMCE), first launched in 1988, replaced the PER. School-level results of the first SIMCE were not published until 1995, however. This is due in part to the fact that teachers initially blocked the publication of school-based results, which they saw as unfair (Delannoy, 2000). Additionally, the *Ley Orgánica de Educación* (LOCE) stipulated that SIMCE results could not be published until the national curriculum had been approved (Cariola et al, 2008).

Despite this rocky start, the SIMCE has since gained widespread acceptance among the Chilean public, and the test is considered one of the most technically advanced and politically influential national assessment systems in Latin America (Delannoy, 2000; Ferrer, 2006). SIMCE results are used to inform curricular design, identify poorly performing schools in order to target state intervention, and incentivize teacher performance through merit-based pay schemes. This national experience in the administration and use of educational assessments is important in understanding why Chile participates in CNAs.

Chile's Participation in Cross-national Assessments

Chile's participation in international tests dates back to 1970, when the country participated in the Six Subjects Study and the First International Science Study (FISS), both of which were conducted by the International Association for the Evaluation of Education (IEA). After a two-decade hiatus from cross-national tests during the military regime, Chile participated in five international studies between 1997 and 2000: (1) in 1997, the first Regional Comparative Exploratory Study (PERCE) (a regional study led by UNESCO); (2) in 1999, the IEA's Third International Math and Science Study (TIMSS); (3) in 2000, the International Adult Literacy Survey (IALS), led by the OECD; (4) in 2000, the IEA's Civic Education Study (IEA 2011a); and (5) the OECD's Programme for International Student Assessment (PISA), also in 2000. Chile has since participated in all subsequent versions of the TIMSS except for the 2007 TIMSS, and all subsequent versions of the PISA except for the 2003 PISA. Figure 1 presents a timeline of these events. This study focuses on Chile's reasons for participating in the TIMSS and PISA from 1998 to 2006.

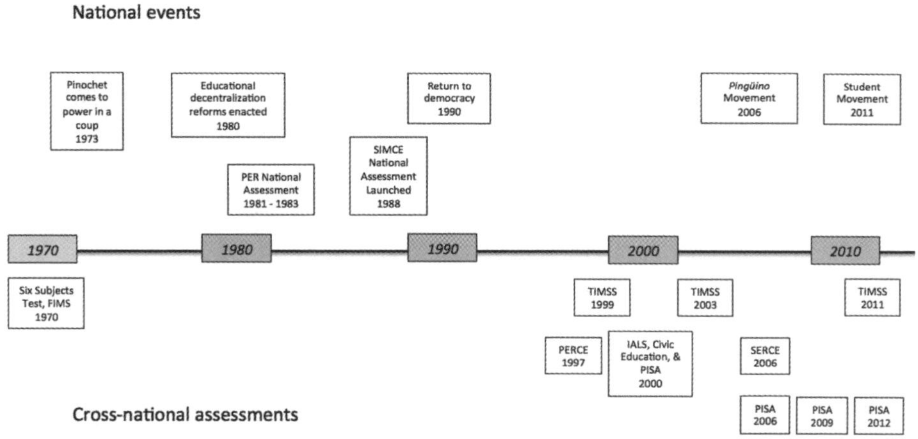

Figure 1. Timeline of national events and participation in cross-national tests, 1970-2012.

Chile's performance in TIMSS and PISA has improved moderately, but the country remains consistently in the bottom 25th percentile or lower when compared with all participating countries. Chile's PISA math scores evolved from 384 (ranked 36th out of 41 countries) in 2000, to 411 (47th out of 57 countries) in 2006, to 421 in 2009 (50th out of 74 countries), to 423 (51st out of 65 countries) in 2012 (OECD, 2004, 2007, 2010, 2012; OECD/ UNESCO Institute for Statistics, 2003). In comparison with other participating Latin American countries (Uruguay, Brazil and Argentina), however, Chile consistently performs at the top. This leads to the following sub-questions: Do the perceived benefits of performing better than regional neighbors offset the costs of poor performance relative to the OECD average? Besides the possibility for regional and international comparison, what other factors motivate the Chilean government's decision to participate in CNAs? Our research seeks to address these sub-questions through various theoretical lenses, as discussed in the following section.

Conceptual Framework

In this section, we highlight three theories that can explain why countries participate in CNAs. The first is neo-institutional world society theory. Following this theory, nation-states that are immersed in world culture are more likely to adopt similar patterns of modernization, thus giving rise to worldwide assimilation and isomorphism (Ramirez & Boli, 1987; Meyer et al,

1992; Strang & Meyer, 1993; Meyer & Ramirez, 2000). Under this logic, countries participate in CNAs in order to be seen as a legitimate actor in the international community (Kamens & McNeely, 2010). Neo-institutional world society theorists would argue that states choose to participate in CNAs because an increasingly greater number of governments buy into the global testing culture, in which participation in large-scale standardized testing has become synonymous with education quality (Balwanz, 2016). While this theory is useful in explaining the rise of a global phenomenon like international assessments, it does not explain the domestic political factors that influence countries to adopt CNAs.

In contrast, scholars who draw from political science constructivist theory highlight the role that international organizations play in setting global norms and frameworks (Finnemore & Sikkink, 1998; Ruggie, 1998). These scholars argue that countries participate in CNAs because of the influence of multilateral aid agencies. Less-developed countries – and even middle-income countries like Vietnam – are often pressured by multilateral agencies to participate in CNAs as a condition of aid funding (Kijima, 2013). This claim is supported by evidence of a correlation between foreign aid to education and participation in CNAs (Kijima, 2010). Constructivist theory is less likely to be relevant in the case of Chile, however, considering the country's upper-middle-income status. Nonetheless, organizations like the World Bank and UNESCO still play an influential role in Chile's educational development, primarily by providing technical assistance (Interview #622015).

Unlike neo-institutional world society theory and constructivist theory, state theory emphasizes the state's interests in policy decisions. State theory is particularly useful in understanding the domestic political forces that influence the Chilean government's decision to participate in CNAs. Specifically, state theory posits that citizens' demands for better resource allocation are mediated by state bureaucrats in order to strengthen the State itself (Carnoy, 1984). In this sense, we argue that participation in CNAs serves to inform the public about the direction of education reforms, which in turn demonstrates the State's competency as a legitimate actor in the education sector.

Legitimization of the State Apparatus

To further refine our conceptualization of Chile's participation in CNAs, we draw our analytical framework from compensatory legitimization, a form of state theory first developed in the 1980s by Hans Weiler. We argue that this theory offers the best explanation for Chile's participation in national, regional and international assessments. In compensatory legitimization theory, governments enact specific policies designed to address the deficit that arises from the disconnect between citizens' expectations of socioeconomic progress and the State's capacity to meet these expectations (Weiler, 1983).

Given the critical role of education in determining social status and socializing citizens, education policy is particularly vulnerable to this 'deficit'. That is, citizens are often unhappy about the perceived failure of education policy to contribute to sustained economic growth and poverty reduction. As such, education policy requires especially high levels of legitimization (Weiler, 1983).

Weiler posits that there are three strategies by which countries enact compensatory legitimization: legalization, utilization of scientific evidence, and citizen participation in policy decisions. Likewise, we offer three usages of assessments from the perspective of the state in order to argue that participation in CNAs provides a mechanism of compensatory legitimation.

First, Chile regularly participates in both national and cross-national assessments, which sends an important signal to Chilean citizens. While Chile's participation in CNAs is not legally mandated, a strong track record of regular participation in international and regional assessments publicly demonstrates the government's commitment to improving the quality of education. CNAs are a convenient way for the Chilean state to demonstrate that its domestic decisions are informed and shaped by international standards supported by norm-setting organizations like the OECD and IEA (Kijima, 2013).

Second, regular participation in CNAs institutionalizes the use of scientific knowledge in education policy. Because assessments are generally considered to be grounded in scientific inquiry and methods that yield objective results, participation in CNAs demonstrates the State's commitment to scientific, evidence-based education planning. This concept is also captured by scholars of neo-institutional world society theory in their explanation of the rationalization of science (e.g. Drori, 2003).

Weiler's theory, however, is much more grounded in the interests of the state, in which the state determines education policies that ultimately serve its own political interests. There are two ways by which the State uses participation in CNAs to standardize the use of scientific expertise. First, government leaders learn from international leaders in assessment administration and analysis in order to strengthen their own assessment systems (Lockheed, 2012). Second, policy officials use the knowledge gained from participating in CNAs to align national curriculum with international curricular standards. This enables the State to legitimize its education policies by framing them as being 'evidence based', regardless of the political or economic factors that may also play a role.

Third, assessment is a mechanism through which public participation, an important aspect of compensatory legitimization, becomes possible. Assessments encourage forms of public discourse around education policy formation. The publication of test results often stirs political debate about the state of education, which in turn serves to either support or critique existing education policy agendas (Takayama, 2010). In this sense, assessments open up political space for citizens and even enable opposing groups to voice their concerns regarding education. Even when assessments are used to protest *against* the state's education policies (as is the case in Chile), the public dissemination of assessment results demonstrates the State's commitment to accountability and citizen participation. As Weiler argues, when facing credibility crises, the state may attempt to reclaim its legitimacy by 'tolerating or actually instituting various schemes for citizen participation' (1983, p. 272). Thus, however real or superficial this commitment may be, the state's publication of assessment results generates participation and public debate, which further legitimizes the state's role as a competent policy maker in a democratic society.

Compensatory legitimization theory is particularly fitting in the case of Chile because of the country's recent political history. In the transition to democracy, the Chilean state faced pressure to demonstrate both its political power and its commitment to restoring democracy and social justice. The role of education in this legitimacy process is pivotal. After the major privatized and decentralized expansion of education during Pinochet's military dictatorship (1973-90), the new coalition government had to reclaim education on its own terms. Participation in CNAs is thus a mechanism through which the Chilean state demonstrates its 'scientific expertise' and 'development of planning mechanisms' to maintain legitimacy in the education sector (Weiler, 1983). Meanwhile, student movements use the results of CNAs to place demands on the state to improve educational equity and quality, while political opposition parties use the government's decision to participate (or not participate) in CNAs as a way to de-legitimize the governing party. In this way, participation in CNAs promotes public participation in education policy and is, therefore, one way through which the democratic state addresses its legitimacy dilemma.

Data and Method

The data from our case-study analysis come from interviews with respondents who have extensive knowledge about Chile's involvement in international, regional and national assessments. Because policy decisions are often made by a handful of high-ranking individuals, only a small number of interviews were needed to understand the decisions and processes behind the country's decision to participate in CNAs. Collecting data from these primary decision-makers enabled us to explore the global and domestic factors associated with participation in CNAs.

We used snowball sampling to identify a total of eight respondents, including former and current senior government officials, a former Minister of Education, officers at international organizations and a Chilean academic. We used a semi-structured interview protocol, and each interview lasted between 45 and 90 minutes. Interviews were conducted at an international conference and online (via Skype) between June 2012 and June 2015. All interviews were transcribed and analyzed using grounded theory (Charmaz, 2006) in order to identify emerging themes and concepts.

Results

We find four main reasons for Chile's participation in international assessments: (1) to compare the country's achievement against other countries; (2) to build institutional capacity; (3) to align the curriculum with 'the international standard'; and (4) to improve public accountability.

Reason 1: International and Regional Comparison

One of the main reasons for Chile's participation in CNAs is the country's desire to compare its educational performance regionally and internationally. If the Chilean government were primarily interested in gaining an understanding of its own educational program, policymakers would continue to rely on the country's extensive national assessment system. This is not the case, however. We find that Chile participates in international assessments in order to understand how the Chilean education system compares with that of the country's regional neighbors and, in particular, with the OECD average.

> For Chile, it's clear that it's absolutely crucial to have this kind of possibility to compare our students and their learning, and results of the educational system, with other countries … We compare with other Latin American countries … and then we have the comparison with the [top OECD performers], and that is a very important lesson, also to compare how far we are in terms of the OECD average. (Interview #56151)

> Well, in our reports we almost always compare with Latin American countries, and then we also choose some of the best countries, and the [lowest] countries. That is something you could see in our reports. And we also look for those that perform the worst. (Interview #56131)

Similarly, participation in CNAs provides international 'benchmarks' that the country can use to determine national performance targets.

> So another big reason was to have a test with international parameters to see how our quality was. This is not only in terms of, 'Okay, let's see how, internationally, we are positioned,' which is also important, but it was also, I would say, an interest in seeing different benchmarks. (Interview #564311)

Reason 2: Institutional Capacity Building

The second reason for Chile's participation in CNAs is to build institutional capacity. In particular, respondents highlight the desire to strengthen the country's national assessment capacity through exposure to the international standards in achievement testing.

> So, our interest in participating in international studies came from trying to have a good way of getting feedback for the national tests. It was seen as an opportunity to learn from different areas involved in the standard assessments. That's the reason why these tests, the international assessments, were introduced in the ministry. (Interview #564311)

> I also think it is important – in terms of the national capabilities for assessment. It's very, very important to participate in these kinds of tests ... [We need] technicians and professionals in our country that can understand better the main tendencies and the trends used in the assessments in this form, and to have our national assessment also aligned with these international tools. (Interview #56151)

Chilean officials involved in the administration and analysis of the national test (SIMCE) benefit from the chance to learn from what respondents considered the 'club of the best assessments in the world of education' – that is, the IEA (Interview #56111). Respondents describe how their national assessment capacity improved through the use of 'item constructions, coding, scoring, analysis reporting, everything' that they learned through participating in the TIMSS (Interview #56111).

> It was not very wise to be out of that club [the IEA]. We wanted to be in that network, we wanted to be with the global leadership in the educational assessment, in terms of national testing of learning results. (Interview #56111)

Importantly, Chile's existing assessment capacity facilitated the government's desire to participate and learn from 'the best'. The government did not have to rely on foreign consultants to implement the TIMSS and PISA. Rather, participation in these tests was seen as an opportunity to strengthen the country's already strong national assessment capacity.

> But we did have testing capacity; we didn't have to resort to foreign consultants ... And we had been doing that for more than a decade, so we had those capacities. (Interview #56111)

In addition, assessments were already publicly accepted. By the late 1990s, teachers and students were used to frequent testing. Some teachers even preferred the international tests because the results were not as high stakes for teachers and students as the national tests, the results of which are posted publicly.

> When we decided to participate in the IEA studies, the country had a decade, more than a decade of experience with assessments of school results, and the communication of those results to society. (Interview #56121)

> [It] is very important to understand why international studies are not so much ... disregarded by teachers ... Teachers are not so much against international studies as they would be against national studies. By now we're starting to have problems ... with getting the agreement from schools for testing because they have so many tests, there are so many tests going on that they do not want to have their students being tested anymore. (#56131)

Reason 3: Alignment of Curriculum to International Standards

Third, education officials use CNAs to ensure that the newly designed Chilean national curriculum is well aligned with what respondents consider to be the 'international standard' – that is, the subjects and competencies covered in the TIMSS and PISA assessments.

> I think we use all of these tools in different matters ... for example, the group of people that work in the curriculum unit analyze not only the results, but also the battery of subjects and competencies. We try to align our curriculum with the international opinion. The reason, I think, is that we used the framework of TIMSS or PISA in trying to analyze whether or not our curriculum covers the matters that these international tests cover. (#56151)

The need to incorporate 'international standards' into the national curriculum is imperative, and participating in CNAs gives education officials the means by which to achieve this goal.

> We didn't want to develop our standards only according to our own national assessment, because then our students would continue knowing the same things they already know. We wanted to raise our standards ... our goals are not to improve our own education, but to be nearer to the educational international standards. (#56131)

> You cannot afford to be outside the PISA definition of competencies that schools need to communicate to the next generation. (#56111)

Reason 4: Public Accountability and Voice

Following the return to democracy in the early 1990s, education officials needed to differentiate the new government's practices from those of the previous authoritarian regime, particularly with regard to transparency and equity. The commitment to testing, and to making the results of both national and international tests publicly available, contrasted with the authoritarian regime's failure to publish SIMCE results. Moreover, given the decision to continue decentralization and privatization reforms that were initiated under the military regime, the government faced extra pressure to address the gap between the public's expectations and the government's capacity to meet these expectations. Participation in CNAs, therefore, announced to citizens the government's capacity to meet these expectations.

> In that context [the return to democracy], to have an international, cross-national examination ... that shows your relative position as these tests developed, announces to you and your population if you are advancing or not, or if you are going backwards in terms of results. It's of extreme importance. When the [TIMSS] results are published ... the whole Chilean press, for a week, dedicates pages and pages to the test results, and comparisons between schools, and the relationship between the new information with the policy-making of the government. (Interview #56111)

Furthermore, one of the first international tests Chile participated in after the fall of Pinochet was the IEA's Civic Education Test, which was used as a tool to gauge the capacity of Chilean schools to prepare students for participation in a democratic society (Interview #56111). This further served to demonstrate the new government's commitment to democracy via transparency and public participation.

In turn, respondents discuss how Chile's participation is CNAs is re-packaged and further legitimized by citizens as a tool to contest the State's education policies. There was public uproar, for example, against the government's decision *not* to participate in the 2007 round of the TIMSS.[2]

> Politically, it was a disaster. From there onwards, there's no major international assessment that Chile skips. No Chilean government can afford to skip an international assessment of education ...
> Because the risks of opting out are immense. Immense. (Interview #56111)

> We joined TIMSS in 1999, then we took 2003, and we skipped 2007, and then we're back in 2011. It was a big issue, that position. We were also in PISA. PISA started in 2001-2000 really – but ... 2003 we did not participate, and we participated in 2006. Especially ... skipping [the TIMSS] after 2 cycles, this was a big

issue. Politicians really discussed why this decision was made. (Interview #564311)

Political opposition parties used the government's decision not to participate as a means to question the government's capacity in the education sector, by suggesting that the decision not to participate was based on a concern that the results would demonstrate the inadequacy of the governing party's education policies (Interview #56111). Participation in CNAs has come to be expected and even taken for granted, and governments cannot risk the political backlash that comes from not participating.

Similarly, respondents discuss how teachers and students learn to 'speak the language' of CNAs in order to articulate their demands for educational reform.

> The results of these tests, they have become part of the country, of the policy-making, of the political culture regarding education ... When I say the political system that includes, of course, the teacher's unit ... And they also speak the language of these results and articulate their views. (#56111)

Student movements, too, use the PISA and TIMSS results to legitimize their claims that the Chilean government does not do enough to address the socioeconomic disparities in educational achievement. Most notably, students in the *Pingüino* movement of 2006 used an OECD publication citing Chile's poor performance in educational equity to support their demands.

> There's a part of the population that has a very crucial use of this data, and they demand and put pressure [on the government] in terms of [whether or not] the country has good or bad results ... the examination report of the OECD, for example, this ... policy report was used by the students, and they had a very important mobilization ... The name of this movement – it was an enormous movement – the name of the movement was 'The Penguin's Revolution'. (Interview #56151)

Indeed, when asked how participation in PISA and TIMSS influences policymaking, respondents describe how the results of these tests affect policy vis-à-vis their incorporation into the public discourse surrounding education. The public's use of CNAs is perhaps just as important for policy making as the government's intended use of CNAs.

> But I'm sure that the research does not have a direct impact in policy-making ... research impacts through public opinion, through the press, through people making noise, through our students in the streets – they are much more knowledgeable now than they were before ... the social movement is educated by research results. (#56131)

In sum, education officials participate in CNAs in order to increase the state's legitimacy. The Chilean state uses participation in CNAs to compare and 'benchmark' the country's educational development relative to international standards, improve national assessment capacity, and align the national curriculum to international norms regarding the competencies and knowledge that students should learn in order to compete in the global economy. In doing so, the state demonstrates its expertise and commitment to education planning – a commitment that the Chilean state faced particularly strong pressure to meet given the dramatic restructuring of the Chilean education system that began in the 1980s. The public then uses Chile's participation and performance in CNAs to question the legitimacy of the state. Political opposition parties claim that the party in power has something to hide if political leaders choose not to participate in a particular CNA. Meanwhile, teachers and students use the results of CNAs to voice their discontent with the status quo. Thus, participation in CNAs to a certain extent institutionalizes civic participation. Even when this participation is directed against the state, by virtue of enabling this public dialogue, the new democratic state differentiates itself from the previous government and secures further legitimacy.

Discussion

Our findings indicate that global factors are not the only reason why Chile participates in CNAs. While it is clear that Chile has been influenced by the international discourse regarding the link between CNAs and educational quality, there are domestic political factors that are equally important in Chile's decision to participate in CNAs.

Chile's interest in maintaining its legitimacy through regular participation in regional and international assessments is clear. As our respondents state, the costs of not participating are too high, the country cannot afford to be 'out of the club'. Neo-institutional world society theory partially explains this need to belong to the 'club' of CNA participants, as participation bolsters Chile's international legitimacy. However, compensatory legitimization is better at explaining the domestic forces associated with this need for legitimacy. Through participating in CNAs, the Chilean government is able to justify its education reforms to its citizens by referring to 'best practices' around the world. In this way, participation in CNAs facilitates policy borrowing (Steiner-Khamsi, 2004). Policy makers' interest in data-driven decisions – based on the results from CNAs – is one example of a 'borrowed' policy. The commitment to evidence-based policy demonstrates the new government's interest in internationally sanctioned forms of transparent policy-making, representing a sharp contrast from the previous authoritarian regime.

Chile also participates in CNAs in order to build national capacity through the technical assistance provided by international organizations like the OECD, UNESCO and IEA.[3] This finding provides limited support for constructivist theory, given that Chile is undoubtedly influenced by these organizations. However, constructivist theory falls short, as it is clear that the Chilean government is in no way coerced to participate in CNAs. Rather, the decision to participate is a strategic one, based primarily on the state's interests. Through membership in the 'club of the best assessments', education officials adopt internationally recognized methods to improve the country's national assessment system. Likewise, participating countries are invited to technical seminars and conferences that are organized with the purpose of improving national capacity to conduct, analyze and utilize CNAs. By associating with these organizations, the Chilean government improves its reputation, both internationally and domestically.

Another key finding is the role of CNAs as a tool for political contestation between the state and the citizens. According to compensatory legitimization theory, in the face of political crisis, the state may tolerate or even promote space for public contestation, so long as these spaces ultimately serve to demonstrate the state's commitment to transparency and accountability.

This is evident in the case of Chile, where participation in CNAs has been used against the state in some of the largest protest movements the country has seen since the return to democracy. Both the *Pingüino* movement in 2006 and the student movement in 2011 presented major legitimacy challenges for the Bachelet government and the Piñera government, respectively. However, despite the crises these movements caused for individual governments, one could argue that the student movements ultimately enhanced the legitimacy of the state itself – especially considering that both movements demanded *increased* state regulation in the education sector.

Recent events in Chile highlight the success of the student movements in reinstating the role of the state in education. In February of 2015, the Chilean government passed a law that will gradually ban profits, tuition fees and selective admission practices in private state-subsidized primary and secondary schools. This reform is considered an important step towards dismantling Pinochet's market-based education reforms (Achtenberg, 2015).

Conclusion

Participation in CNAs is growing. With over 70 countries currently engaged in CNAs, the increasing impact that these assessments have on education policy around the world is undeniable. This study reveals the motives and rationales that explain countries' participation in CNAs through an in-depth analysis of Chile's involvement in CNAs. Drawing from various theories to explain the reasons why countries participate in CNAs, we argue that Chile's involvement in CNAs is explained by the new democratic state's efforts to demonstrate its legitimacy. Our findings move beyond previous studies by casting the state as an active decision maker in the CNA process.

One question that remains is why countries continue to participate in CNAs even when their performance does not improve – such as Yemen, which tends to score at the bottom of the rankings, or Malaysia and Finland, both of which experienced a drop in their overall scores and ranking. This question is beyond the scope of this study. Nonetheless, we can draw some hypotheses from Chile's case. Chile consistently ranks below the international average in PISA, but above most other participating Latin American countries. The fact that Chile is a high performer relative to its regional neighbors likely strengthens the state's local legitimacy. Moreover, regardless of performance, our findings suggest that the act of participation sends an important signal both internationally and domestically.

Research on governments' rationales for participating in CNAs is limited. By analyzing Chile's involvement in CNAs, our findings contribute to an understanding of the political, socioeconomic and educational contexts that influence a country's decision to participate in CNAs. In doing so, we offer a compelling description of the multiple uses of CNAs beyond simply measuring the quality of education.

Notes

[1] In this chapter, cross-national assessments refer to both international and regional assessments. This distinction is necessary because Chile participates in both international assessments (e.g. PISA, TIMSS, etc.) and regional assessments (e.g. PERCE, SERCE, etc.).

[2] Respondents stated that the decision not to participate in TIMSS in 2007, as well as the decision not to participate in PISA 2003, stems from the fact that the country was already participating in multiple other international tests during the same year, and simply did not have the capacity to effectively administer and analyze the results of multiple international tests. There was thus a need to prioritize. In 2003, the TIMSS was prioritized because the officials were particularly interested in assessing the new curriculum, which had been designed partly on the basis of the results of the 1998 TIMSS. In 2006, PISA was prioritized, largely because the country was trying to gain acceptance as a member of the OECD during the same period.

[3] OECD administers PISA, IEA offers TIMSS and PIRLS, and UNESCO moderates the Latin American regional assessments.

References

Achtenberg, E. (2015) Chilean Students Struggle to Deepen Educational Reforms. 3 March. https://nacla.org/blog/2015/03/03/chilean-students-struggle-deepen-educational-reforms

Balwanz, D. (2016) The Discursive Hold of the Matric: is there space for a new vision for secondary education in South Africa? In W.C. Smith (Ed.) *The Global Testing Culture: shaping education policy, perceptions, and practice.* Oxford: Symposium Books.

Bellei, C., Cabalin, C. & Orellana, V. (2014) The 2011 Chilean Student Movement against Neoliberal Educational Policies, *Studies in Higher Education*, 39(3), 426-440. http://doi.org/10.1080/03075079.2014.896179

Cariola, M.L, Cares, G. & Rivero, R. (2008) Sistemas de Evaluación Como Herramientas de Políticas, *Revista Iberoamericana de Evaluación Educativa*, 1(1).

Carnoy, M. (1984) *The State and Political Theory*, vol. 11. Princeton, NJ: Princeton University Press. http://dx.doi.org/10.1515/9781400853458

Charmaz, K. (2006) *Constructing Grounded Theory: a practical guide through qualitative analysis.* London: SAGE.

Cox, C. (2006) Policy Formation and Implementation in Secondary Education Reform: the case of Chile at the turn of the century. World Bank. http://www-wds.worldbank.org/external/default/WDSContentServer/WDSP/IB/2006/08/28/000090341_20060828093017/Rendered/PDF/370140CL0Secondary0ed0reform01PUBLIC1.pdf

Delannoy, F. (2000) *Education Reforms in Chile, 1980-1998: a lesson in pragmatism*, 1(1). World Bank. http://www-wds.worldbank.org/servlet/WDSContentServer/IW3P/IB/2000/09/01/000094946_00081805551098/Rendered/PDF/multi_page.pdf

Donoso, S. (2013) Dynamics of Change in Chile: explaining the emergence of the 2006 Pingüino movement, *Journal of Latin American Studies*, 45(1), 1-29. http://doi.org/10.1017/S0022216X12001228

Drori, G.S. (2003) *Science in the Modern World Polity: institutionalization and globalization.* Redwood City, CA: Stanford University Press.

Ferrer, G. (2006) *Educational Assessment Systems in Latin America: current practice and future challenges*, 1st edn. Washington, DC: PREAL.

Finnemore, M. & Sikkink, K. (1998) International Norm Dynamics and Political Change, *International Organization*, 52(4), 887-917. http://dx.doi.org/10.1162/002081898550789

International Association for the Evaluation of Educational Achievement (IEA) (2011a) IEA: First International Science Study (FISS). http://www.iea.nl/fiss.html (accessed 12 April 2015).

International Association for the Evaluation of Educational Achievement (IEA) (2011b) IEA: Six Subject Survey: literature education. http://www.iea.nl/six_subject_literature.html (accessed 12 April 2015).

Kamens, D.H. & McNeely, C.L. (2010) Globalization and the Growth of International Educational Testing and National Assessment, *Comparative Education Review*, 54(1), 5-25. http://dx.doi.org/10.1086/648471

Kijima, R. (2010) Why Participate? Cross-national Assessments and Foreign Aid to Education, in *The Impact of International Achievement Studies on National Education Policymaking*, vol. 13. Bingley: Emerald. http://dx.doi.org/10.1108/S1479-3679(2010)0000013005

Kijima, R. (2013) The Politics of Cross-national Assessments: global trends and national interests. PhD dissertation, Stanford University.

Lockheed, M. (2012) Policies, Performance and Panaceas: the role of international large-scale assessments in developing countries, *Compare*, 42(3), 512-518. 10.1080/03057925.2012.670480

Matear, A. (2007) Equity in Education in Chile: the tensions between policy and practice, *International Journal of Educational Development*, 27(1), 101-113. http://doi.org/10.1016/j.ijedudev.2006.06.015

McEwan, P.J. & Carnoy, M. (2000) The Effectiveness and Efficiency of Private Schools in Chile's Voucher System, *Educational Evaluation and Policy Analysis*, 22(3), 213-239. http://doi.org/10.3102/01623737022003213

Meyer, J.W., Kamens, D.H. & Benavot, A. (1992) *School Knowledge for the Masses: world models and national primary curricular categories in the twentieth century.* Washington, DC: Falmer Press.

Meyer, J.W. & Ramirez, F.O. (2000) The World Institutionalization of Education, in *Discourse Formation in Comparative Education*, pp. 111-132. Frankfurt am Main: Peter Lang.

Organisation for Economic Cooperation and Development (OECD) (2004) *Learning for Tomorrow's World: first results from PISA 2003.* Paris: OECD Publishing.

Organisation for Economic Cooperation and Development (OECD) (2007) *PISA 2006: Science Competencies for Tomorrow's World.* Paris: OECD Publishing.

Organisation for Economic Cooperation and Development (OECD) (2010) *What Students Know and Can Do: student performance in reading, mathematics and science.* Paris: OECD Publishing.

Organisation for Economic Cooperation and Development (OECD) (2012) *PISA 2012 Results in Focus: what 15-year-olds know and what they can do with what they know. Key results from PISA 2012.* Paris: OECD Publishing.

Organisation for Economic Cooperation and Development (OECD)/UNESCO Institute for Statistics (2003) *Literacy Skills for the World of Tomorrow: further results from PISA 2000.* Paris: OECD Publishing.

Ramirez, F.O. & Boli, J. (1987) The Political Construction of Mass Schooling: European Origins and Worldwide Institutionalization, *Sociology of Education*, 2-17. http://dx.doi.org/10.2307/2112615

Ruggie, J.G. (1998) What Makes the World Hang Together? Neo-utilitarianism and the Social Constructivist Challenge, *International Organization*, 52(4), 855-885. http://dx.doi.org/10.1162/002081898550770

Steiner-Khamsi, G. (2004) *The Global Politics of Educational Borrowing and Lending.* New York: Teachers College Press.

Strang, D. & Meyer, J.W. (1993) Institutional Conditions for Diffusion, *Theory and Society*, 22(4), 487-511. http://dx.doi.org/10.1007/BF00993595

Takayama, K. (2010) Politics of Externalization in Reflexive Times: reinventing Japanese education reform discourses through 'Finnish PISA Success', *Comparative Education Review*, 54(1), 51-75. http://dx.doi.org/10.1086/644838

Valenzuela, J.P., Bellei, C. & de los Ríos, D. (2014) Socioeconomic School Segregation in a Market-oriented Educational System: the case of Chile, *Journal* of *Education Policy*, 29(2), 217-241. http://doi.org/10.1080/02680939.2013.806995

Weiler, H.N. (1983) Legalization, Expertise, and Participation: strategies of compensatory legitimation in educational policy, *Comparative Education Review*, 27(2), 259-277. http://dx.doi.org/10.1086/446371

CHAPTER 4

Teaching the World that Less is More: global education testing and the Finnish national brand

HILLA AURÉN & DEVIN JOSHI

ABSTRACT Finland's impressive performance on international education tests has led to considerable interest in Finland's education model and education-related exports. Moreover, Finland stands out because it has completely eschewed a *disciplinary* testing culture involving high-stakes standardised testing in basic education. Rather, as the authors argue in this chapter, Finland's long-lasting educational success has been achieved by means of a *supportive* testing culture emphasising educational equality. They analyse this development through in-depth interviews with Finnish education experts and systematic content analysis of global media reports covering Finland since the year 2000. The evidence reveals that through international testing Finland has successfully developed a positive global reputation in education, which has enhanced its national brand and demand for its educational exports. However, the successful adoption of Finnish educational practices outside Finland appears to depend on the extent to which others are willing to embrace equality as a means and end of education.

Introduction

Finland's remarkable performance in basic education is unrivalled among Western countries and has drawn much international attention in recent years. As demonstrated in this chapter, this reputation is largely a result of high scores on international education tests. Moreover, Finland stands out because, unlike some other countries performing well on such tests, it does not employ a *disciplinary* testing culture involving high-stakes standardised testing. Rather, as we argue here, Finland's long-lasting educational success has been achieved by means of a *supportive* testing culture. As a result, educational success 'without inspections' has become a major component of

Finland's national brand, prompting an increase in Finnish educational exports. As discussed below, what this chapter reveals is that there are still multiple testing cultures around the world, and it is not inevitable that *disciplinary* approaches will win out over *supportive* ones in the long run.

We begin this chapter by briefly summarising core features of the Finnish education model (FEM) and how its supportive testing culture impacts its success. Illustrating the power of international assessments to identify and legitimate educational practices, we then examine how international testing has contributed to Finland's positive reputation in education, as captured by global media reports. Sharing our findings from recent interviews with 21 Finnish education experts from the government, academia and the private sector, we then discuss the emergence of a positive feedback loop, whereby Finland's education reputation has enhanced both its national brand and demand for exports of its education-related products and services.

The Finnish Education Model

The international appeal of the FEM originated in Finland's impressive performance on the Organisation for Economic Co-operation and Development's (OECD's) challenging PISA (Programme for International Student Assessment) examinations of 15-year-olds that have been held in several dozen countries every three years since 2000 (Sahlberg, 2007; Dobbins & Martens, 2012). As shown in Table I, between 2000 and 2012, with only one exception, Finland has consistently scored among the top five countries in the world in reading, mathematics and science.[1] In addition to remarkable exam results in all three subjects tested by PISA, Finland is the only European country consistently at the top (Telhaug et al, 2006). There is also relatively little variation in student performance across Finnish schools, with 'the proportion of between-school variance in Finland at about one tenth of the OECD average' (Sahlberg, 2007, p. 159). As a result, both PISA tests and the Finnish model have had an increasing impact on education policy reforms in countries around the world (e.g. Sahlberg, 2007; Grek, 2009; Rautalin & Alasuutari, 2009; Toots, 2009; Takayama, 2010; Kauko & Diogo, 2011; Dobbins & Martens, 2012). The impact of the OECD here as a catalyst for the development of Finnish educational policies, especially in serving as a political forum for national discussion, cannot be overestimated (Niukko, 2006).

Evidence of Finland's educational success is not limited to PISA. Finland ranked near the top (second place out of 45 countries) in the 2011 Progress in International Reading Literacy Study (PIRLS), which examines the literacy skills of fourth-graders. In the 2011 Trends in International Mathematics and Science Study (TIMSS), Finnish fourth-graders also scored highly in science (third best out of 50 countries), as did Finnish eighth-graders (fifth highest in science and eighth best in mathematics).

Moreover, out of all countries participating in the TIMSS, Finland had the smallest gaps in performance among students (University of Jyväskylä, 2012).

	2000	2003	2006	2009	2012
Reading	1. Finland 2. Canada 3. New Zealand 4. Australia 5. Ireland	1. Finland 2. Korea 3. Canada 4. Australia 5. Liechtenstein	1. Korea 2. Finland 3. Canada 4. New Zealand 5. Ireland	1. Korea 2. Finland 3. Singapore 4. Canada 5. New Zealand	1. Singapore 2. Japan 3. Korea 4. Finland 5. Canada, Ireland, Taiwan
Science	1. Korea 2. Japan 3. Finland 4. UK 5. Canada	1. Finland 2. Japan 3. Korea 4. Liechtenstein 5. Australia	1. Finland 2. Canada 3. Taiwan 4. Japan 5. Estonia	1. Finland 2. Singapore 3. Japan 4. Korea 5. New Zealand	1. Singapore 2. Japan 3. Finland 4. Estonia 5. Korea
Math	1. Japan 2. Korea 3. New Zealand 4. Finland 5. Australia	1. Finland 2. Korea 3. Netherlands 4. Liechtenstein 5. Japan	1. Taiwan 2. Finland 3. Korea 4. Netherlands 5. Switzerland	1. Singapore 2. Korea 3. Taiwan 4. Finland 5. Liechtenstein	1. Singapore 2. Taiwan 3. Korea 4. Japan 5. Liechtenstein 9. Finland

Note: The table does not include sub-regions of countries that participate in the assessment, such as Hong Kong, Macau, and Shanghai in China.

Table I. Top-scoring countries on PISA examinations (2000-12).
Source: OECD, 2013.

To understand which components of the FEM may have contributed to such high scores on international education tests and to gain an insider perspective on how international test performance has impacted national self-understanding of the FEM, we conducted semi-structured interviews with 21 Finnish education experts (see Appendix), including leading members of the Finnish Ministry of Education and Culture, Finnish National Board of Education, Finnish Education Evaluation Centre, Ministry for Foreign Affairs, Ministry of Employment and the Economy, Future Learning Finland, and educational businesses. These experts were selected by first compiling a list of the major Finnish institutions related to educational testing and exports, emailing all of them to request contact persons, meeting with those who were available, and then snowballing to identify new informants.

We asked all of our interviewees a completely open-ended question (no prompts were given) to identify the guiding principles behind the FEM. Given the opportunity to provide as few or as many answers as they wished, almost all (18 out of 21) interviewees expressed that *equality* is the single most important factor in the success of the Finnish education model, followed by teacher quality, free education, trust, social support for child development, and inclusive education (Figure 1).

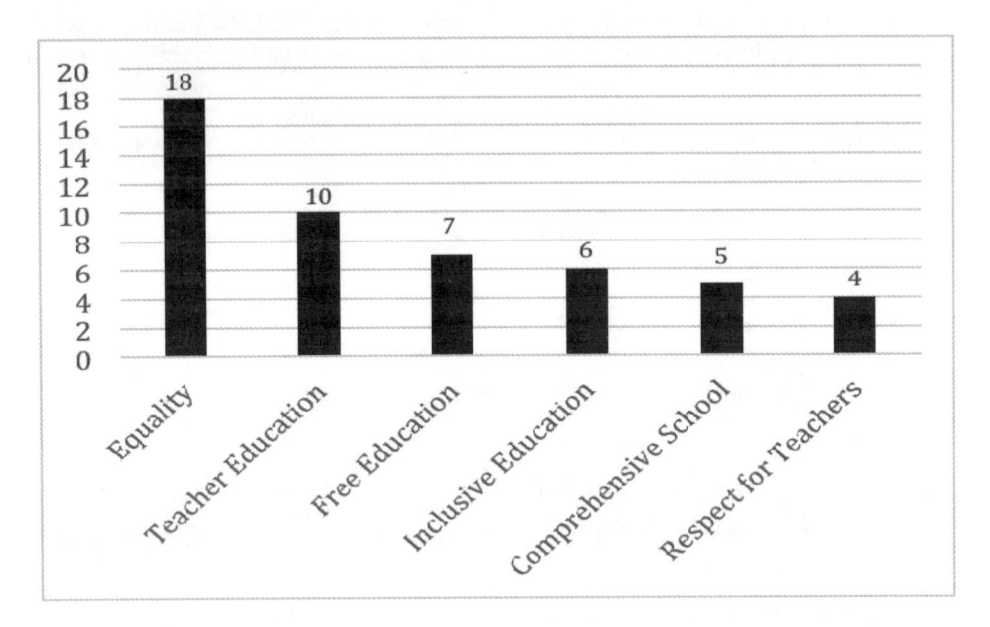

Figure 1. Most common answers to the interview question, 'What are the core components of the Finnish Education Model?'
Source: Authors' interviews.

Equality

In describing the Finnish education model, Jaana Palojärvi, Director for International Relations at the Ministry of Education and Culture (MoEC), answered, 'If I had to choose one word, I would choose equality. It is the biggest defining factor' (Interview 2). The Finnish National Board of Education's (FNBE's) former Director General likewise argues that 'equality in opportunities *and* outcomes is what drives the first nine years of schooling' (Sarjala, 2013, p. 32). Aapo Koukku, Counselor of Education at the FNBE, remarked during our interview: 'In the 1970s, the government decided to establish the comprehensive school, to provide an equally good, quality school for everyone, regardless of where they live, what the parents' financial situation is, and so on' (Interview 1).

Compared with other countries, quality of education varies little across Finnish schools. Finland has very few private schools, voucher programmes or charter schools (Sahlberg, 2011; Simola et al., 2013), and only about 2% of money invested in education in Finland is private – the smallest figure in the world (Interview 15). It is the universally free, nine-year publicly funded and managed 'comprehensive school' (*peruskoulu*) where all students between grades one and nine study that is widely regarded as the foundation of Finland's education success.[2] There is a small achievement gap in performance on PISA, with variance between Finnish schools at 5% –

significantly less than the OECD average of 33% (Darling-Hammond, 2010). As Grek argues, 'non-differentiation is the secret of the success of the Finnish comprehensive school' (2009, p. 28). In Finland, no child is subjected to an inferior education or to sub-standard teachers due to their neighbourhood, socio-economic status, ethnicity or income level of their parents. All schools receive equal public funding on a per-pupil or per-lesson basis (Simola et al., 2013, p. 619).

Equity is supported by free daily meals, health care, transportation, learning materials and counselling (Interview 11; see also Darling-Hammond, 2010). There is also a variety of professionals, including psychologists, social workers and health-care professionals, available in schools to serve the needs of all students. In Finland, it is a top priority to ensure that each student can get through school and receive the necessary supports so that no one is left behind (Interview 1). This principle of equal opportunity extends beyond basic education to higher education, where policies have consistently aimed 'to provide equal opportunities for students from all socioeconomic backgrounds' (Cai & Kivistö, 2013, p. 57).

World-class Teachers

High-quality teaching is integral to the FEM. As Figure 1 shows, the majority of our interviewees (14 out of 21) highlighted either the high education level of teachers (10) or high degree of respect for teachers (4) as key to Finland's education success. In Finland, all primary and secondary school teachers must have at least a master's degree and write a master's thesis. Secondary school teachers major in the subject matter they teach, while primary school teachers major in pedagogy (Jyrhämä et al, 2008; Tryggvason, 2009). Teacher training emphasises diagnosing students' special needs quickly (Interview 1) and 'learning how to teach students who learn in different ways, including those with special needs' (Darling-Hammond, 2010, p. 171). Comprehensive school teachers are well trained, socially respected, highly unionised, decently paid and 'relatively satisfied and committed to their work' (Simola, 2005, p. 463). When a 2013 study asked over 2000 Finnish high school students for their preferred occupation, teaching was the second most popular answer (at 28%) after culture and entertainment (at 30%) (Taloudellinen tiedotustoimisto, 2013). With a status comparable to that of lawyers and doctors, the teaching profession is very popular, reflected by the fact that only 10% of applicants are admitted yearly to teacher education programmes at Finnish universities (Interview 8; Silander & Välijärvi, 2013).

Trust and Autonomy

Finnish comprehensive school teachers are highly trusted and given much autonomy in curriculum design and pedagogy (Silander & Välijärvi, 2013). School curriculum is based on National Core Curriculum standards, but municipal-level education providers have much influence over designing curricula and quality assurance evaluations (QAE) (Kyrö & Nyyssölä, 2006; Simola et al, 2013). Finnish teachers are regularly included in the process of education policy reforms and school development, which also fosters trust (Sahlberg, 2007). Finnish education expert Pasi Sahlberg elaborated on the strong culture of trust in Finland during our interview, including trust between teachers, principals and parents in the education system:

> In Finland, there is no need for the accountability measures that other countries have to have because they lack trust. In the US, I'm often asked how trust can be built, and my answer is that 30 years ago we had an entirely different culture, there was no trust, and there were regulations for everything. We took concrete actions – removing school inspections and requirements to get approval for teaching materials, and even the top-down control of curricula – and allowed schools and teachers to make these decisions. It took 20 years to develop the culture of trust. When teachers feel that they are controlled, that they have to act under strict regulations, it is hard to build trust. Trust has to extend to students as well – they have to feel that they are trusted. This is how the culture of trust starts to grow. (Interview 15)

Sahlberg further noted that Finnish students are recipients of great trust. As an example, while students in the United States often have only 3-5-minute breaks between classes, Finnish students starting from first grade have 15 minutes of recess between classes spent outside in the schoolyard. When Sahlberg enquired why students do not get longer breaks in the United States, he was told, 'We cannot let the students out; they are going to hurt each other and do bad things!' Sahlberg commended the Finnish system, saying that 'this is a great feature of our system. We trust that the students will be okay, and if something happens, we will deal with it' (Interview 15).

Social Support for Child Development

The FEM also rests on widespread social consensus and public support for education and child development among Finns. This is reflected in a wide array of policies and social safety nets supporting the healthy growth of children, including universal, high-quality health care, child allowances, extensive paid maternity and paternity leaves and state-supported day care (Schwartz & Mehta, 2011). These policies reveal a deeply rooted belief in and respect for child development, education and knowledge as a channel for social mobility (Interview 2; Andrews, 2013). When asked why Finland has such a strong national commitment to education, interviewees almost unanimously answered that education is Finland's most important asset. 'We do not have anything else. Our only wealth is a well-educated population,' said Kristiina Volmari from the FNBE (Interview 3). 'The foundation that

Finland has is strongly based on education and knowledge' (Interview 2). 'Education is the key to success for a small nation; only through education can we adjust to rapid global changes, which have a very fast and strong impact on a small economy' (Interview 18). As Ari-Matti Auvinen, CEO of the education consulting firm HCI Productions, pointed out, 'the equal comprehensive school system has allowed us to make use of all of our capacity. Education has enabled us to make use of the diverse reserve of talents in this nation' (Interview 11).

Educational Assessment and Supportive Testing Culture

As Smith (2014, 2015) has pointed out, the currently dominant 'global testing culture' functions as a *disciplining* testing culture (DTC), incentivising students, teachers, administrators and parents to reallocate their time, money and energies towards raising scores on increasingly frequently administered standardised national tests in order to avoid various forms of punishment. By contrast, as illustrated in Table II, Finland has developed a *supportive* testing culture (STC) designed to support student learning and teacher professionalisation rather than to inflict discipline and punishment.

	Finnish testing culture	Global testing culture
Subjects evaluated	17 subjects (almost all subjects in the curriculum).[a]	Three subjects only (math, science, reading).
Sampling method	Uses scientific sampling criteria (proportional to population).	No use of scientific sampling.
Students tested	5-10% tested every four years.	100% tested at least once per year.
Schools tested	10-20% tested every four years.	100% tested at least once per year.
Teacher professionalization	All teachers must have a master's degree and write a research-based master's thesis.	Not all teachers required to complete master's thesis or to have extensive pedagogical training.
Teacher consequences	Teachers not penalized for student performance.	Teachers and administrators frequently penalized for low student performance.
Public ranking/League tables of schools	None – aim is to have no bad schools in the whole country.	Common – parents can choose between good and bad schools (based on test-results).
Pre-schools	Focus on play-based learning, no focus on test-taking.	Prepare child for test-taking.

After-school tutoring	Uncommon; not seen as necessary.	Children spend long hours, and parents bear high costs for after-school classes to get ahead of other children on test-taking.
Overarching goal	To nurture and support student learning and teacher development.	To discipline teachers, administrators, and students by external means.
PISA performance	High	Varied

[a]Evaluated on a rotating basis, these subjects include nine languages: Finnish and Swedish (the two national languages), English, three minor national languages (Romani, Sammi, Sign language), three additional foreign languages (Russian, French and German) plus mathematics, biology, chemistry, geography, home economics/life skills, arts, music, and health education (Interviews 19 and 20).

Table II. Comparing Finland's supportive testing culture with the global testing culture.
Sources: Authors' interviews; Smith (2014, 2015).

This culture also has historical roots. Already in the 1930s the idea that 'it was not the purpose of the school to educate examinees but to produce functional citizens' was emerging in Finland (Vuorio-Lehti & Jauhiainen 2008, p. 153). Thus, Finland has only one standardised national exam: the national high school graduation exam (*ylioppilastutkinto*), which is not taken by everyone, as about half of secondary school students go into vocational education. It is also the case that although Finland does have a social democratic form of government, as in neighbouring Sweden (Joshi & Navlakha, 2010; Joshi, 2013), its testing culture differs from other Nordic countries, as exemplified by Denmark's recent adoption of national computer-based standardised testing (Kousholt & Hamre, 2015) and Sweden's education reforms of the early 1990s which liberalised school choice to make schools compete for students (Burns et al, 2015).

Finland's approach to national education assessments is relatively cost effective because it relies on randomised, 'scientific' sampling of a small and proportionally representative share (typically 5-10%) of a cohort, rather than testing every single student nationwide (Interview 20). Each four-year evaluation cycle involves a two-stage stratified sample involving two out of Finland's five provinces. The evaluating team comprised of experts takes a completely randomised selection of (a) municipalities, towns, villages and rural areas, (b) big and small-size schools, and (c) sampling unit(s) within the bigger schools. Focused on improving learning outcomes, these assessments include interviews with teachers and principals, questionnaires given to students, and controls for factors such as parents' educational backgrounds (Interviews 19 and 20). As the director of Finland's National Education Evaluation Centre (FINEEC) explained in an interview, 'the purpose is not to force every single student and school to take a test, but rather to assess learning outcomes in a way that is supportive and encouraging of student learning ... There are no school ranking lists or "league tables". There is collective school responsibility for learners who are struggling' (Interview 19). FINEEC's findings also feed directly into teacher training, with some evaluation reports used as university course books in teacher education (Interview 19). Additionally, FINEEC cooperates closely with its European counterparts in the European Association for Quality Assurance in Higher Education (ENQA) to promote sharing of expertise in evaluating higher education.[3]

Finland's Global Education Reputation

Finland's educational success has been labelled 'paradoxical' because the high scores on international education assessments have been achieved 'without school inspection, standardized curriculum and high-stakes student assessments, test-based accountability, or a race-to-the-top mentality in terms of educational change' (Varjo et al, 2013, p. 53). As a result, the FEM has influenced education policy reforms in several countries, bringing thousands of 'education pilgrims' to Finland to 'find out the secret of Finland's success' (Takayama, 2010, p. 51). For example, France has instituted education policy reforms modelled after Finland on (a) comprehensive teacher training, (b) social integration, adaptability and pedagogical flexibility, (c) giving weak-performing students more support, and (d) designing classes more flexibly and individually (Dobbins & Martens, 2012, p. 35). Likewise, Estonia, a country which scored among the top five countries in science on PISA 2012, has drawn education lessons from Finland, particularly in curriculum reform, internal evaluation and preprimary education (Toots, 2009).

Presently, international interest in the FEM is so high that the Finnish Ministry of Education and Culture is unable to receive all international visitors. As shown in Table III, it hosts dozens of international delegations every year. Likewise, since 2005 the FNBE has hosted approximately 1200 delegations with about 12,000 visitors from 111 countries.[4] FINEEC has also attracted a noticeable number of international visitors. In 2014, its first year of operation, it hosted 50 visitors representing five continents, followed by 89 international visitors in the first half of 2015 (Interview 19).

In assessing global interest in the FEM, we also conducted a content analysis of annual media reports compiled by the Finnish Ministry for Foreign Affairs from 2001 to 2012. Finnish diplomatic missions abroad compile annual 'Finland in Foreign Media' reports assessing how Finland is portrayed by media in their host countries. These reports provide a comprehensive (although not exhaustive) summary of media outlets in local languages worldwide. Briefly summarised, the reports reveal considerable influence of the FEM in overall reporting on Finland. The first two reports, issued in 2001 and 2002, were titled, respectively, 'Nokia, Doping, Literacy' and 'Nokia, Kaurismäki, Literacy'. Although in these early years Finland was praised for its high level of literacy, it was only after 2003 PISA results were announced in 2004 that education began to feature as a major focus of the global media's reporting on Finland. Figure 2, which shows the number of times the words 'school' (*koulu*), 'education' (*koulutus*) and 'teacher' (*opettaja*) [5] were mentioned in each report, demonstrates the astounding growth over time in global media coverage of Finnish education. As the figure reveals, there are noticeable spikes in the years when PISA assessments were made public in 2004, 2007 and 2010.

Year	Number of delegations	Number of countries
2005	116	44
2006	67	29
2007	89	44
2008	110	42
2009	91	41
2010	93	42
2011	81	42
2012	72	36
2013	86	43
2014	94	54
2015 (first half)	56	39

Table III. International visitors to the Ministry of Education and Culture 2005-15. *Source*: Correspondence with Helena Lalu-Toivio, MoEC Visitor Coordinator (16 June 2015).

Qualitatively analysing the reports' descriptions of education coverage, we found Finnish education to be portrayed overwhelmingly positively. The 2008 report states that 'Finland was again portrayed in foreign media as a model country in teaching', and the success of Finnish children in school was attributed to 'the professionalism of teachers, free school lunches and special education' (Ministry for Foreign Affairs, 2008, p. 29). Debates over education reforms in multiple countries clearly inspired local media to examine the Finnish education system and factors behind its success. As shown in Figure 3, European, Asian and South American countries most frequently featured Finnish education in their media. The MoEC's Director for International Relations also confirmed that this corresponds closely with the nationalities of educational visitors received by Finland (Interview 2).

In East Asia, where governments put much stress on education to advance national development (Joshi, 2012), there have been significant increases in newspaper and television coverage of Finnish education, especially when PISA assessments were made public in 2007 and 2010. In 2001, Finnish education was only mentioned three times in reports from

TEACHING THE WORLD THAT LESS IS MORE

Asian countries, whereas in 2007 it was mentioned 31 times. The media in China, Japan, South Korea and Thailand all have considerable coverage of PISA rankings and demonstrated particular interest in the FEM, frequently comparing it with their own national systems. For example, in South Korean media the fact that education, school lunches and teaching material are all free in Finland has caused much astonishment (Ministry for Foreign Affairs, 2008). Many Asian countries have also looked to Finland as an example for national education reforms.

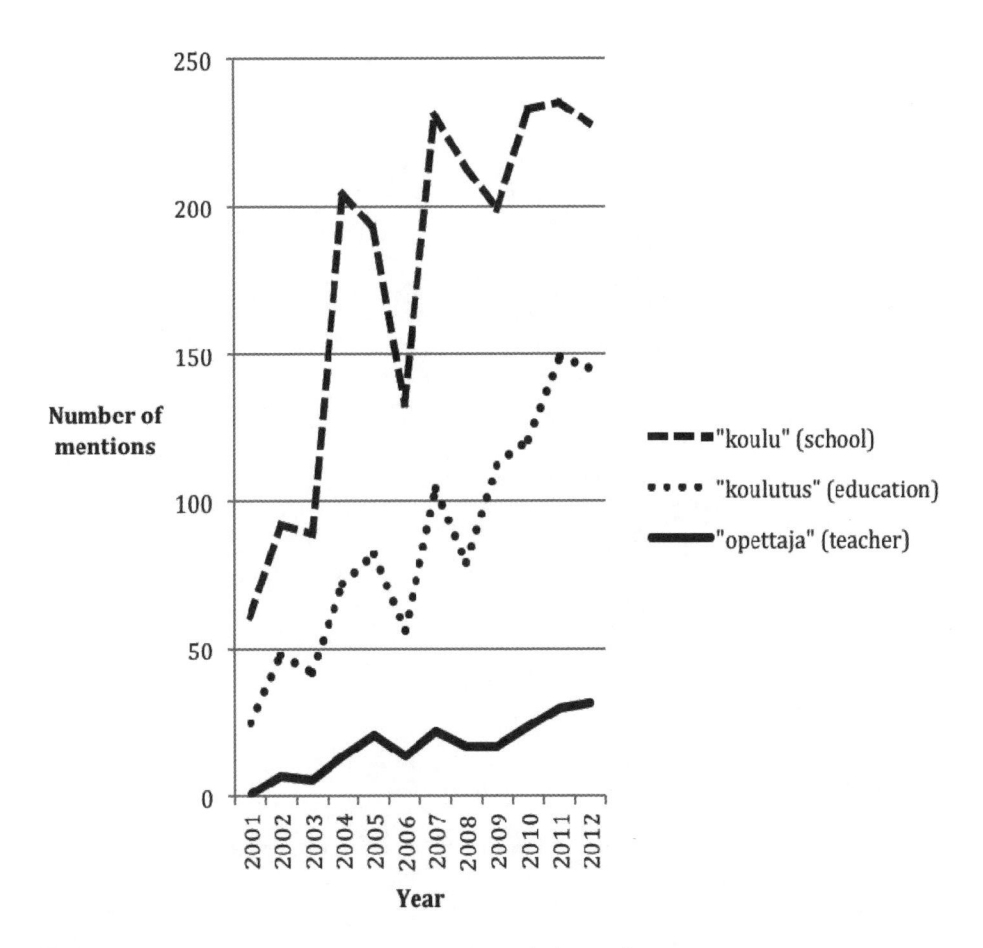

Figure 2. Frequency of Education-related words in media reports.
Source: Authors' analysis of reports by the Finnish Ministry for Foreign Affairs 2001-12.

In Europe, we saw similar increases in the visibility of the FEM. In 2011, Finnish education was mentioned 65 times by different European countries compared with only 16 times in 2001. Austria, Germany, Greece, Kosovo and the UK all featured Finnish education heavily in their media. In many

European countries the Finnish education system was presented as a model during debates over national education reforms. The contrast between the FEM and domestic education models was often evident in European media, such as the Portuguese magazine *Diário de Notícias*, which published an 11-page article titled, 'Portugal versus Finland: what do they have, what don't we have?' (Ministry for Foreign Affairs, 2011, p. 87). The Finnish education system was also frequently portrayed as a model in Sweden and Denmark, and even utilised to defend the education policies of a number of political parties.

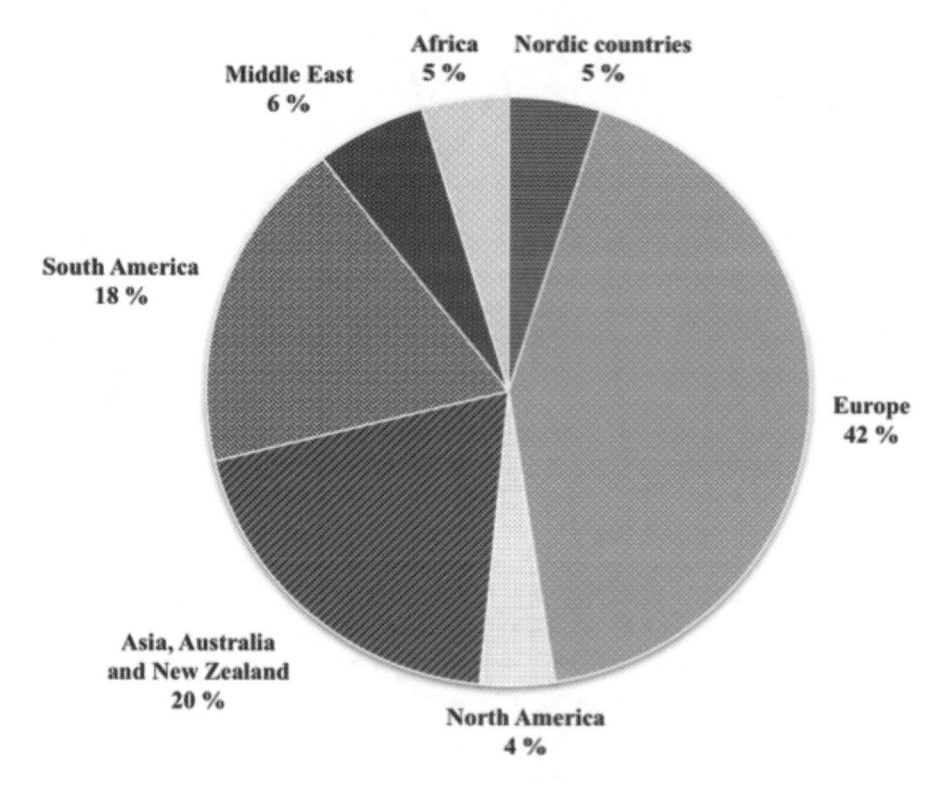

Figure 3. Finnish education featured in media by region (in percentages of total number of mentions).
Source: Ministry for Foreign Affairs 2001-13.

The FEM also attracted increasing attention in the Americas. Mentioned only twice in 2001, education appears 37 times in reports from South America in 2009 and 2011. Media in Brazil, Chile, Mexico and Peru all demonstrated strong interest in Finnish education, with Finland often portrayed as a model country for its welfare model, of which education is a key component. In North America, Finnish education began receiving increased exposure in the late 2000s. In the United States, political pressure to improve the education system, especially during presidential election campaigns, increased curiosity about the FEM. Many American journalists discovered that Finland has 'an equal and well-working society that has schools worth envying' (Ministry for Foreign Affairs, 2008, p. 81).

Comparatively speaking, we found less coverage of Finnish education in the Middle East and Africa. However, Finnish education received significant media attention in Israel, the United Arab Emirates (UAE) and Saudi Arabia. In Israel, Finnish education has become a favourite topic of the media, sparking much interest in Finland's social policies and welfare system (Ministry for Foreign Affairs, 2011). In the UAE, the media has increased reporting on Finnish education as a result of ongoing Finnish education export projects in Abu Dhabi. The 2011 report mentions that the UAE is trying to build a world-class education system and it values highly the FEM, which has ranked well in international assessments (Ministry for Foreign Affairs, 2011, p. 58).

Education Exports and the Finnish National Brand

Global demand for Finnish education expertise appears to be largely due to Finland's performance on international education tests like PISA. As Jari Poikonen, the director of consulting group FCG Education, told us, 'PISA lifted the Finnish brand to a new level. Some other countries would have had to invest a lot to get to the same level as Finland is known in the education sector ... It's hard to find a person in these circles anymore who does not know that Finland has had success in education' (Interview 16). According to Matti Lassila, Finland's former Ambassador of Education Export, 'If we talk about Abu Dhabi, the Emirates would not have bought Finnish schools unless they knew about PISA, and knew about Finland's good schools. I can easily imagine that throughout Europe and the world our embassies are using this reputation, because it is a good reputation, and based on it they can organise conferences, distribute materials, and make Finland more known' (Interview 6). The Permanent Secretary of the MoEC, Anita Lehikoinen, also noted, 'Finland's success in education has produced an image that Finland is something other than cold, far away and expensive. For small countries especially, it shows they can be competitive. This is very much based on our reputation as an education country. But it has not been realised financially as much as it should have, or could have, been' (Interview 8).

With the success of Finnish education validated by PISA, affirmed by academic studies, and trumpeted by global media, Finland and its businesses have been offered new opportunities to sell goods and services internationally, both in education and in other sectors. Figure 4 illustrates this positive feedback loop of national brand promotion and education export.[6] After Finland became a popular destination for thousands of 'PISA tourists', the Finnish government has been strategizing how to promote Finnish education expertise as a major new export industry (MoEC,

2010, p. 29; Sahlberg, 2012, p. 20). One major step towards operationalising a national strategy was the 2011 establishment of Future Learning Finland (FLF) [7], a national education export programme aiming to export Finnish expertise in the form of education-based products, services and solutions for foreign clients. Recent examples include: a Finnish primary school set up in Qatar; a vocational learning centre in Shanghai; training programmes for nurses and physiotherapists from Abu Dhabi offered by a Finnish university; digital learning platforms and materials exported to China; online teacher training programmes offered in Vietnam; virtual music teaching tools sold in Spanish-speaking countries; and live online teaching ongoing in Brazil, the Philippines and China (Finpro, 2015; Kauppalehti, 2015). According to FLF estimates, Finnish companies could receive up to 100 million euros in revenue over the next few years from education exports to China and Qatar alone (Kauppalehti, 2015).

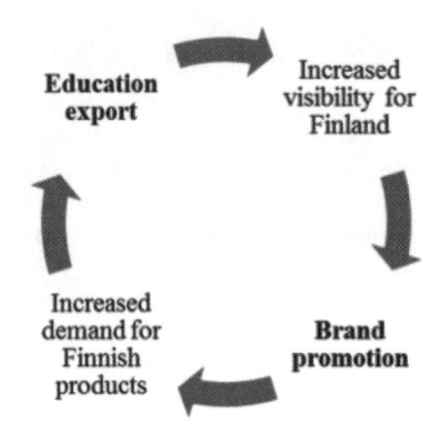

Figure 4. Virtuous cycle of education export and brand promotion.

Although Finnish education exports are on the rise (Kauppalehti, 2015), a number of experts we interviewed stated it is not possible to export the FEM wholesale. Aapo Koukku argued that 'rather than exporting a model, we should export the good ideas that we have – for example, wide collaboration between employers and schools' (Interview 1). Jussi Karakoski of the Ministry for Foreign Affairs likewise warned that it might be impossible to take the factors that have made the Finnish system successful and export them to another country, because factors such as trust, egalitarianism and a strong social commitment to investing in child development are tightly related to the rest of the society (Interview 7). A recent study at Finnish universities confirms what some of the interviewees expressed:

> The results indicate that PISA-studies have formed a reputation for Finland that can be used for commercial purposes, if the

commercialization and exporting stem from commercial interests and are done using the proper expertise. The experts feel that the Finnish primary education system cannot be taken out of its cultural and societal context; however, certain innovations in the primary education field and teacher expertise can be commercialized for export purposes. (Immonen, 2012)

For example, Ambassador Matti Lassila, who worked together with the Finnish education export company EduCluster to pilot an education export project in the UAE, explained how two Finnish schools in Abu Dhabi and Al Ain operate with Finnish principals and teachers working side by side with local teachers:

> I believe that there is something in the Finnish system that can be condensed or distilled – what we know and what we can do – and exported to another country [but ultimately] it is up to the country and their culture and history if they want to take something Finnish … [e.g.] you cannot just take the Finnish model to a country and expect people to suddenly respect teachers – it is up to the receiving country, and these kinds of changes do not happen quickly. (Interview 6)

In the case of the UAE, which follows the UK model of heavy exams on students and inspections of teachers, it has also not been possible to fully implement the Finnish model, as the Finnish schools there have ended up being test-focused in contrast to schools in Finland (Interview 21), perhaps a testament to the global influence of a disciplining testing culture.

Conclusion

This chapter examined how global education testing has impacted the Finnish export of educational practices, goods and services. With a reputation for educational excellence, the Finnish model has impacted education reforms in a number of countries and Finland's influence in the educational sphere is considerably greater than its relative size. Although the main education exporters are English-speaking countries, Finland is beginning to leverage its reputation into the lucrative education export industry in areas such as teacher training programmes and select education-related products such as education technology and online teaching tools. At the same time, exporting the Finnish education model wholesale is difficult, because it takes time to build a lasting social consensus in favour of equality, trust and child development, which many see as the cornerstones of the FEM (Interview 3). Nevertheless, as Poikonen suggested in his interview, 'what Finland should do is believe that education export is a fantastic thing', as education offers an arena where a country the size of five million people with few natural resources has the chance to be an international superpower, while contributing to long-term positive global change (Interview 16).

We conclude with the observation that although a disciplining testing culture has considerable global influence at present, a supportive 'less is more' testing culture emphasising educational equality, as in Finland, may spread internationally in the future as indicated by the large number of foreign delegations coming to learn about Finland's education system. We also note that there is a potential for backlash in attempting to export a model not easily adaptable to other countries – and this applies equally to both disciplining and supportive testing cultures. Nevertheless, we find that Finnish education authorities are deeply interested in the fact that Finnish boys' scores dropped in the 2012 PISA round (Interview 19). This illustrates how PISA scores are taken seriously in Finland not only as a measure of education performance, but also because of their role in validating and legitimating Finland's supportive educational practices and increasing demand for its education-related products and services.

Notes

[1] While still performing among the highest-ranking European countries, in 2012 Finland's ranking in mathematics declined to ninth place.

[2] The *peruskoulu* was enacted by legislation in 1963 and implemented between 1972 and 1979, first in the sparsely populated North, and then gradually in the South (Schwartz & Mehta, 2011, p. 55).

[3] Several Finns are members of the ENQA board and secretariat, including Dr Helka Kekäläinen from FINEEC, who is ENQA's vice president (Interview 19).

[4] Correspondence with Hanna Laakso, FNBE Special Expert (1 July 2015).

[5] Due to the grammar of the Finnish language, we used only that part of the word included in all conjugations. Thus, searching for '*koulutu*' and '*opettaj*' also included *koulutuksen, koulutuksesta* (education's, of education) and *opettajien, opettajista* (teachers', of teachers), etc.

[6] The concept of 'education exports' is a broad one that includes not only direct sales of goods and services but also income and non-income benefits earned through faculty and student exchanges, internationalisation of curricula, and students studying abroad (Heyneman, 2001; Larsen et al, 2002).

[7] FLF is co-directed by three ministries: the Ministry of Employment and the Economy, the Ministry of Education and Culture, and the Ministry of Foreign Affairs. In 2015 it had over 40 members, with a focus on four fields of expertise: teacher training, vocational training, learning environments, and education technology (edtech).

References

Andrews, P. (2013) What Does PISA Performance Tell Us about Mathematics Teaching Quality? Case Studies from Finland and Flanders, in M. Heinz-Dieter

& A. Benavot (Eds) *PISA, Power, and Policy: the emergence of global educational governance*, pp. 99-116. Oxford: Symposium Books.

Burns, T., Blanchenday, P. & Koester, F. (2015) Horizontal Accountability, Municipal Capacity, and the Use of Data: a case study of Sweden, in W.C. Smith (Ed.) *The Global Testing Culture: shaping education policy, perceptions, and practice*. Oxford: Symposium Books.

Cai, Y. & Kivistö, J. (2013) Tuition Fees for International Students in Finland: where to go from here? *Journal of Studies in International Education*, 17(1), 55-78.

Darling-Hammond, L. (2010) *The Flat World and Education*. New York: Teachers College Press.

Dobbins, M. & Martens, K. (2012) Towards an Education Approach à la Finlandaise? French Education Policy after PISA, *Journal of Education Policy*, 27(1), 23-43.

Finpro (2015) Suomen koulutusviennissä merkittäviä läpimurtoja [Major breakthroughs in Finnish education export]. Press release, 12 March 2015.

Grek, S. (2009) Governing by Numbers: the PISA 'effect' in Europe, *Journal of Education Policy*, 24(1), 23-37.

Heyneman, S. (2001) The Growing International Commercial Market for Educational Goods and Services, *International Journal of Educational Development*, 21(4), 345-359.

Immonen, J. (2012) PISA-tutkimukset suomalaisen perusopetusjärjestelmän tilan kuvaajana ja koulutusosaamisviennin perustana.' [PISA-studies as indicators of the state of Finnish primary education system and as a basis for exporting education expertise]. Master's thesis, University of Eastern Finland.

Joshi, D. (2012) Varieties of Developmental States: three non-western paths to the millennium development goals, *Journal of Developing Societies*, 28(3), 355-378.

Joshi, D. (2013) The Protective and Developmental Varieties of Liberal Democracy: a difference in kind or degree?, *Democratization*, 20(2), 187-214.

Joshi, D. & Navlakha, N. (2010) Social Democracy in Sweden, *Economic and Political Weekly*, 45(47), 73-80.

Jyrhämä, R., Kynäslahti, H., Krokfors, L., et al (2008) The Appreciation and Realisation of Research-based Teacher Education: Finnish students' experiences of teacher education, *European Journal of Teacher Education*, 31(1), 1-16.

Kauko, J. & Diogo, S. (2011) Comparing Higher Education Reforms in Finland and Portugal: different contexts, same solutions?, *Higher Education Management and Policy*, 23(3), 115-133.

Kauppalehti (2015) Koulutusvienti rajussa kasvussa [Education export is growing drastically]. 12 March. http://www.kauppalehti.fi/uutiset/koulutusvienti-rajussa-kasvussa/Cd8RAQUy

Kousholt, K. & Hamre, B. (2015) Testing and School Reform in Danish Education: an analysis informed by the use of the 'dispositive', in W.C. Smith (Ed.) *The Global Testing Culture: shaping education policy, perceptions, and practice*. Oxford: Symposium Books.

Kyrö, M. & Nyyssölä, K. (2006) Attitudes towards Education in Finland and Other Nordic Countries, *European Journal of Education*, 41(1), 59-70.

Larsen, K., Martin, J.P. & Morris, R. (2002) Trade in Educational Services, *The World Economy*, 25(6), 849-868.

Ministry for Foreign Affairs (2001-2012) *Suomi ulkomaisissa tiedotusvälineissä* [Finland in foreign media]. http://www.formin.fi/public/default.aspx?contentid=50407

Ministry for Foreign Affairs (2008) *Suomi ulkomaisissa tiedotusvälineissä 2008* [Finland in foreign media 2008].
http://formin.finland.fi/public/download.aspx?ID=41815&GUID={68EC96D9-50BE-4584-AD97-1200BE8A5672}

Ministry for Foreign Affairs (2011) *Suomi ulkomaisissa tiedotusvälineissä 2011* [Finland in foreign media 2011].http://formin-origin.finland.fi/public/download.aspx?ID=92777&GUID={D1D6E903-3A87-401C-B7A2-37CCA8BBA7FD}

Ministry of Education and Culture (MoEC) (2010) *Kiinnostuksesta kysynnäksi ja tuotteiksi: Suomen koulutusvientistrategia* [From interest to demand to products: Finland's education export strategy]. Working group for education export, publication no. 11.
http://www.minedu.fi/OPM/Koulutus/artikkelit/koulutusvienti/liitteet/koulutusvientistrategia.pdf

Niukko, S. (2006) *Yhteistyötä ilman riskejä? OECD:n rooli Suomen koulutuspolitiikassa* [Cooperation without risks? The role of OECD in Finnish education politics]. Turku: Annales Universitatis Turkuensis.

Rautalin, M. & Alasuutari, P. (2009) The Uses of the National PISA Results by Finnish Officials in Central Government, *Journal of Education Policy*, 24(5), 539-556.

Sahlberg, P. (2007) Education Policies for Raising Student Learning: the Finnish approach, *Journal of Education Policy*, 22(2), 147-171.

Sahlberg, P. (2011) *Finnish Lessons: what can the world learn from educational change in Finland?* New York: Teachers College Press.

Sahlberg, P. (2012) Kuka ostaisi suomalaista koulutusosaamista [Who would buy Finnish education expertise], *Ammattikasvatuksen aikakauskirja*, 4, 17-27.

Sarjala, J. (2013) Equality and Cooperation: Finland's path to excellence, *American Educator*, Spring, 32-36.

Schwartz, R.B. & Mehta, J.D. (2011) Finland: superb teachers – how to get them, how to use them, in M.S. Tucker (Ed.) *Surpassing Shanghai: an agenda for American education built on the world's leading systems*, pp. 51-75. Cambridge, MA: Harvard Education Press.

Silander, T. & Välijärvi, J. (2013) The Theory and Practice of Building Pedagogical Skill in Finnish Teacher Education, in M. Heinz-Dieter & A. Benavot (Eds) *PISA, Power, and Policy: the emergence of global educational governance*, pp. 77-98. Oxford: Symposium Books.

Simola, H. (2005) The Finnish Miracle of PISA: historical and sociological remarks on teaching and teacher education, *Comparative Education*, 41(4), 455-470.

Simola, H., Rinne, R., Varjo, J. & Kauko, J. (2013) The Paradox of the Education Race: how to win the ranking game by sailing to headwind, *Journal of Education Policy*, 28(5), 612-633.

Smith, W.C. (2014) The Global Transformation toward Testing for Accountability, *Educational Policy Analysis Archives*, 22(116), 1-29.

Smith, W.C. (2016) An Introduction to the Global Testing Culture, in W.C. Smith (Ed.) *The Global Testing Culture: shaping education policy, perceptions, and practice.* Oxford: Symposium Books.

Takayama, K. (2010) Politics of Externalization in Reflexive Times: reinventing Japanese education reform discourses through 'Finnish PISA Success', *Comparative Education Review*, 54(1), 51-75.

Taloudellinen tiedotustoimisto (2013) *Kun koulu loppuu: Tiivistelmä nuorten tulevaisuuden suunnitelmista* [When school ends: A summary of future plans of the youth]. http://www.tat.fi/wp-content/uploads/2012/06/KKL_tulokset_2013_tiivistelm%C3%A4.pdf

Telhaug, A.O., Medias, O.A. & Aasen, P. (2006) The Nordic Model in Education: Education as a Part of the Political System in the Last 50 Years, *Scandinavian Journal of Educational Research*, 50(3), 245-283.

Toots, A. (2009) Brussels Comes via Helsinki: the role of Finland in Europeanisation of Estonian education policy, *Halduskultuur*, 10, 58-73.

Tryggvason, M.-T. (2009) Why is Finnish Teacher Education Successful? Some Goals Finnish Teacher Educators Have For Their Teaching, *European Journal of Teacher Education*, 32(4), 369-382.

University of Jyväskylä – Institute for Educational Research (2012) Suomalaisten oppilaiden kouluosaaminen kansainvälistä kärkeä [Finnish students' school performance is internationally at the top]. Press release. https://ktl.jyu.fi/tiedotteet/tiedotteet-2012/suomalaisten-oppilaiden-kouluosaaminen-kansainvalista-karkea-tiedote-11.12.2012

Varjo, J., Simola, H. & Rinne, R. (2013) Finland's PISA Results: an analysis of dynamics in education politics, in M. Heinz-Dieter Meyer & A. Benavot (Eds) *PISA, Power, and Policy: the emergence of global educational governance*, pp. 51-76. Oxford: Symposium Books.

Vuorio-Lehti, M. & Jauhiainen. A. (2008) Laurin Zilliacus and the 'War' against the Finnish Matriculation Examination, in M. Lawn (Ed.) *An Atlantic Crossing? The Work of the International Examination Inquiry, its Researchers, Methods and Influence*, pp. 137-156. Oxford: Symposium Books.

APPENDIX. List of Interviews

	Title	Name	Organization	Date
1	Counselor of Education	Aapo Koukku	Finnish National Board of Education	12 July 2013
2	Director for International Relations	Jaana Palojärvi	Ministry of Education and Culture	18 July 2013
3	Counselor of Education	Kristiina Volmari	Finnish National Board of Education	18 July 2013
4	Project Director	Eeva Nuutinen	Future Learning Finland	8 August 2013
5	Director General of the Department of Development Policy	Pekka Puustinen	Ministry for Foreign Affairs	8 August 2013
6	Ambassador	Matti Lassila	Ministry for Foreign Affairs	8 August 2013
7	Senior Education Adviser	Jussi Karakoski	Ministry for Foreign Affairs	8 August 2013
8	Permanent Secretary	Anita Lehikoinen	Ministry of Education and Culture	9 August 2013
9	Head of Division, Enterprise and Innovation Department	Severi Keinälä	Ministry of Employment and the Economy	26 August 2013
10	Senior Adviser	Mari Hakkarainen	Ministry of Employment and the Economy	26 August 2013
11	CEO	Ari-Matti Auvinen	HCI Productions	26 August 2013
12	Director of Teacher Education	Jari Lavonen	University of Helsinki	26 August 2013
13	Senior Adviser	Marita Aho	Confederation of Finnish Industries	27 August 2013
14	Managing Director	Lars Eltvik	Haaga-Helia Global Education Services Ltd.	27 August 2013

15	Director General	Pasi Sahlberg	Centre for International Mobility and Cooperation (CIMO)	28 August 2013
16	Director	Jari Poikonen	FCG Education, Finnish Consulting Group Ltd.	28 August 2013
17	CEO	Jan-Markus Holm	EduCluster Finland Oy Ltd	10 September 2013
18	Director	Jouni Välijärvi	Finnish Institute for Educational Research, University of Jyväskylä	20 September 2013
19	Director	Harri Peltoniemi	Finnish National Education Evaluation Centre (Karvi)	8 June 2015
20	Senior Researcher	Juhani Rautopuro	Finnish National Education Evaluation Centre (Karvi)	8 June 2015
21	Teacher/Student	Sirja Rissanen	University of Helsinki	9 June 2015

CHAPTER 5

Student Achievement and PISA Rankings: policy effects or cultural explanations?

JI LIU

ABSTRACT A central assumption underlying international large-scale testing, such as the Organisation for Economic Co-operation and Development's (OECD's) Programme for International Student Assessment (PISA), is that cross-national variation in student test scores is attributable to national policy environments. This assumption, coined as PISA reasoning, has taken center stage at the heart of the global testing culture. Feniger and Lefstein's (2014) critical analysis of this assumption suggests that cultural and historical background may be a more powerful alternative explanation. This chapter presents important limitations to the current dichotomous debate in two major ways. First, by adding school fixed effects, the effects of cultural origin were reduced by half, indicating that the country-of-origin effect is taking credit for school-level variances. Second, findings from an exhaustive list of origin–destination pairs indicate an inconsistent pattern cross-nationally, and suggest that prior results may not be generalizable to global student achievement patterns.

Introduction

Large-scale international standardized tests have attracted the attention of increasingly more policy makers, who compare the achievement of children in other countries with those in their own (McKinsey & Company, 2010; OECD, 2011; Sahlberg, 2011). Fueled by a growing global testing culture, politicians and policy makers often cite league standings, both good and poor, on such international test score comparisons as evidence to justify domestic reform agendas (Carnoy & Rothstein, 2013; Sellar & Lingard, 2013). The policy significance and importance of these international tests have taken center stage at the heart of the global testing culture, and have been the motivation for increasingly more policy attention. For instance, a central discussion in the United States has been the debate about various reform approaches to increase America's international competitiveness, especially utilizing lessons drawn from league leaders who have achieved better results at lower costs (Tucker, 2011b). A premise to such logic dwells on 'PISA reasoning', which applauds superior test performance as a testimony for superior policies (Feniger & Lefstein, 2014, p. 1). Subscription to this logic has profound consequences, and often requires poorly performing countries to import policies that are administered in the best-performing school systems (Barber & Mourshed, 2007; Schledicher & Stewart, 2008; Tucker, 2011a). Thus, questions surrounding the quickly rising popularity of PISA reasoning and the large numbers of travelling reforms that appear in various corners of the world generate special incentives to decompose PISA results and re-examine the interpretations.

Many scholars have published a great deal of work to criticize this oversimplified PISA reasoning, yet political demand for such standardized testing comparisons and media craving for best-performing policies have just started to increase (Feniger & Lefstein, 2014). Some of this critical commentary has focused on the fact that solely attributing successes in international testing is inattentive to the education effects of national history and culture (Alexander, 2010). The world that we live in is diverse and different, in many ways corresponding to the differences in culture and national history. Students who come from distinctively different cultural backgrounds may have drastically different views and varying family resources in their education. Such is the cultural influence hypothesis, which ascribes variation in student achievement to historical, social, economic and educational background (Condron, 2011). The presence of the cultural influence hypothesis presents an important challenge to the widely popular PISA reasoning.

In order to problematize and challenge the PISA reasoning with the cultural influence hypothesis, Feniger and Lefstein (2014) set up a dichotomy between two opposing views of what accounted for the difference in student achievement across countries. Feniger and Lefstein (2014) attempted to refute the most central element of the PISA logic that differences in student achievement are the result of national educational policies. In Feniger and Lefstein's (2014) analysis using PISA 2009 results, the cross-national immigration that occurred between China and Australia and New Zealand offered an opportunity to observe students who were exposed to a similar policy structure but who were of different cultural origins.

More specifically, Feniger and Lefstein (2014) found that the high academic success of students with Chinese origin is observed universally across policy contexts, even after controlling for a series of family characteristics. In broad strokes, Feniger and Lefstein's (2014) result supports the cultural influence hypothesis and offers a plausible alternative to

PISA reasoning, as cultural background seems to be more explanatory of student achievement. Feniger and Lefstein's (2014) analysis provides substantial evidence for the problematic nature of PISA reasoning and the overinterpretation of international testing comparisons.

Nonetheless, immigration by nature does not happen randomly (Borjas, 1987). Based on this premise, the purpose of this chapter is to contribute to the current literature on the understanding of cultural context and social structures that led to existing conclusions, and to contribute to the ongoing debate between PISA reasoning and the cultural influence hypothesis. It is worth noting that this chapter is not set out with a positivistic agenda to test either of the hypotheses; its aim is to present arguments for more rigorous research on each side.

The significance of this chapter lies precisely at the intersection between these two competing hypothesis. For one, different culture groups have different views and values associated with education, and varying schooling choices. Thus, it is important to unpack the immigrant schooling decisions and their achievement outcomes. In the first research question, this chapter explores to what extent culture or country of origin can explain variations in schooling outcomes by accounting for all differences at the school level using fixed effects. Another key aim of this chapter is to expand the discussion and examine whether Feniger and Lefstein's (2014) results would still hold for a different origin–destination pair. In the second research question, this chapter investigates whether different cultural groups present the same findings as Feniger and Lefstein's (2014) Chinese immigrant example.

In order to answer the proposed questions and compare the policy environment versus cultural influence framework, this chapter examines this topic step by step. First, I use identical sample restriction strategies as Feniger and Lefstein's (2014) to derive the sample of interest. Second, I replicate Ordinary Least Squares (OLS) analysis for Australia and New Zealand using data from the 2012 wave of the Programme for International Student Assessment (PISA). Third, because immigration, culture and school choice are intertwined, I add school fixed effects to Feniger and Lefstein's (2014) OLS model, in order to account for all observed and unobserved between-school differences. Fourth, to answer the second research question regarding generalizability of the findings to other culture–policy or origin–destination pairs, I reproduce the culture–policy exercise using PISA 2012 data for all major diaspora groups with at least 100 valid immigrant student cases in the destination country.

The following sections of the chapter proceed as follows. First, I summarize Feniger and Lefstein's (2014) study and findings. Second, the data and methodology section will provide an overview and details of the data and empirical strategies used in this chapter. Third, the findings section presents results for both research questions, and finally, the discussion and conclusion section draws on the implications of these results.

A Brief Summary of Feniger & Lefstein (2014)

In 'How Not to Reason with PISA Data: an ironic investigation', Yariv Feniger and Adam Lefstein (2014) aimed to elucidate the relationship between policy and culture, and show how these factors interact to consequently affect student achievement. The general public, the media and government agencies have developed a heavy reliance on PISA results in assessing education systems. The underlying assumption accepted by many policy makers is that higher PISA scores are attributable to better education policy structures. Therefore, many believe that poorly performing systems should change their policies and adopt those of high-achieving countries. Nonetheless, there is no clear causal relationship between PISA scores and education policy. As Feniger and Lefstein (2014) summarize, the policy and structure assumption fails to acknowledge the effect of the backdrop of social, cultural, demographic and economic conditions. Yet policy makers are keen to adopt the seemingly simplistic logic. Feniger and Lefstein (2014) set out to challenge the idea of using PISA as the central instrument for assessing policies and justifying reform.

An alternative explanation for the differences in test scores among participating countries is the cultural historical assumption. In comparing the average student scores, this assumption takes 'social, economic, and educational development', as well as 'cultural values, beliefs, and practices', into account (Feniger & Lefstein, 2014, p. 3). Feniger and Lefstein believed that academic achievement cannot be compared solely through differences in policy and structure; rather, other aspects such as culture, history and economic background should be considered. In an effort to offer an alternative explanation to variation in performance on the PISA test, the two authors investigated PISA score differences between natives and students of Chinese origin in Shanghai, Australia and New Zealand. If the cultural historical assumption is sound, it is plausible to hypothesize that PISA scores for students of Chinese origin in these three countries would be similar. To investigate this hypothesis, they used data from PISA 2009. In their analysis, two main case-selection criteria were implemented: student were either born in the host country but their parents emigrated from China or Hong Kong, or they moved to the destination country before the age of five. Due to the fact that large immigrant-receiving countries, such as the United States, do not report details on students' country of origin, and those countries which do report often have too few immigrant cases, the authors picked Australia and New Zealand for the purpose of their exercise. In order to eliminate possible socio-economic confounders, the OLS regression model was used to control for highest parental education in years, highest parental occupational status, and home educational resources.

Through this investigation, Feniger and Lefstein (2014) found that students of Chinese origin who live in Shanghai, Australia and New Zealand did not obtain math scores that are statistically different. The average PISA score for students who tested in Shanghai was around 600, while students of

Chinese origin received average scores of 615 and 571 in Australia and New Zealand, respectively. The differences between these scores were not statistically significant at .05 level – in other words, they were largely due to chance. However, students of Chinese origin in Australia and New Zealand both scored significantly higher than the non-Chinese-origin students in their respective destination countries, after controlling for family characteristics.

In their analysis of Chinese-origin students in Shanghai, Australia and New Zealand, Feniger and Lefstein (2014) find evidence that supports the cultural-historical assumption and largely refutes the policy-and-structures assumption. They conclude that this finding offers an important point of departure for the cross-national comparative studies of education systems, where the policy-and-structure assumption tends to dominate. In their own words, cultural origin seems to be 'more consequential' compared with exposure to the destination education system for these students (Feniger & Lefstein, 2014, p. 6).

Data and Methodology

The data used for the analysis in this chapter are drawn from the PISA 2009 and 2012 student dataset, which collected student achievement scores for reading, math and science, and also surveyed family and school background information on 15-year-old students in more than 60 countries and regions (OECD, 2014). Background questionnaires covered topics regarding students' family, activities and school, and their own attitudes towards various topics. Using PISA 2009 data allows for a close replication of Feniger and Lefstein's (2014) study, which was also based on the 2009 wave, whereas using PISA 2012 data for the second research question will help illustrate the latest patterns.

The case-selection criteria for this analysis follow those of Feniger and Lefstein's (2014) study. More specifically, this chapter focuses on students who either were born in the destination country to parents who emigrated from their respective origin countries, or themselves emigrated to the destination country before the age of five, which is the last year before beginning compulsory education in most countries. In addition, immigrant students who arrived in the destination country after age five and those who had at least one parent who was born in the destination country were removed from the following analysis. A native student is defined as someone who is born in the destination country to parents who are both born in the destination country.

Following Feniger and Lefstein's (2014) study, the outcome of interest is students' math achievement, or First Plausible Value in Math (PV1MATH) [1], which has an international mean of 500 points and a standard deviation of 100 points. Similar to Feniger & Lefstein (2014), all OLS regression models control for three PISA indices: Highest Parental Education in Years; Highest Parental Occupational Status (HISEI); and

Home Educational Resources. In addition, I also consider important individual-level controls, such as gender, grade level and whether the student is an only child.

In order to answer the first research question, I first employ the PISA 2009 dataset. As indicated in Equation (1), this study first demonstrates the country-of-origin effect (β) on student achievement within Australia and New Zealand by taking account of a vector of covariates (X_i), then compares this model with Equation (2), which includes school fixed effects (μ_j). These two equations are depicted as follows:

$$Y_{ij} = \alpha + \beta Origin_i + X_i\gamma + \varepsilon_{ij} \quad (1)$$

$$Y_{ij} = \alpha' + \beta' Origin_i + X_i\gamma' + \mu_j + \varepsilon'_{ij} \quad (2)$$

In Equation (2), by adding school fixed-effect dummies, all variations that occur between schools are accounted for, and the country-of-origin effect in this model (β') now represents differences between native Australian students and immigrant students after controlling for all observed and unobserved school characteristics (and is conditional on observed individual and family characteristics). It is worth noting that any observed difference between β and β' is not simply the effect of schools, but instead is a combination of effects attributable to school-related factors, such as school quality, selectivity in attendance, peer effects, etc. Nonetheless, the change in the coefficient can illustrate whether there is a sizeable overlap between school-related factors and country-of-origin effects. Intuitively, if there is substantial difference between the two coefficients, then it is likely that the country-of-origin effects stated in previous studies have been overstated.

To explore the second research question, I turn to PISA 2012 data to illustrate the latest patterns. First, I identify all origin–destination pairs that have statistically significant differences in mean math achievement at the country level, and have at least 100 valid immigrant student cases, in order to have sufficient statistical power. There are six origin–destination pairs that satisfy this criteria. Then, I report the coefficients of interest by origin–destination pairs. For each origin–destination pair, I run OLS regression with the origin-country students as the reference group, and compare them with immigrant students and with destination-country students, after holding family characteristics constant.

Findings

Table I presents four different OLS regression models. The first two models are based on the PISA 2009 Australian subsample, while models 3 and 4 are computed using the PISA 2009 New Zealand subsample.

In model 1, I present differences in math achievement between students of various countries of origin and the reference category, native Australians, after controlling for individual and family characteristics. The results indicate that students of Chinese origin on average score 65 points, or .65 standard deviations, higher than native Australians. This result is consistent with Feniger and Lefstein's (2014) findings, even after adding additional individual-level variables, such as grade level, sex and whether the student is an only child. Students from other countries of origin who score statistically significantly higher than native students in Australia are those who originate from South Korea (54 points), India (28 points), and other unidentified origins (25 points).

In model 2, school fixed effects are included to account for all observed and unobserved between-school differences. The inclusion of fixed-effect dummies resulted in a sharp reduction in several coefficients. Most notably, the country-of-origin-effect dummy for Chinese students falls by about 45% to 34 points, indicating that conditional on attendance in the same school, students of Chinese origin on average only score .34 standard deviations higher than native Australian students. Also worth noting is that the coefficients of all the family characteristic measures have also shrunk, suggesting that there is also an overlap between school-related factors and family socio-economic status. This result underscores that between-school variation explains a substantial portion of the lead that students of Chinese origin have on native students, and these factors are likely a combination of school-related variation, cultural effect and influence of socio-economic status. In addition, this result is also suggestive that the large effects observed for cultural and county-of-origin effects by Feniger and Lefstein (2014) are likely overstated. Interpreting the large differences between Chinese immigrant and native students as predominantly culturally based is problematic as it fails to consider the school-related and socio-economic factors at play.

In comparing model 1 and model 2, one may also notice similar observations for various origin groups. For Chinese, Korean, Indian and other unidentified-origin groups, between-school differences seem to capture a large share of the origin effects. Especially for Indian students, after accounting for school-level differences, the origin effect becomes statistically insignificant. This seems to indicate that for Indian students in Australia, school-level differences seem to form a key part of the explanation for their higher math scores over native students.

	Australia subsample			New Zealand subsample		
	Model 1	Model 2		Model 3	Model 4
Immigrant Origin (Ref: Australians)			*Immigrant Origin* (Ref: New Zealanders)		
China (including Hong Kong)	65.19 ***	34.59 ***	China (including Hong Kong)	38.07 **	25.63 *
	(13.97)	(7.74)		(12.20)	(10.61)
South Korea	54.29 *	31.64	South Korea	48.37	32.52
	(26.48)	(19.46)		(24.66)	(24.48)
USA	19.39	6.59	-	-	-
	(14.27)	(11.89)	-	-	-
South Africa	-4.38	-8.58	South Africa	13.17	3.01
	(10.55)	(8.48)		(29.89)	(26.42)
India	28.18 **	9.63	-	-	-
	(10.85)	(8.48)	-	-	-
UK	-5.21	-3.58	UK	13.09	14.01
	(5.55)	(4.98)		(10.14)	(9.56)
Philippines	3.20	5.24	Samoa	-56.00 ***	-32.56 **
	(10.37)	(8.81)		(11.26)	(10.42)
Other (Unidentified Origin)	25.07 ***	12.01 ***	Other (Unidentified Origin)	-20.98 ***	-13.30 *
	(4.44)	(3.50)		(6.36)	(5.94)
Individual Characteristics			*Individual Characteristics*		
Grade Level in School (Grade)	29.95 ***	35.42 ***	Grade Level in School (Grade)	37.14 ***	43.18 ***
	(2.34)	(1.99)		(5.22)	(4.70)
Female (Male = 0)	-12.80 ***	-13.58 ***	Female (Male = 0)	-13.76 ***	-8.36 **
	(1.88)	(1.57)		(4.21)	(3.14)
Only Child (Have Siblings = 0)	-3.28	-1.21	Only Child (Have Siblings = 0)	-2.61	1.21
	(1.77)	(1.61)		(3.49)	(3.05)
Family Characteristics			*Family Characteristics*		
Home Educational Resources (HEDRES)	16.68 ***	12.42 ***	Home Educational Resources (HEDRES)	12.39 ***	8.56 ***
	(1.07)	(.95)		(1.81)	(1.56)
Highest Occupational Status of Parents (HISEI)	1.21 ***	.81 ***	Highest Occupational Status of Parents (HISEI)	1.70 ***	1.38 ***
	(.06)	(.06)		(.12)	(.12)
Parent Education (PARED)	7.39 ***	4.55 ***	Parent Education (PARED)	4.55 ***	3.76 ***
	(.61)	(.53)		(.90)	(.81)
School Fixed-Effects	No	Yes	School Fixed-Effects	No	Yes
Intercept	**	**	Intercept		
n	11726	11726	n	3107	3107
Adj. R-Squared	.2002	.1875	Adj. R-Squared	.1981	.1926

Note: Feniger and Lefstein (2014) included students from Hong Kong in the China category; [*p < .05, **p < .01, ***p < .001].

Table I. Unstandardized coefficients from OLS regression on math achievement among students in Australia and New Zealand.

In models 3 and 4, similar patterns are observed. In New Zealand, students of Chinese origin, on average, performed 38 points higher than their native counterparts. After including school fixed effects, the country-of-origin coefficients not only decrease substantially, but all three measures of socio-economic status effects are also noticeably smaller. These results indicate that the patterns observed for Chinese immigrants in Australia hold for the case in New Zealand, and that the effect of origin that Feniger and Lefstein (2014) reported in their study is a combination of cultural and origin, as well as school-level factors. The current evidence presented demonstrates that culture, origin and school effects are substantially intertwined, and adopting either a dominant-policy-environment or a cultural-historical interpretation is misleading.

In order to decide which origin–destination pairs to report on in Table II, I first followed the previously stated case-selection strategy (see data and methodology section) to identify all observed cross-border student immigrants. Then, I shortlisted all origin–destination pairs if their country-level math score mean was statistically different from each other. Finally, I ran Feniger and Lefstein's (2014) OLS model for all origin–destination pairs that have at least 100 immigrant cases, and coefficients of interest are reported in Table II. All origin–destination pairs are listed in alphabetical order.

For each origin–destination pair, the reference group in each regression model is the native students who took the test in the origin country. I report coefficients for immigrant students and native students who took the test in the destination country, after controlling for three family background indices. The intercept represents the average score of students in the origin country who are at the country mean for each of the three family background measures. In Table II, I also report the immigrant sample size n, as well as the total sample size N, and the adjusted R-squared statistic for each regression.

According to Feniger and Lefstein's (2014) analysis and conclusion, after controlling for family background, the cultural influence hypothesis would suggest that immigrant students should perform similarly to students in the origin country and differently from students in the destination country. In the language of coefficients, we should observe the immigrant dummy coefficient to be statistically insignificant and the destination country dummy to be statistically significant. In the succeeding paragraphs, I report the results in detail, using the same model specification for each origin–destination pair.

In the Albania-to-Greece pair, Albanian-origin students in Greece on average score 18 points ($p < .001$) more than native students in Albania, after controlling for family backgrounds. Meanwhile, native students in Greece score about 52 points ($p < .001$) higher than native students in Albania. This finding shows that both native and Albanian-origin students in Greece significantly outperform native students in Albania; however, a larger score margin is observed for native than for Albanian-origin students in Greece. This observation differs from Feniger and Lefstein's (2014) cultural influence hypothesis.

Origin–Destination pair	Variable	Beta	SE	t
Albania to Greece (n=134)	Greece: Albania Origin	18.11***	5.56	3.26
	Greece: Non-Albania Origin	52.07***	1.95	26.70
	Intercept	341.26***	4.83	70.72
	n		9070	
	Adjusted R-squared		.1481	
China (include. Hong Kong) to Australia (n=192)	Australia: China Origin	-15.11*	6.51	-2.32
	Australia: Non-China Origin	-122.96***	1.52	-80.64
	Intercept	484.60***	4.12	117.65
	n		17,244	
	Adjusted R-squared		.3476	
Jordan to Qatar (n=137)	Qatar: Jordan Origin	-6.15	7.59	-.81
	Qatar: Non-Jordan Origin	-44.08***	1.47	-30.04
	Intercept	346.22***	3.81	90.96
	n		10,265	
	Adjusted R-squared		.1406	
Portugal to Switzerland (n=373)	Switzerland: Portugal Origin	.21	4.35	.01
	Switzerland: Non-Portugal Origin	15.4***	1.62	9.5
	Intercept	408.98***	2.67	153.12
	n		14,531	
	Adjusted R-squared		.1720	
Russia to Finland (n=151)	Finland: Russia Origin	-16.13*	6.53	-2.47
	Finland: Non-Russia Origin	31.58***	1.70	18.60
	Intercept	379.81***	5.58	68.07
	n		12,294	
	Adjusted R-squared		.1313	
Serbia to Montenegro (n=164)	Montenegro: Serbia Origin	-28.21***	6.76	-4.18
	Montenegro: Non-Serbia Origin	-34.50***	1.78	-19.37
	Intercept	385.85***	4.91	78.64
	n		8075	
	Adjusted R-squared		.1657	

Note: All models follow same specification as Feniger and Lefstein (2014), descriptive statistics available upon request; Albania did not report HISEI scale, OLS model for Albania to Greece only included PARED and HEDRES as controls; number of immigrant cases for each origin-destination pair reported in parenthesis; [*$p < .05$, **$p < .01$, ***$p < .001$].

Table II. Unstandardized coefficients from OLS regression on math achievement among students, by origin–destination pairs.

In the China-to-Australia pair, Chinese-origin students in Australia on average score 15 points ($p < .05$) lower than native students in Shanghai, after controlling for family backgrounds. As illustrated by Feniger and Lefstein's (2014) analysis, there are several caveats to this comparison; for instance, the assumption that Shanghai is representative of students from China; treating students from Hong Kong as culturally no different to those who originate from other areas of China, etc. Nonetheless, these results are drawn from a direct replication of Feniger and Lefstein's analysis using a newer version of PISA data. These updated results indicate that both China-origin and native students in Australia perform significantly lower than students who took the test in Shanghai, and are contrary to Feniger and Lefstein's (2014) observation of an insignificant coefficient.

In the Jordan-to-Qatar pair, Jordan-origin students in Qatar are on average not statistically different from native students in Jordan in terms of math achievement, after controlling for family backgrounds. The native students in Qatar, however, on average score 44 points ($p < .001$) lower than students in Jordan. This result suggests that Jordanian students who live in Qatar achieved similar scores to those who live in Jordan and obtained much higher scores than native Qatari students. This observation is consistent with Feniger and Lefstein's (2014) cultural influence hypothesis.

In the Portugal-to-Switzerland pair, math scores of Portugal-origin students in Switzerland are on average not statistically different from native students in Portugal, after controlling for family characteristics. The native Swiss students, however, on average outperform native Portuguese students by about 15 points ($p < .001$). Consistent with Feniger and Lefstein's (2014) cultural influence hypothesis, this result show that Portuguese students who live in Switzerland scored similarly to those who live in Portugal, and somewhat lower than native Swiss students.

In the Russia-to-Finland pair, Russia-origin students in Finland score on average 16 points ($p < .05$ level) lower than native students in Russia, after controlling for family backgrounds. The native Finnish students on average score 31 points ($p < .001$ level) higher than native Russian students. This result shows that Russian students who live in Finland score significantly lower than their counterparts in Russia, and native Finnish students score significantly higher than Russian students both in Russia and in Finland. It is worth noting that not only is this result inconsistent with Feniger and Lefstein's (2014) cultural influence hypothesis, which suggests that immigrant students would be more or less the same as native students in the origin country, but Russian students in Finland also score significantly lower than their counterparts in Russia, after taking into account family characteristics.

In the Serbia-to-Montenegro pair, Serbia-origin students in Montenegro on average score 28 points ($p < .001$) lower than native students in Serbia, after controlling for family characteristics. Also, native students in Montenegro score 34.5 points ($p < .001$) lower than native Serbian students. This finding shows that both native and Serbia-origin students in Montenegro score significantly lower than native students in Serbia. However, the performance of native students in Montenegro and that of Serbia-origin students in Montenegro are not statistically different. This observation differs from Feniger and Lefstein's (2014) cultural influence hypothesis, and the fact that students, regardless of country of origin, score similarly in the destination country may even suggest that the policy-environment hypothesis may be true in this case.

To summarize the six origin–destination pairs presented in Table II, there are a few observations that can be made. First, immigrant students are performing statistically differently from native students in five out of six destination countries; Montenegro is the exception, where Serbia-origin and native students are statistically no different. Based on this simple observation, it is plausible to conclude that policy environments do not entirely close the difference in achievement between various countries of origin. Second, only two out of six origin–destination pairs, Jordan–Qatar and Portugal–Switzerland, generate findings that would be suggestive of the cultural influence hypothesis. In both Qatar and Switzerland, it is observed that Jordanian and Portuguese immigrant students perform similarly to students in their respective origin country. Third, replication of Feniger and Lefstein's case study on Chinese students in Australia using 2012 data shows that China-origin students in Australia perform significantly lower than students in Shanghai, but significantly higher than native students in Australia. This result shows that analyses conducted using immigrant students may be subject to temporal trends that vary across time which can complicate interpretation. Fourth, in Finland, Russia-origin students are not only performing lower than their native counterparts in Finland, but also lower than students in Russia. Based on this observation, it is important to acknowledge that analyses concerning immigrant students should be cognizant of effects associated with self-selection, which can be independent of country-of-origin or policy-environment effects.

Discussion and Conclusion

This chapter has presented two important findings. Based on the first research question, analysis shows that the country-of-origin effect on student achievement is reduced by half after accounting for school-level differences. This is an indication that previous analysis which omits school-level differences may be overstating the country-of-origin effect on student achievement. In regard to the second research question, this analysis exhaustively lists all identified origin–destination pairs that have a large enough immigrant sample, with results indicating that there is no uniform pattern in immigrant student achievement cross-nationally. Findings from this exercise suggest that while PISA reasoning and the cultural influence hypothesis are two important and competing explanations for cross-country variation in international tests, and while both have gained attention in recent years, more rigorous work is needed to further this line of research, as the results here suggest that both PISA reasoning and the cultural influence hypothesis are biased and ungeneralizable.

Work on this topic using immigrant data also requires caution, because selection appears to behave quite differently among different cultural groups

(Borjas, 1987). Work on cross-border migration flows has some important implications for the patterns observed in this study. In Gould and Moav's (2010) study on Israeli immigrants to the United States, evidence show that these migrants appear to be positively selected on a set of observable skills. Similar results by Feliciano (2005) and Grogger and Hanson (2008) also indicate that immigrants are positively selected in terms of education attainment by almost all observed sending countries. Although studies indicate that immigration is potentially a positive selection process, Chiquiar and Hanson (2005) find that the patterns may be more complicated; in the case of Mexico, they find that Mexican migrants are more likely to be drawn from the middle of the distribution on observable characteristics. In addition, Abramitzky et al's (2012) analysis, based on historical data of Norwegian immigrants to the United States during the late nineteenth century, suggests that negative selection in immigration may also be observed. As indicated by these studies, immigration can be a positive, neutral, or negative selection process depending on the country of origin and the destination, and even across time periods.

Based on this large body of literature on immigrant selection and on the findings outlined in this chapter, it is crucial to note that results drawn from PISA data regarding both PISA reasoning and cultural influence hypotheses are subject to important limitations. First and foremost, the PISA reasoning that credits student performance to national policy environment is an unwarranted claim. It is worth a word of caution that attributing cross-country variation in student achievement solely to the artifacts of policy design is misguided. Second, simply interpreting the country-of-origin effect as evidence in support of the cultural influence hypothesis is also problematic; it should be interpreted as a mixture of selection, school, and temporal factors. Thus, it is going to the extreme to say that cultural influence is overwhelmingly important and policy environments do not matter. Third, immigrants migrate for many reasons, and international patterns are not uniform. Thus, future research should attempt to better understand these differing observations in their individual context. Lastly, it is important to acknowledge that this chapter is an attempt to problematize and challenge simple answers given by both sides of the culture versus policy dichotomy.

Note

[1] All analyses were performed for all five plausible values (PV1MATH–PV5MATH), and results are available upon request to the author. For simplicity of presentation in this chapter, discussions are based on results using PV1MATH.

References

Abramitzky, R., Boustan, L. & Eriksson., K. (2012) Europe's Tired, Poor, Huddled Masses: self-selection and economic outcomes in the age of mass migration, *American Economic Review*, 102(5), 1832-1856. http://dx.doi.org/10.1257/aer.102.5.1832

Alexander, R. (2010) World Class Schools: noble aspiration or globalised hokum? *Compare*, 40(6), 801-817. http://dx.doi.org/10.1080/03057925.2010.523252

Barber, M. & Mourshed, M. (2007) *How the World's Best-performing School Systems Come Out on Top*. London: McKinsey & Company.

Borjas, G. (1987) Self-selection and the Earnings of Immigrants, *American Economic Review*, 77(4), 531-553.

Carnoy, M. & Rothstein, R. (2013) *What Do International Test Scores Really Show about US Student Performance?* Washington, DC: Economic Policy Institute.

Chiquiar, D. & Hanson, G.H. (2005) International Migration, Self-selection, and the Distribution of Wages: evidence from Mexico and the United States, *Journal of Political Economy*, 113(2), 239-281. http://dx.doi.org/10.1086/427464

Condron, D. (2011) Egalitarianism and Educational Excellence, *Educational Researcher*, 40(2) 47-55. http://dx.doi.org/10.3102/0013189X11401021

Feliciano, C. (2005) Educational Selectivity in US Immigration: how do immigrants compare to those left behind?, *Demography*, 42(1), 131-152. http://dx.doi.org/10.1353/dem.2005.0001

Feniger, Y. & Lefstein, A. (2014) How Not to Reason with PISA Data: an ironic investigation, *Journal of Education Policy*, 29(6), 845-855. http://dx.doi.org/10.1080/02680939.2014.892156

Gould, E. & Moav, O. (2010) When Is 'Too Much' Inequality Not Enough? The Selection of Israeli Emigrants. http://www.ecore.be/Papers/1280145355.pdf

Grogger, J. & Hanson, G.H. (2008) Income Maximization and the Selection and Sorting of International Migrants. National Bureau of Economic Research Working Paper 13821.

McKinsey & Company (2010) *How the World's Most Improved School Systems Keep Getting Better*. New York: McKinsey & Company.

Organisation for Economic Co-operation and Development (OECD) (2011) *Lessons from PISA for the United States: strong performers and successful reformers in education*. Paris: OECD.

Organisation for Economic Co-operation and Development (OECD) (2014) *PISA 2012 Results in Focus: what 15-year-olds know and what they can do with what they know*. Paris: OECD.

Sahlberg, P. (2011) *Finnish Lessons*. New York: Teachers College Press.

Schledicher, A. & Stewart, V. (2008) Learning from World-class Schools, *Educational Leadership*, 66(2), 44-51.

Sellar, S. & Lingard, B. (2013) The OECD and Global Governance in Education, *Journal of Education Policy*, 28(5), 710-725. http://dx.doi.org/10.1080/02680939.2013.779791

Tucker, M. (2011a) *Standing on the Shoulders of Giants: an American agenda for education reform*. Washington, DC: National Center on Education and the Economy.

Tucker, M. (2011b) *Surpassing Shanghai: an agenda for American education built on the world's leading systems*. Cambridge, MA: Harvard Education Press.

CHAPTER 6

Measuring Learning Outcomes and Education for Sustainable Development: the new education development goal

ANGELINE M. BARRETT

ABSTRACT The education Sustainable Development Goal for 2015-2030 will be the first development goal to include targets for learning outcomes. The prevalent global culture of testing has acted to promote standardised measures of literacy and numeracy as the preferred tools for monitoring learning globally. These are not sufficient to the task of ensuring education quality for all, as understood from a social justice perspective. They also do little to promote the kind of social learning that is integral to sustainable development. This chapter contrasts the learning agenda within Education for All with a broader conceptualisation of education quality offered by social justice perspectives and key ideas on learning in the literature on education for sustainable development.

Introduction

At the time of writing, the Education and Lifelong Learning Sustainable Development Goal (SDG) is being negotiated within a global context, where standardised assessments have become a tool for global monitoring and global governance of education (Fukuda-Parr et al, 2013; Sellar & Lingard, 2013). The 2015-2030 education goal will be the first United Nations (UN) development goal to include targets for learning outcomes. Universal in their coverage, these targets represent the single most ambitious and far-reaching manifestation of the global testing culture described by Smith (2016) in the introduction to this book. Globally, most assessments, particularly those used in monitoring Education for All (EFA), focus on a narrow set of foundational skills in literacy and numeracy. By contrast, the challenge of sustainable development in the context of unprecedented environmental change demands interdisciplinary problem-solving and radical departure from the values of neoliberalism (Sterling, 2001). This raises the question of how well the international preoccupation with student performance on standardised tests as an outcome of education serves the broader cross-sectoral agenda of sustainable development. To explore this question, this chapter draws on a social justice framework for education quality and key ideas on learning from the literature on education for sustainable development (ESD). It explores the extent to which they are compatible by adopting a social justice framework for understanding education quality for all. The framework was designed to clarify the meaning and evaluation of education quality at a time when the development objectives were dominated by rights-based and human capital notions of development, so attention is also given to the limitations of the framework and how it may be adapted to evaluate policies for promoting education quality that contribute to sustainable development.

The SDGs conform closely to the proposal of the Open Working Group for Sustainable Development Goals (Open Working 49 Group for Sustainable Development Goals, 2014), henceforth referred to as the OWG. This was the most up-to-date document available at the time of writing in early 2015 and therefore the reference point for this chapter. The education goal is fourth out of 17 goals and is expressed as 'to ensure inclusive and equitable quality education and promote life-long learning opportunities for all' (Open Working Group for Sustainable Development Goals, 2014, p. 10). Learning outcomes have a prominent place within the goal. The first of its seven associated targets aims for 'all girls and boys to complete free and equitable primary and secondary education leading to relevant and effective learning outcomes' (Open Working Group for Sustainable Development Goals, 2014, p. 10). Three other targets are also expressed in terms of outcomes. The adult literacy target, to 'ensure all youth and [x] percent of adults, both men and women, achieve literacy and numeracy', is also defined in terms of narrow, supposedly measurable learning outcomes. The other two may be termed the awkward targets. They are expansive in their ambition and scope but have provided the greatest challenge for technical experts charged with proposing feasible indicators. These are the vocational skills target:

> [to] increase by [x] per cent the number of youth and adults who have relevant skills, including technical and vocational skills, for employment, decent jobs and entrepreneurship (Open Working Group for Sustainable Development Goals, 2014, p. 10)

and what I will term the ESD target:

> [to] ensure that all learners acquire the knowledge and skills needed to promote sustainable development, including, among others, through education for sustainable development and sustainable lifestyles, human rights, gender equality, promotion of a culture of peace and nonviolence, global citizenship and

appreciation of cultural diversity and of culture's contribution to sustainable development. (Open Working Group for Sustainable Development Goals, 2014, p. 10)

The chapter starts by charting the rise in recent years of a learning agenda within the international EFA movement and by looking at how measures of learning outcomes are used to monitor and implement EFA. The second part of the chapter turns to a social justice conceptualisation of education quality to present a broader account of educational outcomes in terms of benefits to individuals and society. The framework is expanded through engagement with key ideas on learning in the literature on ESD and consideration of the challenge of measurement presented by the 'awkward targets'.

The Rise of the Learning Agenda within EFA

In the lead-up to 2015, the formulation of a new goal for education was the subject of debate and international consultations. Measurement and its learning was a persistent theme in this debate. The American think tank the Brookings Institute was an influential advocate for monitoring learning outcomes, placing the 'learning agenda' centre-stage early on in its high-profile report 'A Global Compact on Learning' (Center for Universal Education at Brookings, 2011). In the same year, the World Bank headlined the learning theme in its 2020 Education Strategy, 'Learning for All' (World Bank, 2011). The need to focus on 'learning' and not just enrolment in schools continued to be consistently raised in a series of global consultations conducted by various UN bodies and a coalition of civil society organisations (Beyond 2015, 2013; High-level Panel, 2013; UNDG, 2013; UNICEF/ UNESCO, 2013). Behind this powerful consensus lay the recognition of a 'learning crisis' (UNESCO, 2013), a crisis made apparent by the rapid multiplication of assessments of literacy and numeracy. The EFA Global Monitoring Report (EFA GMR) synthesised findings from large-scale international and regional education assessments of learning to conclude that out of 650 million primary school-aged children worldwide, at least 250 million do not learn the basics in reading and mathematics by the end of grade four (UNESCO, 2014). Indeed, nearly half of these never reach grade four. This is largely a crisis of learning in low- and middle-income countries. Three-quarters of children who go to school but do not learn to read live in South and West Asia or sub-Saharan Africa.

The 'learning crisis' discourse may be viewed as the product of a circular reinforcement between data made available as a consequence of a global testing culture and agenda setting. Data from the Programme for International Student Assessment (PISA) and other international and regional learning assessments (identified below) have enabled quantification of the prevalence of low achievement, particularly in literacy and numeracy. Various actors responded by further proliferating learning assessments in order to understand the 'learning crisis' better. The 'learning crisis' is not new but measures of learning had previously be treated as a proxy giving partial information on education quality (UNESCO, 2004). For approximately the first half of the Millennium Development Goal (MDG) era, UN organisations and non-governmental organisations talked about the problem of poor quality and proposed frameworks for conceptualising and setting expectations for quality (GCE, 2002; Myers, 2004; UNESCO, 2004; IATT on Education, 2006; UNICEF, 2008). These frameworks were explicitly based in a rights-based approach to development, some claiming the Convention on the Rights of the Child (UN, 1989) as their point of departure (UNICEF, 2004). They centred on 'the learner' and the fulfilment of her rights to education, within education and through education. Learning outcomes had a place within this discourse but as just one facet of a multidimensional understanding of quality that also took account of participation, inputs and educational processes.

Filmer et al (2006), economists of education associated with the Center for Global Development, another think tank in the United States, were the first to propose that the enrolment-plus-quality MDG agenda be replaced by a learning goal with targets for measurable learning outcomes set at a regional or national level. They demonstrated the feasibility of their proposal through analysis of the PISA data from eleven middle- to high-income countries. Since then, the explosion in learning assessments has broadened out the choice of data sources. Winthrop et al (2015) note the increasing numbers of mainly middle-income countries participating in international large-scale educational assessments, such as the Organisation for Economic Co-operation and Development's (OECD's) PISA; the emergence of hybrid assessments of literacy and numeracy (Wagner, 2010) conducted by civil society organisations, such as Uwezo in East Africa and the Annual Status of Education Report (ASER) in India, often with external financial backing; and the remarkably rapid spread of Early Grade Reading Assessments (EGRA). EGRA has been adapted for implementation in 65 countries, and is often implemented with financial backing from USAID (Dubeck & Gove, 2015).The latest EFA Global Monitoring Report notes an increase in the number of national surveys of learning from 12 in 1990 to 101 in 2013, 64 of which were conducted in low- or middle-income countries (EFA Global Monitoring Report Team, 2015). Much of this new activity in assessing learning measures skills in literacy and mathematics.

These new data on students' test performance have been used in three ways, which often overlap or work in tandem with each other. These are: to inform policy and practice and sometimes to influence policy debates and decision-making; to hold governments to account for the quality of education they deliver; and to monitor progress towards equity in education. The EGRAs in particular have been used in the first way and the proliferation of their use is closely associated with heavy investment by USAID in improving literacy instruction in the early years. In some places they have been used as a diagnostic tool to identify the specific 'missing' reading skills and design teacher training to address these (Dubeck & Gove, 2015; Dubeck et al, 2015). Some researchers have drawn out policy recommendations from analysis of EGRA data. For example, Piper et al (2015) compared results from EGRA tests conducted in different languages to deduce implications for the use of mother tongue and introduction of languages of wider use in education. Overall, EGRA has been instrumental in directing international aid and national or local interventions towards strengthening literacy and numeracy teaching in the early years of primary education.

The use of assessments for accountability purposes is illustrated by Languille's (2014) case study of development partners' deployment of results-based management strategies in Tanzania. They scored the government's performance in improving education quality according to results from national examinations and the Uwezo survey. Languille shows how the logic of results-based management infuses the relationship between donors and recipient government, becoming a mechanism for external influence on policy. She also identifies the actors involved with the Uwezo study, showing how a network of international actors funds and strengthens the influence of a study, sometimes referred to as 'citizen-led assessment' (EFA Global Monitoring Report Team, 2015; Winthrop et al, 2015). Languille (2014) argues that an international learning goal will intensify the practice of results-based management and with it the promotion of neo-liberal education policies. The World Bank has recently announced that it is taking this kind of results-based management to a further extreme through 'results-based financing', whereby 'a resource transfer is made only when performance or results criteria have been met' (World Bank Group, 2015, p. 5).

The third use of findings – to probe educational equalities – arguably provides the strongest rationale for such assessments (Rose, 2015). It is demonstrated by the analysis of data of international and regional large-scale assessments reported in successive Education for All Global Monitoring Reports. For example, analysis of PISA data reveals strong associations between the economic wealth of countries and students' performance in the PISA tests as well as between individuals in different income quintiles within a country (Bloem, 2013). The Uwezo survey has highlighted the magnitude of disparities in the measured reading ability of children living in rural and urban districts (Uwezo, 2010). The surveys have done much to make disparities in quality visible to policy makers, particularly at the international level.

A key feature of the global testing culture as it pertains to monitoring the education SDG is the narrow range of skills that are assessed, with an overwhelming focus on literacy and numeracy. While large-scale studies have addressed other competencies, these are mainly, although not exclusively, conducted by OECD countries, or else are very specific in their focus. For example, the Southern and East African Consortium for Monitoring Education Quality (SACMEQ) included an HIV and AIDS Knowledge Test its 2007 study. When it comes to monitoring progress towards Education for All, basic literacy and, to a lesser extent, numeracy have been the main focus. National surveys of learning often cover a wider range of skills and curricular subject areas, although literacy and numeracy are still by far the most commonly assessed competencies (EFA Global Monitoring Report Team, 2015).

Learning and the Education SDG

The concept of education quality within Education for All – that preceded the emergence of learning agenda – can be distilled into three ideas: inclusion or equity; relevance; and participation. In previous work with Leon Tikly, we drew on the social justice theories of Amartya Sen (2009) and Nancy Fraser (2008) to more precisely define these concepts and give them a basis in moral philosophy (Tikly, 2011; Tikly & Barrett, 2011, 2013). Like other theorists using the capabilities approach (Unterhalter, 2005; Vizard et al, 2011), we operated social justice theories to supplement and clarify rather than displace human rights. Since then, however, the international agenda for development has shifted significantly. The poverty reduction agenda that drove the MDGs has been broadened out into a sustainable development agenda that embraces environmental as well as economic and social progress. The Education for All targets of 2000 to 2015, which ran in parallel to the Education MDG, are enfolded within an Education and Lifelong Learning SDG. The target for universal primary education is replaced by a basic education target that looks for progress in relevant learning outcomes as well as enrolment.

In the second part of this chapter, I evaluate the extent to which measurement of learning outcomes is fit for the purpose of monitoring education quality. The argument focuses on the two aspects of quality – equity and relevance – that are explicitly referenced in the OWG proposal. I also consider how the sustainable development agenda expands the social justice framework.

Equity and Relevance from a Social Justice Perspective

Equity in education, when informed by Sen's capability approach, is understood not as parity of access to educational institutions and resources as but parity in terms of the opportunities these afford to individuals (Barrett, 2011; Tikly & Barrett, 2011). Evaluating equity in terms of benefits rather than provision rationalises targeting investment at groups historically marginalised within education systems. For example, individuals living with disabilities that affect their participation in education require the learning aids and extra support that enable them to benefit from educational programmes. Similarly, learners who do not have fluency in a language of wider use require mother-tongue education or bi/multilingual education to enable learning across the curriculum. This view of equity implies that outcomes are a more appropriate evaluative space for equity than enrolments (Barrett, 2011). Indeed, in the run-up to 2015, robust arguments have been put forward for using indicators for the basic education targets that disaggregate data from assessments of learning according to variables associated with marginalisation, such as rural/urban locality, socio-economic quintile and gender (Education for All Global Monitoring Report, 2013; EFA Steering Committee TAG on the Post-2015 Education Indicators, 2014; Rose, 2015). Nonetheless, measures of learning outcomes are partial for two reasons. First, they focus on a narrow subset of the proficiencies acquired through schooling. Second, learning outcomes are not equivalent to benefits.

Unterhalter and Brighouse (2007) identify three types of benefits from education – intrinsic, instrumental and positional – arguing that progress towards Education for All should be assessed using indicators for all three. Intrinsic benefits relate to the rewards of participating in education, irrespective of any gain that follows as a consequence. This is education as an end, rather than means, of development, the intrinsic reward of exercising our senses, of imagining, thinking and reasoning that Nussbaum (2011) identifies as a central capability for human dignity and flourishing. Put more simply, it is learning for learning's sake. Following Nussbaum's reasoning, the opportunity to engage in learning should be an entitlement across a lifetime. It may be fulfilled through formal, non-formal or informal education. While lifelong learning is now integrated into the Education SDG, it does not have a dedicated target and so is at risk of neglect (Langford, 2012). However, as argued below, the ESD target may be interpreted to have implications for lifelong learning.

Instrumental benefits of education are the capabilities acquired through education. This is education as the means of development. They include the skills, knowledge and values that enable a person to be socio-economically active and to participate constructively in society. Instrumental benefits relate to relevance. From a social justice perspective, a relevant education expands learners' capabilities for pursuing sustainable livelihoods and participating in the benefits of globalisation. Relevance concerns knowledge, skills and values for socio-economic participation (Tikly & Barrett, 2011). Additionally, it has a socio-cultural element. A relevant education also recognises the diverse socio-cultural identities of learners such as the cultural value to students of the languages they use outside of school, and the history, indigenous knowledge, artistic and cultural life of their communities. Within the Education SDG the target for skills for work addresses the economic dimension of relevance. Instrumental benefits relating to an individual's contribution to society are addressed through the ESD target. The socio-cultural recognition dimension of relevance is not explicitly addressed, although the reference to ESD and peace education may be interpreted to require recognition justice in education. Both the ESD and the skills for work target construct education as enabling of instrumental benefits for individuals.

Finally, positional benefits relate to the status that a person gains in society by dint of the titles, certificates and group memberships acquired through engaging in an education programme. This could be characterised as the social and symbolic capital accrued through education. The positional benefits of education play a profound role in reproducing or transforming social inequalities. Yet they are largely absent from debate around EFA with the important exception of basic literacy and numeracy skills, valued for enabling learners to claim their rights as citizens. So, for example, the adult literacy target in the Muscat Agreement [1] specifies 'literacy and numeracy to fully participate in society' (Global Education for All Meeting, 2014, p. 3). The OWG, however, misses an opportunity to link the adult literacy target (quoted above) to any kind of broader benefit despite it being widely recognised that adult literacy is most successful when embedded within a programme addressing participants' identified knowledge needs – for example, in relation to agriculture (EFA Global Monitoring Report, 2015). To understand how formal education contributes to positional benefits requires analysis not just of learning outcomes but of how different groups perform in selective examinations and with what consequences for transition to successive levels of education and into various types of occupation.

From a social justice perspective, measures of learning give valuable information on equity and inclusion, provided data are disaggregated according to learners' characteristics. However, such measures are not on their own sufficient to monitor quality. In particular, a reliance on measurement of learning overlooks or takes for granted the relevance of education.

Learning within Education for Sustainable Development

ESD, like human rights, is concerned with processes of, as well as outcomes from, education. Indeed, Fien and Tilbury (2002) argue that sustainable development itself is not a product or outcome but a process. Like social justice theories, ESD aspires for learners to be agents in constructing a different trajectory for societies. However, ESD adds an environmental dimension to social transformation. How the environmental dimension is framed varies. Bangay and Blum (2010) discuss the quality of education that prepares learners to face a future made uncertain by climate change. They argue that uncertainty demands that learners are equipped with skills such as critical thinking and problem solving, which can only be acquired through transformational learning that 'expand[s] the learner's understanding of him/herself and of the world around him/her, and potentially lead[s] to individual or social change' (Bangay & Blum, 2010, p. 363). They critique oversimplified understandings within EFA of the relation between inputs, learning and social change. They point instead to a long tradition of educational research that explores the complexity of learning, including social-constructivist theories of learning and critical pedagogies.

Some sustainable development theorists call for a more radical view of learning for sustainable development. Scott and Gough (2010) highlight John Foster's contribution in defining sustainable development as itself a process of social learning. For Scott and Gough, whose work focuses on ESD within formal education, this is the point of departure for arguing that ESD within each level of formal education should build on previous learning. It may equally be argued that sustainable development as social learning justifies lifelong learning, conceived as ongoing participation across the lifetime in communities of inquiry. Morgan (2009) is sceptical of the potential of western forms of schooling to support ESD as social learning but rather envisages its implementation through globally minded action-based community projects. For Morgan, ESD is not just a matter of individual learning but is about communities coming together to identify and resolve or ameliorate an issue of concern. The outcome of ESD therefore does not stop with individuals' acquisition of creativity, critical-thinking or problem-solving skills but is seen in collaborative learning that is intrinsic to transformative social actions. This position leads Morgan to give up on formal education as institutionally and structurally inimical to sustainable development. Nonetheless, his view of learning is compatible with social-constructivist theories of learning, highlighted by Bangay and Blum (2010) and held close by large numbers of teachers, that conceptualise learning as participation in a community of inquiry (Daniels, 2001). Morgan's arguments and those of other ESD scholars (Sterling, 2001; Breidlid, 2013) challenge the privileged position of individual achievement as the form of outcome valued within the culture of global testing (Smith, 2016). By contrast, they draw attention to the value of collaborative achievements and actions that contribute to sustainable and socially just societal change.

Hence, the scholarship on ESD presents a view of learning that contradicts the results-based logic which currently influences global monitoring of the education SDG targets and has shaped their formulation. I include within this the rather long-winded ESD target within the OWG proposal quoted in the introduction to this chapter. The ESD target is the one target that attempts to explicitly link education to the broader sustainable development agenda. However, it still focuses on individual outcomes in the form of knowledge and skills, although the sidelined Muscat proposal also included values and attitudes. Regrettably, it is probable that the ESD target, like the life skills EFA goal before it, will gain less traction than the other education targets. This is because ESD, like the life skills EFA goal, is not widely understood as a concept, and measurable indicators have yet to be identified (Rose, 2015). Nonetheless, it has been accepted as a target because it is considered feasible to develop indicators over the lifetime of the SDGs. For example, it has been suggested that household surveys could be used to collect information on attitudes related to sustainable lifestyles, peace, gender and citizenship (EFA Steering Committee TAG on the Post-2015 Education Indicators, 2014; Unterhalter, 2014). Over the lifetime of the education MDG and EFA goals, our understanding of quality and our capacity for measurement have changed. Indeed, the education SDG and its associated metrics of learning may be viewed as a product of that change. The new education SDG also contains within it the spaces for re-defining quality and creating new metrics. These spaces are provided by the awkward targets, the ones for which technical experts operating within the global testing culture cannot find indicators – namely, the target for ESD quoted above and the target for relevant skills for decent employment and entrepreneurship. Over the next 15 years, the opportunities presented by these targets may be quietly neglected. Or alternatively, they may be taken up by the experts and implementers of EFA to push back against the constrictive limitations of evaluating quality solely in terms of measurable individual achievement.

Conclusion

By drawing on previous work on social justice perspectives on education quality and ideas about learning in the literature on education for sustainable development, this chapter has pointed out some limitations of learning metrics for monitoring the new education SDG. Within the goal itself, there is a tension between an emphasis on learning test results as the evaluative space for quality and an overarching sustainable development agenda that dissolves the distinction between outcomes and processes. The logic of results-based management, which prevails within the international governance of education, leads inexorably to a focus on instrumental benefits to the individual. The overarching purpose of sustainable development, however, demands change through social learning. Certainly, measures of learning outcomes yield important information on inclusion and equity in education and, therefore, should continue to be a part of global monitoring. However, as we move into the future, their inadequacy for ensuring a quality of education that addresses contemporary challenges of social justice and sustainability will become ever more apparent.

Acknowledgements

I am grateful to an anonymous reviewer and William C. Smith for the tactful suggestions for polishing this chapter. I would also like to thank Tore Bernt Sørensen for calling my attention to results-based financing.

Note

[1] The Muscat Agreement contains a proposal for an education goal and associated targets. It was formulated through a consultative process led by UNESCO culminating in the Global Education for All Meeting, held in

Muscat in May 2014. This process ran in parallel with the formulation of the OWG proposal, coordinated from New York.

References

Bangay, C. & Blum, N. (2010) Education Responses to Climate Change and Quality: two parts of the same agenda?, *International Journal of Educational Development*, 30(4), 359-368. http://dx.doi.org/10.1016/j.ijedudev.2009.11.011

Barrett, A.M. (2011) A Millennium Learning Goal for Education Post-2015: a question of outcomes or processes, *Comparative Education*, 47(1), 119-133. http://dx.doi.org/10.1080/03050068.2011.541682

Beyond 2015 (2013) *Making Education for All a Reality: global thematic consultation on education and the post-2015 development framework*. Pretoria: Beyond 2015.

Bloem, S. (2013) PISA in Low and Middle Income Countries. OECD Education Working Paper, no. 93. Paris: OECD Publishing.

Breidlid, A. (2013) *Education, Indigenous Knowledges, and Development in the Global South: contesting knowledges for a sustainable future*. Oxford: Routledge.

Center for Universal Education at Brookings (2011) A Global Compact on Learning: taking action on education in developing countries. Washington, DC: Center for Universal Education at Brookings.

Daniels, H. (2001) *Vygotsky and Pedagogy*. London: RoutledgeFalmer.

Dubeck, M.M. & Gove, A. (2015) The Early Grade Reading Assessment (EGRA): its theoretical foundation, purpose, and limitations, *International Journal of Educational Development*, 40, 315-322. http://dx.doi.org/10.1016/j.ijedudev.2014.11.004

Dubeck, M.M., Jukes, M.C.H., Brooker, S.J., Drake, T.L. & Inyega, H.N. (2015) Designing a Program of Teacher Professional Development to Support Beginning Reading Acquisition in Coastal Kenya, *International Journal of Educational Development*, 41, 88-96. http://dx.doi.org/10.1016/j.ijedudev.2014.11.022

Education for All (EFA) Global Monitoring Report (2013) Proposed Post-2015 Education Goals: emphasizing equity, measurability and finance. Initial draft for discussion. Paris: UNESCO.

Education for All (EFA) Global Monitoring Report Team (2015) Education for All 2000-2015: achievements and challenges. EFA Global Monitoring Report. Paris: UNESCO.

Education for All (EFA) Steering Committee TAG on the Post-2015 Education Indicators (2014) Monitoring the Post-2014 Education Targets: a note on indicators. Paris: UNESCO.

Fien, J. & Tilbury, D. (2002) The Global Challenge of Sustainability, in D. Tilbury, R.B. Stevenson, J. Fien & D. Schruder (Eds) *Education and Sustainability: responding to the global challenge*, pp. 1-12. Gland, Switzerland: International Union for Conservation of Nature and Natural Resources (IUCN).

Filmer, D., Hasan, A. & Pritchett, L. (2006) A Millennium Learning Goal: measuring real progress in education. Working Paper 97. Washington, DC: Center for Global Development.

Fraser, N. (2008) *Scales of Justice: reimagining political space in a globalizing world*. Cambridge: Polity Press.

Fukuda-Parr, S., Yamin, A.E. & Greenstein, J. (2013) *Synthesis Paper – The Power of Numbers: a critical review of MDG targets for human development and human rights*. FXB Working Paper. Cambridge MA: Harvard School of Public Health/Harvard University/The New School.

Global Campaign for Education (GCE) (2002) *A Quality Education for All: priority actions for governments, donors and civil society*. Brussels: GCE.

Global Education for All Meeting (2014) 2014 GEM Final Statement: the Muscat Agreement. Paper presented at the Global Education for All Meeting, Muscat, Oman.

High-level Panel (2013) A New Global Partnership: eradicate poverty and transform economies through sustainable development. The Report of the High-level Panel of Eminent Persons on the Post-2015 Development Agenda. New York: United Nations.

Inter-Agency Task Team (IATT) on Education (2006) Quality Education and HIV & AIDS. Paris: UNESCO.

Langford, M. (2012) *The Art of the Impossible: measurement choices and the post-2015 development agenda*. Governance and Human Rights: criteria and measurement proposals for a post-2015 development agenda, OHCHR/UNDP Expert Consultation. New York: UN Sustainable Development Knowledge Platform.

Languille, S. (2014) Quality Education through Performativity: 'learning crisis' and technology of quantification in Tanzania, *International Journal of Educational Development*, 29, 49-58. http://dx.doi.org/10.1016/j.ijedudev.2014.06.002

Morgan, A.D. (2009) Learning Communities, Cities and Regions for Sustainable Development and Global Citizenship, *Local Environment*, 14(5), 443-459. http://dx.doi.org/10.1080/13549830902903773

Myers, R.G. (2004) In Search of Quality in Programmes of Early Childhood Care and Education (ECCE). Paper prepared for the 2005 EFA Global Monitoring Report.

Nussbaum, M.C. (2011) *Creating Capabilities: the human development approach*. Cambridge, MA: Belknap Press. http://dx.doi.org/10.4159/harvard.9780674061200

Open Working Group for Sustainable Development Goals (2014) Proposal of the Open Working Group for Sustainable Development Goals. New York: UN Sustainable Development Knowledge Platform. https://sustainabledevelopment.un.org/sdgsproposal (accessed 15 July 2015).

Piper, B., Schroeder, L. & Trudell, B. (2015) Oral Reading Fluency and Comprehension in Kenya: reading acquisition in a multilingual environment, *Journal of Research in Reading*, published online 21 April. http://dx.doi.org/10.1111/1467-9817.12052

Rose, P. (2015) Three Lessons for Educational Quality in Post-2015 Goals and Targets: clarity, measurability and equity, *International Journal of Educational Development*, 40, 289-296. http://dx.doi.org/10.1016/j.ijedudev.2014.11.006

Scott, W.A.H. & Gough, S.R. (2010) Sustainability, Learning and Capability: exploring questions of balance, *Sustainability*, 2, 3735-3746. http://dx.doi.org/10.3390/su2123735

Sellar, S. & Lingard, B. (2013) PISA and the Expanding Role of the OECD in global educational governance, in H.D. Meyer & A. Benavot (Eds) *PISA, Power, and Policy: the emergence of global educational governance*, pp. 185-206. Oxford: Symposium Books.

Sen, A. (2009) *The Idea of Justice*. London: Allen Lane.

Smith, W.C. (2016) An Introduction to the Global Testing Culture, in W.C. Smith (Ed.) *The Global Testing Culture: shaping education policy, perceptions, and practice*. Oxford: Symposium Books.

Sterling, S. (2001) *Sustainable Education: re-visioning learning and change*. Totnes: Green Books.

Tikly, L. (2011) Towards a Framework for Researching the Quality of Education in Low Income Countries, *Comparative Education*, 47(1), 1-23. http://dx.doi.org/10.1080/03050068.2011.541671

Tikly, L. & Barrett, A.M. (2011) Social Justice, Capabilities and the Quality of Education in Low Income Countries, *International Journal of Educational Development*, 31(1), 3-14. http://dx.doi.org/10.1016/j.ijedudev.2010.06.001

Tikly, L. & Barrett, A.M. (2013) Education Quality and Social Justice in the Global South: towards a conceptual framework, in L. Tikly & A.M. Barrett (Eds) *Education Quality and Social Justice in the Global South: challenges for policy, practice and research*, pp. 11-24. London: Routledge.

UNESCO (2004) *Education for All Global Monitoring Report 2005: Education for All, the quality imperative*. Paris & Oxford: UNESCO & Oxford University Press.

UNESCO (2013) *The Global Learning Crisis: why every child deserves a quality education*. Paris: UNESCO.

UNESCO (2014) Teaching and Learning: achieving quality for all. EFA Global Monitoring Report 2013/4. Paris: UNESCO.

UNICEF (2004) Child-friendly Schools. http://www.unicef.org/lifeskills/index_7260.html#A%20Framework%20for%20Rights-Based,%20Child-Friendly (accessed 22 January 2010).

UNICEF (2008) Basic Education and Gender Equality: quality of education. http://www.unicef.org/girlseducation/index_quality.html (accessed 22 January 2010).

UNICEF/UNESCO (2013) Making Education a Priority in the Post-2015 Development Agenda. Report of the Global Thematic Consultation on Education in the Post-2015 Development Agenda. New York/Paris: UNICEF/UNESCO.

United Nations (UN) (1989) Convention on the Rights of the Child, ratified by General Assembly of the United Nation in Resolution 44/25 of 20 November 1989 C.F.R.

United Nations Development Group (UNDG) (2013) *A Million Voices: the world we want. A Sustainable Future with Dignity for All.* New York: UNDG.

Unterhalter, E. (2005) Global Inequality, Capabilities, Social Justice: the millennium development goal for gender equality in education, *International Journal of Educational Development*, 25(2), 111-122.
http://dx.doi.org/10.1016/j.ijedudev.2004.11.015

Unterhalter, E. (2014) Measuring Education for the Millennium Development Goals: reflections on targets, indicators, and a post-2015 framework, *Journal of Human Development and Capabilities*, 15(2-3), 176-187.
http://dx.doi.org/10.1080/19452829.2014.880673

Unterhalter, E. & Brighouse, H. (2007) Distribution of What for Social Justice in Education? The Case of Education for All by 2015, in M. Walker & E. Unterhalter (Eds) *Amartya Sen's Capability Approach and Social Justice in Education*, pp. 67-86. New York: Palgrave Macmillan.

Uwezo (2010) Are Our Children Learning? Annual Learning Assessment Report Tanzania 2010. Dar es Salaam: Uwezo, TENMET & Hivos/Twaweza.

Vizard, P., Fukuda-Parr, S. & Elson, D. (2011) Introduction: the capability approach and human rights, *Journal of Human Development and Capabilities*, 12(1), 1-22.
http://dx.doi.org/10.1080/19452829.2010.541728

Wagner, D.A. (2010) Quality of Education, Comparability, and Assessment Choice in Developing Countries, *Compare: a journal of comparative and international education*, 40(6), 741-760.

Winthrop, R., Anderson, K. & Cruzalegui, I. (2015) A Review of Policy Debates around Learning in the Post-2015 Education and Development Agenda, *International Journal of Educational Development*, 40, 297-307.
http://dx.doi.org/10.1016/j.ijedudev.2014.11.016

World Bank (2011) Learning for All: investing in people's knowledge and skills to promote development. World Bank Group Education Strategy 2020. Washington. DC: World Bank.

World Bank Group (2015) *The Rise of Results-based Financing in Education.* Washington DC: World Bank Group.

CHAPTER 7

The International Space of the Danish Testing Community in the Post-war Years

KAREN E. ANDREASEN & CHRISTIAN YDESEN

ABSTRACT International forums and organisations, as well as non-governmental organisations, have played a considerable role in societal developments since the end of World War II. Many changes in post-war Danish public schools, such as standardised educational testing, were formed in dialogue with or initiated in such forums or organisations. This chapter explores the importance of these connections by focusing on the period from 1945 to around 1990 – that is, from the end of World War II, when Danish education was characterised by a high degree of national unity as a contrast to the strife of the inter-war years, and up to the end of the Cold War. Exploring the transnational angle is a highly relevant and interesting research topic because it contributes to a deeper understanding of the origin, development and design of Danish school policy and school practice, and the influence from transnational spaces.

Introduction

International forums and organisations have played a considerable role in societal developments since the end of World War II. This is true in Danish society in general and in education in particular. Many changes, initiatives and activities in post-war Danish public schools, such as education for peace and democracy, the comprehensive school, the establishment of educational psychology, and the rise of standardised educational testing, were shaped in dialogue with or initiated in such forums (Hamre & Ydesen, 2014; Andreasen & Ydesen, 2015). Cooperation in different forums for supranational and international organizations such as the United Nations Educational, Scientific and Cultural Organization (UNESCO), the Organisation for Economic Co-operation and Development (OECD) and the

European Economic Community (EEC), has played a prominent role in this regard. One example is the ground-breaking Bernadotte School in Copenhagen, also known as The International School, founded in 1949 with UNESCO's educational ideas and psychological approaches to pedagogy and internationalism as its core (IOE 1).

The same goes for cooperation in or influence from various non-governmental organisations (NGOs) and epistemic communities, such as the New Education Fellowship (NEF). Exploring international cooperation – its channels, routes, spaces and influence – is, therefore, a highly relevant and interesting research topic because it contributes to a deeper understanding of the origin, development and design of school policies and practices.

Ever since the interwar years, struggles and negotiations have taken place over evaluation in the Danish public school system, concerning, for instance, assessment and evaluation of pupils' skills, abilities and academic progress. Some protagonists advocated traditional exams, while educators associated with the global progressive education movement argued for replacing exams with standardised tests. In the post-World War II era, growing criticism of some test types – like intelligence tests – emerged, while a strong build-up on the educational research front on the other hand called for expansion of standardised testing. Denmark's first participation in an international comparative survey came in 1992 and kicked off a political development in terms of increased focus on subject knowledge (Andreasen & Ydesen, 2014). However, it was not until the shocking PISA results in the 2000s – as indicated by William Smith's introductory chapter in this volume (Smith, 2016) – and the introduction of the national testing scheme in 2010 that Denmark truly joined the ranks of the contemporary global testing culture. Given these historical characteristics as a background, Denmark constitutes an interesting case because it sheds light on transnational transformation processes in terms of what travels and what has an impact and how transnational currents are received in a national context.

The chapter focuses on the years 1945-1990, a period when the character of the international cooperation and influence that was of importance for education and national educational test regimes changed in significant ways. At the beginning of the period, these processes were dominated by cooperation in NGOs and between institutions, but international organisations steadily increased their dominance.

The research focuses on standardised educational tests and evaluations because these phenomena have constitutive effects and have proven to be effective tools in controlling, managing and governing education. They mediate pedagogical values and visions as well as economic interests and control their implementation (Hopmann, 2008; Dahler-Larsen, 2014; Smith, 2014), and are thus pivotal for the interplay between society's macro level (e.g. national and international initiatives and policies) and micro level (e.g. schools and classrooms). In this respect, standardised educational testing and evaluation in national contexts may be viewed as manifestations of a global testing culture. Our analysis of the workings of this culture from a historical perspective shows that it must be understood as a result of multiple developments and multivariate explanations.

Throughout the period covered here, the Danish public school's evaluation practices have been in focus (Andreasen & Ydesen, 2014). Evaluation practice here means the use of different forms of evaluation, such as mandatory as well as non-mandatory tests, during a school year and with different purposes: assessment (formative and summative), advancement, accreditation, and accountability. Evaluation practice does not have one specific origin, but has grown out of many different factors, and there is no doubt that Denmark's international connections have had significant influence.

We will examine the links to the international education space in a chronological review of the undergrowth of networks of agents, spaces and relations that have surrounded and shaped the Danish testing community – that is, the community of like-minded protagonists advocating the introduction of tests in the Danish education system. This community consisted of a diverse group of professionals, such as educational psychologists, teachers, headmasters and university psychologists, and was formed around the time of World War I (Ydesen, 2012). These individuals were tied together by an ambition to introduce testing practices in the Danish public school systems. However, various central agents with influence in the development of the public school system did not relate to this agenda and were not interested in introducing educational testing. In other words, the shaping of the educational system was characterised by ongoing struggles and negotiations over the definition of educational problems and appropriate solutions. Still, questions about how to organise educational evaluation remained high on the agenda. This particular setting will allow us to uncover how the Danish test and evaluation agenda has interacted with and been influenced by the global and regional testing cultures historically. In this respect, the chapter contributes specifically to the understanding of the regional testing culture in north-western Europe and how it has intermeshed with a national context in the shaping of education policy, perceptions and practices.

The chapter thus opens up for reflection on many contemporary debates and issues concerning education – for example, the significance of and reasons for introducing test and evaluation technologies, and the rationales behind the demand for national and international comparisons.

Theoretical Approach and Methodology

The chapter finds analytical inspiration in 'the spatial turn', a prominent approach in the social sciences and the humanities which looks beyond nation-state boundaries to focus on the spaces within which policies, ideas, knowledge and practices travel and move across borders (Cowen, 2009;

Fuchs, 2014; Christensen & Ydesen, 2015). The spatial turn transcends the notion of place, which is intimately connected with the idea of nations as subjects and national narratives (Warf & Arias, 2009). A spatial approach discards the nation-state as the prime frame of reference and focuses on the analytical identification of trading spaces. The chapter is thus based on three specific institutions – or trading spaces: the Emdrupborg Experimental School (founded in 1948); the Danish National Institute of Education (founded in 1955); and the National Centre for Pedagogical Experiments (founded in 1964). All three were important hubs for exchange of international ideas, knowledge and practice, not least in relation to tests and evaluation, via memberships, correspondence, study trips, visits from abroad and arguments based on international ideas and research.

In order to treat these institutions empirically the chapter draws on their archives, which are available in the Copenhagen City Archives (CCA), the Danish National Archive (DNA) and the private archive of the former head of the National Centre for Pedagogical Experiments (PA), respectively. These archives have been studied with specific focus on international relations, connections and idea development. The methodological strategy has been to track the movement of ideas and knowledge and follow their interpretations into these institutions. The structure of the chapter follows an analysis of the spaces emerging around the three national institutions. The relevance of links to the global and regional education spaces will be determined empirically.

The focus on the interplay between key national institutions and the global and regional education spaces characterised by connections with key agents, institutions and organisations finds additional justification in neo-institutionalism. The core of neo-institutionalism is to understand global developments as highly motivated by institutions and organisations functioning and acting as central arbiters and brokers of educational ideas, knowledge and practices (Meyer, 2005; 2010; Smith, 2014). These interplays between institutions and organisations generate common approaches to education through standardisations of problem identification, solutions and even mind-sets. In other words, they create and shape fellowships of like-mindedness, epistemic communities or even a world culture (Hass, 1992; Smith, 2014). Such fellowships or communities are often central features of a transnational space.

However, it is important to note that travelling ideas, knowledge and practices undergo transfer, translation and transformation processes en route and as a consequence of the conditions in the receiving context (Cowen, 2009; Steiner-Khamsi, 2013). In the words of David Livingstone, 'meaning is always constructed locally' (Livingstone, 2003, p. 88), and hence in studying the interplay between national institutions and international organisations we must account for local mediations having an impact on what pass for acceptable ideas, knowledge and practice. A 1:1 transfer of ideas, knowledge and practices is extremely rare.

We will, therefore, focus analytically on the key agents that populate and constitute the very space that engulfs the national institutions and the global and regional education spaces. These agents serve as entries into understanding specific movements because they define meaning in the space, they are situated in a historical context, and they are positioned in relation to other agents. This amounts to a prosopographic endeavour. According to Verboven et al (2007, p. 39), 'Prosopography is a *collective biography*, describing the *external* features of a population group that the researcher has determined has something *in common*' (original emphasis). In Ydesen's (2012) terminology, we will focus on the work of 'the Danish testing community' – more specifically, the transfer, translation and transformation of educational tests into the Danish educational field as a manifestation of the global and regional testing cultures.

The Emdrupborg Experimental School

Right from its foundation in 1948 and well into the 1960s, the Emdrupborg Experimental School took the role of an international educational hub as manifested in close affiliations with the NEF and frequent visits to the school by teachers and researchers with an interest in the concept. Between 1948 and 1965, some 2774 guests from Denmark and 51 other countries visited the school (Ydesen, 2011b). A key component of the Emdrupborg concept was the comprehensive educational evaluation programme covering all sorts of tests to document the results of the educational experiments. In its heyday, the experimental school employed four educational psychologists who conducted a comprehensive testing programme of the approximately 800 pupils enrolled in the school.

The educational psychologists were all part of what we denote 'the Danish testing community'. Two of the most important spaces binding the community together were the one-year course in applied psychology established in 1940 of the Royal Danish School of Education [*Danmarks Lærerhøjskole*] and the three-year educational psychologist academic study programme founded in 1944 at the University of Copenhagen (Ydesen, 2012).[1] Danish educational psychologists were introduced to a common curriculum of applied psychology with a very strong emphasis on intelligence testing and, via this schooling, imbued with a sense of professional competence and dedication. The teachers in the one-year course and the subsequent three-year study programme were the first generation of the Danish testing community, counting, among others, Henning Meyer (1885-1967), the first educational psychologist in Scandinavia, and Sofie Rifbjerg (1886-1981), the headmistress of two Copenhagen remedial schools – both keen admirers of the prominent, but nowadays controversial, British educational psychologist Professor Cyril Burt (1883-1971).

The school was founded on the knowledge that other countries undertook comprehensive educational experiments, and Emdrupborg was seen as a vital component in necessary national experimental work (Nørvig, 1955). According to Jørgen Egedal Poulsen (1921-), one of the educational psychologists at the school, international research results and school experiments were translated and adapted to a Danish educational tradition (PA 1). Disseminating international research results to the Emdrupborg teaching staff was one of the central tasks of the Emdrupborg educational psychologists. They collaborated via personal contacts with English, Scottish and German researchers and obtained annual accounts from research centres in these countries (Nørvig, 1955). It was seen as a prerequisite for the school's ability to retain and expand its status as a pedagogical flagship in the Danish educational field through innovation and the dissemination of well-founded ideas and practices (PA 2).

Anne Marie Nørvig (1893-1959), Emdrupborg's progressive headmistress and also an educational psychologist, was heavily influenced by what she called 'test-psychology', and she described herself as a true disciple of the progressive American educationalist Professor William Heard Kilpatrick (1871-1965), who had studied under John Dewey (PA 3). Nørvig's inspiration from the Unites States was also expressed in her comparison of the educational goals of Emdrupborg, where student guidance was central, with the goals of the famous American Eight Year Study conducted by the Progressive Education Association during the 1930s and 1940s (CCA 1, p. 3).

Nørvig had been on study trips to Italy, Belgium, the United States, Switzerland and Yugoslavia, and in 1957 she studied comprehensive schools in England (CCA 2). She most frequently visited Norway and Sweden and observed teaching at numerous schools (Nørvig, 1949), and a direct result of her trips to Sweden was the introduction of the Uppsala school readiness test at Emdrupborg right from the start of the school (CCA 1).

Other educational psychologists of the experimental school also travelled abroad. Ejvind Jensen (1918-2009) studied for one year at the University of California at Berkeley in 1951/52. American pragmatic educational thinking served as a powerful source of inspiration at Emdrupborg because it stipulated that experiences and results had to be described in such a way that they could easily be translated into everyday school practice (PA 2).

Another example is the third of the four educational psychologists, Wilhelm Marckmann (1919-2009), who in 1955/56 studied the selection of pupils and the comprehensive school in Britain. He studied at the University of Bristol and visited London, Cambridge, Oxford and Edinburgh (Nørvig, 1955; Marckmann, 1999). During his stay in Britain, Marckmann benefited from his acquaintance with Professor Joseph Albert Lauwerys (1902-81), who was Deputy Chairman of the NEF and an often-used expert working for UNESCO, and Dr C. Willis Dixon, head of the London Institute of Education's Department for Comparative Education. Both had previously been to Emdrupborg. Lauwerys and Dixon functioned as Marckmann's academic hosts during his stay, and they introduced him to the British educational field (Marckmann, 1999).

In May and June 1950, the fourth educational psychologist, Jørgen Egedal Poulsen, visited schools, universities and educational institutions in Holland, Belgium and England to seek inspiration for school experiments (CCA 3). Poulsen acquired a number of tests from Utrecht, London and Birmingham to use as inspiration at Emdrupborg. In his critical report, Poulsen wrote about a secondary modern school in Hounslow: 'There is a strong tendency to differentiate pupils according to abilities and too little consideration for social and perhaps also emotional factors' (CCA 3, p. 16). According to Marckmann, Poulsen was also enthusiastic about the tests he encountered, and, like Marckmann, spoke of their objectivity and great value. The reading tests used for the middle school experiment at Emdrupborg were designed on the basis of material obtained by Poulsen in England (CCA 4).

In their joint work at Emdrupborg comparing British and Danish experiences with streaming tests, Marckmann and Poulsen referred extensively to English experiments with streaming at age 11, describing them as successful and with great prognostic value. In this assessment, they referred to the articles published in the *British Journal of Educational Psychology* in 1954 (Burt, 1954; Vernon, 1954) and to a Scottish streaming test – most likely the widely used Moray House intelligence test (CCA 5).

These references and conclusions reveal a strong Anglo-Saxon inspiration for the evaluation practice at Emdrupborg. The six-year report explicitly mentions that 'ideas for tests derive partly from foreign research literature, especially English and American, and partly from the rather voluminous collection of tests at the disposal of the educational psychologists' [2] (Nørvig, 1955, p. 234). The analysis of the Emdrupborg experimental school lodestars and international contacts has drawn a picture of a space very much oriented towards Scandinavia, Britain and the United States. The fact that Emdrupborg's educational psychologists operated without borders in this space is a critical contributing factor to the school's status as an educational flagship. The Emdrupborg professionals shared many values from foreign progressive educational settings such as comprehensive evaluation of the individual child and its social context, student guidance, solicitude and the use of education for social engineering purposes. The experimental school inspired thoughts on comprehensive education expressed in the 1958 education act, but it also served as an arbiter for the expanded use of tests. By 1958, approximately 7000 out of approximately 73,400 Danish pre-schoolchildren were tested with the Uppsala school readiness test stemming from Emdrupborg (CCA 6). Undoubtedly, the Emdrupborg Experimental School's comprehensive international network and well-versed knowledge about the latest international research provided the school with significant capital in the Danish educational field. These ideas and tendencies strongly influenced the decision to establish a Danish National Institute of Education to further develop and spread the use of testing in basic education in the following years.

The Danish National Institute of Education

The Danish National Institute of Education [*Danmarks Pædagogiske Institut*] (DPI) began its operations in 1955. However, the Danish testing community had called for its establishment since 1920 (Tybjerg, 1920). A central characteristic of the DPI was its strong international outlook as reflected in the work of the Institute of Education Establishing Committee, which gathered comprehensive information about pedagogical research institutions in the United States, England, Scotland, France, Holland, Belgium, Finland, Norway and Sweden before submitting its recommendations to the government (Ministry of Education, 1953). After its foundation the DPI retained its international outlook and engaged in comprehensive international correspondence and exchange about testing. The academic staff joined the global community of educational research where comparative studies were a strong current. One example is the leading test psychologist Børge Prien's visit to Moray House in Edinburgh in 1959, which resulted in several exchanges about tests and extended contact (DNA 1). In 1956, the DPI wrote to UNESCO to obtain contact information on foreign educational research institutions as it was interested in achievement tests and aptitude tests for learning languages (DNA 1). The institute received input from Norway, France, the United Kingdom and the United States. Moreover, DPI staff visited foreign colleagues and hosted international visits. In a spirit of reciprocity, the institute even received requests for its own tests from foreign institutes. The requests often concerned the work of the famous Danish statistician Georg Rasch (1901-1980). This exchange of knowledge is also conspicuous in the long-running project on applying military personality tests to children, an area that has been cultivated for many years in the United States.

Thus, educational testing and measurement was a vital focus area for the new institute, and testing was a common element in many of the inputs received from abroad. In connection with its establishment, the key educational organisations devised inputs to tasks for the new institute. One department was dedicated to the development and revision of tests, the value of psychological and educational tests as criteria for selection, as well as children's reactions to tests and the prognostic value of tests (CCA 7).

Testing and evaluation formed the core of one of the main purposes of the institute – namely, to 'prepare and disseminate test material and the like' [3] (Act No. 221, dated 11 June 1954) and to assist in the planning, coordination and analysis of educational experiments in the Danish educational field and thus provide scientific support for school experiments (Nørr, 2009). This task was conducted according to a strictly positivist paradigm of science, with measurement and evaluation of outcomes and results as a central feature (Ljungstrøm, 1985).

One example is from the former Danish colony of Greenland. Educational psychologist Jesper Florander (1918-1988) of the DPI raised severe criticism of the intensified efforts to select the right Greenlandic children for a one-year school stay in Denmark based on an intelligence test claiming to be culture neutral (Ydesen, 2011a). A Greenlandic version of the Non-Verbal Test Battery (NVTB) was included in the test in the school year 1969/70. This special Greenlandic version was standardised on Greenlandic pupils and was based on a test developed by Professor Kaj Spelling during his time as a UNESCO educational advisor in Malaysia (Spelling, 1963).

This positivistic paradigm, centred on mathematics and statistics, was common in many similar foreign institutes of education at the time. Together with the strong international outlook described above, this made transfer, translation and transformation in education a key concern of the Danish National Institute of Education. In fact, the very establishment of the DPI might be seen as an expression of transfer, since it was based on arguments of international comparison and competition (Ydesen, 2011b). However, translation issues played a vital role in the concrete design of the new institute because it had to consider the many competing wishes of Danish educational institutions, which proposed no less than 262 tasks for the new institute (Ministry of Education, 1953).

This very broad backing for the new Danish National Institute of Education also shows that pedagogy rooted in psychology research had become conventional. It was simply very difficult to disagree with this line of thinking. The hegemonic paradigm now called for scientific evidence to support the political ambitions of educational optimisation, and both the Emdrupborg Experimental School and the Danish National Institute of Education were part of that wave orchestrated by the Danish testing community, whose members held vital positions in Danish education and kept close ties with the Social Democratic and Social Liberal parties, which were often in government.

The formation of the Danish National Institute of Education heralded a new era for the Danish testing community. The testing community participated increasingly in decision-making processes in the educational field, but the efforts resulted in something qualitatively different – namely, a state institute of education that, by necessity, would no longer allow the testing community to play first fiddle. However, the DPI did give the testing community an institutional backing that would promote transfer, translation and transformation of knowledge and ideas with foreign peers. Another central development was the founding of the Danish Psychological Publishing House [*Dansk Psykologisk Forlag*] (DPF) in 1949 by a group of psychologists, many of whom were closely affiliated with the DPI. The key significance of this development was the commercialisation of educational tests (Bonde, 1992). The publishing house would distribute standardised tests of various kinds to the Danish educational field on market terms. While the establishment of the DPI meant a higher level of state control compared with the interwar years, the formation of the independent publishing house indicates that the Danish testing community still kept educational testing on a short leash.

The National Centre for Pedagogical Experiments

The National Centre for Pedagogical Experiments [*Statens Pædagogiske Forsøgscenter*] (SPF) was founded in 1964/65.[4] A new act for the public school from 1958 defined the framework for comprehensive education and implied a large reform of the entire school system and its pedagogy. The purpose of the SPF was to support and experiment with the practical pedagogic implementation of the new 1958 act as it was described in a subsequent executive order from 1960 (Ministry of Education, 1960). The executive order was inspired by the NEF's reform pedagogical ideas and UNESCO's resolution to counter 'discrimination in education' (UNESCO, 1960), which Denmark had just ratified and which matched the political visions to make the educational system more democratic.

Jørgen E. Poulsen, former educational psychologist and teacher at the Emdrupborg Experimental School, became head of the new centre, and several of his Emdrupborg colleagues followed him to SPF. The pedagogy and experiments at SPF were highly inspired by Emdrupborg's practices, which of course were developed and revised in several areas, such as the use of testing.

The pedagogical ideas and activities at SPF were strongly influenced by international inspiration and collaboration via international organisations such as UNESCO, the OECD and the Centre for Educational Research and Education (CERI) (PA 4). A report from the centre (PA 5) describes contents and activities of different conferences from 1966 to 1990, for instance: participation in a conference in Ohio and discussions about the centre's information system (student evaluation) on that occasion; UNESCO's initiatives on lifelong learning in 1974; innovation methods based on a visit to a school in Bristol in 1974 that also conducted pedagogical experiments; participation in a conference in Berlin; a visit by education scholar Lloyd Trump in 1967; a meeting with a British principal in 1969; and discussions about a proposal from Sweden in 1974. The report reflects the mutual inspiration as well as the parallel development that characterised school systems in the western world during that period. Apparently, these forums were occupied with the same types of questions and were thus able to exchange experiences and select themes for future experiments.

Many experiments conducted at SPF were either initiated in or inspired by the collaborative relations in international forums like CERI and the International Association for the Development of Adolescent Schooling (IADAS). CERI, a sub-organisation of the OECD, was founded in 1968 to help the member countries' educational systems adapt to new demands and challenges brought on by social developments (Bengtsson, 2008). IADAS was a forum for experimental schools in Europe. An annual conference was held to exchange experiences and select common themes for the following year's experiments, which were then discussed at next year's conference.

The centre was obligated to work closely with schools nationwide – for example, by communicating experiences from its work in reports, giving lectures, and sparring with schools on launching and implementing experiments in school classes. As a consequence, SPF's ideas and practices, including test practices, were spread to and implemented at local schools via many different channels.

As mentioned, Emdrupborg was a major inspiration for SPF's pedagogy and experiments, but the centre also applied new and different approaches – for example, a mix of tests and pedagogic evaluations in teaching. Types of testing were a prominent topic for experiments throughout the life of the centre, which is clear in its reports. Intensive experiments were conducted to renew evaluation types and grading with emphasis on dialogue and evaluation contexts and evaluations that were more qualitatively inspired than tests. In addition, the centre took a critical stance on more intensive use of academic testing (Christoffersen, 2007).

In the period after World War II, dominant actors in pedagogy and education were very focused on the use of tests in daily public school teaching and saw great potential in this. However, this focus did not manifest itself strongly until after the 1960s, even though the DPI had been established precisely to develop test materials for the public school system, was a highly respected institution, and advocated such test practices. The reason that it did not manifest itself in daily teaching during that period – this did not happen until after the 1990s – may be the approach to the pedagogical evaluation represented by SPF. Via its mandate to contribute to new and modern pedagogical practices in Danish public schools, the centre gained a significant influence in this development, which in this respect had been a contrast, or at least an alternative, to the DPI and what it represented. However, it is also clear that the centre in its capacity as a government institution to some extent has had its activities defined and delimited by the political level.

Conclusion

This chapter has examined how evaluation practice in the Danish public school system has developed in the specified period through influence from and relations with the global and regional education spaces and national political agendas and conditions.

Throughout the period, the educational system, and especially the public school, has been subject to great political attention, nationally and internationally. After World War II, education was selected to play a prominent role in securing economic stability and progress in competition with the eastern bloc, avoiding internal conflicts, and developing democratic and peaceful societies in general. Especially during the years immediately following World War II and up to the 1960s, political agendas with a focus on democracy, peace and stability played an important role and influenced the approach to school and education and to the use of tests in different ways. Researchers were interested in what might characterise good teaching from a general perspective and took the initiative to develop some of the first large comparative quantitative surveys – for example, under the auspices of the International Association for the Evaluation of Educational Achievement (IEA). The hope was that the results of the surveys would reveal some general features of a pedagogy that correlated with higher scores in the academic tests that were used in these studies, that were developed for the purpose and that would enable comparability. The idea was that the individual countries would be able to improve the pedagogy in the public school, depending on which factors proved particularly important. This also reflects ideas about turning pedagogy into a science, and in that connection it is fair to mention the importance of the growing research field in comparative education studies in terms of facilitating international comparisons between national education systems.

If we look at the manifestations of the global and regional testing cultures in Denmark it is clear that standardised testing as a practice never replaced end-of-year exams in the Danish educational field. But testing lived a life in special education, and in a wider sense in the handling of those who were different (e.g. the Greenlandic children), as well as in school experiments, as demonstrated at Emdrupborg. A political will to replace traditional examinations with intelligence tests as gatekeepers of secondary education never materialised in Denmark. With the launch of the DPI and the DPF, the Danish testing community gained a stronger voice in the Danish educational system, which was open to change due to effectiveness problems and new educational ideals. This process was characterised by significant path dependencies along which developments in the educational spheres of Scandinavia and the Anglo-Saxon world became significant and mutual sources of inspiration.

The use of academic standardised tests only became mandatory in Denmark with the introduction of national tests in 2010 even though such tests had been accessible and used in many contexts since the interwar years. However, already from the interwar years, standardised tests were imported and domesticated for use in pedagogical practice in the Danish public school and eventually became dominant in special education. In that sense it can be seen as a manifestation of a regional test culture. This development should be seen in the light of several interacting and decisive conditions. First, the inspiration that key actors and networks brought back to Denmark from studies abroad and international research. Second, the growing significance of initiatives by international organisations that Denmark joined. Third, the ideas about and interest in turning pedagogy into a science. Fourth, a commercialisation of pedagogical materials such as tests. Using material produced by recognised publishers allowed schools and teachers to legitimise a qualification of their own pedagogical practice. Fifth and finally, the DPI's huge role as a societal institution during the period in terms of developing standardised tests and introducing them in pedagogical practice and schools.

In sum, we are looking at a historical movement in testing and evaluation in the Danish public school system from a group of pioneers coming from semi-governmental institutions and large international institutions. The result appears to be – in accordance with world culture theory – that the basic differences that have existed between countries, and that have characterised individual countries' educational systems over time and through the influence of such trends, may become differences in degree rather than differences of nature.

Notes

[1] Between 1944 and 1952, 175 educational psychologists graduated from the University of Copenhagen (Ministry of Education 1953, p. 14).

[2] Our translation.

[3] Our translation.

[4] The act on the establishment of a national centre for pedagogical experiments was passed in 1964.

References

Andreasen, K.E. & Ydesen, C. (2014) Accountability Practices in the History of Danish Primary Public Education from the 1660s to the Present, *Education Policy Analysis Archive*, 22(120). http://dx.doi.org/10.14507/epaa.v22.1618

Andreasen, K.E. & Ydesen, C. (2015) Educating for Peace: the role and impact of international organisations in interwar and post-war Danish school experiments, 1918-1975, *Nordic Journal for Educational History*.

Bengtsson, J. (2008) *OECD's Centre for Educational Research and Innovation – 1968 to 2008*. Paris: OECD.

Bonde, T (1992) Var der ikke noget Dansk Psykologisk forlag, måtte man stifte et, *Psykolog nyt*, 46(8), 288-292.

Burt, C. (1954) The Differentiation of Intellectual Ability, *British Journal of Educational Psychology*, 24, 76-90. http://dx.doi.org/10.1111/j.2044-8279.1954.tb02882.x

Christensen, I.L. & Ydesen, C. (2015) Routes of Knowledge: towards a methodological framework for tracing the historical impact of international organizations, *European Education*, 47(3), 274-288. http://dx.doi.org/10.1080/10564934.2015.1065392

Christoffersen, P.E. (2007) Vurdering – uden Mål & Med, *CRIT*, 4, 48-51.

Cowen, R. (2009) The Transfer, Translation and Transformation of Educational Processes: and their shape-shifting?, *Comparative Education*, 45(3), 315-327. http://dx.doi.org/10.1080/03050060903184916

Dahler-Larsen, P. (2014) Constitutive Effects of Performance Indicators: getting beyond unintended consequences, *Public Management Review*, 16(7), 969-986. http://dx.doi.org/10.1080/14719037.2013.770058

Fuchs, E. (2014) History of Education beyond the Nation? Trends in Historical and Educational Scholarship, in B. Bagchi, E. Fuchs & K. Rousmaniere (Eds) *Connecting Histories of Education – Transnational and Cross-cultural Exchanges on (Post-)Colonial Education*, pp. 11-26. New York: Berghahn Books.

Haas, P.M. (1992) Epistemic Communities and International Policy Coordination, *International Organization*, 46, 1-35. http://dx.doi.org/10.1017/S0020818300001442

Hamre, B. & Ydesen, C. (2014) The Ascent of Educational Psychology in Denmark in the Interwar Years, *Nordic Journal of Educational History*, 1(2), 87-111.

Hopmann, S. (2008) No Child, No School, No State Left Behind: schooling in the Age of Accountability, *Journal of Curriculum Studies*, 40(4), 417-456. http://dx.doi.org/10.1080/00220270801989818

Livingstone, D.N. (2003) *Putting Science in Its Place: geographies of scientific knowledge.* Chicago: University of Chicago Press.

Ljungstrøm, C. (1985) *En kritisk skitse over Danmarks Pædagogiske Instituts tidligere arbejder.* Copenhagen: DPI.

Marckmann, W. (1999) Skoleforsøg, *Uddannelseshistorie*, 33, 89-112.

Meyer, J.W. (2005) *Weltkultur: wie die westlichen Prinzipien die Welt durchdringen*, ed. G. Krücken. Frankfurt: Suhrkamp.

Meyer, J.W. (2010) World Society, Institutional Theories, and the Actor, *Annual Review of Sociology*, 36(1), 1-20. http://dx.doi.org/10.1146/annurev.soc.012809.102506

Ministry of Education (1953) *Betænkning angående oprettelse af et pædagogisk institut* [Report on the Establishment of the Danish National Institute of Education]. Copenhagen: Ministry of Education.

Ministry of Education (1960) *Undervisningsvejledning for Folkeskolen* [Guidelines for teaching in the national public school system]. Betænkning nr. 253 [Report no. 253]. Copenhagen: Ministry of Education.

Nørr, E. (2009) Hvorfor blev skoleloven af 1937 først gennemført i 1950'erne og 1960'erne?, in E. Hansen, & L. Jespersen (Eds) *Samfundsplanlægning i 1950'erne – tradition eller tilløb?*, pp. 153-225. Copenhagen: Museum Tusculanum.

Nørvig, A.M. (1949) Forsøgsskole – forsøgsklasser (ed. F. Bøgh & P. Müller), *Vor Ungdom*, 70, pp. 68-73.

Nørvig, A.M. (1955) *Beretning om Emdrupborg skoles første 6 år 1948-1954.* Copenhagen: Det danske forlag.

Smith, W.C. (2014) The Global Transformation toward Testing for Accountability, *Education Policy Analysis Archives*, 22(116). Special Issue, *The Comparative and International History of School Accountability and Testing*, guest co-ed. Sherman Dorn & Christian Ydesen. http://dx.doi.org/10.14507/epaa.v22.1571

Smith, W.C. (2016) An Introduction to the Global Testing Culture, in W.C. Smith (Ed.) *The Global Testing Culture: shaping education policy, perceptions, and practice.* Oxford: Symposium Books.

Spelling, K. (1963) *Miljøets indflydelse på intelligensudviklingen – specielt med henblik på 'racemæssige' forskelle.* Copenhagen: Nyt Nordisk Forlag Arnold Busck.

Steiner-Khamsi, G. (2013) What is Wrong with the 'What-went-right' Approach in Educational Policy?, *European Educational Research Journal*, 12(1), 20-33. http://dx.doi.org/10.2304/eerj.2013.12.1.20

Tybjerg, C. (1920) Forslag om Oprettelse af et pædagogisk Laboratorium og en Forsøgsskole, *Tidsskrift for eksperimental Pædagogik*, 85-97.

UNESCO (1960) Convention against Discrimination in Education. http://portal.unesco.org/en/ev.php-URL_ID=12949&URL_DO=DO_TOPIC&URL_SECTION=201.html

Verboven, K., Carlier, M. & Dumolyn, J. (2007) A Short Manual to the Art of Prosopography, in K.S.B. Keats-Rohan (Ed.) *Prosopography Approaches and Applications. A Handbook*, pp. 35-69. Oxford: Unit for Prosopographical Research (Linacre College).

Vernon, P.E. (1954) Symposium on the Effects of Coaching and Practice in Intelligence Tests: V conclusions, *British Journal of Educational Psychology*, 24, 57-63. http://dx.doi.org/10.1111/j.2044-8279.1954.tb02880.x

Warf, B. & Arias, S. (Eds) (2009) *The Spatial Turn: interdisciplinary perspectives.* New York: Routledge.

Ydesen, C. (2011a) Educating Greenlanders and Germans: minority education in the Danish Commonwealth, 1945-1970, in H. Niedrig & C. Ydesen (Eds) *Writing Postcolonial Histories of Intercultural Education*, pp. 239-267. Frankfurt: Peter Lang.

Ydesen, C. (2011b) *The Rise of High-stakes Educational Testing in Denmark, 1920-1970.* Frankfurt: Peter Lang.

Ydesen, C. (2012) The International Space of the Danish Testing Community in the Interwar Years, *Paedagogica Historica*, 48(4), 589-599. http://dx.doi.org/10.1080/00309230.2011.644428

Unpublished Sources

CCA 1 (Copenhagen City Archives): ESA (Emdrupborg School Archive), Nørvigs papirer [Nørvig's papers]. Manuscript for Nørvig's talk at the Pedagogical Society, 21 January 1955.

CCA 2: ESA, Korrespondance og sager [Correspondence and cases] 1948-1968: letter from Nørvig to Headmaster Em. Andersen, Skibby School, dated 27 February 1957.

CCA 3: ESA, Psykolog [Psychologist] 1950-1962: report of the study trip dated October 1950.

CCA 4: ESA, Marckmanns papirer [Marckmann's papers] III 1954-1965: note concerning a possible cooperation between the DPI and Emdrupborg.

CCA 5: ESA, Prøveudvalget [The Test Committee] 1954-1959: letter from Wilhelm Marckmann and Jørgen Egedal Poulsen to the Emdrupborg test committee dated 30 November 1954.

CCA 6: ESA, Korrespondance og sager [Correspondence and cases] 1948-1963: letter to Headmaster Eivind Jørgensen, Oslo, from Ejvind Jensen dated 4 June 1959. *Statistisk Årbog* [Statistical Yearbook] 1959, p. 17.

CCA 7: ESA, Memorandum, 1955-1961: material concerning the DPI.

DNA 1 (Danish National Archive): HPS (Historisk Pædagogisk Studiesamling [Historical Pedagogical Study Collection], journaliseret korrespondance 1955-1974, sign. 22i: correspondence between Moray House and the DPI, February and March 1959.

IOE (Institute of Education London Archive) 1: World Education Fellowship II/81, pamphlet titled 'The International School, Denmark'.

PA 1 (Private archive of J.E. Poulsen): report written by J. Egedal Poulsen titled 'Forsøgsvirksomheden på Emdrupborg 1949/50-1963/64' [The Experimental Work at Emdrupborg], July 2005, p. 10.

PA 2: Draft chapter written by J. Egedal Poulsen titled 'Inspiration fra England og USA' [Inspiration from England and the United States].

PA 3: Report written by J. Egedal Poulsen titled 'Kontinuitet i forsøgsarbejdet i sidste halvdel af det 20. århundrede' [Continuity in the Experimental Work in the Latter Half of the 20th Century], May 1998, p. 11.

PA 4: Draft chapter written by J. Egedal Poulsen, Om internationalt samarbejde [About International Collaboration], chapter 9.

PA 5: Report written by J. Egedal Poulsen titled 'Konferencer indhold 1966/67-1989/90. Interne drøftelser' [The content of conferences 1966/67-1989/90].

CHAPTER 8

Facilitating Student Learning: a comparison of classroom and accountability assessment

SUMERA AHSAN & WILLIAM C. SMITH

ABSTRACT Student learning should be a central feature in any educational activity. Drawing from the social constructivist learning theory and the work of Vygotsky, this chapter explores the type of assessment most likely to facilitate student learning by comparing classroom assessments with accountability assessments. The comparison makes it clear that classroom assessments have space for the spontaneous social interaction necessary for learning, while accountability assessments tend to be independent isolated activities. Through engagement with teachers and opportunities for self-reflection, students taking classroom assessments are better able to connect the assessment with their socio-historical context and teachers are able to adapt assessment prompts to make them culturally relevant to their students. Accountability assessments, on the other hand, tend to be monolithic in origin, lacking the flexibility to capture cultural differences. Although accountability assessments may be able to address secondary educational goals, such as efficiency or identifying demographic trends, we fear that real student learning will wither away in a global testing culture where classroom assessments are reduced, accountability assessments entrenched, and learning superseded by achievement.

Introduction

Testing and assessments are often the most applied tools in investigating the success of education, be it in a classroom, a school or a national education system. With students across the globe exposed to an increasing number of tests and assessments (Benavot & Tanner, 2007; Kamens & McNeely, 2010; Smith, 2014; UNESCO, 2015), it is important to investigate the impact of tests and the place they have in education. To effectively evaluate the utility of tests, assessments or other school structures, activities or policies, one must first answer the underlying, but often unspoken, question, 'What is the goal of education?' Although a bevy of potential goals exists, the often-assumed goal of education is aiding children's learning about specific subjects themselves, and about the wider society in which they participate (Schuyler, 1997).

With learning identified as the primary goal of education, we must further ask ourselves, 'What do we mean by learning?' In essence, how do people learn? The answer to this question is determined by a fundamental epistemology, or set of beliefs about what constitutes knowledge, that dictates what is identified as effective or appropriate practice. In this chapter we understand learning as a socially constructed process which is culturally and contextually specific (Palinscar, 1998).

If learning is the goal of education and learning is socially constructed, it is important to explore which educational practices facilitate this goal. Assessing students' learning, which historically has been approached in many different ways with many different aims, has over the past thirty years been significantly reduced to large-scale standardized tests, often used for accountability purposes (Smith, 2014). The number of tests, assessments and exams students have been exposed to is due, in part, to the positivist notion that standardised tests are objective, making them the appropriate apparatus for accurately evaluating the goals and outcomes of education (Shepard, 2000). Testing and assessments have become so engrained in education that participation in testing is often seen as synonymous with learning (Shepard, 2000), accountability (Froese-Germain, 2001), and educational quality (Balwanz, 2016).

Using the work of Popham (2009) to categorize tests and assessments into two broad categories – classroom assessments and accountability assessments – this chapter addresses which of these assessment categories is most likely to facilitate learning. We start by exploring the prerequisites of learning, using social constructivism and, specifically, the work of Vygotsky to identify a set of best practices that support student learning. This is followed by a section identifying the characteristics of classroom assessments and using the best practices to examine the reported effects of classroom assessment on student learning. The subsequent section follows a similar pattern of inquiry for accountability assessments. Finally, we directly compare the two assessment types to understand their role in facilitating students' learning.

What Are the Prerequisites of Learning?

Learning is a complex individual process which happens through interaction between people and their environment. Researchers and education practitioners have tried to understand what constitutes learning, how learning happens and how learning can be fostered, which, over time, has led to different theories to explain learning. For example, in the past, learning was thought to have occurred through the direct instructional practices of teachers transmitting information to students or through behaviorist stimulus–response models that often led to rote memorization (Shepard, 2000). Still now, for factual and discrete learning, this approach is used in many occasions. More recently, learning has been understood as an 'active process of mental construction and sense making' (Shepard, 2000, p. 6). Our chapter continues this line of thinking by recognizing that knowledge is the co-construction of individual and social processes, in which individuals interact with and make meaning from the wider social context (Bruner, 1990; Palinscar, 1998).

Social-constructivist Learning Theory

Drawing from cognitive, constructivist and socio-cultural theories of learning, social constructivism posits that learning is developed through socially supported interactions (Shepard, 2000). Social constructivism is based on the assumption that reality, knowledge and learning are socially produced through human interaction (Kim, 2001). As reality is context specific, there is not one underlying truth to be discovered but multiple dynamic truths dependent on shared understanding. Through engaging in their reality, individuals relate meaning to objects and individuals, thus socially constructing knowledge. The interaction of individuals with this socially agreed-upon knowledge represents the active process of learning.

Table I identifies the major practices that support learning, taken from the core tenets of social constructivism. Social constructivism argues that cognition is inherently social and that learning is an element of a system of cultural practice (Vygotsky, 1978, Zimmerman & Schunk, 2001; Cobb & McClain, 2006). For this reason, learning must be deeply rooted in culture, allowing students to make authentic connections between the school and the outside world (Shepard, 2000). Learning is a cooperative dialogic process that happens between students and more knowledgeable members of society – for example, teachers and/or peers in a classroom context. These more knowledgeable others (MKOs) are essential, as students' thinking is refined by engaging with individuals who have more practice in interpreting the symbols of the culture (Kim, 2001). One important role of MKOs is to guide others through the zone of proximal development (ZPD). The ZPD refers to the distance between actual learning level – tasks an individual can complete independently – and potential learning level – tasks that require assistance (Palincsar, 1998). Learning therefore occurs as students progress through the ZPD, moving from actual to potential.

Providing guidance for students as they transcend the ZPD, MKOs engage in continual rounds of scaffolding and fading. Scaffolding involves meeting individual students at their actual level of learning and setting assisted intermediary goals. In this process, the instructor offers the needed support by providing tasks/feedback that will enable a learner to build on prior knowledge. As the student recalibrates their actual level of learning, support is reduced and guidance is gradually removed, a process known as fading (Vygotsky, 1978). Timely and constructive feedback is important in the learning process. As student's progress through their ZPD, they must receive descriptive feedback that provides for alternative approaches (Shepard, 2000). Additionally, teachers and MKOs must receive continual feedback, providing the necessary information about what worked and make adjustments accordingly. Finally, the learning process is best accomplished through collaboration with both the MKOs and their peers: 'as learners participate in a broad range of joint activities and internalize the effects of working together, they acquire new strategies and knowledge of the world and culture' (Palincsar, 1998, pp. 351-352). In summary, social constructivism emphasizes a process of learning where individuals have their own ZPD, participate in collaborative activities, and are engaged in spontaneous dialogue that is supported through positive feedback in a social context, like a classroom.

Practices that support learning
Social interaction and dialogue
Environment deeply rooted in culture
More Knowledgeable Other (MKO) helping students
Scaffolding
Progressing through the zone of proximal development (ZPD)
Constructive and timely feedback
Collaboration among students

Table I. Practices that support learning based on the social constructivist theory.

What Tests Facilitate Student Learning?

Using the previously explored social-constructivist theoretical framework, the following sections explain how two very different types of assessments – classroom assessment and accountability assessment – influence students' learning and thus how much they foster or deter students' learning in an educational context.

Classroom Assessment

What are the characteristics of classroom assessment? Popham (2009) defines classroom assessment as: 'formal and informal procedures that teachers employ in an effort to make accurate inferences about what their students know and can do' (p. 6). Classroom assessment tends to be teacher created or shaped and may include activities such as tests, oral questioning, creation of portfolios, homework, group work or informal observation. Teachers ideally use this continuous stream of data for formative purposes, guiding student learning and further instruction in the classroom (Earl & Katz, 2006).

The formative nature of classroom assessment makes it possible for teachers not only to know their student's learning status, needs, difficulties, style and interests, but also to enhance their learning through effective feedback (Sadler, 1989; Doyle, 2003). It also gives teachers feedback on their teaching so that they can help their students learn more effectively. Black and Wiliam (1998a) described the formative role of classroom assessment as both 'Assessment for Learning' and 'Assessment as Learning', as opposed to summative, high-stakes and accountability assessments, which mainly play the role of 'Assessment of Learning'. While assessment of learning considers assessment a final measure, providing summative scores, grades, certificates or rankings, assessment for learning is used over time to help students further enhance their learning by providing meaningful feedback with guidance for improvement. Assessment as learning goes further, suggesting that the assessment process itself can be a way to help students learn. From this paradigm, self-assessment, peer assessment and other alternative ways of assessment not only measure learning, but can also be a rich learning process for the students and thus an integral part of the classroom learning environment.

The formative feature of classroom assessment is its most central feature, acting as a diagnostic in providing feedback to teachers and students over the course of instruction. The goal of formative assessment is to learn about what students have and have not understood by using techniques that provide continuous feedback, allowing teachers to change their instructional support of prioritized content instantaneously. Because formative assessment is tightly linked with instructional practices, teachers must consider how their classroom activities, assignments and tests support learning aims and allow students to communicate what they know. This reflective exercise, in which teachers reimage their instruction after reviewing the immediate feedback from classroom assessments, is what Earl and Katz (2006) refer to as professional accountability.

What are the effects of classroom assessment on students' learning? Past research has compared classroom assessment with high-stakes accountability assessment by juxtaposing these two types of assessment (see Guskey, 2003). Here, we explore and explain the effects of classroom assessment on students' learning using the social-constructivist theoretical framework.

Learning through social interaction and dialogue. Social constructivism argues that learning is a social process. It does not happen passively within an individual, but is a dynamic, social activity (McMahon, 1997). Classroom assessment offers ample opportunity for the students to interact with their peers and teachers through well-planned assessment activities. It gives them the opportunity to observe, interact with people and the environment, reflect, engage in dialogue and construct their own knowledge. Assessment for learning and assessment as learning, the core values of an ideal classroom assessment, provide students with opportunities to interact with people and the environment through dialogues to co-construct knowledge. Crossouard (2011), drawing from in-depth case studies with pupils and teachers in Scotland, found that formative assessments produce multiple opportunities for teacher-and-pupil dialogue, promoting complex learning in socially deprived schools.

Classroom assessment is an ongoing and continuous process that can provide teachers with opportunities to develop and refine the assessment activities. With this knowledge, teachers can guide students through the meaningful step-by-step interactions necessary to construct their own learning in the classroom. The resultant dialogues are very important here both for students and teachers as they refine their own thinking. Haertel et al (2008) re-emphasize the importance of peer interaction and engagement with the surrounding environment as essential elements for learning. Classroom assessments can include a variety of activities that foster experiential learning through hands-on experiences and student self-reflection (Wilson, 2004). The diversity of classroom assessment can help overcome the poverty of uniform assessment practices by encouraging dialogue between pupils and teachers that is 'thoughtful, reflective, focused to evoke and explore understanding, and conducted so that all pupils have an opportunity to think and to express their ideas' (Black & Wiliam, 1998b, p. 144).

Learning rooted in a cultural context. Social constructivists believe that knowledge is constructed on the basis of our understanding of the surrounding culture and context (McMahon, 1997; Derry, 1999). Classroom assessment happens inside the classroom, where there is scope for giving students the opportunity to situate their own learning in a cultural context. Parameters of this cultural context are set by the shared meaning co-constructed by educational actors. In education this may include each student's or group of students' home culture, classroom culture, school culture or the village culture. This environment is not standardized, where all classes, schools or states need to assess the same thing in the same way, but can be differentiated by the socio-historical context of the students in a school or a specific class, or even of a specific student. This flexibility increases the learning opportunity for students from different backgrounds (ARG, 2002). Hilberg (2012) confirmed the association between classroom assessment and learning by conducting two studies designed to examine formative assessment from a sociocultural perspective. The first study introduced the Formative Assessment and Interaction Record (FAIR), a measure for documenting teachers' use of formative assessment and additional research-based instructional strategies. FAIR was created to be a reliable tool that could support district administrators and site principals in their collaborative efforts to increase teachers' use of formative assessment and equity-focused strategies. The second study explored a collaborative effort between site and district leaders to engage teachers in inquiry and analysis of teacher performance data and student assessment results, with a focus on formative assessment practices and their relationship to equity and opportunity to learn. Results from both studies suggested that formative assessment promoted equity through its classroom-based social learning and assessment exercises that involved all students and monitored and ensured that each student was learning.

Help from More Knowledgeable Others (MKOs). A More Knowledgeable Other (MKO) is described by Vygotsky (1981) as anyone who has better knowledge, experience or skills in a particular matter of learning. In the classroom setting, it can be teachers, peers, guest speakers or even a technological device that can provide students with an opportunity to construct knowledge and understand the surrounding reality. Classroom assessment gives students an opportunity to get help from MKOs through interaction with their teachers and peers, a practice explained by some as 'opportunity to learn' (OTL) (Gee, 2008; Mehan, 2008).

Classroom assessment, if planned and conducted properly by incorporating MKO interaction, can enhance the effectiveness of students' learning. Classroom assessment is a continuous process through which teachers collect data about students' learning. It also helps the teachers to identify their instructional challenges, allowing them to adjust and revise their teaching in the classroom. Additionally, classroom assessment is done on a regular basis, by the teachers who know the students best, and using tools and methods appropriate to the individual student's level of understanding. As teachers are in the best position to effectively understand students and adapt and implement necessary tools and assessment, they should be the individuals primarily responsible for assessing students' learning in the classroom context (Wilson, 2004; Black & Wiliam, 2005).

Support learning through scaffolding. Scaffolding involves giving learners the necessary external support to complete a task. When the learner can do the things by himself/herself the support is removed. In an instructional scaffolding process, students take a more active role in their own learning by asking questions, providing feedback and supporting their peers. Students share the responsibility of teaching and learning through scaffolds that require them to move beyond their current skill and knowledge levels. Teachers use scaffolds when they realize that a student is not progressing on some aspect of a task or is unable to understand a particular concept. Classroom assessment can be effectively used as a scaffolding tool as teachers are made aware of students' need for support and provide them with the necessary aid through extra tutoring, or other differentiated instruction

(Northern Illinois University, n.d.). Once proficiency has been established, the teacher can then remove the temporary support by gradually fading it out of instruction.

Classroom assessment has been shown to be effective in promoting specific higher-order learning such as creativity, problem solving and critical thinking. The continuous monitoring of student learning and self-reflection by students on provided feedback is essential for developing critical thinking. Classroom assessment through its incremental nature builds on lower-order learning to teach higher-order cognitive skills. It ensures learning at every stage so that students do not face difficulty or a conceptual gap in transitioning to higher-order thinking skills (Angelo, 1995). Scaffolding therefore helps overcome the tendency of some students become stuck at a single development level (Chan et al, 2014) by guiding student learning across subjects or to more complex concepts.

Zone of proximal development (ZPD). Vygotsky (1978) described the zone of proximal development (ZPD) as a means of explaining the relationship between learning and development. The ZPD is the distance between independent and assisted performance, the first being at the individual developmental level and the latter representing the individual's potential development. Classroom assessment can be a transparent process where students are aware of learning objectives, what is expected from them, and on what criteria their work will be evaluated. As Guskey (2003) points out, classroom assessment does not surprise students because it provides students with meaningful sources of information on expectations, ways to achieve the expectations, and their progress compared with the expectations. In other words, classroom assessment can clearly articulate the present development level, helping teachers and peers progress through the ZPD toward the potential development goal.

Classroom assessment, if practiced properly, can promote students' intrinsic motivation for learning. Students can see the real meaning and purpose of learning and, as the objectives of the learning are shared, they can see the connection between where they are and where they want to go. In this process students learn to visualize the path or paths they can take for learning (Wongsri et al, 2002; Woytek, n.d.).

The transparent objectives tied to incremental steps in a student's ZPD increase the trust teachers and students have in classroom assessment. Guskey (2003) argues that teachers can trust the classroom assessment results more than external assessments because of their direct relation to classroom instructional goals. Students also find classroom assessment trustworthy as they receive useful suggestions for improving their learning from teachers (Bloom et al, 1981; Stiggins, 2002). Using Sadler's (1989) three elements of effort, Black and Wiliam (2001) argue that self-assessment of students is crucial for their learning. They find that classroom assessment is one of the most efficient and effective tools in the classroom because it helps students think through all three elements – the desired goal, evidence about their present position, and understanding ways to close the gap between the desired goal and current position. Students not only know what they learn, they also know 'how they can learn effectively' (p. 7).

Effective feedback process. One of the most important features of classroom assessment is meaningful feedback. Classroom assessment can provide useful and meaningful feedback to students, which includes information about their learning status, what went well, what needs more attention, and ways to improve (Hattie & Timperley, 2007; Chan et al, 2014). Classroom assessment can also play an important role in diagnosing students' learning difficulties, important in providing appropriate support or scaffolding (Guskey, 2003). It also provides teachers with feedback about their teaching, allowing teachers insight to revise their plan and create more effective lessons (Steadman, 1998). Feedback from classroom assessment is not only immediate, it also does not tend to require a high level of statistical understanding, providing both teachers and students with access to readily usable information without having to acquire the complex skills and knowledge usually necessary for data usage (Guskey, 2003).

Collaborative learning environment. Social constructivism emphasizes the need for collaboration among learners and with practitioners in society (Lave & Wenger, 1991; McMahon, 1997). Social constructivists argue that classroom assessment should include collaborative practices such as reciprocal teaching, peer collaboration, cognitive apprenticeships, problem-based instruction, webquests, anchored instruction, and other methods that involve learning with others (Zimmerman & Schunk, 2001).

Classroom assessments are more likely to elicit a cooperative environment as the assessment is generally less formal and the stakes involved are low – final decisions about students and teachers are not based on their performance. These characteristics make the classroom assessment more comforting and authentic for students, increasing trust and, ultimately, improving student learning (Black & Wiliam, 1998b).

Accountability Assessment

What are the characteristics of accountability assessment? Popham (2009) defines accountability assessments as 'measurement devices, almost always standardized, used by governmental entities such as states, provinces, or school districts to ascertain the effectiveness of educational endeavors' (p. 6). Examples of accountability assessment include high-stake student exams that determine whether a student advances to the next education level; national assessments which aggregate student scores at the school level and hold educators accountable by publishing school-level results and creating market pressure that shapes educator behavior; and sample-based international assessments, such as the Programme for International Student Assessment (PISA), which holds countries accountable for the state of their education system. The main purpose of accountability assessment is to hold different stakeholders of education accountable. As the world looks to improve the quality of education, accountability assessments are often used as a measure of efficiency, ensuring that resource investments are not wasted. Student achievement, measured through the process of student assessment, is the most relied-upon and globally legitimated indicator of education quality (Linn et al, 2008). The common features of accountability assessments include: administration by a bureaucracy above the classroom level; high stakes for some or all education stakeholders; standardization and formal application; summative nature (Gareis, 2007). The underlying assumption in systems focused on accountability assessments is that the incentives embedded in the accompanying accountability will promote professional development of school personnel and increase commitment and effort from all stakeholders, which will eventually enhance student learning. Figure 1 illustrates the process through which proponents of accountability assessments envision quality education will be achieved.

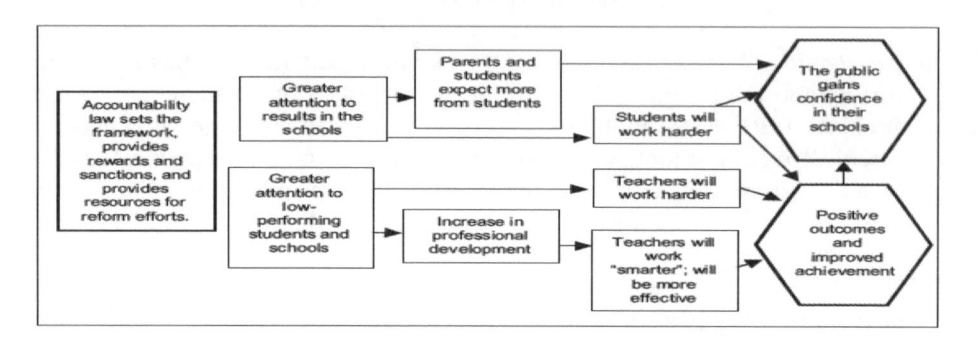

Note: Taken from Perie (2007)

Figure 1. A simplified theory of action: how accountability expectations and actions lead to higher achievement.

What are the effects of accountability assessment on students' learning?

Learning through social interaction and dialogue. Accountability assessments are usually large-scale assessments administered using multiple-choice questions (MCQs) or questions that require short-response answers. Tests using MCQs are increasing in popularity as the format is associated with notions of 'fairness' and 'objectivity' (Carneson et al, 2002). The restricted format, however, does not generally give students an opportunity to dialogue with peers or teachers. Rather, accountability assessments tend to be a very impersonal, formal way of summarizing what students have learned at a given point in time. To prepare for the isolated activity of test taking, some teachers have reshaped their classroom to mimic the testing environment, seating students in rows and eliminating the group work that promotes engaged dialogue (Yarema, 2010). Additionally, in preparation for lower-order MCQs, test-taking strategies often emphasize rote memorization or repeat-after-me parroting (Jones et al, 1999; Somerset, 2016), both reducing the meaningful interaction of students with their environment.

Learning rooted in a cultural context. To maintain their veil of objectivity, accountability assessment questions tend to represent one monolithic culture, which is often equivalent to that of the privileged or more powerful group. Standardized testing promotes a homogeneous knowledge and pedagogy, and thus discourages multicultural values. It squeezes non-tested multicultural knowledge out of the curriculum (Agee, 2004), and silences the voices, cultures and experiences of children, which are not included in the accountability assessment (McNeil, 2000). Research also shows that schools in high-stakes accountability assessment systems are more likely to exclude low-income or low-achieving students. Smith (2015) suggests that this exclusion is incentivized in accountability systems that use school aggregate test scores to punish or reward educators. Administrators and teachers then put practices in place that reduce the testing pool in an attempt to increase the school mean score and ensure their professional livelihood.

Researchers and practitioners argue that accountability assessment does not provide a fair and just tool for teachers and schools (Slee et al, 1998; Ball, 1999; McNeil & Valenzuela, 1999; Linn, 2000). These researchers view the entire accountability policy approach as problematic because such accountability assessment policy is based on a biased norm that overrates the more powerful group in society to the detriment of others (Knight, 1999). Accountability systems therefore do not possess the flexibility necessary to incorporate the cultural context of students with diversified backgrounds, an important prerequisite to student learning.

Help from MKOs. For accountability assessments, MKOs are important for preparing tests and grading the student responses; however, they have little influence on facilitating students' learning as they are limited to providing summative grades, marks and certificates. Accountability assessments also tend to be disconnected or exogenous to the school or classroom objectives. Local MKOs lose authority to centralized bureaucratic processes, often leading to less democratic participation from local stakeholders (Au, 2009). Au (2009) suggests that this may be a deliberate attempt to re-center power away from the periphery. According to Au, the high-stakes assessments reinforce three beliefs: teachers are not to be trusted; diversity is bad; and local conditions are unimportant. Apple (1995) also argues that the way high-stakes accountability assessments control classroom practice portrays the hierarchy of institutional power and dominance: 'High stakes testing thus manifests bureaucratic control, or control embodied within the hierarchical social relations of the workplace' (p. 128). MKOs in accountability assessments do not disappear but are revalued. Local MKOs are relegated to shaping their classroom practice to ensure successful test scores, while those with authority at the central level create and manage the assessment.

Support learning through scaffolding. Unlike classroom assessment, accountability assessment cannot offer scaffolding to students. It gives the students final grades, numbers or certificates. The multiple-choice approach to standardized tests make it difficult to measure higher-order learning, generally limiting prompts to those that promote lower-order learning and are easier to test, such as recalling facts or simple tasks involving basic understanding. As a result, teachers focus only on the information that will be tested and neglect other aspects of learning valuable for a student's overall development. In addition to reducing the complexity of concepts under investigation, narrowing the curriculum has been identified as an unintended consequence of accountability assessment (Hammond, 1991; Ben Jaafar & Anderson, 2007; Figlio & Loeb, 2011). Through limiting the subjects covered and identifying what students need to focus on (Hursh, 2007), accountability assessments influence teachers, which often leads to a restraint in meaningful support or scaffolding for students, as well as to teaching to the test (Popham, 2001).

Zone of proximal development (ZPD). The uniformity of standardized accountability assessments inhibits teachers from providing the individual instruction students need to progress through their ZPD. Underlying standardized tests there is an assumption that to provide an equally valid measure, all students must be evaluated in the same way on the same material. Although computer-adapted assessments are starting to show some promise in adjusting for students' learning level (see Kousholt & Hamre, 2016), the majority of accountability assessments are unable to capture the student's actual development level. Pressing all students to reach the same potential development level without understanding their actual development level may create a situation where students feel hopeless or disheartened, increasing the likelihood that they drop out of school (Natriello & Pallas, 2001). The negative consequences that occur when a student's ZPD has not been accurately identified can be exacerbated when scaffolding is discouraged, removing attainable incremental goals from the learning process. ZPD is closely dependent on the dialogue and feedback processes which, in accountability assessments, are almost absent or are given in such an indirect and general way (e.g. as grades, percentage, pass/fail) that it is not immediately helpful for students (Guskey, 2003).

Effective feedback process. Though the accountability assessment can draw a bigger data set and can give a more general idea about the achievement status of a group of students, it generally does not provide individual students with useful feedback for improvement. Unlike classroom assessment, an end-of-semester grade or certificate does not tell a student about what specific aspects of his or her learning were rich and where more improvement is needed. Specific feedback about achievement is crucial in improving student learning (Chan et al, 2014). In addition to the lack of specificity, the prolonged feedback loop for accountability assessments, ranging from a couple of months to a couple of years, indicates that information comes too late to be useful in adjusting classroom instruction (Chapman & Snyder, 2000; Paris & McEvoy, 2000; Supovitz, 2009).

Collaborative learning environment. Accountability assessments, in most cases, are used for ranking and labeling schools, teachers and students. Schools and teachers compete for higher rankings, more students and higher-performing students. The competitive environment contrasts sharply with the collaborative environment in which teachers, schools and systems share best practices and learn from each other (Sahlberg, 2010). Fearing stigmatization for working in a lower-performing school or with lower-performing students, some teachers leave (Jones et al, 1999), while others place blame on earlier-grade teachers for inadequately preparing their students (Wiggins & Tymms, 2000). Rowntree (1987) captures the fundamental problem with providing school-level rankings for accountability purposes: everyone wants to go ahead in the ranking and the only way to do this is to remove someone else ahead. In this scenario, competition winners are more likely to be those in a better socio-economic position, with more options than others and able to buy a good education, a private tutor and supplementary materials.

Comparing Classroom and Accountability Assessments

Re-centering the goal of education on learning produces a stark contrast between classroom and accountability assessment. Table II expands the previously introduced Table I by setting both types of assessment against the practices that support learning. From the table we can see that classroom assessments have space for the spontaneous social interaction that is necessary for learning, while accountability assessments tend to be independent, isolated activities. Through engagement with teachers and opportunities for self-reflection, students taking classroom assessments are better able to connect the assessment with their socio-historical context and teachers are able to adapt assessment prompts, making them culturally relevant to their students. Accountability assessments, on the other hand, tend to be monolithic in origin, lacking the flexibility to capture cultural differences.

MKOs are present in both classroom and accountability assessments, although the role of local MKOs – namely, teachers – is substantially different. For classroom assessments, teachers as MKOs actively engage with students, guiding them from their present level of understanding to their potential development level through a series of differentiated exercises and instructional sessions. For accountability assessments, the authority of teachers as MKOs is diminished as assessments are created, implemented and monitored by a more centralized bureaucracy. The result is an influential but distant MKO who is unable to adjust to contextual factors, and a local

MKO who adapts to ensure assessments are completed and requirements are met, with less invested in individual students.

Practices that support learning	Classroom assessments	Accountability assessments
Social interaction and dialogue	Spontaneous, social interaction	Independent, isolated activity
Environment deeply rooted in culture	More culturally relevant	Monolithic culture
More Knowledgeable Other (MKO) helping students	Local MKOs have authority	Authority placed in centralized MKOs
Scaffolding	Continuous cycle of interaction, feedback, and refinement make scaffolding more common	Standardization make scaffolding difficult or impossible
Progressing through the zone of proximal development (ZPD)	Can be shaped to individual students, helping students progress through uniquely identified ZPDs	Tend to assume all students start at the same actual development level
Constructive and timely feedback	Compressed feedback loop	Extended feedback loop
Collaboration among students	More likely to foster collaboration	More likely to foster competition

Table II. Supporting learning in classroom and accountability assessments.

Scaffolding is more common in classroom assessments as teachers have the ability to adjust items and questions for the individual student's development level through a continuous process of student interaction, relevant feedback and lesson refinement. In contrast, the standardized approach and the singular summative attempt associated with accountability assessments do not provide space for scaffolding. Without being met at their present level and being guided through a set of incremental steps, students are more likely to feel hopeless and uncared for, and ultimately to drop out.

Progressing students through the ZPD is a cornerstone of Vygotsky's (1978) social-constructivist approach. A student's ZPD can be seen as his or her roadmap for learning; in order to effectively navigate the map, we must first know where they are starting (actual development level) and where they are going (potential development level). The goal for teachers, then, is to aid students as they progress through their ZPD. Ideally, with proper support at the appropriate level, the teacher can eventually fade to the background and the potential development level can be achieved by the student independently. Unfortunately for accountability assessments, all students are placed on the same starting point, often based on normative developmental level or subject standards. While this may be appropriate for many students, a large proportion of students, primarily lower-achieving ones, will be starting at a point they are not ready for and struggle to progress. Classroom assessments can overcome these shortcomings by engaging with students, establishing a baseline starting point, and developing a specialized learning map for students that takes their individual needs into account.

Many of the benefits of classroom assessments come through their compressed feedback loop, providing teachers with timely and important feedback which can direct their instruction and provide students with concrete information about their strengths and what they need to work on. Accountability assessments, alternatively, have a feedback loop that typically lasts from a few months to a few years. By the time information returns to the teacher, students have often moved on, limiting the worth of the results. Additionally, accountability assessments are generally reported by overall score or sub-score, limiting the ability of teachers and students to identify areas of focus for further exploration or re-teaching.

Finally, the ranking of various stakeholders by student achievement score, commonly associated with accountability assessments, creates a competitive atmosphere where individuals compete against each other for accolades and resources. Although supporters promote competition on the grounds that it will encourage stakeholders to change their practice, improving quality and efficiency, past results suggest that whatever changes occur often come at the expense of equity. These include excluding low-performing and low-income students, narrowing the curriculum, and teaching to the test. In contrast, classroom assessments are more likely to encourage student–student, teacher–student and teacher–teacher collaboration as individuals don't feel forced into a zero-sum game but instead can work collectively towards a common goal.

From the discussion above, it is evident that accountability assessments ignore or hinder the co-constructed social process of learning advocated by social constructivism. Since there is not sufficient scope for feedback, students do not have an opportunity for scaffolding; as a result, their proximal development is not supported. On the other hand, classroom assessment builds on a less formal spontaneous social environment that provides ample room for interaction. The presence of incremental feedback promotes the process of scaffolding and maximizes students' proximal development. Moreover, the classroom assessment provides students with opportunities for self-reflection and the development of meta-cognition. These individual cognition development opportunities, along with complex social interactions, advance higher-order learning. Therefore, from a social-constructivist point of view, classroom assessment better facilitates student learning.

Conclusion

To accept the argument presented here – that classroom assessments are a better tool for facilitating learning and should be encouraged over accountability assessments in measuring the effectiveness of education – one must first agree that the goal of education is student learning and that students learn through a process of social construction. This, of course, is not the only goal of education. We believe, however, that it is, or should be, the primary goal. This sentiment has been echoed by others, including Black and Wiliam (2004), who note that 'assessment must first promote learning' (p. 20). It is possible, and it has been discussed elsewhere, that the goal of accountability assessment involves a secondary goal of education, such as increasing efficiency, measuring resources or distinguishing demographic trends. While these goals have merit on their own, increasingly classroom assessments are being replaced by or transformed into accountability assessments (Smith, 2014; Tichá & Abery, 2016). If this trend continues, we fear that real student learning, at the heart of education, will wither away as classroom assessments are reduced, accountability assessments become entrenched, and learning is superseded by achievement.

Finally, we outline the potential of classroom assessments. To fulfill this potential, teachers must be valued in society and adequately trained in social-constructivist learning theory. This may entail an overall reconstruction of evaluation in society, with views of testing and assessment moving from apathy or punishment towards utility and insight (Shepard, 2000). Re-skilling the teaching force is challenging during an era of expanding accountability assessment. At the same time that teachers need to acquaint themselves with the tools for creating dynamic classroom assessments, the profession of teaching is being undercut by accountability practices that remove teachers' authority and question their competency, making it challenging for many teachers to fend off 'the distorting and de-motivating effects of external assessments' (Shepard, 2000, p. 7). To succeed, teachers must be well trained, trusted to do their job and given autonomy. Increasing teachers' capacity to ask probing questions, anticipate and identify conceptual gaps, and create a differentiated assessment program that meets students at their development level is the first step toward ensuring that classroom assessments, and the benefits they bring to student learning, remain central in education.

References

Agee, J. (2004) Negotiating a Teaching Identity: an African American teacher's struggle to teach in test-driven contexts, *Teachers College Record*, 106(4), 747-774. http://dx.doi.org/10.1111/j.1467-9620.2004.00357.x

Angelo, T.A. (1995) Beginning the Dialogue: thoughts on promoting critical thinking: classroom assessment for critical thinking, *Teaching of Psychology*, 22(1), 6-7. http://dx.doi.org/10.1207/s15328023top2201_1

Apple, M.W. (1995) *Education and Power*, 2nd edn. New York: Routledge.

Assessment Reform Group (ARG) (2002) *Assessment for Learning: 10 principles*. London: Institute of Education.

Au, W. (2009) High-stakes Testing and Discursive Control: the triple bind for non-standard student identities, *Multicultural Perspectives*, 11(2), 65-71. http://dx.doi.org/10.1080/15210960903028727

Ball, S.J. (1999) Performativities and Fabrications in the Education Economy: toward the performative society? Paper presented at the annual meeting of the Australian Association for Research in Education, Melbourne.

Balwanz, D. (2016) The Discursive Hold of the Matric: is there space for a new vision for secondary education in South Africa? In W.C. Smith (Ed.) *The Global Testing Culture: shaping education policy, perceptions, and practice*. Oxford: Symposium Books.

Benavot, A. & Tanner, E. (2007) The Growth of National Learning Assessments in the World, 1995-2006. Background paper for the Education for All Global Monitoring Report 2008: Education for All by 2015: will we make it? Geneva: UNESCO-IBE.

Ben Jaafar, S. & Anderson, S. (2007) Policy Trends and Tensions in Accountability for Educational Management and Services in Canada, *Alberta Journal of Educational Research*, 53(2), 205-225.

Black, P. & Wiliam, D. (1998a) Assessment and Classroom Learning, *Assessment in Education*, 5(1), 71-74. http://dx.doi.org/10.1080/0969595980050102

Black, P. & Wiliam, D. (1998b) Inside the Black Box: raising standards through classroom assessment, *Phi Delta Kappan*, 80(2), 139-148.

Black, P. & William, D. (2001) Inside the Black Box: raising standards through classroom assessment, *Phi Delta Kappan*, 80(2), 139-148.

Black, P. & William, D. (2004) Classroom Assessment is Not (Necessarily) Formative Assessment (and vice-versa), in M. Wilson (Ed.) *Towards Coherence between Classroom Assessment and Accountability*, pp. 183-188. Chicago: National Society for the Study of Education.

Black, P. & William, D. (2005) Lessons from around the World: how policies, politics, and cultures constrain and afford assessment practices, *The Curriculum Journal*, 16(2), 249-261. http://dx.doi.org/10.1080/09585170500136218

Bloom, B.S., Madaus, G.F. & Hastings, J.T. (1981) *Evaluation to Improve Learning*. New York: McGraw-Hill.

Bruner, J. (1990) *Acts of Meaning*. Cambridge, MA: Harvard University Press.

Carneson, J., Delpierre, G. & Masters, K. (2002) Designing and Managing Multiple Choice Questions. University of Leicester. http://www.le.ac.uk/castle/resources/

Chan, P.E., Konrad, M., Gonzalez, V., Peters, M.T. & Ressa, V.A. (2014) The Critical Role of Feedback in Formative Instructional Practices, *Intervention in School and Clinic*, 50(2), 96-104. http://dx.doi.org/10.1177/1053451214536044

Chapman, D. & Snyder, C. (2000) Can High Stakes National Testing Improve Instruction: re-examining conventional wisdom, *International Journal of Educational Development*, 20, 457-474. http://dx.doi.org/10.1016/S0738-0593(00)00020-1

Cobb, P. & McClain, K. (2006) The Collective Mediation of a High-stakes Accountability Program: communities and networks of practice, *Mind, Culture, and Activity*, 13(2), 80-100. http://dx.doi.org/10.1207/s15327884mca1302_2

Crossouard, B. (2011) Using Formative Assessment to Support Complex Learning in Conditions of Social Adversity, *Assessment in Education: Principles, Policy & Practice*, 18(1), 59-72.

Derry, S.J. (1999) A Fish Called Peer Learning: searching for common themes, in A.M. O'Donnell & A. King (Eds) *Cognitive Perspectives on Peer Learning*, pp. 197-211. Mahwah, NJ: Lawrence Erlbaum Associates.

Doyle, D. (2003) Data-driven Decision-making, *T.H.E Journal Online*. https://thejournal.com/Articles/2003/05/01/DataDriven-DecisionMaking.aspx?Page=1

Earl, L. & Katz, S. (2006) *Leading in a Data Rich World: harnessing data for school improvement*. Thousand Oaks, CA: Corwin.

Figlio, D. & Loeb, S. (2011) School Accountability, *Handbook of the Economics of Education*, 3, 383-421.

Froese-Germain, B. (2001) Standardized Testing + High-stakes Decisions = Educational Inequity, *Interchange*, 32(2), 111-130. http://dx.doi.org/10.1023/A:1011985405392

Gareis, C.R. (2007) Reclaiming an Important Teacher Competency: the lost art of formative assessment, *Journal of Personnel Evaluation in Education*, 20, 17-20. http://dx.doi.org/10.1007/s11092-007-9044-5

Gee, J.P. (2008) A Sociocultural Perspective on Opportunity to Learn, in P.A. Moss, D.C. Pullin, J.P. Gee, E.H. Haertel & L.J. Young (Eds) *Assessment, Equity, and Opportunity to Learn*, pp. 76-108. New York: Cambridge University Press.

Guskey, T.R. (2003) How Classroom Assessments Improve Learning, *Using Data to Improve Student Achievement*, 60(5), 6-11.

Haertel, E.H., Moss, P.A., Pullin, D.C. & Gee, J.P. (2008) Introduction, in P.A. Moss, D.C. Pullin, J.P. Gee, E.H. Haertel & L.J. Young (Eds) *Assessment, Equity, and Opportunity to Learn*, pp. 1-16. New York: Cambridge University Press.

Hammond, L.D. (1991) The Implications of Testing Policy for Quality and Equity, *Phi Delta Kappan*, 220-225.

Hattie, J. & Timperley, H. (2007) The Power of Feedback, *Review of Educational Research*, 77(1), 81-112. http://dx.doi.org/10.3102/003465430298487

Hilberg, S. (2012) Formative Assessment, Equity and Opportunity to Learn. Dissertation, University of California Santa Cruz.

Hursh, D. (2007) Assessing No Child Left Behind and the Rise of Neoliberal Education Policies, *American Educational Research Journal*, 44(3), 493-518. http://dx.doi.org/10.3102/0002831207306764

Jones, M.G., Jones, B., Hardin, B., Chapman, L., Yarbrough, T. & Davis, M. (1999) The Impact of High-stakes Testing on Teachers and Students in North Carolina, *Phi Delta Kappan*, 81(3), 199-203.

Kamens, D.H. & McNeely, C.L. (2010) Globalization and the Growth of International Educational Testing and National Assessment, *Comparative Education Review*, 54(1), 5-25. http://dx.doi.org/10.1086/648471

Kim, B. (2001) Social Constructivism, in M. Orey (Ed.) *Emerging Perspectives on Learning, Teaching, and Technology*. http://projects.coe.uga.edu/epltt

Knight, S.L. (1999) Using Evaluation in the Service of Student Learning: diverse perspectives on detecting and diminishing achievement disparities. Paper presented at the annual meeting of the American Educational Research Association, Montreal, Canada.

Kousholt, K. & Hamre, B. (2016) Testing and School Reform in Danish Education: an analysis informed by the use of the 'dispositive', in W.C. Smith (Ed.) *The Global Testing Culture: shaping education policy, perceptions, and practice*. Oxford: Symposium Books.

Lave, J. & Wegner, E. (1991) *Situated Learning: legitimate peripheral participation*. New York: Cambridge University Press.

Linn, R.L. (2000) Assessments and Accountability, *Educational Researcher*, 29(2), 4-16. http://dx.doi.org/10.3102/0013189X029002004

Linn, R., Miller, M. & Gronlund, N. (2008) *Measurement and Assessment in Teaching*, 10th edn. Upper Saddle River, NJ: Prentice Hall.

McMahon, M. (1997) Social Constructivism and the World Wide Web: a paradigm for learning. Paper presented at the ASCILITE conference. Perth, Australia.

McNeil, L. (2000) *Contradictions of School Reform: educational costs of standardized testing*. New York: Routledge.

McNeil, L. & Valenzuela, A. (1999) The Harmful Impact of the TAAS System of Testing in Texas: beneath the accountability rhetoric. Unpublished paper.

Mehan, H. (2008) A Sociocultural Perspective on Opportunity to Learn and Assessment, in P.A. Moss, D.C. Pullin, J.P. Gee, E.H. Haertel & L.J. Young (Eds) *Assessment, Equity, and Opportunity to Learn*, pp. 42-75. New York: Cambridge University Press.

Natriello, G. & Pallas, A.M. (2001) The Development and Impact of High-stakes Testing, in G. Orfield & M.L. Kornhaber (Eds) *Raising Standards or Raising Barriers? Inequality and High-stakes Testing in Public Education*, pp. 19-38. New York: Century Foundation Press.

Northern Illinois University. (n.d.) Instructional Scaffolding to Improve Learning. Faculty Development and Instructional Design Center.

Palincsar, A.S. (1998) Social Constructivist Perspectives on Teaching and Learning, *Annual Review of Psychology*, 49, 345-375. http://dx.doi.org/10.1146/annurev.psych.49.1.345

Paris, S. & McEvoy, A. (2000) Harmful and Enduring Effects of High-stakes Testing, *Issues in Education*, 6(1), 145-159.

Popham, W.J. (2001) Teaching to the Test, *Educational Leadership*, 58(6), 16-20.

Popham, W.J. (2009) Assessment Literacy for Teachers: faddish or fundamental? *Theory into Practice*, 48(4), 4-11. http://dx.doi.org/10.1080/00405840802577536

Rowntree, D. (1987) *Assessing Students: how shall we know them?* London: Kogan Page.

Sadler, D.R. (1989) Formative Assessment and the Design of Instructional Systems, *Instructional Science*, 18(2), 119-144. http://dx.doi.org/10.1007/BF00117714

Sahlberg, P. (2010) Rethinking Accountability in a Knowledge Society, *Journal of Educational Change*, 11, 45-61. http://dx.doi.org/10.1007/s10833-008-9098-2

Schuyler, G. (1997) A Paradigm Shift from Instruction to Learning. Los Angeles: Eric Digests.

Shepard, L.A. (2000) The Role of Assessment in a Learning Culture, *Educational Researcher*, 29(7), 4-14.

Slee, R., Weiner, G. & Tomlinson, S. (1998) *School Effectiveness for Whom? Challenges to the School Effectiveness and School Improvement Movements*. London: Falmer Press.

Smith, W.C. (2014) The Global Transformation toward Testing for Accountability, *Education Policy Analysis Archives*, 22(116). http://dx.doi.org/10.14507/epaa.v22.1571

Smith, W.C. (2015) Exploring Educator-based Testing for Accountability: national testing policies and student achievement, in T. Burns (Ed.) *Modern Governance in Education: the challenge of complexity*. Paris: OECD Publishing.

Somerset, A. (2016) Questioning across the Spectrum: pedagogy, selection examinations and assessment systems in low-income countries, in W.C. Smith (Ed.) *The Global Testing Culture: shaping education policy, perceptions, and practice*. Oxford: Symposium Books.

Stiggins, R.J. (2002) Assessment Crisis: the absence of assessment for learning, *Phi Delta Kappan*, 83(10), 758-765. http://dx.doi.org/10.1177/003172170208301010

Supovitz, J. (2009) Can High Stakes Testing Leverage Educational Improvement? Prospects from the Last Decade of Testing and Accountability Reform, *Journal of Educational Change*, 10, 211-227. http://dx.doi.org/10.1007/s10833-009-9105-2

Tichá, R. & Abery, B. (2016) Beyond the Large-scale Testing of Basic Skills: using formative assessment to facilitate learning, in W.C. Smith (Ed.) *The Global Testing Culture: shaping education policy, perceptions, and practice*. Oxford: Symposium Books.

UNESCO (2015) EFA Global Monitoring Report. Education for All 2000-2015: achievements and challenges. http://unesdoc.unesco.org/images/0023/002322/232205e.pdf

Vygotsky, L.S. (1978) *Mind in Society: the development of higher psychological processes*, ed. M. Cole, V John-Steiner, S. Scribner, & E. Souberman. Cambridge, MA: Harvard University Press.

Vygotsky, L.S. (1981) The Genesis of Higher Mental Functions, in J.V. Wertsch (Ed.) *The Concept of Activity in Soviet Psychology*, pp. 144-188. Armonk, NY: Sharpe.

Wiggins, A. & Tymms, P. (2000) Dysfunctional Effects of Public Performance Indicator Systems: a comparison between English and Scottish primary schools. Paper presented at the European Conference on Educational Research, Edinburgh.

Wilson, M. (2004) Assessment, Accountability and the Classroom: a community of judgment, in M. Wilson (Ed.) *Towards Coherence between Classroom Assessment and Accountability*, pp. 1-19. Chicago: National Society for the Study of Education.

Wongsri, N., Cantwell, R.H. & Archer, J. (2002) The Validation of Measures of Self-efficacy, Motivation and Self-regulated Learning among Thai Tertiary Students. Paper presented at the Annual Conference of the Australian Association for Research in Education, Brisbane. http://www.aare.edu.au/02pap/won02083.htm

Woytek, A. (n.d.) Utilizing Assessment to Improve Student Motivation and Success. Chaminade University of Honolulu. http://www.usca.edu/essays/vol142005/woytek.pdf

Yarema, C.H. (2010) Mathematics Teachers' Views of Accountability Testing Revealed through Lesson Study, *Mathematics Teacher Education and Development*, 12(1), 3-18.

Zimmerman, B.J. & Schunk, D.H. (2001) Reflections on Theories of Self-regulated Learning and Academic Achievement, *Self-regulated Learning and Academic Achievement: theoretical perspectives*, 2, 289-307.

CHAPTER 9

Beyond the Large-scale Testing of Basic Skills: using formative assessment to facilitate student learning

RENÁTA TICHÁ & BRIAN ABERY

ABSTRACT Assessment is an integral part of educational accountability at the local, national and international level. Educational assessment can have many forms and be administered for a variety of purposes. This chapter outlines the characteristics and functions of summative and formative assessment, two key assessment types in education. The authors point out the strengths and limitations of each of the assessment types and discuss a recent trend of 'adapting' formative assessments for use as screening tools of basic skills administered to large numbers of students. The chapter concludes with recommendations focused on the use of assessments for the purposes for which they were intended and the need to validate assessments for implementation in local contexts to monitor teacher instruction and student learning.

Introduction

In the United States, one result of the No Child Left Behind (NCLB) Act of 2001 (NCLB Act, 2001) has been a surge in the assessment of student academic outcomes. Often implemented in response to demands on of local, state and federal authorities for greater educational accountability, this form of high-stakes assessment in many areas of the United States now extends well beyond the requirements of federal and state systems. In addition to required summative assessments at key grade levels, districts and schools are also frequently administering different types of formative assessments on an ongoing basis with the goal of predicting student performance on high-stakes tests, and monitoring the progress of learners experiencing difficulties mastering basic educational skills related to literacy and numeracy.

The increased interest in all forms of educational assessment has led many organizations, both in the United States and internationally, to contract with large educational testing groups that have, in recent years, cornered the testing market. Although that has made additional options available for local, state and national assessment purposes, it has also resulted in much misunderstanding with respect to the types of assessments available, their intended purpose, and their technical adequacy and utility. As Chappuis and Chappuis (2008) have noted, we currently see assessment products claimed to be formative that are no more than a series a mini-summative assessments. In addition, approaches to assessment whose original purpose was for use in individual classrooms are now being implemented on an international scale and being used to develop national 'benchmarks', as well as make global comparisons of the efficacy of national educational systems. Beyond creating multimillion-dollar/-euro markets for tests, these developments have contributed to considerable confusion about test development and the use of assessment in education. This includes questions regarding whether tests themselves are formative or summative (Chappuis, 2005), the use of assessments for purposes other than those for which they have been validated, and how in a world of limited resources classroom teachers, local schools, education districts, states and national education agencies can most effectively collect and use data to improve the day-to-day instruction received by children and youth as the ultimate consumers of education, as well as their academic outcomes.

Chapter Overview

The goal of this chapter is to heighten readers' awareness of recent developments in, and the implementation of, educational assessments in general, and in particular of their use within an international context. The impetus for writing this chapter is twofold. It stems from: (a) the authors' research and implementation experience both in the United States and internationally with formative assessment used with students with disabilities and those without disability who are struggling academically; and (b) international efforts by government agencies, non-governmental organizations (NGOs) and others to improve basic literacy skills in developing countries.

The chapter begins with a discussion of differences between using assessments for summative versus formative purposes. The authors argue that even though summative assessments play an important role in education through providing comparisons between academic performance of students, classrooms, schools and even states and countries, formative assessments have a greater utility for teaching and learning. The case is made that unlike infrequently administered summative assessments, formative assessments have been designed for frequent monitoring of students' learning progress. The underutilization in education of standardized formative assessments with sound psychometric properties is then discussed, as well as how, in an international context, these formative assessments (e.g. curriculum-based measurement) have been re-purposed as summative assessments and used to report basic literacy and numeracy rates in developing countries. The authors argue against such efforts and propose that energy would be more wisely invested in implementing formative assessments as originally intended (i.e. to be used to directly improve teacher instruction and student learning). The case is then made that in order to successfully accomplish this goal, formative assessments need to be localized at the school and classroom level and capacity built such that teachers and school administrators are able to administer, appropriately interpret and effectively utilize these data to improve student learning.

The Basics of Educational Assessment

Assessment refers to the long-term systematic process of gathering, analyzing and interpreting data. In education, it entails the manner in which teachers (and those who are administratively responsible for the educational endeavor) gather data about the instruction and the learning that has taken place among students (Hanna & Dettmer, 2004). Data collected can be based on different forms of assessment (e.g. pre-tests, observations and examinations) and used in a variety of ways to evaluate the performance of both learners and teachers. Assessment of educational achievement is therefore a set of processes designed to improve, demonstrate and inquire about student learning (Mentkowski, 1999), evaluate educational growth and guide educators in decision-making.

Assessments in education can be categorized on the basis of their characteristics and purposes as either *summative* or *formative*. The following section will outline the differences and similarities between the two assessment types in education.

Summative Assessment

Summative assessment entails an evaluation *of* learning mastery. It typically takes place at the end of a unit, semester or year and is administered in an attempt to determine what students have or have not learned to proficiency. It provides global feedback on the knowledge students have acquired across a specific time period. The typical goal of summative assessment is not to *evaluate student learning* in isolation, but rather, to compare it against some standard or benchmark. Rubrics, developed around a set of standards or expectations, are often used for this purpose. Summative assessments are often *high stakes*, and are used to determine whether students, schools, educational districts or states are meeting learning goals and standards. Grades/scores are usually an outcome of summative assessment and are intended to indicate whether students have accumulated a sufficient degree of knowledge to pass on to the next level, grade or instructional unit. Examples of summative assessments include: a midterm exam; a final project; a state or national exam.

Summative assessment methods have, in most countries, been the traditional way of evaluating learner outcomes. Well-developed summative assessments typically are the product of years of development and multiple, independent research efforts that have established their reliability and validity, and that they are non-discriminatory (Angelo & Cross, 1993). In the United States, the National Assessment of Educational Progress (NAEP) is an example of a thoroughly researched, psychometrically sound summative assessment administered on a national level. Internationally, the Progress in International Reading Literacy Study (PIRLS) and Trends in International Mathematics and Science Study (TIMSS) are used in similar ways. Other types of assessment typically used for summative purposes include national or state exams; university/college entrance exams (ACT, SAT); a final examination for a course; term papers; and portfolios. Due to their high-stakes nature, the 'learning' evaluated in summative assessments is often limited with respect to experimentation with ideas and concepts or being creative (Biggs & Tang, 2007), with test-takers often asked to provide no more than the answers they believe are expected of them.

It should be remembered that summative assessments are 'after the fact', product oriented, and assess final outcomes. They serve a purpose and can be used to help make broad policy decisions based on results that, if interpreted properly, provide one with a snapshot at a single point of how well nations, educational districts and schools are doing in comparison with each other, as well as with respect to achieving educational equity (as long as data can be disaggregated). They do, however, have limited classroom utility in that they: (a) are designed to focus on a final or finished product; (b) do not provide sufficient instructional guidance due to their inadequate alignment with the curriculum and infrequent administration; and (c) are often insufficiently sensitive to determine whether learning growth has occurred, especially when used with low-performing children and those with disabilities (Johnson & Jenkins, 2009; Wixson & Valencia, 2011).

Summative assessments, when adequately constructed, normed and standardized, can be useful in measuring learner progress toward national or state academic standards and in predicting future performance on similar summative tests. A caveat to the use of this approach is that if a summative assessment is to be utilized to assess the degree to which students have developed specific skills or learned academic content, it must reflect that which they have been taught in the classroom. The tacit assumption made when children take such tests is that the students in question have in fact been exposed to the material on which they are being tested (Johnson & Jenkins, 2009) or, as stated in the work of Schmidt and colleagues, been provided with an 'opportunity to learn' (OTL; Schmidt et al, 2011). In countries in which there is a national or state curriculum and where what occurs in the classroom on a daily basis is tightly controlled by central authorities, this assumption is most often satisfied. In situations in which there is a low goodness-of-fit between the content classroom instruction and that of a summative assessment, however, such measures are not a good indicator of the 'learning' that has occurred. This is one reason why teachers have, for years, developed their own summative assessments. Compared with state and district tests, these classroom assessments are more likely to cover the learning targets most recently taught, but they have not been standardized or formally evaluated.

Formative Assessment

Formative assessment provides feedback and information *during and about* the instructional process, throughout the period during which instruction and hopefully learning are taking place. Its purpose is to *monitor student learning*. Formative assessments have been implemented and evaluated most thoroughly when used with students with mild disabilities and students struggling academically or behaviorally (Black & William, 1998; Madison-Harris & Muoneke, 2012). As such, they are often referred to as assessment *for* learning. Formative assessment is characterized by its frequent measurement (e.g. weekly, monthly) and its relatively short administration time, and by the fact that it provides information about student learning, instructional effectiveness and the need to modify instruction to improve student outcomes. Rather than focusing on final learning outcomes, a primary use of formative assessment is to identify areas of both learning and instruction that are in need of improvement. This allows teachers to make more informed decisions with respect to whether and how they may need to redeliver material that students have not understood. Formative assessment provides a linkage between assessment, teaching and learning, as each informs the other (Johnson & Jenkins, 2009; Madison-Harris & Muoneke, 2012). Formative assessment alone has a positive impact on student learning (effect size between .4 and .7) that is larger than many educational interventions (Black & William, 1998). Based on formative assessment, both teachers and learners are provided with feedback that focuses on intended learning, identifies specific strengths and areas needing improvement, and suggests a route of action that can be taken to close the gap between where students are now and where they need to be.

There are myriad formative assessments used in education settings, including: observations during in-class activities; homework exercises; classroom discussions; end-of-unit tests; portfolios; and curriculum-based measurement (Johnson & Jenkins, 2009). In order to be most effective, any form of assessment needs to include a standardized approach to administration and scoring as well as instruction on how to most appropriately and accurately interpret the data that it provides. Unfortunately, although a high degree of formative assessment takes place within the typical classroom, the vast majority of it is informal in nature, with little information available as to whether teachers in the same school, using the same curriculum, and providing instruction at the same grade level are using this assessment approach in a similar manner (Shinn, 2013).

An exception to the informal nature of many formative assessments and an example of a well-researched approach to monitoring student progress with sound psychometric properties is 'curriculum-based measurement' (CBM; Deno, 1985, 2003). CBM was originally developed in the United States at the University of Minnesota to help special education teachers monitor whether their instruction in reading was resulting in student learning. Since then, CBM research and implementation initiatives have expanded into other academic areas, including early literacy, mathematics and written expression (Foegen et al, 2007; McMaster & Espin, 2007; McCormick & Haack, 2010). CBM consists of multiple passages (in reading) or probes (in mathematics and writing) sampled from the curriculum at each grade level that are of equivalent difficulty to be able to measure progress over time. The probes are typically administered weekly or biweekly to students struggling in a specific academic area. Frequent administration is made possible by the measures' short duration (i.e. 1-5 minutes).

From its inception, teachers have been using CBM scores to graph students' progress over time, modify their instruction, and provide additional supports based on the data. Used in this manner, CBM can be utilized to gauge the effectiveness of current instruction for specific groups and subgroups of students. This approach is differentiated from summative approaches to assessment and more informal approaches to formative assessment in that it has established reliability and validity; is sensitive to small changes in performance; is easy to administer and thus can be administered frequently; possesses clearly specified, objective scoring standards; and is inexpensive, time efficient (1-5-minute assessments) as well as unobtrusive to instruction. The outputs of CBM are easy to understand graphic representations of student growth across time that provide information relevant to the effectiveness of instruction with individual students.

Over the past 30 years, CBM measures have been developed and their psychometric properties thoroughly investigated primarily in the United States in the areas of letter naming and letter-sound fluency, oral-reading fluency, reading comprehension (maze), early math fluency, math computation and written expression, such that schools can be assured of their reliability and validity (Deno, 2003; Hosp et al, 2007; Jenkins et al, 2007). A number of commercial versions of assessment systems based on the CBM approach (e.g. EasyCBM, AIMSWeb, DIBELS and FAST) are now available for monitoring the progress of learners in both reading and math, and the assessment approach is now being used as an integral part of the Response to Intervention (RTI) framework. More recently, CBM has also been used for screening of student performance and for predicting their scores on high-stakes assessments (Deno, 2003). Research has demonstrated that regular use of CBM measures is associated with improved academic outcomes for learners, more effective instruction, increased student responsibility for learning, and more effective communication between parents and teachers (Fuchs et al, 1984; Fuchs et al, 1993, 1994; Good et al, 2001; Stecker & Fuchs, 2000).

A form of CBM developed more recently, referred to as 'general outcome measures' (GOMs), was created out of a need to assess specific sub-groups of students using materials other than those taken from the school curriculum (e.g. students in kindergarten and early grades) (Kaminski & Good, 1998), and students with significant cognitive disabilities (Wallace & Tichá, 2012). These sub-groups are typically assessed on their proficiency and progress with respect to their development of basic skills in reading and math rather than in terms of specific curriculum materials. The GOM approach to formative assessment has become popular in education in general with the rise of commercially available packages available online (e.g. AIMSWeb, EasyCBM) from educational organizations that have invested resources in creating sets of grade-level passages from materials sampled across multiple curricula.

Substantial resources have been invested in establishing CBM benchmarks that now make it possible to identify students who are struggling academically in comparison with their peers (Hosp et al, 2007). Similar efforts, however, have been very limited when formative assessments have been used under the auspices of US Agency for International Development (USAID), World Bank or UNESCO funding. In spite of the fact that the concept of using CBM or GOM internationally to aid student learning is a noble goal, the rigor and utility of approaches currently being used needs to be questioned.

Differentiating Formative and Summative Assessment

The main difference between summative and formative assessment lies in the purpose for which it is conducted. Chappuis and Chappuis (2008) make the point that almost any assessment instrument can be used for summative or formative purposes and that the two types of assessment are best differentiated based on how the results are used. Scriven (1967) notes that it is a fallacy to assume that formative and summative represent two types of assessment. Instead, they refer to interpretations of information within two differing time frames – that is, interpretations that can then lead either to changing a program of learning, or to making a statement about student learning at the end of the program. Some instruments, however, on the basis of their design and how quickly feedback can be provided to key stakeholders, are better suited for summative or for formative use. Problems arise either when assessments are used for purposes other than for which they have been designed or when there is little research to support assessments for such use. State and national assessments, for example, are typically designed to provide accountability data and can legitimately be used to compare schools, districts, states and even nations with respect to educational outcomes at a given time. However, they are ill suited to drive instructional decision-making in *the classroom*, and few data exist to support this use of these assessments. Their primary purpose is to compare groups of students with each other (e.g. schools or school districts). In addition, the large majority of these instruments were not developed, nor do they possess the necessary psychometric characteristics, to support their use as measures of *individual student growth*. As a result, although such assessments may be adequate to make long-term policy decisions, they fail to possess a high degree of classroom utility. Paraphrasing Clarke (2001), who used the garden as a metaphor, plants in a garden can be assessed summatively to simply compare their size with other plants, but, in themselves, such measurements do not affect the growth of the plants. *Formative assessment*, on the other hand, serves as an indicator of when there is a need for feeding and watering the plants, and thus leading to directly affecting their growth (Clarke, 2001).

Assessments of Elementary Students in International Contexts

International Assessment of Basic Academic Skills

Currently, there are two large-scale efforts taking place at an international level to assess the basic academic skills (i.e. reading and mathematics) of elementary-level students. The first consists of the Trends in International Mathematics and Science Study (TIMSS) and Progress in International Reading Literacy Study (PIRLS) international assessments overseen by the International Association for the Evaluation of Educational Achievement (IEA). IEA is an international cooperative of national research institutions and governmental research agencies headquartered in the Netherlands whose mission is to carry out comparative research studies in education on an international scale in multiple subject areas. TIMSS has been utilized since 1995 to measure math and science performance among fourth and eighth graders every four years. In 2011, 63 countries participated in the assessment. PIRLS has been used every five years to assess the reading comprehension of fourth graders since 2001. In 2011, students in 49 countries took part in PIRLS (Loveless, 2013).

Students taking TIMSS or PIRLS from developed as well as developing countries represent probability samples using a two-stage stratified cluster design, both at the school and the classroom level. Students are assessed in the primary language of instruction in each country. The tests and their items are carefully constructed, and have established scoring reliability and multiple validity studies to substantiate their use. Data are reported using item response theory (IRT) scaling methods (Kadijevich, 2006; Martin et al, 2006; Marsh et al, 2013).

These large-scale summative assessments possess good psychometric properties, but provide only very general, snapshot-like descriptive comparisons of reading and math performance between countries and regions through the assessment of students within participating countries twice each decade. Data from these assessments are often used by governments to inform national education policies and practices (Grilli et al, 2014).

A second line of effort consists of assessments funded primarily by USAID, the World Bank, UNESCO and UNICEF in response to international education initiatives – namely, Education for All (EFA). The purported overarching goal of these governmental and international agencies is the improvement of education and the quality of life for all children, especially in developing countries where a high percentage of students are from underprivileged backgrounds (Braun & Kanjee, 2006). These organizations contract with large research and service delivery institutions (e.g. Research Triangle International – RTI), whose efforts span many fields and countries. Such institutions have adopted and adapted formative assessments (e.g. CBM) developed at US universities through years of research to maximize their psychometric properties (i.e. reliability and validity) and usability in *the classroom*. The purpose of these assessments, however, has often been altered from that for which they were initially designed, with their use quickly expanded to multiple countries. Implementing organizations all too often have neglected to devote sufficient resources to validate the utilization of these assessments in international contexts that are decidedly different from the educational, cultural and linguistic environments in which they were developed and for which there is clear evidence of effectiveness.

Under the EdData II initiative of USAID and the World Bank, RTI has developed its own version of CBM and GOM measures for reading and math (i.e. Early Grade Reading and Math Assessments (EGRA and EGMA) (Linan-Thompson, 2012). Even though the original function of CBM was for teachers to monitor student academic progress in the classroom (Deno, 1985, 2003), this purpose was dramatically altered when the EGRA system adapted these measures. Gove and Wetterberg (2011) state:

> the EGRA instrument was first developed to be a sample-based 'system diagnostic' measure. Its purpose was to document student performance on early grade reading skills to inform ministries and donors regarding system (including national, state, or district) needs for improving instruction. This system-level version of EGRA was not intended either for direct use by teachers or for screening of individual students. (p. 20)

EGRA and EGMA have been conceptualized for purposes similar to the large international summative assessments, such as TIMSS and PIRSL, to provide governments with an overall picture of student achievement in their country and to compare literacy or numeracy proficiency and performance of students across countries.

NAEP, intended for use in a single country and language, was developed over the course of nine years. EGRA and EGMA protocols on the other hand, which were first rolled out in 2006, have been implemented in over 50 countries and 70 languages in the same period of time (Gove & Wetterberg, 2011). In spite of the head start EGRA developers had in relying on earlier research on CBM, the speed with which these measures have been put into use has resulted in insufficient research being conducted to confirm their psychometric properties. In their report on EGRA and guidelines for implementation, Gove and Wetterberg (2011) and Frazier and Pflepsen (2012) describe a process of adaptation, administration and evaluation of the measures for implementing in their own national and language contexts in countries interested in using EGRA. The fact that such guidelines have been created is commendable. They do not, however, call for an evaluation of the assessments with the necessary research rigor to be able to conclude that they are reliable, valid and sensitive to growth, as has been the tradition in the development of the CBM measures in the United States (Foegen et al, 2007; Wayman et al, 2007). Although it is desirable to provide interested educational staff in developing countries with inexpensive and efficient tools to assess their students, one has to question the quality and meaningfulness of the data that are being presented to and used by stakeholders.

A more recent focus of EGRA has been to use its sub-components for screening, progress-monitoring and instruction modification, the original purpose of the measures adapted for EGRA (i.e. CBM). In only a handful of countries (e.g. Nicaragua), however, have EGRA sub-components been utilized for these purposes through the creation of alternate forms of measures for screening (Linan-Thompson, 2012). Moreover, the available public literature on EGRA suggests that only in Liberia have the measures approached the purpose for which they were originally developed (i.e. to monitor the acquisition of and progress in basic academic skills; Davidson et al, 2011), a purpose for which at least 10 alternate forms of each measure need to be developed, and subsequently evaluated for reliability, validity and sensitivity to growth.

In their extensive review of assessment in an international context, Braun and Kanjee (2006, p. 23) concluded:

> The problematic characteristics of both the technical and substantive aspects of assessments (especially examinations) are a persistent problem in the developing world. The questionable quality of the data collected through the use of unreliable instruments or mediocre administration procedures leads to system inefficiencies and to cynicism among stakeholders. This cynicism is deepened when the integrity of the assessment system is compromised, a widespread phenomenon in many countries.

Looking to the Future: limitations of large-scale assessments

Large-scale efforts at an international level to assess basic academic skills of elementary school students have their place in the world of education. Making between-country comparisons using sound assessment data, such as those which can be gleaned from TIMSS and PIRLS results, can inform national education policies and practices. Assessment initiatives under the auspices of international development, however, often have a more complicated legacy and agenda. In this chapter we have focused on the need to improve such efforts in the context of international development initiatives.

The EFA global initiative has noble goals. In addition, there is a genuine interest among many educators, researchers, parents and policy makers and a tremendous momentum that has been generated toward improving the lives of children in every country, including those in the developing world. Along with such a momentum, there is also a great opportunity for an examination and evaluation of the effectiveness of current assessment systems to support the achievement of EFA goals. It is beyond question that international human development agencies and educational organizations have a genuine desire to improve the outcomes and prospects of children and youth, especially those who are members of marginalized populations. This chapter has attempted to point out some of the shortcomings of assessment efforts taking place on a large scale in developing countries.

When intervening at a societal level, it is tempting to attempt to make as big a difference as possible as quickly as possible. It can be very rewarding and satisfying when this occurs. The impact of most large-scale educational and assessment efforts has, in many respects, fallen short of the intended impact. As described in this chapter, international assessment efforts, primarily as implemented in developing countries, have serious limitations due to a variety of factors. These include: (a) limited investment with respect to resources and efforts to assure that assessments adopted and adapted from other contexts have been adequately evaluated for their psychometric characteristics in each country and language in which they are used; and (b) the fact that large-scale efforts undertaken at considerable cost by international agencies have typically done nothing more than assess the basic literacy and math skills of large numbers of children at a single point. Such efforts have all too often failed to use the assessments they have adapted for the formative functions for which they were intended (i.e. to inform and improve instruction within the classroom).

The outlined limitations of large-scale assessments currently used in international contexts call for specific strategies and serious efforts to remedy them. In the absence of such efforts, large sums of international development funding will continue to be used in a manner that does little to improve the lives of the children and youth for which such support is intended.

The Need for Quality Assessments Validated for their Intended Purpose

Large-scale national efforts in developing countries have used formative assessments (e.g. EGRA) to provide 'snapshots' of educational systems. This is a purpose for which, to date, these assessments have neither been designed nor validated. Based on the information published in international education journals, it appears that, thus far, such efforts have resulted in little substantive impact on the learning of children in these areas of the world. Insufficient resources and effort have been invested to evaluate the reliability, validity and sensitivity to growth of these assessments, nor their linkage with instructional decision-making in the classroom. This has transpired in spite of the fact that there are university faculty worldwide specializing in assessment development and research who have the necessary expertise to ensure that assessments used in national and international contexts have the capacity to produce quality data which make a real difference in instruction.

Recently, several international efforts on a smaller scale in countries such as South Korea (Kim, 2012; Shin, 2012) have been reported that provide a model for studying the best ways to adapt CBM and similar formative assessments to the cultural and linguistic contexts of the country. This limited number of studies has also resulted in the development of benchmarks of student academic performance specific to the country's education system. In India, the Annual Status of Education Report (ASER) assessments (Vagh, 2012) have been developed and evaluated with good psychometric rigor by the ASER Centre, which was established as an autonomous unit within the Pratham network in 2008.

The Need to Utilize Formative Assessments as Originally Intended

Once the formative measures used in international contexts have been sufficiently evaluated for their quality, the next step in improving educational outcomes of students is to scale down mass assessment efforts and refocus resources on the local needs of school districts, schools and instructional staff. Such localized projects focusing on the needs of teachers and school administrators have a higher likelihood of resulting in real improvements in instruction and student learning. Hoffman (2012), in his article 'Standpoints: why EGRA – a clone of DIBELS – will fail to improve literacy in Africa', expressed a similar vision for more localized, evidence-based and accountable international education initiatives in his critique of EGRA. Hoffman points out one of the reasons why efforts to enhance the learning of children in developing countries have often failed. Citing the work of Easterly (2006), who categorized people into 'planners' and 'searchers' to support his contentions, Hoffman states that planners tend to apply global blueprints to local conditions without understanding the local needs. Searchers, on the other hand, study local conditions carefully and utilize local capacity to implement a strategy. To date, it would seem, far more planners than searchers have been involved in international projects designed to enhance the learning outcomes of children in developing countries.

An example of a localized international education effort that in our view is implemented by searchers is a current project funded by the United States–India Educational Foundation – the Obama–Singh 21st Century Knowledge Initiative (OSI): the *Implementation of a Sustainable Response to Intervention Model*. This project, a collaborative effort between the Avinashilingam University for Women in Tamil Nadu India and the University of Minnesota in the United States, focuses on the development and validation of a sustainable Response to Intervention (RTI) model to enhance the learning of all students, including those with disabilities. The goal is to create a small number of model elementary schools with staff trained to administer, interpret and effectively use CBM in reading and mathematics. Assessments, as well as interventions, have been adapted for use in the Tamil Nadu educational and cultural context and are being used for progress monitoring and data-based decision making to improve instruction. As part of the project, local teachers are being trained to use data to guide their implementation of evidence-based instructional strategies in reading and math to help under-performing students close the achievement gap that currently exists with their peers.

Projects such as OSI that invest a substantial proportion of resources in local teachers, school administrators, students and their communities can truly build the capacity of education agencies. Those agencies can, in turn, not only adapt and adopt the assessment systems to determine how their students are performing in relation to age or grade-level peers in other countries, but also utilize acquired skills and understanding to make sound instructional decisions based on formative data to facilitate student progress regardless of the level of proficiency or ability. This includes the development of culturally appropriate instructional programs that both meet the needs of learners and are capable of being implemented with high fidelity given the availability of local resources.

Recommendations

The Education for All (EFA) movement is one of the most important global initiatives to promote and implement instructional strategies for all learners, regardless of gender, socioeconomic status or ability, that provides equitable opportunities to learn. One of its primary goals is to ensure that best practices, backed by state-of-the-art research, are used to educate children and youth. It is clear that, at the current time, the need for EFA goal enforcement is greatest in developing countries. This should not, however, require educators in these countries to settle for instructional and assessment strategies that do not measure up to the highest-quality standards.

In this chapter we echo a plea by Hoffman (2012), who calls for a re-examination of global literacy assessments (e.g. EGRA) and intervention efforts that do not utilize evidence-based and sustainable approaches to literacy suited to local needs.

This chapter reviewed the differences between summative and formative assessment, their intended uses and their misapplications. Based on this examination, it is proposed that a number of changes are needed in our approach to educational assessment at the international level in order to better support the development of literacy and numeracy skills among children and youth. These changes include: (1) investing greater energy and resources to develop *locally validated assessments* that possess robust psychometric characteristics and can be used for formative purposes; and (2) building local capacity to use formative assessments in the manner for which they were initially intended (i.e. to drive instructional decision making). This includes linking the results of formative assessments to culturally and linguistically appropriate instructional strategies that fit the educational needs of local schools and students with diverse abilities. Taking this approach is a logical next step to the development of effective, sustainable teaching and learning in an international context.

It is further proposed that there is a need for the international development community to come together with researchers and educators responsible for the development of assessments and instructional strategies, a proposition similar to the one recently proposed by Hoffman (2012). We believe that the goal of that collaboration should be the generation of a databank of psychometrically sound assessment tools used for their intended purpose and instructional strategies that have undergone a thorough scientific peer-review process, and that comply with national and international evidence-based standards. The fact that 'the need is now' and time is critical is acknowledged. We also appreciate that some in the international development community have a desire to intervene quickly, and at as large a scale as possible, because of their concern about educational inequities that exist across the globe. As researchers, teachers and administrators, however, we need to ensure that the millions of dollars invested in international education are well spent and have the potential to support the achievement of the goals we all support.

References

Biggs, J. & Tang, C. (2007) *Teaching for Quality Learning at University*, 3rd edn. Maidenhead: Society for Research into Higher Education and Open University Press.

Black, P. & William, D. (1998) Inside the Black Box: raising standards through classroom assessment, *Phi Delta Kappan*, 80(2), 139-144, 146-148.

Braun, H. & Kanjee, A. (2006) Using Assessment to Improve Education in Developing Nations, in H. Braun, A. Kanjee, E. Bettinger & M. Kremer (Eds) *Improving Education through Assessment, Innovation, and Evaluation*. Cambridge, MA: American Academy of Arts and Sciences.

Chappuis, S. (2005) Is Formative Assessment Losing its Meaning?, *Education Week*, 24(44), 38.

Chappuis, S. & Chappuis, J. (2008) The Best Value in Formative Assessment, *Informative Assessment*, 65(4), 14-19.

Clarke, S. (2001) *Unlocking Formative Assessment*. Philadelphia: Trans-Atlantic Publications.

Davidson, M., Korda, M. & Collins, O.W. (2011) Teachers' Use of EGRA for Continuous Assessment: the case of EGRA Plus: Liberia, in A. Gove & A. Wetterberg (Eds) *The Early Grade Reading Assessment: applications and interventions to improve basic literacy*, pp. 113-138. Research Triangle Park, NC: RTI International.

Deno, S.L. (1985) Curriculum-based Measurement: the emerging alternative, *Exceptional Children*, 52, 219-232.

Deno, S.L. (2003) Developments in Curriculum-based Measurement, *Journal of Special Education*, 37(3), 184-192. http://dx.doi.org/10.1177/00224669030370030801

Easterly, W. (2006) *The White Man's Burden: why the West's efforts to aid the rest have done so much ill and so little good*. New York: Penguin.

Foegen, A., Jiban, C. & Deno, S.L. (2007) Progress Monitoring Measures in Mathematics: a review of the literature, *Journal of Special Education*, 41, 121-139. http://dx.doi.org/10.1177/00224669070410020101

Frazier, J. & Pflepsen, A. (2012) Tools & Tips for Planning and Implementing an Early Grade Reading Assessment. https://www.eddataglobal.org/reading/

Fuchs, L.S., Deno, S.L. & Mirkin, P.K. (1984) Effects of Frequent Curriculum-based Measurement of Evaluation on Pedagogy, Student Achievement, and Student Awareness of Learning, *American Educational Research Journal*, 21, 449-460. http://dx.doi.org/10.3102/00028312021002449

Fuchs, L.S., Fuchs, D. & Hamlett, C.L. (1993) Technological Advances Linking the Assessment of Students' Academic Proficiency to Instructional Planning, *Journal of Special Education Technology*, 12, 49-62.

Fuchs, L.S., Fuchs, D. & Hamlett, C.L. (1994) Strengthening the Connection between Assessment and Instructional Planning with Expert Systems, *Exceptional Children*, 61, 138-146.

Good, R.H., Simmons, D.C. & Kameenui, E.J. (2001) The Importance and Decision Making Utility of a Continuum of Fluency-based Indicators of Foundational Reading Skills for Third Grade High Stakes Outcomes, *Scientific Studies of Reading*, 5(3), 257-288. http://dx.doi.org/10.1207/S1532799XSSR0503_4

Gove, A. & Wetterberg, A. (2011) The Early Grade Reading Assessment: an introduction, in A. Gove & A. Wetterberg (Eds) *The Early Grade Reading Assessment: applications and interventions to improve basic literacy*, pp. 1-38. Research Triangle Park, NC: RTI International.

Grilli, L., Pennoni, F., Rampichini & Romeo, I. (2014) Exploiting TIMSS and PIRLS Combined Data: multivariate multilevel modelling of student achievement. Paper presented at the VI European Congress of Methodology, Utrecht, Netherlands, July.

Hanna, G.S. & Dettmer, P.A. (2004) *Assessment for Effective Teaching: using context-adaptive planning*. Boston, MA: Pearson A&B.

Hoffman, J.V. (2012) Standpoints: why EGRA – a clone of DIBELS – will fail to improve literacy in Africa, *Research in the Teaching of English*, 46(4), 340-357.

Hosp, M.K, Hosp, J.L. & Howell, K.W. (2007) *The ABCs of CBM*. New York: Guilford Press.

Jenkins, J.R., Hudson, R.F. & Lee, S.H. (2007) Using CBM-Reading Assessments to Monitor Progress, *Perspectives on Language and Literacy*, 33(2). http://www.rtinetwork.org/essential/assessment/progress/usingcbm

Johnson, E. & Jenkins, J. (2009) Formative and Summative Assessment. http://www.education.com/reference/article/formative-and-summative-assessment/

Kadijevich, D. (2006) Developing Trustworthy TIMSS Background Measures: a case study on mathematics attitude, *The Teaching of Mathematics*, 9(2), 41-51.

Kaminski, R.A. & Good, R.H. (1998) Assessing Early Literacy Skills in a Problem-solving Model: dynamic indicators of basic early literacy skills, in M.R. Shinn (Ed.) *Advanced Applications of Curriculum-based Measurement*, pp. 113-142. New York: Guilford Press.

Kim, D. (2012) Current Status of Curriculum-based Measurement in Korea, in C.A. Espin, K.L. McMaster, S. Rose & M.M. Wayman (Eds) *A Measure of Success: the influence of curriculum-based measurement on education*, pp. 307-314. Minneapolis: University of Minnesota Press.

Linan-Thompson, S. (2012) Expanding the Use of Curriculum-based Measurement: a look at Nicaragua, in C.A. Espin, K.L. McMaster, S. Rose & M.M. Wayman (Eds) *A Measure of Success: the influence of curriculum-based measurement on education*, pp. 321-328. Minneapolis: University of Minnesota Press.

Loveless, T. (2013) How Well Are American Students Learning? Washington, DC: Brookings Institution Brown Center on Education Policy. http://www.brookings.edu/research/reports/2013/03/18-brown-center-report-loveless

Madison-Harris, R. & Muoneke, A. (2012) Using Formative Assessment to Improve Student Achievement in the Core Content Areas. Southeast Comprehensive Center at SEDL. http://secc.sedl.org/resources/briefs/formative_assessment_core_content/Formative_Assessment.pdf

Marsh, H.W., Abduljabbar, A.S., Abu-Hilal, M.M., et al(2013) Factorial, Convergent, and Discriminant Validity of TIMSS Math and Science Motivation Measures: a comparison of Arab and Anglo-Saxon countries, *Journal of Educational Psychology*, 105(1), 108-128. http://dx.doi.org/10.1037/a0029907

Martin, M.O., Mullis, I.V.S. & Kennedy, A.M. (2006) PIRLS 2006 Technical Report. Boston, MA: TIMSS & PIRLS International Study Center.

McCormick, C.E. & Haack, R. (2010) Early Literacy Individual Growth and Development Indicators (El-igdis) as Predictors of Reading Skills in Kindergarten through Second Grade, *International Journal of Psychology: A Biopsychosocial Approach*, 7, 29-40.

McMaster, K.L. & Espin, C. (2007) Technical Features of Curriculum-based Measurement in Writing: a literature review, *Journal of Special Education*, 41(2), 68-84. Http://dx.doi.org/10.1177/00224669070410020301

Mentkowski, M. (1999) *Learning that Lasts*. San Francisco: Jossey-Bass.

No Child Left Behind (NCLB) Act (2001) Pub. L. No. 107-110, § 115, Stat. 1425 (2002).

Schmidt, W.H., Cogan, L. & Houang, R. (2011) The Role of Opportunity to Learn in Teacher Preparation: an international context, *Journal of Teacher Education*, 62(2) 138-153.

Scriven, M. (1967) The Methodology of Evaluation, in R. Tyler, R. Gagne & M. Scriven, *Perspectives on Curriculum Evaluation*. AERA Monograph Series – Curriculum Evaluation. Chicago: Rand McNally.

Shin, J. (2012) Footprints of Curriculum-based Measurement in South Korea: past, present, and future, in C.A. Espin, K.L. McMaster, S. Rose & W.M. Wayman (Eds) *A Measure of Success: the influence of Curriculum-based measurement on education*, pp. 315-320. Minneapolis: University of Minnesota Press.

Shinn, M.R. (2013) *Measuring General Outcomes: a critical component in scientific and practical progress monitoring practices*. Pearson: Aimsweb. Http://www.aimsweb.com/Wp-content/uploads/Mark-Shinn-gom_Master-Monitoring-White-paper.pdf

Stecker, P.M. & Fuchs, L.S. (2000) Effecting Superior Achievement Using Curriculum-based Measurement: the importance of individual progress monitoring, *Learning Disability Research and Practice*, 15, 128-134. Http://dx.doi.org/10.1207/SLDRP1503_2

Vagh, S.B. (2012) *Validating the ASER Testing Tools: comparisons with reading fluency measures and the Read India measures*. New Delhi: Pratham, ASER Centre.

Wallace, T. & Tichá, R. (2012) Extending Curriculum-based Measurement to Assess Performance of Students with significant disabilities, in C.A. Espin, K.L. McMaster, S. Rose & W.M. Wayman (Eds) *A Measure of Success: the influence of Curriculum-based measurement on education*, pp. 211-224. Minneapolis: University of Minnesota Press.

Wayman, M.M., Wallace, T., Wiley, H.I., Tichá, R. & Espin, C.A. (2007) Literature Synthesis on Curriculum-based Measurement in Reading, *Journal of Special Education*, 41(2), 85-120. Http://dx.doi.org/10.1177/00224669070410020401

Wixcon, K.K. & Valencia, S.W. (2011) Assessment in RTI: what teachers and specialists need to know, *The Reading Teacher*, 64(6), 466-469. Http://dx.doi.org/10.1598/RT.64.6.13

CHAPTER 10

Questioning across the Spectrum: pedagogy, selection examinations and assessment systems in low-income countries[1]

ANTHONY SOMERSET

ABSTRACT This chapter presents an overview of the spectrum of contexts in which questioning is employed to assess student learning, ranging from the grassroots level of the classroom to the central level of the national examinations authority and the national or international assessment agency. The respective roles of formative and summative questioning are compared, and an example of the effective use of formative questioning in the development of problem-solving skills discussed. Following an analysis of the negative backwash effects of low-quality, high-stakes selection examinations on the quality of classroom pedagogy, the chapter concludes with suggestions as to how various initiatives, across the full assessment spectrum, could contribute to the strengthening of student learning, in low-income countries especially.

Introduction

Selection examinations have a deep history. They were first employed in China well over a millennium ago, as a means of selecting recruits to the imperial civil service on the basis of their scholastic achievement rather than through patronage. Acceptance of the new system, however, was far from universal: almost from its inception, critics complained that the examinations tested only the power to memorise, not the capacity to understand or to solve problems (Dore, 1976).

Identical charges are frequently levelled against contemporary national selection examinations but, nevertheless, they remain an integral component of most formal education systems.[2] In low-income countries especially they are often deeply entrenched, largely because competition for the well-rewarded opportunities to which they control access is so intense.

National selection examinations focus mainly on measuring performance at the student level, whereas, by contrast, assessment studies focus on performance at the system or sub-system level. They are of comparatively recent origin. The first international assessment study, of mathematics achievement in 12 developed countries, was conducted during the 1960s (Husen, 1967). Similar assessments of science and literacy followed in the ensuing decade. With powerful advocacy from the World Bank and other donor agencies (Lockheed & Verspoor, 1991; Greaney & Kellagan, 1996), the number of countries participating in international learning assessments, or running their own national assessment studies, escalated rapidly over the final decade of the old millennium and the first decade of the new one (Kamens & McNeely, 2009). In 2012, as many as 65 countries and economies – 31 of them from outside the Organisation for Economic Co-operation and Development (OECD) – took part in the fifth round of testing for the Programme for International Student Assessment (PISA); while between 1995 and 2013, nearly 150 countries conducted a total of more than 1000 national assessment studies (UNESCO, 2015). The great majority of the studies, both international and national, have focused on three core curriculum areas: language (or literacy), mathematics (or numeracy) and science. These striking trends have given rise to concerns that the emergent global testing culture may lead to a narrowing of curriculum objectives, and to a reductionist acceptance of quantitative test scores as sufficient measures of educational quality (Goldstein, 2004; Sahlberg, 2011).

Selection examinations and assessment systems differ in many respects, but they share an important feature in common. In both, a central authority is responsible for all the major professional activities: for setting the questions, for evaluating students' responses, and for analysing and reporting the results. Skill in the asking of questions, however, is an essential component in the repertoire of all education professionals, as important for the classroom teacher working at the periphery, in an isolated rural school, as it is for the testing specialist working at a national or international centre.

This chapter attempts a preliminary scanning across this broad assessment spectrum. The analysis draws on two studies carried out and published in the Philippines (see Somerset et al, 1999; Somerset, 2002). Neither report is readily available elsewhere. But it also draws, to a much greater degree, on 'tacit' knowledge (Erault, 2000) built up incrementally over the course of five decades of experience as an educational practitioner, initially in East Africa and more recently in South and South-East Asia.

Questioning across the Spectrum

Educators ask questions for two main sets of reasons: formative and summative. Formative assessment is prospective. It aims at informing future pedagogy by probing students' current levels of understanding, identifying any misconceptions which need to be tackled, and providing stimulus for further learning (Wiliam, 2011). It is essentially a 'soft' activity, concerned with guiding the learning process and offering remedial support to those needing it.

Summative assessment, on the other hand, is retrospective. It aims at measuring learning already achieved, often with the purpose of grading students along a performance scale, sometimes as a basis for promotion or selection decisions. Summative assessment is also frequently used as a tool for appraising the effectiveness of teachers, principals, local education managers – or even entire national systems. It is essentially a 'hard' activity, concerned with making judgements as to relative success or failure – judgements which, in low-income countries especially, often have profound consequences for the futures of those being judged.

Questioning activities, both formative and summative, take place in a variety of different contexts. In Figure 1 these are arranged along a spectrum, according to the period of time which elapses before feedback from the questioning is available. To the left side of the spectrum are 'grassroots' assessment activities which take place in the 'black box' of the classroom (Black & Wiliam, 1998). These include oral questions asked during teaching and learning, mainly by the teacher but also by students, and written questions set in teacher-constructed tests. Feedback from these activities is rapid. The teacher knows the students' responses immediately or almost immediately.

Immediate feedback ←――――――――――――――――――――――――――――→ **Delayed feedback**

Questions during teaching & learning	Questions at end of lesson	Questions in class-, school-level tests	Questions in national examinations	Questions in national assessment studies	Questions in international assessment studies
Oral *Asked by teacher & students*	*Oral, written* *Asked by teacher & students*	*Mainly written* *Set by teacher(s)*	*Mainly written* *National setters*	*Written* *National/int. setters*	*Written* *International setters*
Formative: *-Construction of concepts, skills* *-Identification, remediation of misconceptions*	**Formative:** *-Reinforcement of concepts, skills* *-Identification, remediation of misconceptions*	**Formative:** *-Reflection on, modification of practice*	**Formative:** *-Exam. feedback reports (topic, question-level analysis)*	**Formative:** *-Nat. assess. reports (topic-, question-level analysis)*	**Formative:** *Int. assess. reports (topic-, question-level analysis)*
Summative: *Should not be used summatively*	**Summative:** *Should not be used summatively*	**Summative:** *-Record of achievement (students)*	**Summative:** *-Selection (students)* *- Accountability (teachers, principals)*	**Summative:** *-Accountability (local managers)*	**Summative:** *-Accountability (central managers, politicians)*

Figure 1. A spectrum of assessment activities.

To the right side are centrally managed assessment activities: questions asked in national examinations, and in national and international assessment systems. Feedback is delayed, with results from national examinations generally not known for several months, while in assessment systems the delay may be up to two years or more.

The number of assessment categories shown is of course to some degree arbitrary. Additional boxes could be added, or existing boxes combined. For example, a case could be made for inserting an additional box at the centre of the spectrum, to include questions set in local-level examinations. These examinations are features of many education systems, particularly in low-income countries.

The quality of questioning during classroom transactions, and in class- and school-based testing (left side), has massive effects on the levels of competence displayed in national examinations and in national and international assessment studies (right side). However, in many low-income countries, relatively little attention is paid to strengthening these 'left-side' assessment activities. I discuss these activities in more detail in the next section, before switching our attention to 'right-side' activities, at the national and international levels, in the section that follows.

'Left-side' Activities:
assessment at the classroom and school levels

Activities at all points along the assessment spectrum can and should generate formative feedback of various kinds. Towards the left side, however, feedback originating from teaching and learning activities, and from informal testing at the end of a learning session, should not be used summatively. Students should not be judged by the mistakes they make during the learning process: if they are, they will be inhibited from responding to the teacher's questions, or from initiating questions of their own. In consequence, communication between teacher and students will be reduced towards a one-way flow, and the construction of meaningful concepts, and effective skills, placed in jeopardy.

Head teachers, education managers and parents can on occasion be insistent that teachers produce 'results' – by which they generally mean lists of test scores, ranking the students in performance order. The skilled teacher will delay making such summative assessments for as long as it is practicable.

It can be argued, in fact, that at the classroom level there is an inescapable tension between the teacher's formative and summative roles. If she is an effective practitioner, her main concern will be to ensure that as many of her students as possible grasp the concepts, or master the skills, she is aiming to develop. But to the extent that she is successful, the scores will bunch towards the top end, making it increasingly difficult for her to differentiate among them along a summative performance scale. If, on the other hand, many of her students perform poorly, she will regard it as being as much her own failure as theirs and she will renew her formative and remedial efforts rather than rushing to judgement.

One-way and Two-way Pedagogy

Effective use of students' responses for formative purposes is, however, not often seen during classroom observations in many, if not most, low-income countries. At the primary level especially, 'one-way' pedagogy, from the teacher to the students, is the dominant mode. The teacher is the expert transmitter of knowledge and the students are the passive, and largely undifferentiated, recipients. 'Two-way', or 'dialogic', pedagogy (Alexander 2008a,b), in which, by contrast, teacher and students engage jointly in the construction of meaning through dialogue, is much less frequently encountered.[3]

The closest the students are likely to come to active engagement in lessons based on one-way pedagogy is through the chanted response. The teacher asks a question, typically demanding no more than straightforward recall of previously memorised knowledge, or, in mathematics, a well-drilled formula or number bond. The students respond in chorus:

Teacher: The capital city of Kenya is...
Students: Nairobi.

When the question cannot be answered directly from recall but requires a little thought, the teacher sometimes provides a cue:

Teacher: Nineteen minus six equals thir...
Students: ...teen.

Provided the sound she hears is loud enough, the teacher is likely to be satisfied. Often, however, the response will have come from a relatively small group of students, typically those seated near the front. Other students, especially those seated around the margins of the classroom furthest from the teacher, may well have remained silent.[4]

Akyeampong and his colleagues (2013) characterise the situation in sub-Saharan Africa as follows:

> Discourse analysis of classroom teaching and learning ... generally shows the African teacher as an authoritarian classroom figurehead who expects students to listen and memorize correct answers or procedures rather than to construct knowledge themselves. (Akyeampong et al, 2013)

Likewise Hardman and his colleagues (2012):

> In common with other sub-Saharan African countries, the comparatively few studies that have been carried out into classroom pedagogy in Tanzanian primary schools show a teacher-

dominated discourse promoting rote learning and recitation ... Helping teachers to transform classroom talk into a purposeful and productive dialogue ... is therefore seen as being fundamental to improving the quality of primary education. (Hardman et al, 2012)

One-way pedagogy is also common in many low- and middle-income countries in Asia. In a teacher-needs study carried out in 15 secondary schools in the central Philippines (Somerset et al, 1999), a total of 59 science and mathematics lessons were observed, each taught by a different teacher, and their pedagogy rated along a five-point scale, with each point anchored against a description of typical teacher behaviour. All the teachers, without exception, were college graduates.[5] Table I shows summary results.[6]

Rating	Teachers
1. Pure one-way pedagogy: teacher makes no attempt to monitor students' learning during lesson through oral questioning	2 (3%)
2. Predominantly one-way pedagogy: teacher accepts choral answers to questions. Makes no attempt to check individual students' understanding	19 (32%)
3. Teacher directs some questions to individual students, but does not use the students' responses formatively	20 (34%)
4. Partial two-way pedagogy: teacher directs many or most questions to individual students, but only occasionally uses the students' responses formatively	10 (17%)
5. Full two-way pedagogy: effective dialogue between teacher and students in the construction of knowledge and concepts	8 (14%)

Table I. Pedagogy in the central Philippines:
ratings of 59 secondary mathematics and science teachers.
Source: Somerset et al, 1999, pp. 22-23.

All the teachers except two asked at least some questions during their lessons, but as many as one-third always accepted choral responses. They thus received no feedback from which they could assess the progress of individual students. A further one-third did direct some of their questions to individual students, but made no attempt to use their responses formatively – apart from indicating whether the response was correct or incorrect. Fewer than one teacher in six engaged her students fully in two-way communication, using their responses as building blocks in the construction of knowledge, concepts or skills.

Brief extracts from the record of the lesson taught by one of these outstanding teachers are given below. Practising dialogic pedagogy from the outset, she extracted a formative message from almost every student response – correct as well as incorrect. Throughout the lesson the teacher distributed her questions widely, always asking an individual student after it was posed, and never accepting a choral response. Moreover, the bulk of the questions she asked concerned the decision-making steps in problem solving rather than the routine calculations, and thus challenged the students to think. When routine, well-practised calculations were needed, she left the students to carry out the work unaided. The crux of the lesson came as the class began to tackle the third problem. The first two problems had involved essentially the same procedure: calculating the areas of the two component figures and summing them. If the students had simply memorised this procedure without understanding it, they would almost certainly have tried to apply it to the third problem without modification. In the event, however, virtually the whole class saw the need to change the operation, from addition to subtraction. Their excitement as they reached this insight for themselves, without help from the teacher, was palpable. The classroom had become a pedagogical field which was neither teacher-centred nor student-centred, but learning-centred.

Extract 1. Effective formative questioning in the development of mathematics problem-solving skills

The Grade 7 lesson was at 2 p.m. on a hot afternoon, but the teacher's lively approach soon dispelled drowsiness. We started with rapid revision. Holding up a cardboard template of a square, the teacher asked:

T: Here is a square of dimension 10 cm. What is its area?
S1: 100cm.
T: Is that right?
S2: No, it's $100cm^2$
T: Yes, when we are measuring area we must not forget the measure is squared
T: Here is a triangle. Its base is 10 cm, and its height is 12 cm. What is its area?
S3: $60\ cm^2$
T: Yes. How did Mark get $60\ cm^2$?
S4: The area of the triangle is base times half height

In similar fashion, the teacher reviewed the formulae for the areas of three more plane figures: rectangle, parallelogram and circle. With the scaffolding in place, the new learning began.
The teacher produced a cardboard template of a rectangle, coloured yellow, with a purple semi-circle attached to one of its shorter sides. The diameter of the semi-circle and the side of the rectangle matched exactly.

T: Now we are going to find the area of this figure. Can you tell me what we will do?

S5: *The formula for the area of a rectangle ...*
T: *(Interrupting). No, I don't want the formula. Just tell me what we are going to do*
S6: *Add the area of the rectangle to the area of the semi-circle*

The dialogue continued, until the sequence of steps needed to calculate the area of the total figure had been established. Then, *and only then,* the teacher supplied dimensions:

T: *Now let's put in some numbers. The length of the rectangle is 300 cm and the width 200 cm*

There was some confusion as to the difference between the radius and the diameter of the semi-circle, but this was soon resolved, again with the help of a student response. With the full sequence of calculations displayed on the chalkboard, the teacher told the students to complete the task individually, and gave no further help. About half finished within five minutes.

The teacher then introduced a second figure similar to the first: a rectangle with a triangle adjoining its length. The students had little difficulty transferring the procedure they had just followed to the new figure.

However with a third figure the teacher posed a new task, requiring a new procedure. Holding up a square with a circle inscribed inside, the circumference touching the four sides, she asked:

T: *This time I've got a square, and I'm going to cut a circle from it. How can we work out the area of the pieces that will be wasted?*

There was the briefest of pauses as the students considered this new problem. Then a forest of hands shot up.

S: *We will calculate the area of the square and subtract the area of the circle*
T: *Is she right?*
Students (in chorus, for the only time during the lesson): YES!

The Impact of One-way Pedagogy

The lesson just discussed was of course exceptional. In the bulk of the lessons observed, formative questioning was rare, or absent altogether – as is indeed also the case in many classrooms in other low-income countries. The consequences for student achievement were strongly suggested by results from another component of the same Philippines study. During the 15 secondary school visits, a test of basic number skills was administered to randomly selected samples of 360 eighth-grade and 207 tenth-grade students (Somerset, 2002). The test, based on the primary curriculum, consisted of three main sections: number values and estimation; mechanical arithmetic; and number problem solving.

The responses indicated widespread misunderstanding of basic number concepts or, in the case of the number problems, systematic errors in setting up a valid sequence of steps for reaching the solution. Moreover, these misconceptions were often as common, or nearly as common, among the tenth-grade students, in their final year of secondary schooling, as they were among more junior students in the eighth grade.

In the number values section of the test, for example, where students were asked to rearrange groups of three numbers in ascending value order, there were major misconceptions with decimal number values. Table II sets out the response patterns for two items.

	Question 5c (0.55 0.8 0.14) Response	Grade 8 % n = 360	Grade 10 % n = 207	Question 5h (0.438 0.4 0.44) Response	Grade 8 % n = 360	Grade 10 % n = 207
1	0.14 0.55 0.8 (correct)	4	13	0.4 0.438 0.44 (correct)	3	9
2	0.8 0.14 0.55 (DPI error)	83	73	0.4 0.44 0.438 (DPI error)	84	73
3	0.55 0.14 0.8 (ROD error)	10	12	0.438 0.44 0.4 (ROD error)	9	16
4	All other responses	3	2	All other responses	4	2

DPI: decimal point ignored. ROD: reverse order with decimals.

Table II. Misconceptions in ordering decimal numbers (smallest to largest).
Source: Somerset (2002).

Among the Grade 8 students, the proportion of correct responses to both questions was less than one in 20 – well below the level they would have achieved if they had guessed at random (one in six). But few students did in fact guess – the great majority worked to a consistent, but flawed, conception of decimal number values. More than four-fifths evaluated the decimal numbers as if they were whole numbers, ignoring the decimal point (the DPI error), while around one in ten evaluated them in the reverse direction to the whole-number order (the ROD error).[7] The most frequent source of this latter, more 'advanced' misconception is that students generalise from their knowledge of fractional values. Having learned that, for example, the fraction

¼ is smaller than ½, they argue, by flawed analogy, that the decimal fraction 0.4 is smaller than 0.2.[8]

Aside from their prevalence, the most salient feature of these misconceptions – in this Philippines sample at least – is their *persistence*. Between Grade 8 and Grade 10, progress towards eliminating the misconceptions is only marginal. Despite the fact that they had all completed three years of secondary mathematics education, only about one in eight of the Grade 10 students could evaluate decimal numbers correctly – a competency they should have acquired while still at primary school. Their teachers had clearly focused on 'delivering' the secondary curriculum, leaving these and many other basic misconceptions to persist, undetected and uncorrected. Few of them can have employed formative questioning as a pedagogical tool. The consequences for their students' progress and performance – in the science subjects as well as in mathematics – must have been substantial.

'Right-side' Activities:
assessment at the national and international levels

In the previous section I discussed grassroots activities, on the left side of the assessment spectrum, stressing the essential contribution of formative assessment to effective knowledge construction and skills acquisition in the classroom. I now switch to centrally directed 'right-side' activities, including national examination systems and assessment systems, both national and international.

Table III compares characteristics of national examinations systems, as they function in low-income countries, with those of the main international assessment systems. National assessment systems are more varied than the international systems, so fewer generalisations can be made about them. Although listed separately, many of the points of comparison link to each other. At least two major clusters can be identified, the first centred on issues of resourcing, the second on the contrasted profile of consequences which stem from the results of examinations and of assessment systems for the various stake-holding groups.

Resources

In most if not all low-income countries, national examination systems function under severe resource constraints, both financial and professional. Candidates' fees are often the main – sometimes the only – source of income, while staff with the skills needed to carry out the essential professional work are often in critically short supply.

A recent article outlines the current situation in Kenya:

> When the ... Kenya National Examinations Council [was established] in 1980, it was a relatively small organisation,

responsible for only four major examinations. Its total professional staff numbered fewer than 25. ... Over the past three decades, however, the scope and scale of the Council's work has expanded massively. In 2011 it ran as many as 18 examinations, made up of no fewer than 1893 papers, and examined a total of 1.47 million candidates.

... [T]he effect of such expansion has been to place the Council's professional skill resources under increased strain. The pressures generated by the annual examinations cycle are relentless ... In the Test Development Division especially, these pressures have meant that senior staff must devote themselves increasingly to urgent, but essentially routine, tasks: editing draft examination papers, supervising security printing ... In consequence, less time is available for their core professional function: the development of high-quality test instruments. Many test development officers play little or no part in writing examination questions; some do not even participate in moderation meetings. (Wasanga & Somerset, 2013)

	National Examination Systems (in low-income countries)	International Assessment Systems (PISA, TIMSS, PIRLS)
Geographical scope	Generally confined to a single national state. Exceptions include the West African and Caribbean Examinations Councils	International; participation skewed towards high-income countries, but low-income countries becoming increasingly involved. Some low-income countries participate in regional systems (e.g. SACMEQ)
Core purposes	(a) To *select* students for desirable opportunities, in continued education, training, or employment (b) to *monitor* performance differences among schools/districts/regions as an *accountability* tool	(a) To *monitor* trends in international cognitive achievement, among countries and over time (b) To identify *best educational practices* on the basis of associations between national performance levels and the organisation, management and delivery of education in the participating countries.

Subject coverage	Most curriculum subjects examined	Focus on 'key' subjects: literacy, numeracy, science
Results	Main focus on *student-level* results. Performance of school/districts may also be compared	Main focus on *system-* or *subsystem-level* results (national or regional mean scores; scatter of means among schools/regions)
	Question-level analysis in some countries (formative feedback)	Some question-level analysis, but subordinate to comparative analysis of total scores
	Fairly rapid release of results (typically 2 to 6 months)	Slower release of results (typically 1 to 3 years)
Professional and financial resources	Generally under-resourced. Usually funded, partly or wholly, from candidates' fees. Professional staff with question-writing skills often in short supply. 'Setter fatigue'.	Much better resourced. High-income participating countries carry local costs. International organizations contribute professional support, and subsidise participation of some low-income countries.
Quality of questions	*Variable*, but often *low* in *low-income countries*. Substantial proportion of lower-order recall questions; Infrequent and ineffective use of graphics	*High*. Substantial proportion of questions testing higher-order thinking skills; frequent and effective use of graphics
Testing cycle	*Annual*	*Periodic*: once every 3 to 5 years
Release of questions	*Immediate and complete.* Teachers and principals have access to all questions as soon as examination paper completed	*Delayed and partial.* Majority of questions kept confidential; minority released only after time delay
Consequences: (a) for pupils	*High* stakes. Life chances may depend on performance	*Zero* stakes. Results not analysed at pupil level

(b) for teachers, principals, local school managers	*Fairly high* stakes. School/district performance may be used for accountability purposes, and affect career prospects	*Zero* stakes. Samples too small for analysis at school/district level
(c) for central policymakers/politicians	*Low or zero* stakes, especially when examination grades are standardised or norm-referenced	*High* stakes. Ranking in international assessment league tables has major consequences for national prestige: 'PISA shock'.
Students tested	*Population-based*: all students in final year of major schooling cycle (primary, secondary)	*Sample-based*: only a small proportion of students tested; generally from intermediate year of schooling cycle
Backwash effects on quality of pedagogy	*Strong.* Teachers teach to the examination, to which they have immediate access. Hence quality of questions has major impact on quality of pedagogy, especially in examination grade	*Weak.* Many teachers never see test questions nor results, especially in low-income countries. Results have impact on classroom practice only if transmitted and interpreted by teacher support system

Table III. National examinations and international assessment systems: some comparisons.

The quality of national examinations in low-income countries is often severely affected by these time pressures and resource constraints. Low-demand questions, requiring students to do no more than reproduce remembered facts, in unchanged form, can be set quickly and without great professional skill. By contrast, the construction of high-demand questions, which go beyond simple recall and require students to demonstrate thinking skills, is both professionally challenging and time consuming.[9] As a result, recall questions often predominate in these examinations, while thinking-skill questions are typically few in number, or absent altogether. For the same reasons, questions testing similar or even identical content tend to be repeated, year after year.

The assessment systems, on the other hand, operate in relatively resource-rich environments. They are funded by contributions from the participating, often high-income, countries and they can draw on the substantial professional skills of international panels of testing and measurement specialists for the construction of questions. To anyone who has ever struggled to produce a set of questions tapping higher-order thinking skills rather than recall, the overall quality of the questions employed in the international assessment systems is impressive indeed.

The test developers for the international assessment systems benefit further from working to a relatively leisurely time cycle – generally one of three or four years. They are thus spared the time pressures which confront their counterparts working to the annual cycle of national examination systems. Moreover, only a small proportion of the questions they write are released after the assessment cycle. The majority are kept confidential, and hence available for re-use in subsequent cycles. Examination questions, by contrast, enter the public domain on the day the candidates sit for the exam, and so must be replaced each year.

Consequences

The second group of contrasts between examination and assessment systems centres on the very different consequences they have for the various stakeholding groups: the participating students, their teachers, school principals, local and national education managers, and national politicians.

National examination systems are population based. In virtually all low-income countries all students are required to sit at least one – often two or even three – centrally administered examinations as they pass through the successive cycles of the education system. Furthermore, these examinations nearly always have selection functions. Perhaps because there is no other indicator available, examination performance is widely regarded as the fairest, most objective measure of student 'merit', and is thus commonly used as the main criterion – often the only criterion – for allocating the most desirable opportunities in the subsequent education cycle, or in the job market.

Hence, national examinations carry major consequences for the life chances of the students sitting them. A student who successfully surmounts all the examination barriers in a low-income country and emerges with a tertiary-level qualification in a subject for which there is labour-market demand can anticipate lifetime earnings many times – or many tens of times – higher than another who falls at the first hurdle.

National examinations also carry substantial stakes for teachers and principals, albeit not as high as those for their students. Schools which perform well gain a reputation for excellence, and their staff are likely to be rewarded, in terms of enhanced career prospects – or at least enhanced prestige. For managers, policymakers and politicians functioning at the centre, however, national examinations are generally low stakes, or sometimes even zero stakes. There will be concern if performance levels appear to be declining from year to year, but in many systems such changes are masked by standardisation or norm-referenced grading.

But with assessment systems, by contrast, this stakes hierarchy is reversed. The international systems, and most of the national systems, are based on the testing of samples – generally light samples – rather than whole populations. In any particular locality, the students from no more than one or two schools chosen at random are likely to be included. Hence at the grassroots the tests are low stakes: both for the participating students and for their teachers, no consequences of any importance follow from relative success or failure. Perceptions are very different, however, among the decision makers, power wielders and communicators at the centre. When the findings from any international assessment study (but particularly a PISA study) are published, they receive wide publicity and close scrutiny – although it is the one-dimensional league tables which get the bulk of the attention. Any evidence that the country is slipping in the global rankings is likely to be seen as a blow to national prestige – even, on occasion, as a harbinger of long-term national decline. 'PISA shock' has become a recognised syndrome – even in countries which perform relatively well, such as Japan (Takeyama, 2008).

The disjunction between perceptions at the centre and at the periphery has led to some curious effects. In an attempt to raise the motivational stakes for the grassroots participants, the authorities in Scotland showed students a PISA-preparation video entitled 'Scotland expects'; meanwhile, 'the Welsh Government ... has asked schools to teach to the PISA test in order to raise the standing of Wales in the global league tables of PISA performance' (Schweisfurth, 2015).[10]

There is no need for such motivational messages with national examinations. Given the high stakes they carry both for students and for teachers, they are powerful determinants of the delivered curriculum. Teachers are adept at reading the signals the examination questions convey, and in modifying their classroom strategies accordingly. These backwash effects are strongest during the final year running up to the examination, but are often apparent throughout the preceding education cycle. Both content and pedagogy are affected. No matter how prominently a particular knowledge domain may feature in the formal curriculum, it will receive scant attention in the classroom if it has not featured in the national examination for some time.

But the effects on pedagogy are more profound – and potentially more damaging. An examination paper made up predominantly of low-demand questions testing straightforward recall – or, in the case of mathematics, straightforward number substitution into well-rehearsed formulae – generates strong incentives for teachers to practice didactic, one-way pedagogy. Time spent on memorising quantities of factual material through drilling and repetition is more likely to bring success in such an examination than time spent developing conceptual understanding and thinking skills through dialogic, two-way pedagogy. Low-quality national examinations, in short, promote low-quality pedagogy.

Assessment systems, by contrast, have no direct backwash effects on pedagogy, for the reasons already outlined: they carry no consequences either for the students tested or for their teachers; and the questions set are either kept confidential, or released only after a time delay. Hence, assessment systems can have an impact on classroom practice only if transmission channels are in place through which their results can be communicated to the grassroots practitioners, and interpreted in ways which are meaningful and useful to them. The evidence suggests, however, that these transmission channels often function imperfectly, if at all. During recent school visits in Nepal, a number of principals were asked about a national assessment survey, the findings from which had been published about a year previously. A single principal was aware of the survey – but only because he had been involved in test administration at a neighbouring school which was included in the sample. He had not seen the test questions, nor did he know anything about the findings.[11] Similar enquiries during school visits in Kenya indicated a similar state of affairs.[12]

But even if the transmission channels were open and functioning well, it is doubtful that the findings from most assessment studies, as they are reported at present, would be of much help to a teacher struggling to improve her classroom practice in an under-resourced school in a low-income country. With the international studies in particular, it is the league tables, based on subject-level aggregate scores, which generally receive the most attention. League-table rankings certainly generate *incentives* for performance improvement, but they provide no *information* as to how that improvement might be achieved. Such information can be elicited only from the disaggregated data: analysis of the errors students commonly make in responding to questions tapping particular concepts or cognitive skills can enable teachers to develop insight into the reasons for these misconceptions, and hence to formulate appropriate remedial action. The diagnostic message is in the detail: aggregation muffles it.

Of course, the assessment study reports, both international and national, do include a wide variety of evidence which carries the analysis of student performance well beyond the simplistic level of the league table. Very often, however, the focus of these enquiries is on the identification of the antecedent and contextual correlates of aggregate performance: socioeconomic status, parental education, home language, school location, class size and the like. Studies in which the performance variable is disaggregated – to the concept, skill, or single-question level – are much less frequent.

The findings from multivariate studies in which aggregate performance is the dependent variable can, of course, do much to enrich the teaching of university-level courses in subjects such as the sociology of education. Evidence that the work of the schools is largely constrained by external factors outside their control contributes substantially to the material from which such courses are constructed. But it is not easy to see what useful message a grassroots practitioner – especially one working in an isolated rural area or urban slum – could take from a finding such as the following, from a recent assessment study in Nepal:

> [S]ocioeconomic status plays a strong role in educational processes in Nepal. ... [I]f the social economic standard of the lowest performing students was raised ... the results in these groups would rise remarkably. Especially challenging is the situation in the families where both parents are illiterate or they both work in agriculture. (Metsamuuronen & Kafle, 2013, p. 95)

Summary and Conclusions

I have argued that measures to strengthen formative questioning across the assessment spectrum could contribute to the enhancement of student learning in low-income countries. However, it is at the grassroots level of the classroom, towards the left side of the spectrum, that the need for improvement is most urgent – and the scope greatest. In many, if not most, low-income countries, relatively little professional attention is currently paid to these 'left-side' assessment activities. Most of the questions asked in the majority of classrooms are low demand. They require students to do no more than reproduce factual material – often material they have just heard from the teacher. While such questioning aids memorisation, it contributes little to the construction of conceptual understanding and thinking skill. Moreover, the teacher very often accepts a choral response, which may well have come from only a vocal minority, leaving the majority largely excluded from participation.

The situation is often exacerbated by the powerful backwash effects of high-stakes national examinations. The questions set for these examinations in many low-income countries test predominantly low-order recall skills; questions requiring higher-order thinking skills are often rare, or absent altogether. Teachers have ready access to these undemanding questions, scrutinise them closely, and frequently model their lesson content, pedagogy and class testing on them. By contrast, the questions employed in the national and (more particularly) international assessment studies are for the most part of impressively high quality – not surprising, given the professional resources available for their construction. However, classroom teachers, and other grassroots practitioners who carry the main burden of developing student competencies, rarely get to see these questions, nor the results they produce.

It is evident that if assessment, broadly conceived, is to realise its full potential for strengthening student learning, initiatives across the full assessment spectrum are needed. At least three can be identified:

- First: devoting more attention to the development of teachers' formative assessment skills, both in pre-service programmes and in subsequent professional development programmes. Subject-specific

pedagogy, focused on the identification and remediation of the systematic errors which commonly develop during the acquisition of particular concepts and skills, should be a major component of such programmes.
- Second: strengthening the professional skills of the test-development teams in examinations bodies. The benefits to be gained from closer professional collaboration between examinations and assessment teams might well prove substantial.
- Third: developing ways of analysing the results of assessment studies which are more meaningful and useful to teachers and other grassroots practitioners, and of disseminating these results to them more effectively. Greater attention needs to be paid to student responses at the concept, skill and question level; less to league tables and to multivariate analyses of aggregate performance.

Notes

[1] This chapter explores in greater depth issues concerning the role of assessment in strengthening educational quality previously outlined briefly in Somerset (2011).

[2] The USA is a conspicuous exception.

[3] It should be stressed that the distinction between one-way and two-way pedagogy is not congruent with the more familiar distinction between teacher-centred and student-centred pedagogy. In the overcrowded and under-resourced classrooms typical of most low-income countries, student-centred learning is difficult, sometimes impossible, to implement effectively. In such circumstances, teacher-led direct instruction, *but involving meaningful two-way communication between teacher and students*, is likely to be more successful (Westbrook et al, 2013, p. 37). The teacher whose lesson is outlined in Box 1 below employed such an approach in a highly effective fashion.

[4] Such students are members of Lewin's third zone of exclusion: present in the classroom but not participating, and hence underachieving and at risk of dropping out (Lewin, 2007).

[5] However, about one-third were teaching a subject different from the one in which they had majored.

[6] The teachers had been briefed beforehand about the study, and all had agreed to be observed. Lessons varied in length from 40 to 80 minutes, and were observed in their entirety. The three observers were all university teachers, one a chemistry specialist, the second a biology specialist, and the third a generalist. Ratings were made independently and compared as soon after the lesson as practicable. Discrepancies were surprisingly small, rarely amounting to more than one scale point. They were generally resolved by discussion, or on occasion by using half-point ratings. Teachers' subject content knowledge was also rated. After the observations, the team met separately with each

teacher and provided formative feedback. These sessions often stimulated fruitful discussion of a wide range of issues and concerns.

[7] These misconceptions have, of course, been widely documented. See, for example, the early analysis carried out by the UK Mathematics Assessment of Performance Unit (NFER, 1985).

[8] A Grade 10 student who had consistently made the ROD error gave this explanation in a follow-up interview immediately after the test. It was subsequently confirmed in further interviews.

[9] Such skills are many and varied. They include: the ability to restructure remembered knowledge and apply it to new situations; the ability to assimilate new information and draw valid inferences from it; the ability to develop a coherent argument using connected prose; and the ability to produce original or creative work.

[10] Quoting material from the *Times Educational Supplement* (9 March 2012).

[11] A series of regional seminars had been held to disseminate the findings of the assessment study to district-level staff, but it seems that onward dissemination to the principals and teachers had been patchy – as so often happens with cascaded training.

[12] According to Ravela (2005), however, this issue has been resolved in Uruguay. After testing for the national assessment survey was completed, the test papers were made available to all schools, those outside the national sample as well as those within it, and training workshops were held throughout the country, explaining to teachers how to administer the test and interpret the results. These workshops became the 'starting point for a process of pedagogical reflection'.

References

Akyeampong K., Lussier K., Pryor J. & Westbrook J. (2013) Improving Teaching of Basic Maths and Reading in Africa: does teacher education count?, *International Journal of Educational Development*, 33(3), 272-282. http://dx.doi.org/10.1016/j.ijedudev.2012.09.006

Alexander, R.J. (2008a) EFA, the Quality Imperative and the Problem of Pedagogy. CREATE Pathways to Access Research Monograph No. 20. London: Institute of Education.

Alexander, R.J. (2008b) *Towards Dialogic Teaching: rethinking classroom talk*. York: Dialogos.

Black, P.J. & Wiliam. D. (1998) *Inside the Black Box: raising standards through classroom assessment*. London: King's College London School of Education.

Dore, R. (1976) *The Diploma Disease*. London: Unwin.

Erault, M. (2000) Non-formal Learning and Tacit Knowledge in Professional Work, *British Journal of Educational Psychology*, 70(1), 113-136. http://dx.doi.org/10.1348/000709900158001

Goldstein, H. (2004) Education for All: the globalization of learning targets, *Comparative Education*, 40(1), 7-14. http://dx.doi.org/10.1080/0305006042000184854

Greaney, V. & Kellaghan, T. (1996) *Monitoring the Outcomes of Educational Systems*. Washington, DC: World Bank. http://dx.doi.org/10.1596/0-8213-3734-3

Hardman F., Abd-Kadir J. & Tibuhinda A. (2012) Reforming Teacher Education in Tanzania, *International Journal of Educational Development*, 32(6), 826-834. http://dx.doi.org/10.1016/j.ijedudev.2012.01.002

Husen, T. (1967) *International Study of Achievement in Mathematics: a comparison of twelve countries*. New York: Wiley.

Kamens, D. & McNeely, C. (2009) Globalisation and the Growth of International Educational Testing and National Assessment, *Comparative Education Review*, 54(1), 5-25. http://dx.doi.org/10.1086/648471

Lewin, K.M. (2007) Improving Access, Equity, and Transitions in Education. CREATE Pathways to Access Research Monograph No. 1. Brighton: University of Sussex.

Lockheed, M. & Verspoor, A. (1991) *Improving Primary Education in Developing Countries*. Oxford: Oxford University Press for the World Bank.

Metsamuuronen, J. & Kafle, B. (Eds) (2013) Where Are We Now? Student Achievement in Mathematics, Nepali and Social Studies in 2011. National Assessment of Student Achievement. Education Review Office, Ministry of Education, Kathmandu, Nepal.

National Foundation for Educational Research (NFER) (1985) Mathematics Assessment of Performance Unit: decimal numbers. Reading: NFER.

Ravela, P. (2005) A Formative Approach to National Assessments: the case of Uruguay, *Prospects*, 23, 21-43. http://dx.doi.org/10.1007/s11125-005-6816-x

Sahlberg, P. (2011) *Finnish Lessons: what the world can learn from educational change in Finland*. New York: Teachers College Press.

Schweisfurth, M. (2015) Learner-centred Pedagogy: towards a post-2015 agenda for teaching and learning. *International Journal of Educational Development*, 40, 259-266. http://dx.doi.org/10.1016/j.ijedudev.2014.10.011

Somerset, A. (2002) Basic Number Skills: why students fail in math. A Diagnostic Survey of Fifteen High Schools in Central Visayas, Philippines. Quezon City, Philippines: University of the Philippines, National Institute for Science and Mathematics Education.

Somerset, A. (2011) Strengthening Educational Quality in Developing Countries: the role of examinations and international assessment systems, *Compare*, 41(1), 141-144. http://dx.doi.org/10.1080/03057925.2011.534851

Somerset, A., Alfafara, R.M. & Dalman, T. (1999) *Teaching and Learning Science and Mathematics in the Classroom: effective and ineffective pedagogy compared*. Cebu City, Philippines/Amsterdam: University of San Carlos, Science and Mathematics Education Institute/Free University of Amsterdam.

Takeyama, K. (2008) The Politics of International League Tables: PISA in Japan's achievement crisis debate, *Comparative Education*, 44(4), 387-407. http://dx.doi.org/10.1080/03050060802481413

UNESCO (2015) *Education for All 2000-2015: achievements and challenges*. Paris: UNESCO.

Wasanga, P. & Somerset, A. (2013) Examinations as an Instrument for Strengthening Pedagogy: lessons from three decades of experience in Kenya, *Assessment in Education*, 20(4), 385-406. http://dx.doi.org/10.1080/0969594X.2013.833499

Westbrook, J., Durrani, N., Brown, R., et al (2013) Pedagogy, Curriculum, Teaching Practices and Teacher Education in Developing Countries: final report. Education Rigorous Literature Review. London: EPPI-Centre, Social Science Research Unit, Institute of Education, University of London.

Wiliam, D. (2011) *Embedded Formative Assessment*. Bloomington, IN: Solution Tree Press.

CHAPTER 11

An Evaluation of How the 'Policies of K-12 Testing' Impact the Effectiveness of Global Testing Programs

SEAN W. MULVENON & SANDRA G. BOWMAN

ABSTRACT A culture of testing has evolved globally as societies focus on education as a method to expand opportunities for all students and strengthen local economies. A common metric used to evaluate student achievement, teacher effectiveness and school systems as part of these efforts has been through an expanded use of standardized exams and testing. The use of standardized exams has both advocates and critics, but an element missing in the discussion is the impact of educational policies implemented in support of testing and accountability programs. The purpose of this chapter is to provide a narrative of the role of educational policies on testing programs and their impact on our global testing culture.

Introduction

The term 'global testing culture' conveys an impression or belief that testing dominates our educational systems and is more than just an essential component of the assessment process when evaluating student achievement. The discussion of testing policies in education can lead to a range of emotional displays by parents, teachers and other educational stakeholders. Further, the expansion of mandated standardized testing over the last 20 years has raised additional questions regarding the effectiveness, appropriateness and impact (negative or positive) on student achievement (Grant et al, 2002). It is even difficult to use the term 'global testing culture' without this label presenting a negative representation. What are the implications of testing in education? Is a negative perception of testing simply due to testing? As an educational statistician, it is my (Mulvenon) supposition that educational policies may have contributed to a negative perception of the action of testing in education.

Global testing policies are those practices, principles and philosophies accepted as either appropriate or inappropriate employed in the evaluation of student achievement. The unstated goal of testing systems should be the effective evaluation of student performance. In a vacuum or a perfect world, this process may be reduced to several components: (1) test development; (2) evaluation of performance; and (3) identification of interventions or instructional strategies to improve student achievement. At the core of global testing policies, these components may be assumed as goals of international testing programs. However, the introduction of accountability programs and teacher evaluation systems may have altered these otherwise notable and essential components of testing systems. More specifically, is the emphasis of global testing policies still focused on improving student achievement or are the underlying philosophies and policies designed to represent all schools as providing equitable educational opportunities? Are suspect testing policies having an unrealized impact when interpreting or evaluating student achievement, teacher evaluations or school effectiveness?

The 'Policies of K-12' have had an impact at the local, national and international levels on how students, parents, educators and other educational stakeholders perceive the effectiveness of testing and student achievement (Kane & Staiger, 2002). Much of the criticism of mandated standardized testing may be reduced to two elements: (1) a common belief that the tests do NOT accurately measure student achievement or teacher effectiveness (Tienken & Zhoa, 2013); and (2) a belief that the amount of testing detracts from learning opportunities in the classroom (Kohn, 2000; Cheng & Curtis, 2004). I would support many of the concerns associated with the accuracy and use of testing results to evaluate student achievement or teacher effectiveness, but would not ascribe to the theory cited in element (2) that there is too much testing. However, I do understand the concerns of parents and educators regarding testing. Are the emotions associated with elements (1) and (2) due specifically to mandatory standardized testing or to the impact of global testing policies? Further, how have testing policies influenced test development, scoring and the representations of student achievement in accountability models, teacher evaluations and educational research?

An example of my supposition regarding the impact of educational testing policies can be demonstrated by an editorial published in the *Arkansas Democrat Gazette* on 7 September 2014 (Greenburg, 2014). The editorial questioned the complicated process and validity of the new Arkansas School Accountability GRADES System. In reading this editorial, it became clear to me that the issue was not that parents, educators, politicians or editors of the *Democrat Gazette* need to understand the metrics of accountability systems, but that the results of the new GRADES system have limited 'face validity'. More specifically, many of the GRADES assigned using this system are incongruent when comparing the performance of individual schools on the mandated standardized tests in Arkansas. We will provide a study as part of this chapter that outlines the questions associated with 'face validity' and results of the GRADES system. The seminal point that will be demonstrated is an inconsistent representation of school performance, not due to testing results, but based on educational policy.

The purpose of this chapter is to investigate the development and implementation of global testing policies and their impact on a global testing culture. How does testing policy impact the validity of interpretations of testing results in evaluating student achievement, school performance (accountability) and teacher effectiveness? Educational policies must be developed that effectively use the results of student testing and provide appropriate information to the school system, while concurrently providing a mechanism for evaluating school performance and teacher effectiveness. Global testing policies should be designed to facilitate the development of information that helps improve student achievement and maximizes educational outcomes for all students. This chapter will provide a narrative of the challenges, as well as recommendations on how to improve the face validity of assessment models, and subsequently improve global testing policies in the age of a global testing culture.

The Philosophy, Politics and Mathematics of a Global Testing Culture

In theory, the development of school accountability systems should be focused on evaluating the instructional effectiveness of a school or district (Au, 2013). In practice, these systems become inherently complicated due to the application of flexibility models to assign points to school systems for any number of elements as part of accountability scoring models. Use of flexibility models immediately spirals into attempts to account for poverty, attendance, graduation rates, percentage of licensed teachers and many other factors associated with student achievement. In the United States, the current goal is for all students to be 'proficient', with the term 'proficient' representing an omnibus label rather than an accurate descriptor of performance (NCLB, 2002). However, if a student from a school attains the label 'proficient' on a mandated standardized test, does this really provide a measure of school effectiveness? If a student in poverty attains the label 'proficient', does this represent evidence the school system is effective in educating students from low-income families? In either scenario there is not enough information to determine the instructional effectiveness of the school system. However, in both scenarios the school system will receive points for being effective in its respective accountability system. In reality, accountability systems don't directly measure school effectiveness, they just assign points, and in many cases, for random events associated with flexibility models.

Figure 1 represents a systems approach to how I viewed development of educational policies over a 17-year period of working at the district, state and, specifically, national level on accountability systems. The process starts with a 'philosophy' and the ideals of a committee imposed on the development of an accountability system. Next, 'philosophies' are transformed and operationalized by the committee to implement 'policies'. The 'mathematics' represents the actual science of the system, but the use of the 'mathematics' and science available to accurately assess student achievement and accountability is limited, with the priority being to implement 'policies' based on 'philosophies'.

Philosophy
- How we would like to see things ... for examples, equitable educational opportunities for all students

Policy
- Implementation of policy associated with our philosophy that will facitate attainment of this goal

Mathematics
- The analytics and research on the system as to why there may not be equitable educational opportunities and outcomes for all students

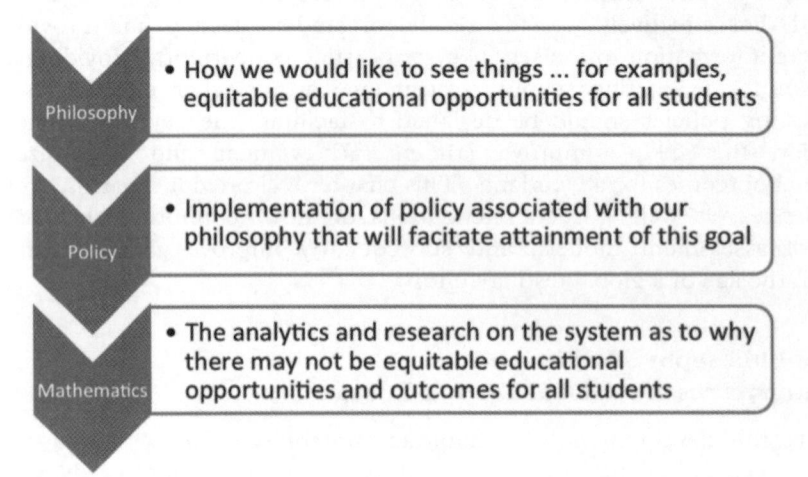

Figure 1. The flow of philosophy, policy and mathematics in educational policy.

The use of philosophy in the development of policy is always well intended, but can be guided by a less-than-perfect understanding of the covariates that impact student achievement and accountability models. As global testing policies are developed, too often the ideals of the committee are used as part of the test development, assessment and scoring models. As an ex officio member of the Arkansas Accountability Committee and senior advisor on numerous NCLB committees at the US Department of Education, it was always my experience that policy may supersede the science when developing educational policies (Mulvenon, 2010). The implications may be overarching when you consider allowing philosophy and policy to overshadow the role of psychometrically sound test development and scoring models. Figure 1 represents a model where the progression is from top to bottom, but the progression should really flow from mathematics to policies to philosophies.

It should also be stated that psychometric theory and statistics represent just a few of the mathematically based sciences used to support the development of tests in K-12 education and global testing policies. Are these methods, or any other mathematically based scientific methods, perfect? No!

All mathematically or quantitatively based methods have measurement error. A goal of any scientific method is to expand the paradigm and reduce both specific and unique error variance. However, a poor scoring model and imperfect rubrics in an accountability program may transform the interpretation of results from a test from meaningful/useful to uninterpretable.

In the development of Figure 1 we elected to use the term 'philosophy' instead of 'ideology'. On multiple occasions we discussed the relative merits of both words in describing this directional hierarchy. We also discussed the issue with numerous colleagues, presenting the case for use of both words. Philosophy was presented as more inclusive and representative of the overall premise of Figure 1. An ideology may be a philosophy, but all ideologies are subsets derived from more global philosophies. A government may implement numerous global warming policies, but there may be even more recommendations of what should be pursued from eclectic ideologies within a philosophy of global warming. Pro-testing, anti-testing, neutral testing views and the subsequent conversations of the merits of testing may be driven based on distinct ideologies, but they all exist under an overarching element of the philosophy of testing.

Development of Psychometrically Sound Tests for Use in Global Testing

The core facet of testing must be the development and use of psychometrically sound tests in education (Patz, 2007). But what does psychometrically sound represent when developing a test? To add clarity I will provide an overview of how I interpret this phrase and provide a definition.

The development of a psychometrically sound test involves much more than just writing items mapped to a curriculum, taking into account student learning expectations, and ensuring the items are racially and culturally unbiased. Individual items must also be aligned and associated with other items while concurrently representing a difficulty along a spectrum that provides educators with an ability to differentiate the knowledge level of students. Good tests don't just exist, they evolve from incorporating these elements into the design, piloting and editing of the items to ensure that what is purported to being tested is actually being tested. In my humble opinion, the science of test development is marginalized by a misguided belief that psychometrically sound testing can be reduced to just writing items, and, further, that all results can be reduced to the lowest common level of understanding (e.g. the use of a mean to interpret the performance of a classroom).

Development of psychometrically sound tests as part of global testing policies may be a fantasyland ideal, but I would like to believe that a major reason for it being a fantasy is the limited role played by an independent panel of academics who are experts in educational statistics and measurement in the development of educational testing policy decisions. Psychometrically sound exams as a practice should go beyond a technical manual that is provided by a testing company, but should be an integrated model of items, constructs, metrics, reports and models that guide professional development, understanding and effective use of testing results. As such, psychometrically sound may be defined as: *Exams that measure what is purported to be measured, as demonstrated through convergent validity; that have item development that supports an ability to identify and differentiate understanding and knowledge of content aligned with student learning expectations; that have metrics and statistical reports that are readily interpretable and presented in a manner to facilitate understanding of context and use of the information; and that readily transition results to student- and classroom-based interventions that will improve student achievement and guide educators in development of their instructional lessons and pedagogical practices.*

As I attempted to write a definition of 'psychometrically sound' it was immediately apparent to me that writing a definition is an incredibly narcissistic activity. My intent is to provide a context or first draft in the hope that this is a dynamic effort, and that the definition will evolve over time with input and support from others invested in improving global testing policies. Regardless, much of the provided interpretation of psychometrically sound is focused on developing from the exam and extends to the discussion to what results are essential to report to parents and educators.

The reporting of testing results is something that contributes to the challenges of developing effective global testing policies (Marsh et al, 2006). The presentation of results and metrics to aid in the interpretation and use of standardized test results is typically limited to the most basic of measures, such as a mean or percentile rank (Arkansas Department of Education Parent Report, 2014). The limited context of the metrics reported and their use may be marginalized by the philosophies and policies associated with testing policy.

Understanding the Metrics of Assessment

Let's take an example, suppose a literacy and mathematics test is developed with 100 multiple-choice questions each worth 1 point and a total of 100 possible points. What constitutes 'passing' or 'proficient'? Traditionally in education a score of 70% on a criterion-referenced test (CRT) is associated with a grade of 'C' or 'passing'. Is this consistent in global testing policy? Does this apply only to CRTs? What does this score represent on a norm-referenced test (NRT)? Use of the labels CRT and NRT may add to the confusion of most parents, educators and other educational stakeholders as they are unclear as to the differences in scaling and scoring that exist between these two types of exams. Regardless, unless you possess an understanding of the underlying metrics, scaling and application of scores within these systems, your ability to interpret results is minimized. A more significant issue in testing policy may be the method selected to provide information from a test which may dramatically alter the perceptions of scores and the representation of performance.

The statistical distributions of scores on a test may also impact global testing policy. For example, the average or mean score for Classroom A was 80 of a possible 100 points on the previously described literacy and mathematics exams. Was the performance of Classroom A equal on both exams? Is the teacher an excellent instructor in both topics? More information is required to answer these questions, but what if the national averages were 85 and 75 for the literacy and mathematics exams, respectively? What if the reported standard error of measurement (SEM) was 2.5 for both exams? Does this impact your opinion of Classroom A's performance? Using the SEM of 2.5 for both exams, Classroom A would be in the bottom 5% in performance for literacy and in the top 5% in performance for mathematics. And, given that these were both point-in-time exams (i.e. one administration of the exam), there is not enough information to make an accurate interpretation of the instructional effectiveness of the teacher. The seminal point is that the interpretation of performance requires statistical context based on the distribution of scores, historical performance, and an assessment of change from past performance.

What percentage of teachers, parents or educational stakeholders understand what a measure of SEM represents and how to use this value correctly? The SEM is an important metric for understanding reported test results, but too often metrics are simplified to facilitate ease of interpretation by consumers. It is at this point that labels are provided as part of testing reports to increase understanding of results. For example, Classroom A may be assigned various labels, such as 'Achieving', 'Meets Standards', 'Meets Growth', 'Excelling', or any number of other descriptors to facilitate understanding of performance. If Classroom A is assigned the label 'Meets Standards', it may convey any number of perceptions, but are those perceptions accurate? Global testing policies are too often driven by simplistic reporting of scores, means and labels with limited attention to the context (NCLB, 2002). In the preceding example, Classroom A had an average score of 80 for both the literacy and mathematics exams. However, it was reported that Classroom A was assigned the label 'Needs Improvement' for literacy and the label 'Excelling' for mathematics. Do you think this may cause confusion among parents? Classroom A had the same average score for both exams. This example represents a situation where more effective global testing policies may facilitate understanding of performance and provide an appropriate context for parents and teachers.

Sean W. Mulvenon & Sandra G. Bowman

Understanding the Statistical Context of Testing Reports

The context of statistical reports is an area that I emphasize in my courses as a professor. I insist that students develop an understanding of the statistical values that are presented in addition to how they are being employed. For example, what is your immediate perception if I share that 85% of students were assigned the label 'Proficient' on an algebra exam? Further, what if the label 'Proficient' represented that a student demonstrated mastery of the core concepts, skills and knowledge consistent with the student learning expectations? Please think about the last two sentences and then your impressions of what both really mean. Next, what if I shared that a student who earned 42 of a possible 100 points on the algebra exam is assigned a label of 'Proficient'? Does this change your perception of performance for a student who is 'Proficient'? Does it make you question what the term 'Proficient' represents, given the definition provided in this paragraph? The limited nature of a guiding philosophy for the development of psychometrically sound tests, reporting and context does have implications for perceptions of global testing policies.

Implications of Philosophy and Policy Guiding Global Testing Policy

At present there may be no better example of the implications of 'philosophy' and 'policy' transcending the mathematics and overall goals of a system than the recent revelations of Dr Jonathan Gruber associated with the Affordable Care Act (ACA), or 'Obamacare', in the United States (*Fox News*, 2014). The reality of Dr Gruber's actions, and subsequent testimony to the US Congress, may actually parallel many of the challenges associated with information used in developing effective global testing policy.

Jonathan Gruber is a professor of economics at the Massachusetts Institute of Technology (MIT) in Boston, Massachusetts. He has admitted that many of the facts and computations he provided in support of 'Obamacare' were designed to mislead perceptions of the benefits of this program. Are his actions uncommon when 'philosophies' are influencing the development of policies? Or is this uncommon in the development of educational reports or in the development of CRTs for use in mandated testing and accountability programs? My experiences would suggest that the actions of Dr Gruber to influence erroneous interpretations of information (or testing results) are not isolated.

A colleague and I were requested in 2000 to visit with a testing company about the development of the Arkansas Department of Education (ADE) fourth-grade benchmark exam. We had raised several questions regarding the distributions and results of the literacy and mathematics sections of this exam, including issues of convergent and face validity of the reported results. At one point during this meeting the vice-president of the testing company stated that they knew that mid-level management at the

ADE did not understand testing or test theory, so as a company they just gave them what they requested. Later, as we followed up with more questions about the psychometrics of the exam, he made the comment: 'I'm not going to let a couple of snot-nosed university professors ruin a $38-$40 million a year business.' We shared these comments with the deputy director of the ADE, Dr Woodrow Cummins [1], and to the credit of the vice-president of the testing company, he later acknowledged to Dr Cummins that our reporting of his comments was accurate.

My point in sharing these comments is only to enunciate that 'philosophy' and 'policy' are used to override or supersede the mathematics and psychometrics associated with test development and directly impact global testing policies. Further, it can be demonstrated that 15 years later, the same challenges in the developing and application of sound psychometrics have an impact on our interpretations of student performance, and may affect teacher evaluations, the perceptions of parents in understanding the performance of their children, and the perceptions of parents and educators concerning the global testing culture.

Key Research Question(s) and Elements of this Chapter

The seminal research questions center on assessing the impact of 'philosophies' and 'policies' employed in student testing, teacher effectiveness and school accountability associated with global testing policy.

- Research Question 1: How does interpretation of student achievement impact evaluation of school and teacher performance?
- Research Question 2: How does face validity of testing results impact the confidence of parents, teachers and other educational stakeholders?
- Research Question 3: How does use of convergent validity impact representation of student performance (e.g. use of SAT, ACT, NAEP or TIMSS scores)?
- Research Hypothesis: An examination of convergent and face validity in a mandated standardized testing system will demonstrate the negative effect of 'philosophies' and 'policies' on the perception of the effectiveness of global testing polices.

Using Interpretation of Student Achievement to Evaluate School and Teacher Performance

'Statistically Significant', 'Meaningful' and 'Readily Interpretable'

An often-used term in education to justify a report, conclusion or recommendation is in citing analytical results as 'statistically significant'. The likelihood of an outcome randomly occurring such that the probability of the event is less than 5% or 1% may be valuable, but is limited in terms of interpretability and meaningfulness. For example, the mean on a mathematics exam is 84.1 and 84.2 for Classroom A and Classroom B, respectively. Is this difference between groups important? Is this difference between groups meaningful? Is a large sample size that homogenizes the distributions of the scores the basis for a difference of 0.1 point being 'statistically significant'? However, is the difference 'meaningful' in terms of needing to take more formal actions or needing to implement an intervention? Many other factors need to be considered to determine the meaningfulness of results and the implications for improving student achievement or instructional practices, or for identifying appropriate academic interventions.

A second area of importance is to provide testing results that are readily interpretable or meaningful (Koretz, 2015). It is common for testing companies to report that raters of open-response questions are highly correlated in the application of scoring rubrics (i.e. assignment of possible points) (Arkansas Department of Education Testing Manual, 2002). The standard process employed by most test development companies is to correlate the responses of raters, and if the degree of correlation is less than desired, additional rater(s) are employed until the degree of association is at an established level. The reporting of a high degree of correlation as evidence of scoring accuracy and reliability is going to happen due to the design and the methodology employed. However, are the ratings congruent with the multiple-choice elements measuring the same learning expectation(s)? Is there evidence of a convergent validity to assess and validate the interrater reliabilities? Our culture in testing at times relies on citing and referencing statistical methods as evidence of validity, but without a convergent validity they have limited meaningfulness and interpretability (Dunn & Mulvenon, 2009).

Context of Test Results in a Report

If we extend from the concept of 'meaningfulness' to the concept of 'context', how does this apply to the present example? If Classroom A had used Instructional Method 1 and Classroom B had used Instructional Method 2, may you claim Method 1 is more effective? And further, that Instructional Method 1 should be implemented districtwide as your results were 'statistically significant'? The declaring of 'statistical significance' may impress certain audiences, but how do you justify this conclusion if you report that a difference between the treatment and control groups is only 0.1 of a point (84.2-84.1 = .1)? What are the cost benefits? Is a difference of 0.1 of a point meaningful?

Understanding Face Validity

Face validity can be described as a parsimonious notion that a basic review of reported results from a mandated standardized test makes sense or is believable based on a cursory review of the information (Kirk, 2008). A challenge or threat to face validity in accountability programs may be the use of labels to describe or represent performance of students, teachers or school systems. No Child Left Behind (NCLB) legislation in the United States mandated that all students must be 'Proficient' on CRT exams and deferred the defining of this term to the individual state educational agencies (SEAs). What does 'Proficient' mean? Is the definition the same in each state? Does use of this term impact the perceptions of parents and teachers regarding student achievement?

The Arkansas Department of Education required an end-of-course (EOC) algebra exam which had 100 possible points. In recent years, if a student attained a score of between 38 and 42 points (i.e. 38-42%) they were assigned the performance label 'Proficient'. Approximately 80-90% of students who attempted this EOC algebra exam were labeled as 'Proficient'. However, annually 50-60% of college-bound seniors in Arkansas are required to complete remedial mathematics in college due to an ACT math score of less than 19. If a student obtained a score of 90 on the EOC algebra exam, I am positive they can successfully do algebra. In contrast, if a student obtained a score of 42 and was assigned the label 'Proficient', I am confident they cannot do algebra. When a parent is told their child is 'Proficient' in algebra, but must take remedial mathematics in college, it will impact their perceptions of global testing policies. The EOC algebra and ACT math sections may both provide excellent assessments of algebra based on the test designs. It is the process of assigning the labels to achievement through educational policy that has created confusion or a misrepresentation of the performance of a student (or students).

Defining Growth in Education

Did a student make annual growth or improve in their performance from one year to the next? An underlying goal of all educational systems is to improve the knowledge, skills and demonstrated performance of students, and this requires an assessment of growth. However, what constitutes improvement and what is an appropriate method to assess growth? The educational policies around assessment and evaluation of growth may be considered suspect and add to a negative perception of the measurement models associated with global testing policies.

In November 2005, then US Secretary of Education Margaret Spellings initiated the Pilot Growth Model Program (PGMP). One aspect of this PGMP was to determine what constituted an acceptable measure of growth (Mulvenon, 2010). As part of the PGMP it was determined that a student could be defined as having 'Made Growth' under two situations.[2] (1) They would be considered to have 'Made Growth' if they achieved the label 'Proficient' for the current academic year. (2) Using the current year's performance goal score, a predicted score (or scores) would be generated for the next one- to three-year period, and if the trajectory for a student exceeded the performance goal score (at any point during this period), the student would be considered to have 'Made Growth'.

As part of NCLB, all students in Grades 3-8 were required to complete mandated standardized CRT exams and attain a performance goal established by the individual SEAs. For example, in Arkansas the benchmark exams were administered to all students in Grades 3-8, and on average the performance goal required was approximately 37% of possible points. The establishment of the performance goal 'cut scores' is for a different chapter, but the selection of the points required has been questioned by many and does add to the debate on educational policies. Regardless, I will now provide examples of the application of the two described scenarios:

> Scenario 1: Student A has a third-grade performance score of 88%, which is above the performance goal of 37%, and will be determined to have 'Made Growth'. This is a point-in-time cross-sectional score, yet a measure of growth is assigned by this single point.

> Scenario 2: Student B has a current-year third-grade score of 22% and this is below the performance goal. However, the projected scores of Student B for 2015, 2016 and 2017 are 29%, 36% and 43%, respectively. Student B is projected to attain the required score for the performance goal of 37% in Grade 6 in 2017. As such, Student B is considered on track and assigned the label 'Made Growth'. As part of the accountability system, did Student B make growth? Yes. Has the student demonstrated any growth from the single point-in-time measure? No.

A third scenario also exists, and was addressed in part by Scenario 1, but the policy decision associated with Scenario 3 demonstrates where lack of confidence in testing and accountability programs may occur with parents and educators.

> Scenario 3: Student C had a score of 88% and 72% on the third- and fourth-grade literacy exams, respectively. In this situation does Student A make 'annual growth'? YES. The fourth-grade performance score of 72% exceeds the performance goal of 37%. Thus, even though Student A declined in performance by 16% from third to fourth grade, he/she is considered to have made growth with the condition that the current-year score is above the identified performance goal.

A final note on use of projected scores is the impact of a statistical effect called 'regression/projection toward the mean' where projected scores for lower-performing students may be 'inflated' while those for higher-performing students may be 'deflated'. As part of NCLB, *all* students had to have 'growth' scores computed, and this led to much discussion regarding Scenario 3. As an NCLB educational policy, it was determined that you had to compute the growth score of Student C and you could report this decline as having 'Made Growth', citing the current-year score as 'Proficient'. Basically, in review of Scenarios 1-3, higher-achieving students may be declining and lower-achieving students may have inflated growth scores, but both events result in a school system receiving 'points' for these students 'Making Growth' in an accountability system.

A Study on Global Testing Policies

A study was conducted to assess the accuracy of the theory and appropriateness of the research questions. Table I provides a brief statistical overview of how face validity can be readily questioned using labels and performance results in an accountability system. High Schools A and B are both markedly outperforming the average performance of the 15 high schools identified as 'Achieving High Schools'. However, School A is identified as 'Needs Improvement', while School B is identified as 'Needs Improvement Focus School'. Of the 'Achieving High Schools' five had an average ACT English score of below 19 and six had an average ACT math score of below 19. As you may remember, a score below 19 on the ACT exam indicates that a college-bound student is required to complete remedial courses when attending college in Arkansas. Yet, these 15 schools systems are identified as 'Achieving High Schools'. Table I may oversimplify the issue of school accountability and assignment of performance labels, but it does an excellent job of demonstrating the issue of face validity. More specifically, as a parent, which of these 17 high schools would you prefer your child to attend?

A convergent validity is also demonstrated relative to the Arkansas literacy and math scores and the ACT English and math scores. The performance scores of High Schools A and B remain much higher than the scores of the 'High Achieving Schools' on each of these measures. As you assess various indicators of performance, it is essential to identify other measures of student performance and evaluate the association of these indicators. High Schools A and B do not attain the label of 'High Achieving' because of issues associated with flexibility models. In contrast, the 'High Achieving Schools' attain this status because of limited cohorts of students and metrics used in flexibility models. As a result, the face validity of the accountability system and the effectiveness of the educational policies may be questioned.

Many factors may have contributed to the performance of the school systems in the previous study. Several chapters within this text emphasize the social conditions of students, high-stakes testing and other covariates as explanatory in the performance of student achievement. These issues are all valid and should be given all due consideration when evaluating student achievement, teacher effectiveness and school evaluations. Use of standardized testing is only one of the many factors that may contribute to our understanding of learning, achievement and performance. Often in educational research we discuss the issue of Type I and Type II errors. Which of these two errors is more desirable in global testing policies or for use in accountability scoring models? Most people would conclude, based on Table I, that Schools A and B are performing better than those schools assigned an 'achieving' label. What are the implications for attribution of Type I versus Type II errors at the student level?

High School(s)	Literacy Proficient %	Math Proficient %	TAGG Literacy Proficient %	TAGG Math Proficient %	Graduation Rate %	*ACT English	*ACT Math
School A (Needs Improvement School)	88.9	92.8	74.6	84.3	85.2	24.0	22.9
School B (Needs Improvement Focus School)	82.3	83.5	73.6	73.6	86.8	24.3	23.4
Achieving High Schools ($n = 15$)	75.4	72.0	71.3	69.3	88.8	20.6	19.7

*Denotes 2012-2013 State Report Card Data (Note: weighted averages employed for ACT comparisons).

Table I. Are High Schools A & B really less effective than ALL the high-achieving schools?
Source: Arkansas Department of Education 2013-2014 School Data Reports.

Recently a cheating scandal in the Atlanta Public Schools (APS) resulted in 11 teachers being convicted and sentenced to jail sentences for improprieties associated with the testing program (WXIA-TV, 2015). As we completed this chapter a colleague expressed an opinion that 'pressure due to high stakes testing' explained the behavior of these 11 teachers in APS. A policy in APS was to provide bonuses and salary increases to teachers and administrators for improvements in standardized test scores. Subsequently, those convicted were all found guilty of manipulating scores to receive these bonuses and increases in their salaries. Was it the pressure of a testing policy or global testing policies or possible financial benefit that motivated their behavior? How many students were impacted by their decisions to alter test answers (Sass et al, 2015)? The goal of testing, and test policies, should be to improve student achievement and outcomes. The manipulation of those polices for personal gain by educators should not be viewed as a result of a social condition or high-stakes testing, but as representative of poor choices by a few educators. Another perspective may be that 99% of APS teachers were dedicated educators who were actively seeking to improve student achievement.

The assignment of performance labels to school systems in NCLB is an inexact science, as demonstrated by the data reported in Table I. In efforts to address the issue of face validity, the Arkansas Department of Education adopted a new letter GRADES system of 'A', 'B', 'C', 'D' and 'F' for use in 2015. The GRADES system is a modified version of Flexibility Models which does not appear to be designed to measure school effectiveness, but appears more to be an effort to limit the representation of schools as 'failing'. In 2013 a total of 931 schools in Arkansas received a performance label, with 8 schools identified as 'Exemplary' and 130 as 'Achieving'; 793 were assigned as 'Needs Improvement' schools. The University of Arkansas and the Office of Education Innovation (OEI) released a report stating that if you used these same schools and the proposed letter GRADES system, the GRADES of 'A', 'B' and 'C' would be assigned to 8, 137 and 790 schools, respectively. Basically, the GRADES system changes the label from 'Needs Improvement' to a grade of 'C' for 790 schools. An effective argument could be made that the rationale for adopting the GRADES scoring model is to transform the perception of a school labeled as 'Needs Improvement' to 'Passing' without changing the demonstrated performance of the school systems (Office for Education Policy Press Release, 2014).

In my experience working with various state educational agencies and foreign educational systems and as a senior advisor to the Deputy Secretary of Education at the US Department of Education, I have been provided with the opportunity to review and analyze a plethora of accountability systems. The following are a few more examples of questionable testing policies:

- The use of transformed scores in North Carolina created a system where negative growth (i.e. declines in performance) by students who were already performing below proficient was considered 'growth' and they were scored as 'meeting growth' under their state accountability program.
- The United Arab Emirates postsecondary system requires all students to pass an English competency exam before formally enrolling in courses that provide college credits. I was asked by the director of the Sharjah campus why after two years of instruction in English only 15% of students were able to pass this exam. As a policy decision, the exam employed was designed to evaluate a student's level of knowledge in English, not their competency or fluency or ability to be taught in English.
- The US Department of Education, when developing policies concerning use of growth models in NCLB, allowed 'index models'.

Index models provide points based on changes in a student's performance category (e.g. 1 point for improving from 'Basic' to 'Proficient'). A requirement was that the SEA had to demonstrate an 'educational effect' to award points. One SEA determined that if a student correctly answered seven questions on a 48-question multiple-choice exam (each question had four possible answers), this would be considered evidence of an 'educational effect'. The SEA had used a 3-parameter IRT model with a guessing parameter value of .10, which resulted in a score of six as the baseline for performance or 'guessing'. However, using random guessing on all 48 items, you would expect a score of 12 points.

Each of these examples represents an issue in standardized testing that is problematic due to policy decisions associated with evaluating performance, not specifically problematic because of the exams or global testing policy.

Summary of the Impact of Global Testing Policies on K-12 Education

The research questions and global hypothesis for this chapter focused on the impact of educational policies and their influence on a global testing culture. The examples provided throughout this chapter are drawn from experience of the impact of educational policies designed in theory to improve educational outcomes for students. Figure 1 presents an overview of a perceived approach employed in developing educational policies, where the philosophies and policies associated with testing and other goals have a tremendous impact on the perceptions regarding use of mandated standardized testing. Too often it is these policies that contribute to a negative perception of testing by students, parents and educators. It is also my experience that when a teacher is able to meet with a parent and meaningfully share the performance of their child, the next steps, the key learning goals, the challenges and the path to improving their child's academic outcomes, this contributes to a positive view of testing. Our local school systems and global testing systems should be dynamic in their efforts to assist in the improvement and support of educational outcomes for all students.

The development of any global testing system should be based on three components: (1) the design of the test; (2) the scoring and labeling of results; and (3) the use of student testing data in the classroom, accountability programs, and subsequently in research designed to improve all aspects of the K-12 systems.

The Design of Tests

How are the tests developed? The theory associated with test development and item response theory (IRT), differential item functioning (DIF) and vertical equating for growth models is well established. Elements to include in reporting are item difficulty, use of open-response versus multiple-choice questions, and content alignment with specific learning expectations and curriculum objectives.

Scoring and Labeling of Results

The use of scoring models has had a profound impact on the relevance of testing outcomes for students and global testing policies. For example, traditional terms such as 'Mastery of Content' are being replaced with terms such as 'Proficient' or 'Advanced'. Does 'passing' mean 'Proficient'? A student 'passing' should be able to demonstrate mastery of content in new and unique learning opportunities. More specifically, systems should develop labels consistent with performance expectations and, where possible, employ use of convergent validity methods.

Accountability Models and Teacher Effectiveness

The use of global testing data in accountability models and teacher effectiveness relies on test development and scoring policies (Koh et al, 2013). If there are questions about the test design and the accuracy of scoring models, this measurement error will transfer to the interpretation of accountability models and evaluation of teacher effectiveness. Systems should develop growth models and scoring frameworks consistent with the stability of the testing data and scoring models using randomized block designs. Additionally, transcend the use of a single-year evaluation to use multiple years of assessment of performance in accountability and teacher effectiveness models. Finally, develop effective data and reporting models that are diagnostic/informative for educators. The current practice of classroom means, percentages, etc. is incredibly simplistic and misleading. I would suggest use of reports that examine classroom performance relative to the learning objectives and curriculum objectives and that are linked to individual student performance. To identify instructional gaps and areas of need, link item difficulty, relative to classroom and individual student performance, and annual growth of the classrooms and students. Yes, this will require multiple pages of reporting, but it can be presented in a way all teachers/parents understand.

Summary

A goal of this chapter was to present an overview of the impact of global testing polices associated with the global testing culture. It is difficult to identify a positive example of the use of the term 'global testing culture' and I am not suggesting that all testing is positive, that there should be more testing, or that all testing is effective. I am attempting to provide an overview of the repercussion of educational policies associated with a global testing culture and the impact of those policies associated with a negative perception of *any* mandated standardized testing. As a professor of educational statistics I have often lamented the impact of poorly contrived and implemented educational policies associated with test development, scoring models, accountability systems and assessment of teacher effectiveness. Too often, I have heard other faculty members attribute problems with testing to the mere act of testing. Tests, statistics, growth models and other areas of research have a valuable role in educational assessment models and should not be readily dismissed/blamed due to poor educational policies.

Notes

[1] Dr Woodrow Cummins was contacted and has confirmed the accounts reported in this chapter.

[2] Under NCLB a performance goal was created for each individual CRT. If the student obtained a score at or above this performance goal the student was considered to be 'Proficient'.

References

Arkansas Department of Education Parent Report (2014) http://www.arkansased.gov/im-looking-for/parents

Arkansas Department of Education Testing Manual (2002) http://repairfilter.com/access/a/arkansas-department-of-education-testing.pdf

Au, W. (2013) Hiding behind High-stakes Testing: meritocracy, objectivity and inequality in US education, *International Education Journal: comparative perspectives*, 12(2), 7-19.

Cheng, L. & Curtis, A. (2004) Washback or Backwash: a review of the impact of testing on teaching and learning, *Washback in Language Testing: research contexts and methods*, 3-17.

Dunn, K. & Mulvenon, S. (2009) A Critical Review of Research on Formative Assessments: the limited scientific evidence of the impact of formative assessments in education, *Practical Assessment, Research and Evaluation*, 14(7). http://pareonline.net/genpare.asp?wh=0&abt=14 (accessed 23 March 2009).

Fox News (2014) Gruber Apologizes for 'Mean and Insulting' ObamaCare Comments. FoxNews.com, 9 December.

Grant, S.G., Gradwell, J.M., Lauricella, A.M., et al (2002) When Increasing Stakes Need Not Mean Increasing Standards: the case of the New York State global history and geography exam, *Theory & Research in Social Education*, 30(4), 488-515. http://dx.doi.org/10.1080/00933104.2002.10473208

Greenburg, P. (Ed.) (2014) Editorial. (A) x 1.25, Carry the 4... : 'Here some of us thought that letter grades for public schools would be a better thing', *Arkansas Democrate Gazette*, 7 September.

Kane, T. & Staiger, D. (2002) The Promise and Pitfalls of Using Imprecise School Accountability Measures, *Journal of Economic Perspectives*, 16(4), 91-114. http://dx.doi.org/10.1257/089533002320950993

Kirk, R. (2008) *Statistics: an introduction*. Belmont, CA: Thomson Wadsworth.

Koh, N., Reddy, V. & Chatterji, M. (2013) Understanding Validity Issues Surrounding Test-based Accountability Measures in the US, *Quality Assurance in Education*, 22(1), 42-52.

Kohn, A. (2000) *The Case against Standardized Testing: raising the scores, ruining the schools*. Portsmouth, NH: Heinemann.

Koretz, D. (2015) Adapting Educational Measurement to the Demands of Test-based Accountability. A working paper of the Education Accountability Project at the Harvard Graduate School of Education. http://projects.iq.harvard.edu/eap

Marsh, J., Pane, J. & Hamilton, L. (2006) Making Sense of Data-driven Decision Making in Education. Evidence from recent Rand research. Occasional paper, Rand Education.

Mulvenon, S. (2010) Assessing Performance of School Systems: the measurement and assessment challenges of NCLB, in G. Walford, E. Tucker & M. Viswanathan (Eds) *SAGE Handbook of Measurement*. London: SAGE. http://dx.doi.org/10.4135/9781446268230.n29

No Child Left Behind Act of 2001 (NCLB) (2002) Pub. L. No. 107-110, 115 Stat. 1425.

Office for Education Policy Press Release (2014) A–F School Letter Grades. http://officeforedpolicy.com/2014/09/17/guest-blog-post-a-f-school-letter-grades/

Patz, R. (2007) Vertical Scaling in Standards-based Educational Assessment and Accountability Systems. Council of Chief State School Officers. http://www.ccsso.org/Documents/2007/Vertical_Scaling_in_standards_2007.pdf

Sass, T., Apperson, J. & Bueno, C. (2015) The Long-run Effects of Teacher Cheating on Student Outcomes. Atlanta Public Schools. http://www.atlantapublicschools.us/crctreport

Tienken, C. & Zhao, Y. (2013) How Common Standardized Testing Widen the Opportunity Gap, in P. Carter & K. Welner (Eds) *Closing the Opportunity Gap: what America must do to give every child an even chance*. New York: Oxford University Press.

WXIA-TV (2015) 11 Atlanta Educators Convicted in Cheating Scandal, *USA Today*, 1 April.

Definitions

Accountability system – a system that allows the public to understand how well their schools are working and that provides information to policymakers on the changes that are needed to make the schools more effective and to continually improve all students' educational opportunities.

Convergent validity – refers to the degree to which two measures of constructs that theoretically should be related are in fact related.

Face validity – the extent to which a test is subjectively viewed as covering the concept it purports to measure. It refers to the transparency or relevance of a test as it appears to test participants.

Flexibility models – used to assign points to school systems for any number of elements as part of accountability scoring models.

Global testing culture – conveys an impression or belief that testing dominates our educational systems and is an essential component of the assessment process when evaluating student achievement.

Growth models – track individual student achievement over time, comparing actual and expected rates of growth or progress in relation to a defined target.

CHAPTER 12

How Much Stakes for Tests? Public Schooling, Private Tutoring and Equilibrium

MARIAM ORKODASHVILI

ABSTRACT The present chapter analyzes the influence of stakes on tests and examinations. It reveals that when public schooling is poor or unsatisfactory, the stage at which students resort to private tutoring may affect TIMSS (Trends in International Mathematics and Science Study) and PIRLS (Progress in International Reading Literacy Study) results. If tutoring starts at an early stage, TIMSS and PIRLS scores may be a by-product of the intensive preparation for high stakes examinations. If tutoring happens at a later stage, the results of TIMSS and PIRLS are low. Therefore, depending on the school grade at which high-stakes examinations appear, in a number of countries, students increasingly resort to private tutoring to succeed at school, or at university or college entry examinations; hence, the influence on international projects can be vividly observed.

Introduction

The present chapter discusses the factor of stakes in tests and examinations. It hypothesizes that the stage at which students start intensive preparation and learning, and the stage at which the stakes become high, could influence the test results. On the one hand, we have high stakes, extremely competitive tests that are mainly parts of entry examinations or requirements to highly selective and prestigious institutions either at secondary or tertiary levels. On the other hand, we have international assessment projects, such as TIMSS (Trends in International Mathematics and Science Study) and PIRLS (Progress in International Reading Literacy Study), that are not high stakes but try to identify pitfalls in individual schools, school districts and countries and identify reasons behind the achievement gaps between the high-scoring and low-scoring countries. In both cases, we can identify the factor of high-stakes versus low-stakes examinations that often influences human behavior, and hence conditions the intensity of preparation for these assessments frequently through private tutoring.

Equilibrium is the optimum balanced condition between multiple interacting forces. The present chapter discusses the possibility of finding the equilibrium point between the two extremes of high-stakes and low-stakes/no-stakes testing programs. It argues that very high-stakes tests engender distortions, manipulations and corrupt cases; however, on the other hand, they stimulate better and more intensive preparation and study processes. Low-stakes/no-stakes assessment projects identify the education drawbacks and reasons for achievement gaps between countries, on the one hand; however, no special preparation or study process is incentivized by them. Hence, we get the results and problems that are often inexplicable, complicated and difficult to deal with.

Naturally, the hypothesis and resulting cases might not be generalizable over all regions and countries in the world. However, certain countries and regions that face similar processes and issues might recognize the picture described here and might give it some consideration before introducing new policies on testing, core curriculum, tutoring or accountability of schools.

Methodology, Data and Sampling

This chapter compares test scores, testing practices and tutoring practices across high-performing and low-performing countries. The main methodologies implemented in the chapter are cross-country comparative analysis, narrative analysis and qualitative analysis of the data and information obtained through the official assessment and education websites and documents of high-achieving and low-achieving countries. In addition, the factor of the spread of private tutoring for high-stakes examination preparation purposes has been taken into consideration. The countries have been selected according to the criteria of having high-stakes tests, widely spread private tutoring and high/low scores on international assessments.

The following countries have been chosen from high-achieving countries: South Korea, Hong Kong, Japan, Chinese Taipei and Singapore. The reason for choosing these countries is that they score high on TIMSS and PIRLS, and have high-stakes testing systems and widely spread private tutoring for preparing for those high-stakes tests.

The following countries have been selected as low scorers on TIMSS and PIRLS: Armenia, Azerbaijan, Georgia, Kazakhstan and Ukraine. These countries score low in TIMSS and PIRLS, and also have high-stakes testing systems and widely spread private tutoring for the preparation purposes for those tests.

Five hundred online surveys and interviews (where possible) have been conducted among schoolchildren, high school students and their parents to ask about the reasons for resorting to private tutoring and about the stage at which they go to private tutors. These questions have been asked to consider the possible influence of the stage at which students participate in private tutoring on both high-stakes and low-stakes tests. The questions asked were: Which grade are you in at school/college? How old are you? Are you going to a private tutor? How long have you been going to a private tutor? What subjects are you preparing with the private tutor? In what subjects do you have to take exams (secondary school entry exam, university/college entry exam)? How important are these exams?

The respondents were approached through school/college websites, administrative staff and personal contacts. On several occasions focus groups were arranged where schoolchildren and high school students brought their peers with them to discuss the high-stakes and test issues. The respondents were entering either selective secondary schools or preparing for university/college entry examinations.

In addition to the above countries, the well-known and widely discussed Finland success case is referred to in the chapter. The chapter discusses the successful public schooling system in Finland, with a high scoring tradition on TIMSS and PIRLS, and notes that there is no spread of private tutoring in Finland. This country is referred to in the chapter for the sake of illustrating the case of effective public schooling that eliminates the necessity for private tutoring and high-stakes testing and produces high results on international assessments. The chapter thus uses the Finland case for the purpose of contrast.

'What ifs' and Counterfactuals for Future Research

The present research in no way claims that private tutoring is a panacea for the improvement of education quality, and does not act as an advocate of private tutors, nor does it claim that the findings and hypotheses expressed in the present research are generalizable over all countries and regions. However, should any country recognize itself in the situation depicted by this article, it could give a thought or two to the problems raised.

The present chapter agrees with the well-established idea that the most efficient, equitable and viable remedy for malfunctioning education systems in low-scoring countries would be to improve public school quality and enable all members of society to participate in high-quality schooling.

However, since this improved condition seems too far away, if not mission impossible, the present chapter puts forward two hypothetical counterfactuals that would be both challenging and intriguing to consider: what if high-stakes tests and intensive private tutoring started at an earlier age in low-scoring countries, as happens in most Asian high-scoring countries? And what if the TIMSS and PIRLS assessments were conducted in the eleventh and twelfth grades across countries and regions? How would the results change in those cases? And how would the overall picture of testing, examinations and schooling alter?

Theoretical Framework

The theoretical framework for this study includes discussions about the types of tests that are taken by students in different countries and achievement gaps that are revealed as a result of these tests. The tests determine how early and how intensively students resort to private tutoring and intensive academic preparation. This largely determines how successfully they perform on international assessments. Tied on to this is the section on achievement gaps that are most vividly visible through tests and assessments, both national and international. The section mentions the widely held beliefs on achievement gaps that are usually related to school effects, socio-economic status (SES), parental education and encouragement and many other factors. The purpose of the section is to provide an overview of the popular theories in this field to relate them to high-stakes and tutoring factors in the research results section.

Types of Tests

The present research develops its arguments within the framework of testing and examinations. The main types of standardized tests are achievement, aptitude, proficiency and diagnostic. Achievement tests measure how well a student has acquired knowledge from a secondary school syllabus. Aptitude tests measure skills and abilities of a student and provide an indication of future performance; they are a kind of prognostic test. Proficiency tests measure an individual's level of proficiency in any given subject and determine whether their level corresponds with specific requirements. Diagnostic tests relate to the use of information obtained and to the absence of a certain skill in a learner. They diagnose future needs of a learner (Ahola & Kokko, 2001; Akey, 2006).

One example of a widely spread examination required for university entry in the USA and many western countries is the Scholastic Aptitude Test (SAT). It is a combination of aptitude, achievement and proficiency tests and contains elements from the different categories. One asset of the SAT is that because it does not have an effect on school curriculum, teachers can be creative and experiment with study programs, whereas academic achievement tests dictate school curriculum significantly. The SAT also fosters higher equity by revealing low-income but bright students. The SAT provides an opportunity for low-income students who did not have high-quality schooling to reveal their abilities and skills. Therefore, it increases equity.

Achievement Gaps

The variations in testing systems and procedures bring us to a further important issue – namely, achievement gaps across countries, school districts and schools. Achievement gaps across countries and their causes have been widely studied and major theories have been revised several times (Coleman et al, 1968; Baker, 1993; Schmidt et al, 2001; Willms & Somers, 2001;

Baker, Goesling & Letendre, 2002; McEwan & Marshall, 2004; Heyneman, 2005; Gamoran & Long, 2006; Marks et al, 2006). In order to touch upon the issue of high-stakes influence and private tutoring, this chapter attempts to describe the popular discussions on the achievement gaps that are usually revealed through national and international assessments and tests.

Lack of teaching resources and materials; low parental encouragement, SES and educational level; wide social stratification; non-standardized curriculum; low teacher quality, etc. – these are usually named as major causes of achievement gaps in different parts of the world that tend to be reflected in TIMSS and PIRLS results (Vickers, 1994; Rinne et al, 2004; Schuller, 2005; Weymann & Martens, 2005; Rivkin et al, 2005; Kallo, 2006 Rinne, 2008; Rautalin & Alasuutari, 2009; PIRLS, 2011).

The issue of factors affecting student achievement has been researched over the past decades, yielding various results depending on the context- and time-specific characteristics of the analyzed data sample (Martin et al, 2001, 2004; Mullis et al, 2003, 2012a, b). However, the influence of the intensity of private tutoring on TIMSS and PIRLS has been studied relatively scarcely. As for the influence of the stage at which the students resort to private tutors on TIMSS and PIRLS results, this has not been studied at all. Therefore, the present research raises this issue.

Research Findings

High-stakes Testing: the cases of high-scoring countries

Interviews and surveys revealed that in high-scoring countries such as Japan, Chinese Taipei, Hong Kong, Singapore and South Korea, children start preparation for high-stakes exams at an early age, and in the most cases the preparation process takes place with private tutors, since the parents are not satisfied with the quality of public schooling. Getting into a highly selective secondary school is associated with social and economic prestige and is mainly regarded as a precondition for entering a prestigious university, and thereafter, for building a successful career.

As one of the parents indicated, 'I wish my child could get into prestigious school because then his future will be guaranteed. He will enter prestigious university and will then get a good job.' Another parent noted the low quality of public schooling and dissatisfaction with the school teacher:

> She never gives them [children] enough homework to prepare for the tests properly. The tests to secondary school are really tough and the school teacher does not prepare the children properly. My friends' children go to private tutors to prepare better. So at the exams they will beat my son and he will be left outside the school. So I decided to take him to a private tutor.

Numerous times parents mentioned peer influence and competition, and insufficient preparation by a public school teacher.

The entry examinations to the selective schools are extremely competitive and have rigid requirements. Therefore, students resort to private tutoring at an early age. This might be anywhere starting at the age of 8-9 and onwards (Bray, 2009). The data on exam preparation courses and private tutoring in these countries testify to the fact that the students by the age of 10-11 are already well prepared in several core subjects, such as mathematics, foreign language, science, reading, literature, and others. As the surveys and interviews have showed, the high-stakes factor and dissatisfaction with public schooling influence the early decision of parents and students to get involved in intensive private preparation processes for the exams because much depends on the ability of students to get enrolled in the highly selective schools.

A few examples can illustrate how widely spread private tutoring and private institutes are in some Asian countries. The famous *Jukus* (private institutes) in Japan (Stevenson & Baker, 1992; Bray, 2009), *hakwons* (private institutes) in South Korea, and intensive preparation courses in Hong Kong and in China all testify to the nationwide obsession with private tutoring in those countries. In South Korea, for instance, in 2007, 45.5 % of students at middle-school stage were attending private institutes called *hakwons* (Bray, 1999, 2003, 2009; Baker & Mori, 2010). All the named examples present high-profile private institutions for secondary school-level students that pave the way into a brighter future for the youth.

Besides this, society in these countries puts considerable emphasis on human capital production. Therefore, the parents do whatever it takes and make whatever sacrifices they need to to push their offspring into the highly prestigious schools. As already mentioned, this preparation process for the high-stakes tests starts at an early age, at around 8-9, so that by the time the tests are to be taken, by the age of 10 or 11, the students are already well trained and prepared in the core curriculum subjects.

The issues of equity and access to private tutoring and highly prestigious schools naturally rise at this point. And there are members of society in these countries who cannot afford either private tutoring or to enter elite schools. However, this chapter tries to show instances of countries where the overwhelming majority of members of society manage to resort to high-profile private education, since education is the number one priority in these countries and is closely associated with high social and academic or career status. Therefore, private tutoring and high-stakes testing create a general atmosphere of high competitiveness that pervades the entire society in these countries.

Low-stakes Testing

TIMSS and PIRLS assessment projects. Assessment projects, such as TIMSS and PIRLS, are low stakes because schoolchildren do not undergo any special preparation for those assessments and they are not graded or assessed based on them. However, these assessments are used to identify education problems and drawbacks in the fourth and eighth grades and find the reasons behind achievement gaps between the countries, schools and school districts. Achievement gaps have become even more vivid since more countries started participating in TIMSS and PIRLS projects (Chrostowski, 2004; Foy & Joncas, 2004; Gonzalez et al, 2004; Joncas, 2004).

*The Cases of High-scoring Countries:
high-stakes influence on low-stakes assessments*

The present chapter hypothesizes that the early private preparation process for high-stakes exams may influence the high achievement on low-stakes/no-stakes tests. Well-prepared students at the age of 10-11 sail through TIMSS and PIRLS smoothly without any special preparation for these assessments. Hence, high scores at TIMSS and PIRLS could be a kind of by-product of the intensive preparation that the students go through with private tutors for entering elite secondary schools. It could be an indirect result, a 'spillover effect', of the preparation process for high-stakes tests. It could even be claimed that the private tutoring sessions act as a kind of remediation for poor public schooling.

Naturally, equity and access issues rise again at this point, meaning that low-SES students have limited or no access to private tutoring. But the overall picture is that since the overwhelming majority of societies in these countries put extremely high emphasis on enabling their children to enter elite schools and on investing in human capital, low-stakes assessments also benefit as an indirect consequence, so that the low quality of public schooling is remediated or improved through private and intensive tutoring courses.

The 2011 data from TIMSS and PIRLS official websites, as shown in Table I, illustrate the scores of high-achieving countries. As the figures in the table illustrate, Hong Kong, Singapore, South Korea, Chinese Taipei and Japan are among the top-scoring countries in TIMSS and PIRLS assessments. And as already mentioned, high-stakes examinations and intensive preparation with private tutors or at private institutes are widely spread in these countries. Readiness for TIMSS and PIRLS could be a kind of natural consequence of the overall situation.

High-stakes Testing: the cases of low-scoring countries

Low-scoring countries, especially transition countries, such as Armenia, Azerbaijan, Georgia, Kazakhstan and Ukraine, are also famous for intensive private tutoring practices (Parental Informal Payments for Education across Eurasia [PIPES], 2010; Orkodashvili, 2010a,b,c, 2012). But the case in these countries is that the students go to private tutors at a later stage – that is, in the eleventh or twelfth grades, when it is time to prepare for the entry examinations for higher education institutions. The ages of students at this stage are mainly 17-19. There are no high-stakes tests in these countries at an early age. The students move from grade to grade relatively smoothly, without stringent assessments in the lower grades. The degree of accountability of public schooling is very low. The students resort to private tutors only to prepare for entry examinations at universities (Orkodashvili, 2012, 2014, 2015).

PIRLS	2011 Grade 4	
Hong Kong	571 (2.3)	
Singapore	567 (3.3)	
Chinese Taipei	553 (1.9)	
PIRLS mean	500	
TIMSS, Science	2011 Grade 4	2011 Grade 8
Hong Kong	535 (3.8)	535 (3.4)
Singapore	583 (3.4)	590 (4.3)
South Korea	587 (2.0)	560 (2.0)
Japan	559 (1.9)	558 (2.4)
Chinese Taipei	552 (2.2)	564 (2.3)
TIMSS mean	500	500
TIMSS, Math	2011 Grade 4	2011 Grade 8
Hong Kong	602 (3.4)	586 (3.8)
Singapore	606 (3.2)	611 (3.8)
South Korea	605 (1.9)	613 (2.9)
Chinese Taipei	591 (2.0)	609 (3.2)
Japan	585 (1.7)	570 (2.6)
TIMSS mean	500	500

Data extracted from the official TIMSS and PIRLS website (http://timssandpirls.bc.edu/).
Standard deviations are indicated in parentheses.

Table I. TIMSS and PIRLS scores, 2011, high-scoring countries.

As already mentioned, the surveys were conducted in low-performing countries as well. The majority of respondents (about 89%) stated that they started going to the private tutors in the eleventh or twelfth grades (whichever was the final grade in their country). The main reasons for going to private classes were the approaching entry examinations in higher education institutions and a low trust level in public schooling which did not provide adequate preparation for those examinations. Therefore, it can be stated that in the transition countries the majority of students do not have the 'luxury' of going to private tutors in the lower grades, and only attend private classes in the case of necessity – that is, in the case of preparation for university entrance examinations.

The lack of alignment between public school preparation and the requirements of the entrance examinations to higher education institutions is the most apparent issue in all the discourses, surveys and interviews with students, their parents and the general public. The low level of trust in public schooling is aggravating the dire situation even more and is demotivating the teachers to conduct high-quality classes at schools. The common reply from a school teacher is that the students will go anyway to a private tutor and cover the material that they missed in school class, so nobody takes much care of instruction accountability and results until the final grades. As one of the parents said, 'The teacher covers only half of the material in class because she knows everyone goes to private tutors. She often misses the classes, not worrying that certain items will be left *un-covered* in class. She knows that the students will learn those items with their tutors anyway. So why bother?' Such was a common reply from the parents who were extremely dissatisfied with public schooling.

Low-stakes Testing: the cases of low-scoring countries

The situation depicted in the previous section has a natural spillover effect on lower grades as well. Regarding the fourth- and eighth-graders, the poor public schooling does not prepare them adequately for achieving high results in international assessments. Since TIMSS and PIRLS are conducted in the fourth and eighth grades, the students in transition countries are not well prepared in these grades. TIMSS and PIRLS results are low there. Public schooling systems function poorly in those countries and the majority of the population has no financial means to resort to private tutoring at lower grades, especially in the case when there is no urgent need to do so (in the fourth and eighth grades or earlier). The low TIMSS and PIRLS results reflect the dire reality of poor public schooling.

Table II illustrates the 2011 results of low-performing countries in TIMSS and PIRLS assessments. As can be seen from the table, Azerbaijan, Georgia, Armenia, Kazakhstan and Ukraine are low-performing countries. This may be due to poor public schooling. However, it should also be noted that since students face high-stakes assessments only in the final grades of schools, they are not prepared well in the lower fourth and eighth grades, hence their low performance on TIMSS and PIRLS.

Finland Case: the optimal equilibrium?

One of the interesting cases is that of Finland, where private tutoring is not widespread and the TIMSS and PIRLS results are high. This is generally attributed to the high quality of public schooling. Therefore, where public schooling is of high quality, there is no need for private tutoring. And inversely, where public schooling is of poor quality, private tutoring may serve as a substitute, but at the stage where the stakes become high and students resort to the services of private tutors. Much has been written and discussed on the miraculous results of the Finnish education system and its public schooling organization that might serve as an exemplary case for countries worldwide. And the present chapter fully agrees with that statement. However, the harsh reality is that Finland is a unique case of its kind and leaves much to be desired and attained by other regions.

PIRLS	2011 Grade 4	
Azerbaijan	462 (3.3)	
Georgia	488 (3.1)	
PIRLS mean	500	

TIMSS, Science	2011 Grade 4	2011 Grade 8
Azerbaijan	438 (5.6)	
Georgia	455 (3.8)	420 (3.0)
Kazakhstan	495 (5.1)	490 (4.3)
Armenia	416 (3.8)	437 (3.1)
Ukraine		501 (3.4)
TIMSS mean	500	500

TIMSS, Math	2011 Grade 4	2011 Grade 8
Azerbaijan	463 (5.8)	
Georgia	450 (3.7)	431 (3.8)
Armenia	452 (3.5)	467 (2.7)
Kazakhstan	501 (4.5)	487 (4.0)
Ukraine		479 (3.9)
TIMSS mean	500	500

Data extracted from the official TIMSS and PIRLS website (http://timssandpirls.bc.edu/).
Standard deviations are indicated in parentheses.

Table II. TIMSS and PIRLS Scores, 2011, low-scoring countries.

The present research hypothesizes that the most significant optimum/equilibrium state that Finland has managed to achieve is through regulating and managing this factor of 'stakes'. Not pressing too hard with high-stakes testing and at the same time concentrating on high-quality public schooling accessible for all members of society sets the equilibrium that yields the results that have been so much desired across countries for years.

Table III illustrates the 2011 TIMSS and PIRLS scores for Finland. High scores at TIMSS and PIRLS and absence of private tutoring testify to the efficient public schooling in Finland.

PIRLS	2011 Grade 4	
Finland	568 (1.9)	
PIRLS mean	500	

TIMSS, Science	2011 Grade 4	2011 Grade 8
Finland	570 (2.6)	552 (2.5)
TIMSS mean	500	500

TIMSS, Math	2011 Grade 4	2011 Grade 8
Finland	545 (2.3)	514 (2.5)
TIMSS mean	500	500

Data extracted from the official TIMSS and PIRLS website (http://timssandpirls.bc.edu/).

Table III. TIMSS and PIRLS scores, 2011, Finland.

Campbell's Law: are high stakes upsetting the equilibrium?

The present chapter assumes that the factor of 'stakes' that incentivizes students to resort to private tutors and to put much emphasis on exam results might be preventing countries from reaching the equilibrium that Finland has achieved. Distortions and biased or dishonest attitudes and practices of teachers are to be particularly mentioned here. Corruption and bribery are yet other challenges that societies with overly high-stakes tests experience. All these deviant practices upset the balance necessary for the proper functioning of an efficient education system. Campbell's law could be useful for explaining the phenomenon and the social behavior at this point.

Campbell's law was named for the social psychologist, evaluator, methodologist and philosopher of science Donald Campbell, who brought the phenomenon in question to the attention of social scientists in 1975. According to Nichols and Berliner (2007), Campbell's law stipulates that:

> the more any quantitative social indicator is used for social decision-making, the more subject it will be to corruption pressures and the more apt it will be to distort and corrupt the social processes it was intended to monitor. Campbell warned us of the inevitable problems associated with undue weight and emphasis on a single indicator for monitoring complex social phenomena. (pp. 26-27)

Madaus and Clarke (2001) noted that if Campbell is right, whenever you have high stakes attached to an indicator, such as test scores, you have a measurement system that has been corrupted, rendering the measurement less accurate. Apparently, you can have (a) higher stakes and less certainty about the validity of the assessment, or (b) lower stakes and greater certainty about the validity. Uncertainty about the meaning of test scores increases as the stakes attached to them become more severe. The higher the stakes, the more likely it is that the construct being measured has been changed (Nichols & Berliner, 2007).

Evidence of Campbell's law is everywhere. Wherever we look, when high stakes are attached to indicators, what follows is the corruption and distortion of the indicators and the people who employ them. In business, economists have long recognized the possibility for corruption when stakes are high. For example, incentives such as big bonuses for increased sales are common in business, but when stakes are attached to sales, the business of selling can become corrupt. Cars may be sold that are lemons, houses may be sold with concealed defects, guarantees may be made that are not genuine. It is the sale that is important (Nichols & Berliner, 2007).

Perhaps it is exactly what Campbell's law postulates that Finland has addressed most efficiently to achieve the results desired by other countries? Therefore, the present chapter states that the issue of stakes as applied to testing and examinations should be approached with due consideration and caution not to overly bend the results in one direction or another and not to make hasty and immature conclusions. However, it should be noted that although it is widely known that the stakes for examinations are a negative phenomenon and bring about multiple undesirable consequences for the public, such as data distortions, information manipulation and corruption, the reality is that they have a certain influence on the testing and examination process across countries and cannot be ignored.

Discussion of Findings

The present research suggests that when public schooling is considered to be of high quality, private tutoring is not necessary. Consequently, in such cases, both high-stakes examinations and TIMSS and PIRLS results are high. However, when public schooling is deemed poor or unsatisfactory, the stage at which students resort to private tutoring might affect the TIMSS and PIRLS results. If tutoring starts at an early stage, the TIMSS and PIRLS scores are a by-product of the intensive preparation for high-stakes examinations and high results are achieved. If tutoring happens at a later stage, the results of TIMSS and PIRLS are low. Therefore, depending on the school grade at which high-stakes examinations appear, in a number of countries students increasingly resort to private tutoring to succeed at school, or in the entrance examinations, and hence the influence of private tutoring on international projects can be vividly observed.

International projects like TIMSS and PIRLS could serve not only as means of setting and checking quality standards in education, but as mediators in closing achievement gaps and in helping increase the accountability of schools towards the wider public. This chapter makes a suggestion that the international assessment projects such as TIMSS and PIRLS could not only produce official data on the rankings of countries and, consequently, reveal the general academic standings of school students (namely, fourth- and eighth-graders), but they could also induce discussions on the possible causes of achievement gaps between the countries and make suggestions on low performance of certain regions and countries in these projects. In this case, they could bring forward such issues as the revision of teaching materials, school textbooks, national curricula, teaching methodologies, teacher qualifications, parental involvement, and high- versus low-stakes examinations.

Concluding Remarks

Public Schooling and Private Tutoring: stakes, quality and equilibrium

Through international education projects and global data availability and comparability, the focus of most national education policies has shifted from access to quality over the past decade. Policymakers, donors and project implementers try to ensure that international, national and local stakeholders perceive education improvement strategies and projects as successful. The present research assumes that the large-scale international data might appear useful for benchmarking the progress made in any individual country. The chapter suggests that the arrows of influence move and operate in both directions, implying that while setting global standards, international projects should base their judgments on identified local challenges in the education systems of individual countries. Lost trust in the quality of public schooling is perceived as a major challenge to education systems in the countries where private tutoring is widely spread.

Stakes and Stage

In summary, the main challenge faced by international projects and donors is the complexity of the definition of education success and quality, the inefficiency of scarce resource allocation and the lack of methods for measuring sustainable outcomes. As the present research has revealed, when public schooling is considered high quality, private tutoring is not necessary. And consequently, in such cases, both high-stakes examinations and TIMSS and PIRLS results are high. However, when public schooling is viewed as poor or unsatisfactory, the stage at which students resort to private tutoring might affect the TIMSS and PIRLS results. If tutoring starts at an early stage, the TIMSS and PIRLS scores are a by-product of the intensive preparation for high-stakes examinations, and high results are achieved. If tutoring happens at a later stage, the results of TIMSS and PIRLS are low. The high-stakes versus low-stakes factor, although undesirable, might be a significant influencing factor both on the testing preparation process and on examination results. Therefore, finding the equilibrium point between the two extremes of high-stakes and low-stakes/no-stakes testing programs might be one of the challenges for education systems across countries.

References

Ahola, S. & Kokko, A. (2001) Finding the Best Possible Students: student selection and its problems in the field of business, *Journal of Higher Education Policy and Management*, 23(2). http://dx.doi.org/10.1080/13600800120088689

Akey, T.M. (2006) *School Context, Student Attitudes and Behavior, and Academic Achievement: an exploratory analysis*. New York: MDRC.

Baker, D. (1993) Compared to Japan, the U.S. is a Low Achiever ... Really, *Educational Researcher*, 22(3), 18-20.

Baker, D.P., Goesling, B. & Letendre, G.K. (2002) Socioeconomic Status, School Quality, and National Economic Development: a cross-national analysis of the 'Heyneman-Loxley Effect' on mathematics and science achievement, *Comparative Education Review*, 46(3), 291-312. http://dx.doi.org/10.1086/341159

Baker, D.P. & Mori, I. (2010) The Origin of Universal Shadow Education: what the supplemental education phenomenon tells us about the postmodern institution of education, *Asia Pacific Education Review*.

Bray, M. (1999) *The Shadow Education System: private tutoring and its implications for planners*. Paris: UNESCO International Institute for Educational Planning.

Bray, M. (2003) *Adverse Effects of Private Supplementary Tutoring: dimensions, implications and government responses*. Paris: UNESCO International Institute for Educational Planning (IIEP).

Bray, M. (2009) *Confronting the Shadow Education System. What Government Policies for What Private Tutoring?* UNESCO: International Institute for Educational Planning.

Chrostowski, S.J. (2004) Developing the TIMSS 2003 Background Questionnaires, in M.O. Martin, I.V.S. Mullis & S.J. Chrostowski (Eds) *TIMSS 2003 Technical Report*. Chestnut Hill, MA: Boston College.

Coleman, J.S., Campbell, E.Q., Hobson, C.J. et al (1968) The Equality of Educational Opportunity Report. Washington, DC: US Printing Office.

Foy, P. & Joncas, M. (2004) TIMSS 2003 Sampling Design, in M.O. Martin, I.V.S. Mullis & S.J. Chrostowski (Eds) TIMSS 2003 Technical Report. Chestnut Hill, MA: Boston College.

Gamoran, A. & Long, D. (2006) Equality of Educational Opportunity: a 40-year retrospective, in R. Teese (Ed.) *Macrosocial Perspectives on Educational Inequality*. New York: Spring Press.

Gonzalez, E.J., Galia, J. & Li, I. (2004) Scaling Methods and Procedures for the TIMSS 2003 Mathematics and Science Scales, in M.O. Martin, I.V.S. Mullis & S.J. Chrostowski (Eds) *TIMSS 2003 Technical Report*. Chestnut Hill, MA: Boston College.

Heyneman, S.P. (2005) Student Background and Student Achievement: what is the right question?, *American Journal of Education*, 112(1), 1-9. http://dx.doi.org/10.1086/444512

Joncas, M. (2004) TIMSS 2003 Sampling Weights and Participation Rates, in M.O. Martin, I.V.S. Mullis & S.J. Chrostowski (Eds) *TIMSS 2003 Technical Report*. Chestnut Hill, MA: Boston College.

Kallo, J. (2006) Soft Governance and Hard Values: a review of OECD operational processes within education policy and relations with member states, in J. Kallo & R. Rinne (Eds) *Supranational Regimes and National Education Policies: encountering challenge*, pp. 261-297. Helsinki: Finnish Educational Research Association.

Madaus, G.F. & Clarke, M. (2001) *The Adverse Impact of High Stakes Testing on Minority Students: evidence from 100 years of test data*. Washington, DC: US Department of Education, Office of Educational Research and Improvement.

Marks, G.N., Cresswell, J. & Ainley, J. (2006) Explaining Socioeconomic Inequalities in Student Achievement: the role of home and school factors, *Educational Research and Evaluation*, 12(2), 105-128. http://dx.doi.org/10.1080/13803610600587040

Martin, M.O., Mullis, I.V.S. & Chrostowski, S.J. (Eds) (2004) TIMSS 2003 Technical Report. Chestnut Hill, MA: Boston College.

Martin, M.O., Mullis, I.V.S., Foy, P. & Stanco, G.M. (2012) TIMSS 2011 International Results in Science. Chestnut Hill, MA: TIMSS & PIRLS International Study Center, Boston College.

Martin, M.O., Mullis, I.V.S., Gonzalez, E.J., O'Connor, K.M., Chrostowski, S.J., Gregory, K.D., Smith, T.A. & Garden, R.A. (2001) Science Benchmarking Report TIMSS 1999 – Eighth Grade: achievement for US states and districts in an international context. Chestnut Hill, MA: Boston College.

McEwan, P. & Marshall, J. (2004) Why Does Academic Achievement Vary across Countries? Evidence from Cuba and Mexico, *Education Economics*, 12, 205-217. http://dx.doi.org/10.1080/0964529042000258572

Mullis, I.V.S., Martin, M.O. Foy, P. & Arora, A. (2012a) TIMSS 2011: international results in mathematics. Chestnut Hill, MA: IEA, Lynch School of Education, Boston College.

Mullis, I.V.S., Martin, M.O. Foy, P. & Drucker, K.T. (2012b) *PIRLS 2011: international results in reading*. Chestnut Hill, MA: IEA, Lynch School of Education, Boston College.

Mullis, I.V.S., Martin, M.O., Smith, T.A., et al (2003) *TIMSS Assessment Frameworks and Specifications 2003*, 2nd edn. Chestnut Hill, MA: Boston College.

Nichols, S.L. & Berliner, D.C. (2007) *Collateral Damage. How High-stakes Testing Corrupts America's Schools*. Cambridge, MA: Harvard Education Press.

Orkodashvili, M. (2010a) From Equity of Access to International Quality Standards for Curbing Corruption in Secondary and Higher Education and Closing Achievement Gaps in Post-Soviet Countries, in A.W. Wiseman (Ed.) *The Impact of International Achievement Studies on National Education Policymaking, International Perspectives on Education and Society (IPES)*, vol. 13, pp. 181-206. London: Emerald Publishers.

Orkodashvili, M. (2010b) Higher Education Reforms in the Fight against Corruption in Georgia, *Demokratizatsiya: the journal of post-Soviet democratization*, 18(4), 357-374.

Orkodashvili, M. (2010c) Leadership Challenges in the Fight against Corruption in Higher Education in Georgia, *John Ben Sheppard Journal of Practical Leadership*, 5(1), 26-44.

Orkodashvili, M. (2012) The Changing Faces of Corruption in Georgian Higher Education: access through times and tests, *European Education: Issues and Studies*, 44(1), 27-45. http://dx.doi.org/10.2753/eue1056-4934440102

Orkodashvili, M. (2014) Access to Higher Education in Post-Socialist Countries: the stories of corruption, standardization, success and failure, in L. Elinor, P.C. Brown, G.L. Gorski (Eds) *Poverty, Class, and Schooling. Global Perspectives on Economic Justice and Educational Equity*. Charlotte, NC: Information Age Publishing.

Orkodashvili, M. (2015) Higher Education Access Policies in the Post-Soviet Region: standardization, testing, and corruption, in V. Stead (Ed.) *International Perspectives on Higher Education Admission Policy. Equity in Higher Education Theory, Policy, & Praxis*, vol. 1. New York: Peter Lang.

Parental Informal Payments for Education across Eurasia (PIPES) (2010) Drawing the Line: parental informal payments for education across Eurasia. Azerbaijan, Georgia, Kazakhstan, Latvia, Moldova, Slovakia, and Tajikistan. OSI's Education Support Program and Network of Education Policy Centers (NEPC), OSI.

PIRLS 2011 Assessment (2011) Released Reading Literacy Items. PIRLS User's Guide, Grade 4. Chestnut Hill, MA: IEA, Lynch School of Education, Boston College.

Rautalin, Marjaana & Alasuutari, Pertti (2009) The Uses of the National PISA Results by Finnish Officials in Central Government, *Journal of Education Policy*, 24(5), 539-556. http://dx.doi.org/10.1080/02680930903131267

Rinne, R. (2008) The Growing Supranational Impacts of the OECD and the EU on National Education Policies, and the Case of Finland, *Policy Futures in Education*, 6, 665-680. http://dx.doi.org/10.2304/pfie.2008.6.6.665

Rinne, R., Kallo, J. & Hokka, S. (2004) Too Eager to Comply? OECD Education Policies and the Finnish Response, *European Educational Research Journal*, 3, 454-484. http://dx.doi.org/10.2304/eerj.2004.3.2.3

Rivkin, S.G., Hanushek, E.A. & Kain, J.F. (2005) Teachers, Schools, and Academic Achievement, *Econometrica*, 73, 418-458. http://dx.doi.org/10.1111/j.1468-0262.2005.00584.x

Schmidt, W.H., McKnight C.C., Houang, R.T., et al (2001) *Why Schools Matter: using TIMSS to investigate curriculum and learning*. Unpublished manuscript.

Schuller, T. (2005) Constructing International Policy Research: the role of CERI/OECD, *European Educational Research Journal*, 4, 170-179. http://dx.doi.org/10.2304/eerj.2005.4.3.2

Stevenson, D.L. & Baker, D.P. (1992) Shadow Education and Allocation in Formal Schooling: transition to university in Japan, *American Journal of Sociology*, 97(6), 1639-1657. http://dx.doi.org/10.1086/229942

Vickers, M. (1994) Cross-national Exchange, the OECD, and Australian Education Policy, *Knowledge and Policy*, 7, 25-47. http://dx.doi.org/10.1007/BF02692814

Weymann, A. & Martens, K. (2005) Bildungspolitik durch internationale Organisationen: Entwicklung, Strategien und Bedeutung der OECD, *Österreichische Zeitschrift für Soziologie*, 30, 68-86. http://dx.doi.org/10.1007/s11614-006-0065-y

Willms, J.D. & Somers, M.A. (2001) Family, Classroom and School Effects on Children's Educational Outcomes in Latin America, *School Effectiveness and School Improvement*, 12(4), 409-445. http://dx.doi.org/10.1076/sesi.12.4.409.3445

CHAPTER 13

Testing and School Reform in Danish Education: an analysis informed by the use of 'the dispositive'

KRISTINE KOUSHOLT & BJØRN HAMRE

ABSTRACT This chapter is in two parts, consisting of both the theoretical development of Foucault's concept of the dispositive and an analysis of documents concerning national standardised tests and school reform in the Danish primary and lower secondary school. The Danish national standardised tests are recently implemented in the school system with different political ambitions. We argue that the tests are a crucial new form of assessment among others based on their adaptive character and of the political intentions connected to them. The article stems from an ambition to contribute with an adequate critique of the tests and related discourses. This is done by reading documents related to the national test through the dispositives ('dispositive' is a Foucauldian term for a rationale of power) of discipline, security and optimisation.

Introduction

This chapter presents an analytical suggestion to how we might understand the political ambition of challenging all pupils 'to reach their fullest potential'.[1] This ambition is expressed in both the Danish School Reform 2014 and in the technologies that are used to cultivate what might be termed 'the desirable pupil'. The desirable pupil is the pupil who continuously works on becoming as capable as possible. The desirable pupil has potential to become more capable – especially in Danish and maths. This chapter is written with the ambition of critically analysing recent movements in the Danish school system and viewing these movements as part of larger transnational movements. The following excerpts are taken from the document explaining the contents of the Danish school reform, on which the 2014 reform of the Danish Folkeskole was based.

> Denmark (has) a relatively small number of academically strong pupils. If their academic level, and thus the professional level of the Danish Folkeskole (primary and lower secondary school) are to be improved, it is essential that all pupils have the opportunity to reach their full potential, so that we can cope with the increasing international competition.[2]

The Danish Folkeskole reform of 2014 was – among many aspects – based on Denmark's belief that they must be more competitive internationally. The reform constitutes an agreement between the government (consisting of the Social Democratic Party, the Danish Social Liberal Party and the Socialist People's Party), the Liberal Party, and the Danish People's Party. The reform was intended to boost primary and lower secondary education in Denmark. Below, we will refer to this document as the reform text. It is stressed that, 'The Danish Folkeskole must challenge all pupils to reach their fullest potential', and that 'the Danish Folkeskole must reduce the significance of social background in relation to academic results'.[3] These objectives should be fulfilled through specific performance goals: (1) at least 80 per cent of the pupils must be good at reading and arithmetic in the national tests, (2) the proportion of excellent pupils in Danish and maths must increase from year to year, (3) the proportion of pupils with bad results in the national reading and maths tests must be reduced from year to year.[4] The goals are related to the role of national testing: 'The professional points of development are measured in national tests'.[5] The content in these excerpts will be further developed in the analysis.

A national battery of tests – so-called Danish national tests – becomes then a relevant technology for documenting whether the new goals are achieved. In that sense, Denmark has become part of the growing number of counties that have adopted a national assessment programme (Smith, 2016). The Danish national tests are so-called CAT tests (Computer Adaptive Tests). The adaptive design indicates that the tests are adapted to the pupils' responses while taking the tests. If a pupil answers an item correctly, they are presented with a more difficult item; if they answer an item incorrectly, an easier item will be presented. The tests are computer based, mandatory and self-scoring. They have a multiple-choice design, which means that open-ended answers are not possible. The intention of the tests is to determine the individual pupil's ability within the tested area. The combination of this adaptive design and the reform focus on pupils reaching their fullest potential is extremely noteworthy, and the design has influenced our choice of analytical point of departure. Both in the reform text and the adaptive design of the national tests, we can observe the conception of the pupils' shapeable potentiality: a political ambition of cultivating and shaping 'the desirable pupil' who can contribute to optimisation.

The empirical material consists of policy documents regarding the reform of the Danish school system and documents regarding national testing. The analysis is informed by Foucault's concept of 'the dispositive' which will be elaborated on below. In addition to presenting theory that can be used for empirical analysis, it is the ambition of this chapter to contribute to further development of the concept of the dispositive within school research. The analytical perspective is further developed with special focus on the school, based on Foucault-inspired analyses of journal texts, including texts produced by school psychologists (Hamre, 2012, 2014). The aim is to show how new technologies of regulation and management, like national standardised tests, are to be found in the area of tension between different dispositives.

The article begins with a presentation of the Danish national tests as part of transnational developments and connections, followed by a presentation of the analytical approach and the concept of the dispositive. Subsequently, we look at the national tests and the attached political documents through the different dispositives.

Contextualising Danish National Tests

As a social technology, the Danish national standardised tests are part of Danish political history, which has increasingly merged with a larger transnational history. The genealogy of Danish national testing draws on recognisable elements across nations, but also illuminates the special nature of Danish national tests.[6] The Danish national tests relate to a genealogy of how international measurements, school criticism and school reforms interfere and create basic changes in the way schools are managed, understood and justified, and how this trinity has different meanings in the local school history of different nations. This genealogy is complex and brings many threads together in multifaceted ways. Denmark has had (and in many aspect still have) a tradition for prioritising internal and formative assessment in education. However, standardised testing is not new in the context of the Danish school, where intelligence tests played a major role in sorting children for various educational programmes in the 1930s (Ydesen, 2011). However, it would be a simplistic reduction to regard the introduction of national tests in Denmark as a revitalisation of former management technologies. The introduction and nature of new social technologies in school creates a link between transnationally influenced policy and national policies, interpretations and discussions. In the Nordic countries and Europe there is a strong tendency to manage through data, numbers and standards (Lawn & Grek, 2012). Introducing standards can be seen as a way of dealing with education and ambitions for lifelong learning in Europe (Lawn & Grek, 2012). In this context, the OECD and PISA measurements play a prominent role, and transnational rankings and national results are part of educational reforms (see also Smith, 2016).

In 1994, the report on the Danish results of an international comparative reading test (an international reading test carried out by the International Association for the Evaluation of Educational Achievement) was published. The disappointing results sent shock waves through the Danish school system, which had regarded itself as one of the best in the world, and led to open criticism of the Danish school system (Pedersen, 2011; Gustafsson, 2012). About a decade later, the results of the PISA tests and the Danish results, which were mainly described as disappointing, became agenda-setting. For instance, the PISA tests showed that the Danish school system did not succeed in supporting social mobility to the extent that was expected. Some political parties saw tests and quality control as part of the solution to the disappointing results. In 2004 an OECD report on the Danish Folkeskole (Ekholm et al, 2004) was published and the implementation of standardised national tests in Denmark cannot be seen in isolation from the conclusions and impact of this report. Among other things, it emphasised that the Danish school system needs a strengthened assessment culture with objective assessments that may contribute to building a self-critical attitude without having a negative influence on the pupils' self-confidence (Ekholm et al, 2004). Drawing on this report, the liberal party's education minister argued that national tests should be an instrument to strengthen the assessment culture, benefit the weakest pupils, and ensure that all pupils benefit from teaching (Gustafsson, 2012, p. 194). National standardised tests became a legitimate political focus and investment across political parties (except for the Red–Green Alliance party placed far on the left wing).

The Dispositive as an Analytical Approach

Our study of the logics that characterise the new understanding of testing is informed by Michel Foucault's concept of the dispositive. We understand the dispositive as a tool to analyse governance and social mechanisms in society. By applying this concept, we will be able to systematise some of the contradictory agendas that, in our opinion, affect the political and educational field and appear in the national tests. Within the past decade, the concept has become an important analytical tool to analyse continuity, fractures and dislocations in social and political rationales, both in international Foucault reception (Rabinow, 2003; Agamben, 2009; Bussolini, 2010) and reception of Foucault in Denmark (Fogh Jensen, 2005; Raffnsøe et al, 2008). From having been relatively unnoticed in Foucault-oriented research, the dispositive as a concept has now been included in various disciplines in political, social policy and educational research (Dahlager, 2005; Øland, 2007; Villadsen, 2011; Hamre, 2012; Bailey, 2013). Foucault defines the dispositive as follows: 'with the term dispositive, I understand a type of – so to speak – formation which in a certain historical moment had as its essential function to respond to an emergency. The dispositive therefore has an eminently strategic function' (Foucault, 1980, p. 194).

The dispositive is a tool in Foucault's attempt 'to incorporate non-discursive elements such as institutions, policies and material objects in a sustainable discourse approach to social and political phenomena' (Howarth, 2005, p. 120, translation by the authors). The dispositive can be analysed as a response to a specific historical situation, but it also works in a prescriptive albeit not determinant fashion. 'Dispositive can be viewed as a possible functional response to a problem that is beginning to emerge; but the answer is not given in advance. A dispositive has a reflectivity that cannot be reduced to pure functionality' (Raffnsøe & Gudman-Høyer, 2004, p. 20, note 27, translation by the authors).

In this chapter, we have chosen to analyse testing through dispositives. This means that we read the empirical data on national tests through three different, predesigned dispositives, each of which makes it possible to highlight different aspects of testing. This will enable us to understand how national tests and their use are characterised and permeated by different logics. In doing so, we will have the opportunity to understand how different dispositives turn out to be assembled and refracted in the analysed material. We will read the test material through the dispositive of discipline, the dispositive of security, and the dispositive of optimisation. These are different approaches, each emphasising different aspects of the way testing is problematised in relation to the role of school in society. In combining these dispositives, we find an analytical approach well suited for critically exploring different, naturalised political assumptions materialised in documents concerning national standardised tests and school reforms. The dispositive of discipline and security are, along with the dispositive of law, essential to Foucault's analysis of the exercise of power in the development of modern society and its institutions (Foucault, 2008). Whereas the dispositive of discipline is setting certain norms for institutions, the dispositive of security has a normalising function in relation to the unexpected. The dispositive of optimisation has been chosen due to its relation to the dynamics of the competition state, and the way in which modern subjectivity is formed (Hamre, 2014).

The dispositive of discipline seeks to explain the distinction between normality and deviancy. Its function is, among others, seen in the normalisation project that is legitimised and practiced through human sciences such as pedagogy, psychology and psychiatry, analysed by Foucault in *Discipline and Punish* (Foucault, 2002). The dispositive of discipline can shed light on how testing functions as normalisation by differentiating between pupils and establishing a relationship of surveillance between individual pupils and teachers. The pupil's awareness of being the object of testing also works as a self-technology, leaving the pupil to recognise themselves as a subject who is governed and aware of their status as a component of productivity in the competition state. In the management of testing in school, knowledge and power are connected in a written documentation of pupils, which in turn allows for comparison and differentiation between pupils who fall within or outside the norm. Following the above definition of the dispositive of discipline, national testing can thus be observed as a phenomenon that sets standards, organises and is based on a normalising practice. This makes testing part of a larger system in school and society that constitutes how pupils are desired to be. The dispositive of discipline illustrates how testing functions as a dividing practice, sorting out those who are not considered skilled or competent.

Whereas the dispositive of discipline involves setting the norms for what should be, the dispositive of security involves reacting to what is already given, i.e. existing. In Foucault's studies of the state management of the relationship between security and freedom, it is illustrated how a range of security technologies became crucial as the population was discovered as a field of intervention. With the need to manage the population, a new type of power technology emerged, designed to handle the unpredictable events of modern society. The welfare state has introduced security technologies intended to anticipate what appears threatening and dangerous, through calculation and minimisation of risks. The intention of the dispositive of security is to perform 'cost accounting' (Foucault, 2008, p. 12). Certain school and testing policies can be seen as means to handle the unforeseen and seek to preserve the status quo. As examples of the function of the dispositive of security, Foucault mentions the normal distribution curve and statistics that provide visibility and construct the dangerous and undesirable in a scheme that makes various interventions possible. The normal distribution curve also illustrates something crucial when it comes to the adaptive testing of pupils. The test differentiates between pupils according to skills and delivers a picture of what deviates from the norm. In this perspective, adaptive testing can be analysed as a security measure that operates by taking account of the occurrence of the unforeseen.

Inspired by Hamre (2012, 2014), we argue that the technologies and practices of school can also be analysed through a dispositive called the dispositive of optimisation. This will enable us to explain a particular form of subjectivity that is prevalent in schools today. We see this kind of subjectivity reflected in the intention of adaptive tests to interact with the individual pupil, in accordance with their level of performance, as well as in the political ambition of challenging all pupils to reach their fullest potential. This includes a performance and an expectation that the pupil's potentiality can and should be unfolded and released. These ideas merge in current school political discourses, including PISA surveys measuring pupils' academic performance, based on economic rationales about the nation's future competitiveness in a global perspective. The dispositive of optimisation shares similarities with the dispositive of security in the sense that it responds to the occurrence of the unforeseen; however, it reflects mainly economic rationales in the sense that it penetrates how subjectivity is constructed in the modern welfare state. In the construction of this dispositive, we partly draw on the tradition in post-structuralism called governmentality studies in education, because we particularly want to emphasise the importance of the economic rationales that have characterised the education agenda, as seen in phenomena like New Public Management, TALIS and PISA surveys, and in adherence to policies from the OECD and the EU, such as the Bologna Process (Fendler, 2001; Krejsler, 2002, 2004; Hultqvist, 2006, 2008; Popkewitz, 2008; Staunæs, 2011).

We also draw on Dorthe Staunæs' analysis of potentiality as an understanding of how subjectivity is created (Staunæs, 2011). We use the term dispositive of optimisation to stress the focus on the individual's potentiality as an educational subject affected by a particular economic and political agenda that characterises modern schooling. It is no longer only about *what you are* – and what kind of skills you are equipped with – but about *what you can become*. The dispositive of optimisation helps us analyze how pupils are constantly challenged to exceed themselves. This is the case both when it comes to optimising knowledge and specific skills, and when it comes to releasing potentiality, i.e. willingness to see oneself as something unfulfilled and constantly on the path of lifelong learning with a never fulfilled learning potential.

Analysis

In the following paragraphs, we present an analysis divided into three themes produced by reading through the perspective of the different dispositives. These themes are: different legitimisations of tests; testing as a project of equality – cleverness and appreciation, and; the launch of national tests. The themes are produced in an analytical process of reading empirical material; wondering how this material appears to draw on different logics; applying the theoretical approach of the different dispositives; and hereby finding an adequate language to analytically visualise and put into words how the material incorporates different, apparently contradictory, political assumptions.

Different Legitimisations of Tests

The traditional understanding of standardised tests is based on the notion that they categorise and normalise, and that they are therefore connected to the dispositive of discipline. Educational testing in general places itself in a discourse of a particularly legitimised science: there is a correlation between the tests and new positivism (or 'instrumental positivism', see Smith, 2016), which strives towards ontological objectivity (the understanding that reality can be recognised independently of the subject (Christensen, 2003 [2002]), reliability, validity and evidence. As such, testing aims at being an epistemological match (Højlund, 2006) to a form of science that is generally acknowledged as legitimate. The new positivistic approach in test technology entails an implicit understanding of what can be termed 'core cleverness' (see Kousholt, 2009). This is a critical based term for the assumption that test technology can identify an existing, essential cleverness in every pupil. This understanding – that cleverness is essentialised, internalised and individual – is related to the accumulation and measurement of cleverness and skills. The reform text focuses on developing and measuring skills and cleverness (especially in Danish language and maths). As such, there is an assumption that core cleverness is so stable that measurement and rating is possible. This assumption of core cleverness, and the faith in tests to reveal what the pupil is actually capable of, can be seen through the categorising and normative functions of the dispositive of discipline.

Concurrently with legitimatisation of tests through a new positivistic discourse of objectivity exists another form of legitimisation that attempts to match what is prioritised and developed in the Danish Folkeskole: formative assessment which can lead to differentiated teaching and the possibility of identifying and helping the pupils considered the weakest learners. This legitimisation is related to political discussions as the basis for introducing national tests in Denmark. In addition to the epistemological match to a new positivistic discourse and ontological objectivity, there is also an epistemological match to progressive pedagogy. The prioritisation of internal usability rather than external ranking is expressed through the fact that the results of the national tests are not currently to be published (even though this has previously been on the political agenda). Even though (or perhaps because) the tests are mandatory, they are also regarded as an option that teachers are welcome to use (it is mandatory to use the tests, but the teachers can use the test results in many different ways, present the tests differently, prepare differently or not at all, or offer their pupils assistance).

The national tests are part of a school system that has many different agendas. These agendas have an impact on the design of the tests and, especially, on how the tests are presented, introduced and identified with regard to population policy. The bill on the introduction of national tests in 2005 states that:

> Studies show that the majority of pupils thrive at school, are motivated to learn ... However, the most recent studies have shown that academic results are still unsatisfactory ... For instance, far too many young people leave primary and lower secondary school without useful reading skills.[7]

The bill mentions the qualities of school and aspects of the pupils' well-being, self-confidence and motivation, moving on to mention a defect necessary to identifying new initiatives (national tests). This defect is to be found in the academic results, which are considered unsatisfactory on the basis of new studies. The bill points to a large group of young people who leave primary and lower secondary school with inadequate reading skills.

This positions the school as a compensatory institution intended to correct inequality, and the phrasing justifies the test as a social project aiming to measure cleverness/skills and create equality. This ambition is also found in the reform text, as quoted initially. Here, we can see how the objectives of the new school involve reducing the significance of social background in relation to academic results, and how national tests are to be used as a tool of measurement to show a reduction in the proportion of pupils with poor results in Danish reading and maths (in national tests).

In the bill it is further stated:

> In order to monitor the individual pupil's acquisition of knowledge and skills, including strengths, weaknesses and potentials, it is proposed that – as part of the assessment of what the pupils learn from the teaching – centrally prepared tests should be used in selected subjects and certain age groups.[8]

The national tests are identified as a useful tool in monitoring the development of knowledge and skills, including strengths, weaknesses and potentials. It is expected that the pupils are already located at various points on the school's stratification of cleverness (Kousholt, 2009). Testing relates to predefined norms of cleverness, which implies disciplining and categorisation of skills as well as differentiation of skills; tests work only through differentiating. Furthermore, the quotation points to a crucial new function of tests: they must also monitor the individual pupil's potential. This is due to the understanding that pupils are capable of constant development – i.e. the desirable pupil as presented initially. Simultaneously, the quotation paves the way for an understanding and launch of national tests as a formative pedagogical tool, which is intended to help teachers plan and differentiate their teaching to reach the individual pupil's next potential stage of development. The quotations show how the tests can be identified and recognised through contemporary claims of inclusion; the school as an institution of social compensation; formative assessment; as well as the ambition to break with negative social inheritance.

Testing as a Project of Equality – Cleverness and Appreciation

The Danish Ministry of Education emphasises the non-differentiation of national tests, based on the fact that all pupils are considered testable because the tests differentiate themselves (the adaptive design), and thus accommodate the pupils' different responses and academic levels. This is reflected in the following quotation from so-called inspirational material from the Danish Ministry of Education with the title 'National tests for pupils with ADHD and/ or autism disorders – challenges, recommendations and inspiration'. This text states that:

> Exemption (from the national tests) is rarely necessary. It will only be necessary to exempt pupils with ADHD or autism from

participation in exceptional circumstances. This is because the tests are adjusted to suit the level of the pupils as they proceed, because the pupils can take the test over several days, and because the pupils are allowed to use any of the aids they use in everyday school life.[9]

This quotation indicates that the special design of the tests constitutes what can be termed test equality, and emphasises the flexibility of the tests and their ability to adapt and provide assistance to the pupils. Within this test design and test performance, it is implied that everyone, regardless of differences, should be incorporated in/ subjected to the test logic. The tests, therefore, compensate for the pupils' differences and imply that the starting point varies to reduce these differences. It is implicit in the differentiated mechanisms of the test design that the pupils are understood and met as different, and that the test design implicitly aims to be able to accommodate and include all these differences. The requirement of inclusion is a contemporary claim to the school. Within this framework can be seen the contours of the test as a compensatory and appreciative technology. In the dispositive of security, it is assumed that something deviates from the norm, and at the same time there is a norm prescribing that all pupils need to become better, which is why technologies have been developed to take care of those who are different. The dispositive of security – that the test differentiates itself and thus performs an inclusive movement towards all pupils' potential testability (Kousholt, 2014, inspired by Foucault, 2002) – is also closely linked to the dispositive of discipline: that the tests measures and normalises.

The national tests do not only imply separation, selection and exclusion; they also accommodate those who would traditionally be excluded. Moreover, the tests differentiate themselves through an adaptive design that is technically able to present any pupil who has answered incorrectly with an easier task. Everyone is included in the test technology; everyone is testable. Concurrently with the tests as a project of equality and appreciation of the pupils' abilities, another function is to place the pupils in the school's stratification of cleverness, as seen in connection with the dispositive of discipline.

While the tests define normality on a broad scale, they categorise and differentiate individually. Everyone is testable, but the individual is rated and stratified in relation to all the others, which points to the traditional function of tests as a dividing practice, as outlined in connection with the dispositive of discipline. If we read the tests through the dispositive of discipline, they function as a technology of discipline based on given standards, while contributing to normalisation by contributing to differentiation. If we read through the dispositive of security, we come to see how the national tests also imply and respond to recognition of what is different. Thus, the tests are not only prescriptive but also legitimised as contributing to inclusion. In this way, it could be said that testing is legitimised as a project of equality.

The Launch of National Tests

From the perspective of the different dispositives, we can now take a closer look at how the national tests have been addressed as something other than control and centralisation. The idea behind national tests has been to give an academic boost of the Danish Folkeskole, and testing thus concerns the intention of doing something to/with someone. At the same time, this 'someone' is also supposed to want to do something themselves. The national tests have been communicated in a way that allows them to fall under the teachers' educational and formative orientation, which can be seen (for instance) in the following extract from the Ministry of Education's inspirational material called 'Use test results. Inspiration for educational use of the results from the national tests' [10]:

> The test results can form the basis of a dialogue with parents on educational objectives for the individual pupil. If the interview is in the autumn, and a test is taken in the spring, the teacher can also talk about the development which has taken place since the test. The parents can support their child's academic development in many ways, and the teacher can give parents ideas for how this can be handled. Depending on the pupil's strengths and weaknesses as identified in the test, the teacher exemplifies what can be done.[11]

Testing as an institutionalised dispositive of discipline does not receive much direct attention in the above. Instead, we see a focus on the tests as connected to the dispositive of optimisation, i.e. potentiality. In the above, there is an implicit expectation of the pupil's development, which the teacher talks about based on the results over time. Read through the dispositive of optimisation, the national tests are made relevant as documentation of development in relation to a formative assessment practice. The teacher can give parents ideas for how they can support their child's academic development – on the basis of test results.

The inspirational material further points to the fact that: the teacher can support the pupil in describing what they are, and are not yet, able to do; the pupils can formulate their own learning objectives on the basis of the test results; and parents can support pupils' academic learning in many ways.[5] In that sense, testing is constituted as an opportunity for the pupil to take responsibility for his or her own learning. At the same time, the teacher is encouraged to take responsibility by providing the pupil with an insight into his own abilities and not-yet-abilities, and differentiating the teaching accordingly. Test results can thus be part of the imperative of the school's encouragement to know yourself and your potential (Juelskjær et al, 2011; Hamre, 2012). Simultaneously, there is an assumption in the inspiration material, as illustrated in the quotation above, that the pupil does not have direct access to knowing his own strengths and weaknesses, and that a test system is necessary to recognise this kind of knowledge as knowledge. The test is expected to reveal something about the pupil's' skills to the pupil's himself and the teacher. Getting to know your self is thus not necessarily an introspective journey with self-assessment as the primary assessment method, but a process involving the relation to the teacher and the aim to differentiate. When the test results are received, it is the political intention that teachers should differentiate their teaching on this basis. This aspect in particular can be read through the dispositive of optimisation. The purpose of the tests is not only to appreciate the individual pupil's academic level, as seen in relation to the dispositive of security, but also to contribute to optimisation of the learning resources available. This can be seen (for example) in the inspirational material 'Use the test results. Inspiration for educational use of the results of the national tests' [13], where the following quotation is part of the section 'From test result to learning':

> The test results can provide a source of content in future teaching because they provide the teacher with information about pupils' academic strengths and weaknesses. If the starting point is the pupils' abilities, they will be more likely to engage in the work. If the results of the class cover a wider spectrum than expected, the teacher can consider whether further differentiation of the teaching needs to be implemented in order to adapt it to the diversity of pupils.[14]

The focus on these strengths and weaknesses reflect the willingness to optimise' the learning of the pupil (see Hamre [2012] about learning as a key problematisation in contemporary education and schooling as a contemporary problem area), so that he/she come to reach their fullest potential. As the quotations above show, the tests aim to contribute to teachers' knowledge about pupils' academic levels and then to differentiate and adapt their teaching to suit the individual pupil's strengths and weaknesses. Read through the dispositive of optimisation, the essential elements are: the movement from test result to expected learning; and, test results contributing to the pupils' commitment and engagement via differentiated teaching. These are the elements that in particular point to an increasing optimisation of the learning resources available and thus to the desirable pupil who is committed to becoming as clever/skilled as possible.

Even though the national tests are compulsory and at first glance connote central management and control, the launch of the tests also connotes opportunities, self-management, self-realisation and empowerment. It is essential that the paradigm of tests does not only imply central control but that the design of the tests and the accompanying texts from the Ministry link to the discourses that are already popular in the Danish Folkeskole because of the historical development of the Danish school system. These are the discourses of progressive pedagogy, where the individual subject is at the centre as the active co-creator of their own learning objectives. The self-governance, which the Ministry encourages in the inspirational material, can be seen as a link between the new national tests and the well-known educational practice. This link to formative educational practice can be seen in the light of the fact that educational standardised testing has traditionally been criticised as an engine of discipline, sorting and selection: a way to centralise and create control. To work – despite this criticism – the national tests have to be and do something else and more. They do this by linking themselves to the discourses of internal and formative assessment practice.

Conclusion

Reading the current testing regime through the three dispositives, we can observe a development that can be seen as a break with the disciplining and norming functions of previous testing regimes, towards another regime that provides the individual with responsibility for their own professional, academic and personal optimisation. Furthermore, the chapter has highlighted the point that the current testing regime works by integrating the understanding of 'core cleverness' with the idea of unlimited development of personal resources. In this integration, the current testing regime reflects the efficiency strategy of the competition state, merged with the idea from progressive pedagogy of the child being at the centre of its own development. The dispositive of optimisation implies specific distinction and categorisation of skills. There is a difference between those who are considered competent and those who are not. Potentiality appears to be unequally distributed, and the educational challenge is to provide an opportunity for the pupils to realise their full potential.

The paradox is that different measuring methods – including national tests – constitute understandings of categorisations and core cleverness, at the same time as seeking to include and optimise the learning resources. The point presented above is that skills and potentiality interact in new ways and that national tests play an important role in this interaction. The tests categorise and differentiate in ways that also contribute to the construction of potentiality over time. The internal balance between the three dispositives is changeable and not easy to predict. The importance of potentiality is emphasised, both in relation to pupils who are already perceived as skilled and competent, and pupils who are perceived as less competent. Regarding the latter, the compensating function of school is stressed; all pupils should have the opportunity to fully realise their potential. Nevertheless, potentiality also contributes to categorisation. We find that the sentence: 'The Danish Folkeskole should challenge all pupils to reach their full potential' reflects all three dispositives: The dispositive of discipline illuminates aspects of standardisation, categorisation and differentiation; there is a standard for being a desirable pupil, which at the same time defines what is not seen as desirable. The dispositive of security illuminates inclusive aspects of the sentence; that is, not some but all pupils need to become as clever as possible. The dispositive of optimisation illuminates that the pupils' potential needs to be released; the pupils should become as clever as possible.

As illustrated, the national tests contain elements of former disciplinary functions of testing. This is supported by the Danish school reform, in which two out three aims are supposed to be achieved through national testing as an assessment tool that functions as a new form of power. Elements of the dispositive of discipline however, constantly merge with features of the dispositive of security (inclusion) and the dispositive of optimisation (to release potentiality): cleverness that seems boundless, since it can always be improved. Our conclusion is that the national standardised tests constitute compulsory testing that satisfies different contemporary demands; therefore, we expect testing to gain more influence and acceptance internationally and thus spread transnationally. Our ambition with this chapter has been to unfold the agenda of the Danish national standardised tests in order to contribute to critical perspectives on such new forms of power. This leads us to conclude that the national adaptive tests are a crucial new technology of power in primary and lower secondary school today.

Acknowledgement

We wish to thank Dorthe Staunæs and John Benedicto Krejsler for their fruitful comments on earlier drafts of this chapter.

Notes

[1] http://www.kl.dk/ImageVault/Images/id_62271/scope_0/ImageVaultHandler.aspx (p. 2, our translation).

[2] http://www.kl.dk/ImageVault/Images/id_62271/scope_0/ImageVaultHandler.aspx (p. 1, our translation).

[3] http://www.kl.dk/ImageVault/Images/id_62271/scope_0/ImageVaultHandler.aspx (p. 2, our translation).

[4] http://www.kl.dk/ImageVault/Images/id_62271/scope_0/ImageVaultHandler.aspx (p. 31, our translation).

[5] http://www.kl.dk/ImageVault/Images/id_62271/scope_0/ImageVaultHandler.aspx (p. 23, our translation).

[6] Our use of genealogy as a concept is influenced by Michel Foucault (Foucault, 1991).

[7] http://www.ft.dk/samling/20051/lovforslag/l101/html_som_fremsat.htm (p. 5, our translation).

[8] http://www.ft.dk/samling/20051/lovforslag/l101/html_som_fremsat.htm (p. 6, our translation).

[9] http://www.uvm.dk/Uddannelser/Folkeskolen/De-nationale-test-og-evaluering/De-nationale-

test/~/media/UVM/Filer/Udd/Folke/PDF11/110921_de_nationale_test_for_ele
ver_med_ADHD_og%20autisme.ashx (p. 3, our translation).

[10] http://uvm.dk/~/media/UVM/Filer/Udd/Folke/PDF11/111111%20Brug%20te
stresultarne.pdf

[11] http://uvm.dk/~/media/UVM/Filer/Udd/Folke/PDF11/111111%20Brug%20te
stresultarne.pdf (p. 12, our translation).

[12] http://uvm.dk/~/media/UVM/Filer/Udd/Folke/PDF11/111111%20Brug%20te
stresultarne.pdf (p. 10).

[13] http://uvm.dk/~/media/UVM/Filer/Udd/Folke/PDF11/111111%20Brug%20te
stresultarne.pdf

[14] http://uvm.dk/~/media/UVM/Filer/Udd/Folke/PDF11/111111%20Brug%20te
stresultarne.pdf (p. 11, our translation).

References

Agamben, G. (2009) What is an Apparatus?, in A. Giorgio (Ed.) *'What is an Apparatus?' and Other Essays*. Stanford, CA: Stanford University Press.

Bailey, P.L.J. (2013) The Policy Dispositif: historical formation and method, *Journal of Education Policy*, 28(6), 807-827.
http://dx.doi.org/10.1080/02680939.2013.782512

Bussolini, J. (2010) What is a Dispositive?, *Foucault Studies*, 10, 85-107.

Christensen, G. (2003 [2002]) *Psykologiens Videnskabsteori*, vol. 2. Frederiksberg: Roskilde Universitetsforlag.

Dahlager, L. (2005) I samtalens rum – en magtanalyse med afsæt i den livsstilsrelaterede forebyggelsessamtale. PhD thesis, Faculty of Health Sciences, Copenhagen University.

Ekholm, M., Mortimore, P., David-Evans, M., Laukkanen, R. & Valijarvi, J. (2004) *OECD-rapport om grundskolen I Danmark – 2004*. Copenhagen: Danish Ministry of Education.

Fendler, L. (2001) Educating Flexible Souls. The Construction of Subjectivity through Developmentality and Interaction, in K. Hultqvist & G. Dahlberg (Eds) *Governing the Child in the New Millennium*, pp. 119-142. London: RoutledgeFalmer.

Fogh Jensen, A. (2005) *Mellem ting, Foucaults filosofi*. Frederiksberg: Det lille forlag.

Foucault, M. (1980) The Confession of the Flesh: interview, in C. Gordon (Ed.) *Power/Knowledge: selected interviews and other writings, 1972-1977*, pp. 194-228. London: Pantheon Books.

Foucault, M. (1991) Nietzsche, Genealogy, History, in P. Rabinow (Ed.) *The Foucault Reader*. New York: Pantheon.

Foucault, M. (2002) *Overvågning og straf*. Frederiksberg: Det lille forlag.

Foucault, M. (2008) *Sikkerhed, territorium, befolkning – Forelæsninger på Collège de France, 1977-1978*. Copenhagen: Hans Reitzels Forlag.

Gustafsson, L.R. (2012) What Did You Learn in School Today? How Ideas Mattered for Policy Changes in Danish and Swedish Schools 1990-2011. PhD thesis, Aarhus: Forlaget Politica & L.R. Gustafsson.

Hamre, B. (2012) Potentialitet og optimering i skolen – Problemforståelser og forskelssætninger af elever – en nutidshistorisk analyse. Institut for Uddannelse og Pædagogik. Aarhus: Aarhus University.

Hamre, B. (2014) Optimization as a Dispositive in the Production of Differences in Schools in Denmark, *European Education*, 45, 7-25.

Højlund, I. (2006) Gennem flere labyrinter. Unpublished PhD thesis, Department of Education, Aarhus University, Copenhagen.

Howarth, D. (2005) *Diskurs – en introduction*. Copenhagen: Hans Reitzels Forlag.

Hultqvist, K. (2006) The Future is Already Here – As It Always Has Been. The New Teacher's Subject, the Pupil and the Technologies of the Soul, in T.S. Popkewitz, K. Petersson, U. Olsson & J. Kowalczyk (Eds) *The Future is Not What It Appears to Be: pedagogy, genealogy and political epistemology*, pp. 20-61. Stockholm: HLS Förlag.

Hultqvist, K. (2008) 'Fremtiden' som styringsteknologi og det pædagogiske subjekt som konstruktion, in J.B. Krejsler (Ed.) *Pædagogikken og kampen om individet – Kritisk pædagogik, ny inderlighed og selvets teknikker*. Copenhagen: Hans Reitzels Forlag.

Juelskjær, M., Knudsen, H., Grønbæk Pors, J. & Staunæs, D. (2011) *Ledelse af uddannelse: at lede det potentielle*. Frederiksberg: Samfundslitteratur.

Kousholt, K. (2009) Evalueret. Deltagelse i folkeskolens evalueringspraksis. PhD thesis, Danmarks Pædagogiske Universitetsskole, Aarhus University.

Kousholt, K. (2014) Testing and Differentiation. A Critical Approach to Standardized Testing in Education. Paper presented at International Society for Cultural and Activity Research, Sydney, 1 October 2014.

Krejsler, J.B. (2002) *Læring, magt og individualitet*. Copenhagen: Gyldendal Uddannelse.

Krejsler, J.B. (Ed.) (2004) *Pædagogikken og kampen om individet – Kritisk pædagogik, ny inderlighed og selvets teknikker*. Copenhagen: Hans Reitzels Forlag.

Lawn, M. & Grek, S. (2012) *Europeanizing Education: governing a new policy space*. Oxford: Symposium Books.

Øland, T. (2007) Grænser for progressive pædagogikformer, Sociologiske undersøgelser af progressive pædagogikformer som middelklassekamp om dominans over det statslige skolegangsfelt & praktisk-epistemologiske undersøgelser af progressiv pædagogik som ledelse af individuel frihed 1970 og 2005. PhD thesis, Copenhagen University.

Pedersen, O.K. (2011) *Konkurrencestaten*. Copenhagen: Hans Reitzels Forlag.

Popkewitz, T.S. (2008) *Cosmopolitanism and the Age of School Reform: science, education, and making society by making the child*. New York: Routledge.

Rabinow, P. (2003) *Anthropos Today – Reflections on Modern Equipment*. Princeton, NJ: Princeton University Press.

Raffnsøe, S. & Gudman-Høyer, M. (2004) Michel Foucaults historiske dispositivanalyse. MPP Working Paper No. 11/2004, Department of Management, Politics and Philosophy, Copenhagen Business School.

Raffnsøe, S., Gudmand-Høyer, M. & Thanning, M.S. (2008) *Foucault*. Frederiksberg: Samfundslitteratur.

Smith, W.C. (2016) An Introduction to the Global Testing Culture, in W.C. Smith (Ed.) *The Global Testing Culture: shaping education policy, perceptions, and practice*. Oxford Studies in Comparative Education series. Oxford: Symposium Books.

Staunæs, D. (2011) Governing the Potentials of Life: interrogating the promises in affective educational leadership, *Journal of Educational History and Administration*, 43(3), 227-247. http://dx.doi.org/10.1080/00220620.2011.586454

Villadsen, K. (2011) Modern Welfare and 'Good Old' Philanthropy – A Forgotten or a Troubling Trajectory? *Public Management Review*, 13(8), 1057-1075. http://dx.doi.org/10.1080/14719037.2011.622675

Ydesen, C. (2011) *The Rise of High-stakes Educational Testing in Denmark (1920-1970)*. Frankfurt am Main: Peter Lang.

CHAPTER 14

South Korea's Accountability Policy System and National Achievement Test

PEARL J. CHUNG & HYEONWOO CHEA

ABSTRACT South Korea made a decision to implement performance-based accountability in 2008 by expanding the national achievement test from a sample-based to a census-based test. The decision influenced schools of all levels across the nation through the use of publicized school report cards, sanctions and rewards, and through the designation of schools as low performing. However, the performance-based accountability policy system has taken a shift under the new administration recently; the national achievement test and corresponding accountability system has been discontinued in elementary schools. Based on a Decision Making Action Cycle, this chapter analyzes factors that have contributed to the implementation and discontinuation of performance-based accountability and discusses their effects at the national, district and school levels.

Introduction

South Korea (hereafter, Korea) has received much recognition around the world for reputable scores in international assessments such as the Trends in International Mathematics and Science Study (TIMSS) and the Programme for International Student Assessment (PISA). In fact, Korean students ranked first in mathematics and second in science in 2011, with an increase of about thirty points in mathematics on TIMSS compared with the mid-1990s (Loveless, 2013). PISA also announced Korea as one of the top five highest-performing countries in mathematics, literacy and science in 2014 (OECD, 2014). To learn more about the Korean education system, scholars have written much about the influence of Confucianism (Martin et al, 2014), shadow education (Lee & Shouse, 2011), and economic development (Byun & Kim, 2010).

Historically and traditionally, Korea's socio-historical context blended with cultural practices and religious beliefs to shape the Korean education system. In particular, education has primarily pursued equity and excellence based on egalitarian ideas and educational zeal, striving to offer equal learning opportunities for upward mobility, higher social status, and academic success (Martin et al, 2014). However, as education became an important factor to one's prosperity in life, academic competition and reliance on external institutions to improve students' academic achievement increased. Korea eventually confronted strong criticisms from the public about the failure of public school systems, in part due to the highly centralized curriculum and standardized instructions. The teachers not only lost authority and suffered from diminished reputation, compared with the past (Kim, 2004) – described in the media as 'school collapse' – but the increased participation in private institutions widened the achievement gap between students from diverse economic backgrounds.

Out of this situation, the 31 May Education Reform Proposal (ERP) was initiated by the Presidential Commission on Education Reform (PCER) in the mid-1990s. It was one of the major education reform proposals in Korea, addressing critical issues that Korea faced in the era of globalization. The aims of the ERP included: (1) increasing accountability measures; (2) curriculum reforms; and (3) expanding educational opportunities for all students (Kim, 2002, 2004). On the one hand, the ERP purported to 'better prepare children, as well as adults, for a knowledge society, where knowledge will be critical for the prosperity of both individuals and society' (Kim, 2002, p. 36). On the other hand, it was criticized for its neoliberal principles, introducing marketism, choice, consumer-based education, autonomy and accountability to the Korean education system (Kim, 2004; Park, 2013).

The ERP provided a framework for education policy, and it affected education at the national, district and school levels (Park, 2013). For instance, Korea revised the national curriculum in the late 1990s and emphasized ability grouping for the first time, tracking students based on academic ability. This was practiced regularly in high schools, offering students differentiated instruction through advanced and regular courses. Indeed, this was a major curriculum reform at the time since the previous national curricula commonly resonated with a standardized approach, focused on uniformity and coherence. The revised curriculum, however, provided teachers with more autonomy to launch diverse academic courses and discretionary activities. As more freedom was given to the teachers, the central education authority (central and local governments) suggested implementing a sample-based national achievement test (NAEA [National Assessment of Education Achievement]) in the late 1990s, monitoring a nationally representative sample of students' performances and academic growth.

However, as the Lee Myung-Bak administration took office in 2008, the accountability policy system underwent a dramatic shift, with salient changes to the NAEA. In fact, the central education authority's conservative political stance concurred with the dominant discourses, such as the standardization movement and the performance-based accountability policies of the United States and United Kingdom (Chung & Hong, 2014; Smith, 2014). In addition, the widespread promotion of the standardization movement affected the central education authority's ability to accentuate the quantitative aspect of academic success, whereby it emphasized choice, rewards and sanctions, and publicized report cards (Sung, 2008).

Despite these crucial changes in education policy, only limited international studies have examined performance-based accountability in Korea, and little is known about the recent policy transition and its effects. Therefore, this chapter analyzes Korea's decision-making process in initiating the outcomes-based accountability policy system and its outcomes at the national, district and school levels. In particular, we focus on the major changes made to the accountability policy system in 2008 and 2013 as well as its impact on education policy and practices in Korea. The study makes use of scholarly literature and official documents, and examines the decision-making process based on Hoy and Miskel's (2013) Decision Making Action Cycle. Based on the analysis, the study attempts to draw wider implications that can be useful to policy-makers, educators and scholars in Korea and other contexts.

Accountability Policy System and National Achievement Test in Korea

Hoy and Miskel's (2013) Decision Making Action Cycle is comprised of five distinct phases: (1) recognize and define the issue; (2) analyze the difficulties; (3) establish criteria for a satisfactory outcome; (4) develop a plan or strategy of action; (5) initiate the action plan. Although these phases occur simultaneously, our analysis of the accountability policy system investigates each phase in a sequential manner, considering the fact that Korea's decision-making process is highly centralized. In order to provide a comprehensive picture, Korea's political stance, social demands, and controversies at the national, district and school levels are delineated as well.

Phase 1: Recognize and Define the Issue

According to Hoy and Miskel (2013), a decision-making process first begins with identifying and defining immediate and long-term issues, placing the problem in perspective. In doing so, decision makers attempt to analyze the problem from various aspects, recognizing necessary sub-problems in the existing situation.

As the Lee Myung-Bak administration took office in 2008, the central education authority addressed the need for a national evaluation system to measure school performances, students' academic growth and the quality of education. In particular, although Korea demonstrated prestigious scores on international exams, tracking individual students' academic progress through a nationwide test was not systematically instituted. A sample-based NAEA was conducted annually, but it was only administered to about 0.5% to 3% of a nationally representative sample of students in grades 6, 9 and 11. The central education authority thus insisted that sample-based NAEA results give inadequate academic data and information to stakeholders and parents (Shin & Shin, 2010; Kim et al, 2011). As a result, the central authority suggested conducting a census-based NAEA to evaluate all students' performances and expand parents' right to know about their child's academic performances (Shin & Shin, 2010).

Phase 2: Analyze the Difficulties

In the second phase of Hoy and Miskel's (2013) decision-making cycle, decision makers further analyze the identified problem. In fact, the problem is classified to make a generic or a unique decision; the difference between the two is that while generic decisions 'arise from established principles, policies, or rules', unique decisions 'require going beyond established procedures for a solution' (Hoy & Miskel, 2013, p. 333). Then, decision makers collect data and relevant facts to determine the significance of the issue.

The central education authority attempted to launch the accountability policy system, yet there was a conflict between two groups with contradicting opinions. On the one hand, the central education authority favored a census-based NAEA, insisting that increased accountability enhances the quality of education for all students. On the other hand, several organizations that had formed around teachers, parents and lawyers raised serious concerns (Park, 2013). They contended that the accountability policy system increases students' participation in shadow education and reduces schools' allocated time for student-centered teaching and learning. They also questioned the effectiveness of outcomes-based accountability in the Korean education system, as a census-based NAEA reinforced more regulations around testing.

Because employing outcomes-based accountability was a critical decision, the central government collected relevant data. Most research studies were conducted through two public institutions – the Korean Institution of Curriculum and Instruction (KICE) and the Ministry of Education. From reviewing related literature and conducting surveys and interviews, they identified three issues. First, research indicated that the existing sample-based NAEA lacks a means to objectively measure all students' achievement as it did not specify academic achievement of individual students, schools and districts across the nation (Kim et al, 2011). Second, research found that inducing 'well-intended' competitions through the accountability policy system is critical in improving school performances in a globalized society (Kim et al, 2009; Kim et al, 2013). Third, research demonstrated that Korea needs valid and reliable NAEA data to implement data-driven policy and instructions and revitalize school members through incentive systems (Shin & Shin, 2010; Kim et al, 2011). However, despite the central education authority's intention to find a satisfactory solution and gain full acceptance from the public, opposing voices to the accountability system were considered to a lesser degree (Park, 2013).

Phase 3: Establish Criteria for a Satisfactory Outcome

Hoy and Miskel's (2013) third phase requires decision makers to establish criteria for a satisfactory solution. That is, decision makers are to develop standards to be achieved in order to 'decide what constitutes an acceptable solution' (Hoy & Miskel, 2013, p. 334). This provides decision-makers with specific guidelines to evaluate the decision as either satisfactory or non-satisfactory.

To set up criteria for a satisfactory outcome, the government proposed the following aims for a census-based NAEA under the accountability policy system: (1) diagnose individual student's academic proficiency level; (2) enhance school competency, including instructional capacity; (3) supplement students with below-basic proficiency through compensatory educational services; and (4) improve curriculum, distribute allocated resources, and support schools financially (Kim et al, 2009). The government ultimately targeted alleviating issues with regard to the achievement gaps and enhancing schools' academic competitiveness.

Based on the above criteria and the legislated accountability system policy, the government solidified its decision. Here, it revised the first clause of Article 9 of the Elementary and Secondary Education Act (ESEA) and employed an agenda called Zero Plan for students with below-basic proficiency (Kim et al, 2011). The agenda was similar to the No Child Left Behind (NCLB) Act in the United States, aiming to move all students out of below-basic proficiency and achieve zero percent of students with low achievement in all schools. Based on the policy, the Minister of Education and the Minister of Education and Human Resource Development obtained full authority over conducting a census-based NAEA. In addition, a tentative plan for the NAEA was created to systematically arrange concrete regulations for the new testing system.

Phase 4: Develop a Plan or Strategy of Action

In the fourth phase of Hoy and Miskel's (2013) cycle, decision-makers specify their actual plan deliberately and choose an action plan. This entails the following steps: (1) specifying alternatives; (2) predicting the consequences of each alternative; (3) deliberation; and (4) selecting a plan of action.

Based on the Zero Plan for students with below-basic proficiency, the government's plan was to financially support schools with low academic performance, called academic improvement schools. The central education authority designated these schools based on the concentrated percentages of students with below-basic proficiency on the NAEA: 5% in elementary schools, 20% in middle and high schools, and 40% in specialized high schools (Ministry of Education, 2012). According to statistics, 1440 schools (elementary, middle and high schools) in 2009, 1660 schools in 2010, and 1520 schools in 2011 were designated as academic improvement schools (Kim et al, 2011). The government's financial support ranged from 50,000 to 100,000 US dollars, allocated by student population and school size. The fund was used for academic support and supplemental educational services such as hiring assistant teachers, developing curriculum and materials, and offering after-school academic programs.

The Ministry of Education also recognized inadequate support for students with emotional, mental or chemical disability. In response, the central education authority implemented personalized instruction, therapy programs and customized interventions to supports students with diverse academic needs. In addition, a voucher program provided increased learning opportunities for students who are at risk due to economic disadvantages and marginalized backgrounds. The programs included after-school services for enriched learning experiences such as field trips, interdisciplinary studies, art, music and sports clubs. Education welfare priority projects also offered additional academic programs targeted at students from families with low socio-economic status. At the district level, academic clinic centers comprised of professional counselors, social workers and teachers provided further academic and emotional assistance to students.

Phase 5: Initiate Action Plan

In the fifth phase of Hoy and Miskel's (2013) decision-making cycle, final decisions are not only implemented in practice, but individuals involved in carrying out the decisions are 'fully aware of their roles and responsibilities ... [and] the success of the plan is appraised in terms of criteria for a satisfactory solution' (Hoy & Miskel, 2013, p. 339).

In initiating the action plan, various roles and responsibilities were disaggregated at the national, provincial and district levels. At the national level, the Ministry of Education established the groundwork for NAEA policy, managed provincial and district education offices, distributed NAEA budget to schools, and reported school performances. KICE took on more technical roles; it developed NAEA questions and assessment tools, disseminated the NAEA to district education offices, created a system to publicize school report cards, analyzed NAEA outcomes and monitored schools' overall academic growth. At the provincial level, Metropolitan and Provincial Offices of Education supervised the NAEA, held professional development sessions for principals, and provided extra support for schools to provide practical information. At the district level, each district education office held regional NAEA training sessions for teachers, collected NAEA answer sheets, and notified individual schools and students about NAEA results.

Over the implementation period, students in the below-basic-proficiency level dropped significantly. The Ministry of Education (2014) reported that the percentage of elementary school students with below-basic proficiency on the NAEA diminished from 2.3% in 2008 to 1.5% in 2010, and to 0.7% in 2012. Middle and high school students with below-basic proficiency also decreased from 10.2% to 3.3% and from 8.0% to 3.4% between 2008 and 2012. Kim and Kim (2012) found that about 92% of all academic improvement schools achieved their academic goal within a year. However, it needs to be noted that the result was not accomplished through the accountability policy system or academic improvement schools alone; rather, it was achieved through a comprehensive effort by teachers, parents and students.

Despite these reputable achievements, some teachers refused to participate in the NAEA as the accountability policy system strictly mandated all students to take the assessment. For instance, several teachers dismissed low-achieving students from taking the NAEA and allowed them to go on a field trip (Park & Ahn, 2011). The central education authority responded immediately and used its legal power to terminate their jobs, as Korean teachers are public service employees (Kim & Kim, 2011). The social pressure to increase students' academic performances heightened along with overheated competition between schools as the NAEA continued until 2012. But the public began to recognize the NAEA's influence on students' affective domains; students with below-basic proficiency experienced negative labeling effects, dealing with low self-concept, self-esteem and motivation. In order to reduce the academic pressure, the central education authority reduced the tested subject areas from five subjects (language arts, social studies, science, mathematics and English) to three subjects (language arts, mathematics and English).

Current Situation: the Park Geun-Hye administration

The following issues were recognized as the new administration took office in 2013, taking the central education authority back to the first phase of the decision-making cycle. First, although the central education authority insisted that low-performing schools launch supplemental educational programs, teacher-centered instruction and rote learning dominated teaching and learning (Kim & Kim, 2010; Kim et al, 2011). That is, in contrast to the government's intention to revitalize schools, administrators and teachers put minimal effort into reinventing curriculum, programs and services to meet students' particular needs. In fact, a testing culture permeated into schools, forcing teachers to meet the standardized goals. District-level support for students with low academic proficiency also appeared to have trivial impact; most schools simply implemented supplemental educational services developed and disseminated by the district education offices, without considering students' different backgrounds. Thus, school districts with high-average and low-average academic performance offered standardized instruction in practice (Kim et al, 2011).

In addition, side effects of the NAEA included a narrowed-down curriculum, teaching to the test, bubbling up the test scores, and neglect of non-tested subjects (Kim & Kim, 2011; Shin & Kim, 2012). In classrooms, opportunities for in-depth discussions, student-centered learning and differentiated instruction decreased (Shin & Kim, 2012). School principals, under heightened academic pressure, also felt the need to increase test scores, creating a test-driven school culture inside schools (Kim & Kim, 2011). Furthermore, because NAEA scores evaluated teacher performances, teachers with low mean scores submitted a statement of reasons to administrators, explaining why their students did not make certain achievements (Kim, 2013).

Despite the outcomes shown at the school level, most parents preferred a census-based NAEA and the accountability policy system. This was because they positively recognized schools' efforts to improve student performances, particularly through receiving additional academic services (Park & Ahn, 2011). From a wider perspective, parents' satisfaction was linked with increased educational opportunities, parental choice and extra supplemental services. Students, on the other hand, illustrated both positive and negative outcomes (Cho & Kim, 2012; Kim & Kim, 2014). For instance, supplemental educational services after regular school hours decreased students' motivation, especially as they received special attention due to low achievement, giving them a negative labeling effect (Cho & Kim, 2012). However, some students mentioned that they valued the time to learn with peers at their academic level because of a lowered ceiling effect (Kim & Kim, 2014). For teachers, instructional methods for teaching and learning appeared to be the same, using didactic and teacher-dominated instructions for drills and memorization to help students increase test scores (Kim & Kim, 2010). In fact, a number of research studies indicated that teachers delivered more teacher-centered instruction rather than student-centered instruction, investing little time in students' development of creativity, problem-solving skills and higher-order thinking skills (Kim & Kim, 2011; Shin & Kim, 2012).

In 2014, PISA indicated Korea as being a country with the lowest student happiness in schools compared with other countries in the Organisation for Economic Co-operation and Development (OECD) (Ministry of Education, 2014). Due to the heightened academic competition along with increased demand on raising NAEA scores, shadow education for additional support also expanded significantly. This ultimately induced education polarization (Yi et al, 2009). That is, the academic gap increased between the students in the top 20% and those in the bottom 20% socioeconomically, widening the achievement gap between the rich and the poor. In response, the government changed the accountability policy system based on a new education theme of 'Happy Education for Students' Dream and Talent'. In addition, the government decided to eliminate sixth-graders from taking the NAEA, but continued the middle and high school NAEA. Thus, the accountability policy system undertook a revision once again, in order to meet social demands and resolve prevalent issues with education in Korea.

Conclusion

Korea initiated outcomes-based accountability largely due to the international promotion of standardized reforms and the government's neoliberal conservative political stance (Kim & Kim, 2010). However, the public raised critical concerns when the central education authority implemented the accountability policy system; it seemed Korea's decision was solely based on the international movement toward the accountability system since Korean students already demonstrated high scores in international assessments. Some teachers, parents and lawyers thus opposed the system that undergirds market logic, deregulation and financialization, concerned about its negative outcomes. Despite the opposition, the central education authority took a top-down approach in making a decision to implement the accountability policy, with an intention to continually improve Korea's academic competitiveness in a globalized society.

The census-based NAEA expanded the notion of outcomes-based accountability, as the test evaluated performances of schools and teachers. In particular, publicizing school report cards and low-performing schools reinforced teachers' desire to improve students' achievement on the NAEA. Making public the reputation of 'competent' and 'non-competent' teachers and/or 'high-quality' and 'low-quality' schools also forced administrators to emphasize test scores, ultimately intensifying a test-driven culture and competitive academic environment inside schools (Kim & Kim, 2011; Lee & Han, 2013). Schools not only launched programs to increase test scores, but the accountability policy affected teaching and learning, curriculum, student motivation and teacher satisfaction. Thus, the NAEA in many ways failed to provide genuine support for students as it strictly encouraged schools to meet certain academic standards.

The central authority recently took a top-down approach once again in eliminating the census-based NAEA in some grades. The decision appears to have been immensely influenced by social demands, the government's aim for education, and the country's international academic reputation. This is because one of the key factors that influenced the decision was PISA's report on Korean students' low score on happiness in schools (Ministry of

Education, 2014). In addition, issues such as education polarization, academic competition and shadow education became crucial as Korea paid increasing attention to test scores, performance and academic credentials (Park, 2013).

Since the discontinuation of the NAEA, both criticism and approval have existed in Korea (Park & Ahn, 2011). Some criticize the abrupt changes in education policy, while others express consent for exempting elementary school students from test pressures. In fact, since Korea's discontinuation of the census-based NAEA at the elementary level, there have been discussions regarding having an objective assessment to screen, monitor and evaluate students with academic difficulties. This is because an assessment to evaluate basic academic skills of all students is still necessary. It does not appear that the central authority would implement the accountability policy any time soon; as previously mentioned, the Park Geun-Hye administration's aim is to enhance students' happiness, reduce academic pressure and support students' academic and emotional development through comprehensive support.

Implications

Most countries around the world have been implementing education policy and programs to ensure basic skills, recognizing that schools are public institutions responsible for teaching students the minimum skills needed to have a good quality of life (Kim & Lee, 2011). However, with the rise of accountability policy, standardized assessment has become the sole determinant in measuring academic achievement of students and schools, resulting in a test-driven culture and negative consequences. Although tests do not always yield negative outcomes, it needs to be noted that how test results are used can significantly change the interaction between teachers and students, and school cultures. Therefore, instead of an outcomes-based accountability with an emphasis on academic achievement, it is crucial to provide students with assistance through collective efforts, robust services and meaningful learning opportunities.

An outcomes-based accountability policy can bring harmful effects to students because it modifies the aim of education towards a standardized lever. The Korean case also demonstrates how the accountability policy system negatively impacts individual teachers' efforts to voluntarily and genuinely help students. As a result, a support system that encourages teachers to assist students and provide services that are personalized and customized is significant. In order for such a system to work, it is important to give teachers adequate support, time, resources and funds to create a positive learning environment. But to make a legitimate decision and implement the appropriate education policy, more research that includes the voices of teachers, students and parents and that understands their needs is critical both in Korea and in other national contexts.

References

Byun, S. & Kim, K. (2010) South Korea: the widening socioeconomic gap in student achievement, *Research in Sociology of Education*, 17, 155-182. http://dx.doi.org/10.1108/S1479-3539(2010)0000017008

Cho, H.R. & Kim, B.C. (2012) A Qualitative Case Study on the Operation Process of an Underachiever's Support Policies, *Korean Journal of Educational Administration*, 30(4), 73-102.

Chung, P.J. & Hong, W.P. (2014) A Comparative Study on Supplemental Educational Services in the United States and Korea, *Korean Journal of Comparative Education*, 24(5), 127-152.

Hoy, W.K. & Miskel, C.G. (2013) *Educational Administration: theory, research, and practice*. New York: McGraw-Hill.

Kim, D.H. (2013) A Study on Side Effect of the National Assessment of Educational Achievement, *Teacher Education Research*, 52(1), 125-138.

Kim, G.J. (2002) Education Policies and Reform in South Korea, *Secondary Education in Africa: strategies for renewal*, 29-39.

Kim, J.E. & Kim, J.H. (2012) Evaluation of the Effectiveness of Academic Improvement School Program on Students' Basic Academic Achievement, *Journal of Elementary Education*, 25(2), 117-139.

Kim, J.W. (2004) Education Reform Policies and Classroom Teaching in South Korea, *International Studies in Sociology of Education*, 14(2), 125-146. http://dx.doi.org/10.1080/09620210400200122

Kim, K., Shin, J., Park, I., et al (2013) Elementary School Academic Achievement Evaluation and Accountability Policy Reform, *Korea Institute for Curriculum and Evaluation: issue paper*, 57(11), 1-24.

Kim, M. & Kim, Y. (2014) Underachievers' Learning Experience, *Korean Journal of Sociology of Education*, 24(3), 31-61.

Kim, M.S. & Kim, K.K. (2011) The Impact of Student Assessment Policy on Educational Practices in Individual Schools, *Korean Journal of Educational Research*, 49(1), 93-121.

Kim, S., Kim, K., Kim, D., et al (2009) *All Testing Methods of the National Achievement Test and Investigation of Educational Context*. Seoul: KICE.

Kim, S., Song, M.Y., Kim, J. & Yi, H.S. (2011) A Further Analysis of Achievement Gap among Districts based on 2009 NAEA (National Assessment of Educational Achievement) Results, *Journal of Educational Evaluation*, 24(1), 51-72.

Kim, S.N. & Lee, B.H. (2011) A Study on Arguments of Accountability of Retarded Students in Learning, *Journal of Educational Administration*, 29(2), 159-183.

Kim, Y.M. & Kim, Y.C. (2010) National Academic Achievement Tests: effects of the national academic achievement test, *Journal of Secondary Education*, 22, 45-59.

Lee, S. & Shouse, R.C. (2011) The Impact of Prestige Orientation on Shadow Education in South Korea, *Sociology of Education*, 84(3), 212-224. http://dx.doi.org/10.1177/0038040711411278

Lee, S.H. & Han, E.J. (2013) Exploring Possibility of School Consulting for Embodiment of Internal Accountability of Education, *Korean Journal of Education Study*, 31(4), 283-308.

Loveless, T. (2013) The Latest TIMSS and PIRLS Scores. Part I of the 2013 Brown Center Report on American Education. http://www.brookings.edu/research/reports/2013/03/18-timss-pirls-scores-loveless (accessed 2 September 2014).

Martin, S.N., Choe, S.U., Kim, C.J. & Kwak, Y. (2014) Employing a Sophistorical Perspective for Understanding the Impact of Ideology and Policy on Educational Achievement in the Republic of Korea, *Closing the Achievement Gap from an International Perspective*, 5, 229-250. http://dx.doi.org/10.1007/978-94-007-4357-1_11

Ministry of Education (2012) Academic Achievement Support System Plan of 2012. Seoul: Ministry of Education, Science and Technology.

Ministry of Education (2014) Accountability Policy to Raise Dreams and Talents of Students with Underachievement. Seoul: Ministry of Education.

Organisation for Economic Co-operation and Development (OECD) (2014) Programme for International Student Assessment (PISA) 2012 Result in Focus: what 15-year-olds know and what they can do with what they know. http://www.oecd.org/pisa/keyfindings/pisa-2012-results-overview.pdf (accessed 2 September 2014).

Park, D.H. & Ahn, H.I. (2011) A Study on the Perception of Elementary School Teacher and Parents about the National Assessment of Education Achievement System, *Ocean and Education Research*, 23(2), 182-197.

Park, N.G. (2013) Analysis on the Background and the Context of Adopting Educational Accountability System to Elementary and Secondary Education, *Korean Journal of Educational Administration*, 31(2), 347-376.

Shin, E.J. & Kim, W.J. (2012) The Impact of National Assessment of Educational Achievement on Class Management, *Journal of Educational Culture*, 18(1), 55-82.

Shin, H.S. & Shin, W.H. (2010) An Analysis of Policy Situation about National Assessment of Educational Achievement (NAEA) by Lee Myung-Bak Government, *Korea Educational Methodology*, 22(1), 121-145.

Smith, W.C. (2014) The Global Transformation toward Testing for Accountability, *Education Policy Analysis Archives*, 22(116). http://dx.doi.org/10.14507/epaa.v22.1571

Sung, K.S. (2008) *National Assessment of Educational Achievement: who is this evaluation for?* Seoul: KICE.

Yi, H., Kim, M., Lee, D. & Son, S. (2009) *Seeking for the Better Instruction and Support for Low Achievers in Schools: a framework for educational policy-making for low achievers*. Seoul: KICE.

CHAPTER 15

The Discursive Hold of the Matric: is there space for a new vision for secondary education in South Africa?

DAVID BALWANZ

ABSTRACT High-stakes secondary school leaving exams are a feature of many national education systems. In many low- and middle-income economies, exam performance, which mediates access to scarce university places and formal-sector jobs, significantly influences the life chances of youth. This chapter draws on a small-scale qualitative study in South Africa to describe the influence of a high-stakes exam, the National Senior Certificate (NSC) exam, in schools in two historically marginalized communities. Data indicate that learners in South Africa's poorest schools are also the least likely to pass the NSC. However, an NSC pass offers these same learners their best chance at securing a bright future. This chapter discusses the influence of a testing culture on conceptualizations of and practices in secondary education and identifies grassroots perspectives which could be drawn on to articulate a new vision for secondary education in South Africa.

Introduction: the discursive hold of the 'matric'

In South Africa, grade 12 learners are generally referred to as 'matrics' – they are considered to be in their matric year, at the end of which they will take the National Senior Certificate (NSC) exam, a secondary school leaving exam, referred to as the 'matric'. Nearly everyone involved in education in South Africa is concerned about the matric. One learner, expressing the sentiment of his peers, argues that 'without matric [a pass] you are doomed' (SS Learner 12). A parent I interviewed recalled that 'when my daughter was writing matric the whole household that year we stopped everything to give her all the support' (Interviewee B). District staff and teachers I interviewed echoed the sentiment of a secondary school principal who lamented that 'the only thing DBE [the Department for Basic Education] cares about is matric [NSC pass rates]' (Interviewee C). University administrators and popular media voices regularly express concern about the 'falling standard' of the matric. During the year in which I conducted research used for this chapter, the DBE put together a task team to investigate concerns about 'the standard and quality of the NSC as a qualification' (DBE, 2014a, p. 5).

These concerns evidence the varied meanings and purposes attributed to and associated with the NSC exam in South Africa, while at the same time situating the matric at the center of discourse on secondary education quality, reform and meaning in South Africa. To many, the matric is valued insofar as a pass provides a *ticket* to further education. Wedekind (2013) notes that historically and up to the present, 'the school leaving certificate had become strongly associated with one function, namely providing access into university level programmes' (p. 7). The ticket is important: nearly 50% of South Africans live in poverty, youth unemployment stands at nearly 50%, fewer than 25% of the school leavers proceed to higher education, and access to formal-sector jobs is highly competitive (Wedekind, 2013; Statistics South Africa, 2014). To youth from historically disadvantaged groups, areas or households, a matric pass may be the surest first step toward escaping poverty. Matric pass rates also serve as the *indicator* of choice for measuring school and education-system quality. Popular discourse, a significant body of academic research, and national and provincial policies, priorities and practices have constructed an understanding of educational quality which is defined by school and provincial NSC pass rates (DBE, 2013, 2014a; GDE, 2013). A matric pass is also supposed to serve as a *signal* that a learner has demonstrated attainment of a particular level of knowledge and skill. Over the past decade, however, voices from universities and the business community have expressed concern that a matric pass no longer serves as an accurate signal of a learners' college or work readiness. It has been argued that the 'low standard' of the matric fosters a culture of mediocrity in secondary schools and undermines the contribution of education to national economic growth objectives (CDE, 2012; Jansen, 2012; DBE, 2014a).

Similar to high-stakes secondary school leaving exams in other countries, the NSC takes on and creates significance and meaning vis-à-vis the social reality in which it exists. The ubiquitous use of the term 'matric' in written and oral policy, and in academic and popular dialogue on secondary education in South Africa, exemplifies the discursive hold of the NSC in shaping expectations of and practices in secondary education. As a researcher troubled by the extent to which high-stakes testing narrows conceptualizations of and practices in secondary education – often to the disadvantage of learners in historically marginalized communities – I conducted a small-scale qualitative study in which I asked students and teachers to 'talk back to discourse' (i.e. dominant perspectives) and re-imagine the purpose of secondary education based on their own priorities and perspectives. While interviewee perspectives shared in this chapter speak to the extent to which matric 'backwash' (i.e. the influence of the leaving exam on schooling in grades 9-12) shapes secondary education, they also identify priorities and interests which could be drawn on to construct a broader, and more humanistic, conceptualization of and practice in secondary education. The remaining part of this chapter is organized into four sections: research methods; background and context on secondary education in South Africa; research findings; and discussion.

Eliciting Grassroots Perspectives (Researcher Perspective and Methods)

My research draws on constructivist-interpretive and critical methodological perspectives which articulate human understandings of truth and knowledge in the social sciences to be partial, contextual, socially constructed and operating in a social reality shaped by unequal power relations (Kincheloe et al, 2011). In this research I identify secondary education, the curriculum and the NSC as social constructions. I argue that dominant understandings of the purpose of secondary education, or of the importance of the matric, reflect discursive practices which privilege some things over others – determining, for example, which knowledge, skills, values and experiences constitute 'secondary education'. In South Africa, education policies which identify English as the language of instruction, emphasize science and mathematics, or allow for schools to charge fees reflect values privileging elite interests. In this research, I also draw on an agency-focused capabilities approach, which offers conceptual tools useful for thinking through how alternative constructions of secondary education may contribute to human development and well-being (Crocker, 2008).

Findings presented in this chapter draw on an extensive literature review and dissertation field research – a small-scale qualitative study completed in 2013-14 at two schools located in townships in South Africa's Gauteng province. One school was an academic secondary school. The second school was a Further Education and Training (FET) college at which I interviewed learners who had dropped out of secondary school and were enrolled in a vocational equivalent to the NSC, called the National Certificate Vocational (NCV). My research questions were exploratory and explanatory: I sought grassroots perspectives from learners and teachers on their experiences in secondary education, on what types of learning they valued, and on what they thought was the purpose of secondary education (Hesse-Biber & Leavy, 2011). My fourth research question was: how do grassroots perspectives compare with the perspectives articulated in the dominant global and national discourses on secondary education? In South Africa, black South African youth living in townships are among the most structurally disadvantaged populations in South Africa: many youth come from high-poverty households, where one or both biological parents are absent, exposure to formal work experience is limited and the home language is not English. Learners coming from poor households are more likely to drop out between grades 10 and 12 and are less likely to pass matric or successfully transition to higher education. Recognizing the multiple disadvantages these youth face, this research sought to offer them a space to contest the social construction of secondary education. During the research period, I was based at the Centre for Education Rights and Transformation at the University of Johannesburg and was supported through a Fulbright Grant.

Data collection involved interviewing fourteen secondary school learners (from the eleventh and twelfth grades), nine learners who had dropped out of secondary school and were enrolled in a NCV course, seven teachers and six other key informants who worked at district and policy levels. All student interviewees were selected by teachers. All secondary school learners interviewed were likely to graduate: they were in the 'sciences stream', which in this school was populated by high achievers. FET college students interviewed had dropped out of secondary school. Interviews were semi-structured and followed an interview guide organized around the research questions. After some general questions about participants' life backgrounds and schooling experiences, I asked students to explain in their own words the purpose of secondary education. The interview protocol also included a card sort, in which learners were given nine cards, each of which had a different type of learning. Participants were asked to pick two or three types of learning which were most important to them.[1] The first exercise allowed interviewees to discuss 'purpose' in their own words; the second created a common framework participants could use to identify priorities. In many cases, the card sort prompted additional discussion on learners' interests, priorities and critiques. The interview closed by asking participants to 'reimagine secondary education' based on the discussion.

Data analysis included the following: writing a research memo immediately after the interview, inductively coding interview transcripts and writing a second memo (organized around the research questions) for each interview based on the transcript and inductive coding (Coffey & Atkinson, 1996; Hesse-Biber & Leavy, 2011). The purpose of memoing and inductive coding was to develop an initial set of codes, which were then used to develop a data matrix which was drawn on to identify key themes and issues arising from the raw data. Codes and concepts were refined through member-checking exercises, triangulation with literature review data, and ongoing dialogue with other education-sector researchers and practitioners. The findings presented in this chapter are informed by the literature review and my epistemological perspective and emerged out of data analysis and member-checking exercises. The quotes included were selected because they articulate findings in the words of the participants. I initiated this research with the hope that participants would offer a humanistic counter-narrative to the dominant discourse on secondary education (which itself is largely constructed around human capital theory). More than I expected, participants spoke of the extent to which local, lived experiences (e.g. violence, drug use and crime; challenges understanding English; adolescent physical and social maturation; child abuse/neglect; parental absence) influence secondary education. While many participants critiqued the matric focus of secondary school, they also appeared quite comfortable with accepting that secondary school could support multiple and overlapping purposes – including instrumental purposes (e.g. test preparation) and existential purposes (e.g. self-exploration, finding purpose).[2] The next section provides background and identifies some of the main debates over secondary education and the matric in South Africa over the last two decades.

Secondary Education and the Matric in a Democratic South Africa

This chapter does not have sufficient space to articulate the long-standing, varied and, in some cases, highly contested material and symbolic effects of apartheid on education in South Africa. South Africa's apartheid era was, in part, characterized by the practice of racial capitalism in which the white minority government violently exploited, oppressed and systematically marginalized non-white peoples. Examples of apartheid-era resistance in education include the Black Consciousness Movement, which sought to promote conscientization and a culture of positive values among black South Africans (Biko, 2004), and the Soweto Uprising, a 1976 protest of over 20,000 Soweto secondary school students against the introduction of Afrikaans as the medium of instruction. During the protest, Bantu education, the education of black South Africans during apartheid, was summarized thus: 'enter to learn, learn to serve' (Kanfer, 1993, p. 321).

The first major education legislation in South Africa's new democracy, the South African Schools Act 1996, argues that South Africa should work toward a vision of 'learners who will be inspired by the values of a society based on respect for democracy, equality, human dignity, life and social justice' (Government of South Africa, 1996, p. 21). Curriculum 2005, popularly known as outcomes-based education (OBE), sought to make manifest this vision through curriculum reform. Jansen and Christie (1999, as cited in Jansen & Taylor, 2003) characterized Curriculum 2005 as:

> [a] direct response to the apartheid curriculum variously described as teacher-centered, authority-driven, content-based, elitist, examination-based, and Eurocentric in orientation. The previous curriculum privileged formal knowledge and encouraged rote learning. It straight-jacketed students for university preparation, not recognizing the diverse interests and pathways actually pursued by the majority of students. (p. 37)

This transformative vision, however, met several obstacles, among them the inheritance of economic crisis and deep social and economic inequalities; the dominance of perspectives which identified education as an instrument to be used to meet economic growth objectives; and pervasive concerns about the quality of education. Chisholm (2012) characterizes the state of the education system in 1994 as follows:

> Massive inequalities in every aspect of educational provision combined with high levels of poverty resulted by 1994 in an inheritance of deep differences between black and white educational provision in school resourcing, infrastructure, teacher quality and post-school and employment futures. (p. 89)

While present inequality is tied to apartheid legacies, it is also perpetuated through a legal framework which allows 'a two-tiered system of state-aided, fee paying and state-funded, non-fee paying public schools in South Africa' (Chisholm, 2012, p. 93). Spaull (2011) argues that South Africa today remains 'a tale of two schools: one which is wealthy, functional and able to educate students, while the other is poor, dysfunctional, and unable to equip students' (p. 26). Results of national exams and international assessments echo this conclusion, showing persistent inequalities by class (by income quintile), race and geographic location (Christie et al, 2007; Spaull, 2012).

From the time of the transition, and into the early 2000s, goals of social justice and redress espoused by the South African Schools Act were eclipsed by urgent concerns about the economic crisis, expression of the need for austerity, and focus on economic growth. Motala and Pampallis (2001) argue that during this era, the state's neoliberal macro-economic policies were irreconcilable with its social justice intentions. The same debates emerged during the design of the new curriculum. According to Spreen and Vally (2010), OBE curriculum designers were to promote knowledge, skills and values for social justice as well as 'align the curriculum to ... "global competitiveness" ... [to promote] economic growth for the 21st century' (pp. 44-45). Linda Chisholm, the then director of the Education Policy Unit at the University of the Witwatersrand, argued that the matric focus of secondary education was a poor fit with the philosophical underpinnings of OBE and argued instead for increasing emphasis on school-based assessment (SBA). Making the argument in an op-ed, Chisholm (1999) writes, 'OBE-speak typically describes "traditional" assessment as "input-based", "norm-referenced" and "summative". An OBE framework prefers assessment to be "outcomes-based", "criterion-referenced" and "formative".' However, this proposal never took off: detractors questioned whether schools could be trusted to fairly and effectively implement and report on SBA.

Efforts by the newly formed Department for Basic Education (DBE) to assert itself across a new national system and improve 'pass rates' amid growing international evidence of the low quality of South Africa's education system may have also played a role in quashing the expansion of SBA during the early transition period. At the time of the transition, 'there were 17 different [education] departments each administering their own examinations and, in some cases, following divergent curricula and assessment regimes' (Wedekind, 2013, p. 5). By the late 1990s, in addition to being tasked with streamlining the secondary certification process, the DBE became increasingly focused on 'the improvement of numbers who pass matric' (Lolwana, 2006, p. 21). During the same period, there was increasing concern about the low quality of education in South Africa. From the late 1990s, matric results and results from international assessments (e.g. PIRLS, PISA, SACMEQ and TIMMS) were drawn on as evidence of the failure of education. In a review of 2003 PISA (Programme for International Student Assessment) scores, Crouch (2005) argues that 'there is little doubt that the biggest two problems South Africa faces are the extreme inequality in actual learning achievement, and the relatively low level in this achievement across all groups' (p. 18).

As 1994 grows more distant, there appears to have been an increasing focus from government on improving matric scores, accepting matric scores as a proxy for quality education, and drawing on human capital and productivist rationales to shape education policy. Recent DBE and Gauteng Department of Education (GDE) strategic plans identify 'preparing learners for the NSC' as one of the main purposes of grades 10-12, and 'improving NSC pass rates' as a critical priority. To make progress toward these goals, GDE funds a Secondary School Improvement Programme (SSIP), a test preparation program for Grade 12 learners, mainly for low-income communities, which takes place during school holidays and on Saturdays and Sundays. Discourse which equates educational improvement with test preparation also underpins recent 'schools that work' studies (see Christie et al, 2007; Jansen & Blank, 2014) and several non-governmental organization (NGO) programs working in low-income communities.

Responding to the critique of 'falling standards' and the cry to increase South Africa's global economic competitiveness, the Ministerial Task Team Report on the National Senior Certificate argues that 'South Africa should communicate a clear and unambiguous vision of its economic future and how it can be reached, and that the education system be shaped by that vision' (DBE, 2014a, p. 13). By 'falling standards', critics mean that the level of the pass (e.g. 40% in English) is too low – that a pass does not accurately signal that a learner has the English (or other) skills necessary to succeed in university (Jansen, 2012; Wedekind, 2013). More generally, over the past decade, concerns about the extent to which the matric *signals* learners' preparedness for university study have led to the development of other assessments designed for this purpose, including the National Benchmark Test (overseen by Higher Education South Africa) and several university-specific entrance exams (Nel & Kistner, 2009; Wedekind, 2013; DBE, 2014a). Before moving to research findings, it is helpful to have more detail on the NSC.

The newest iteration of the matric, the National Senior Certificate (NSC) was implemented in 2008. Over 90% of secondary school students in South Africa are enrolled in courses designed to prepare them for the NSC – the main path for admission to higher education. To obtain an NSC pass a candidate must achieve either a 40% or a 30% score in six of seven subjects. Higher levels of pass (e.g. a 'Bachelor's' pass) require higher scores. All learners are required to take exams in seven subjects: four required (i.e. Home Language, First Additional Language, Life Orientation, and Mathematics or Maths Literacy) and three elective. Learners most frequently take elective exams from the sciences or business studies learning areas, including Life Sciences, Business Studies, Geography, Physical Sciences and Accounting (DBE, 2014b). Less popular exam subjects include History, Dramatic Arts, Religion Studies and Music.

What does the path to the NSC look like? In Grade 10, most learners choose a learning area (e.g. sciences or business studies) from which they will select elective subjects during their Grade 10-12 years. It does not appear to be uncommon for a learner to take biology for three years in a row. Secondary school drop-out and push-out is high: nearly fifty percent (over 500,000) of Grade 9 learners do not end up taking matric. Learners drop out for a variety of reasons (e.g. poverty, pregnancy, health issues, or feelings that 'education is worthless' [Sheppard, 2009]). Many schools 'push out' poorly performing learners to improve school pass rates or, alternatively, encourage poorly performing learners to take easier subjects (Dieltiens & Meny-Gibert, 2008; Jansen & Blank, 2014). The majority of learners have a poor foundational education and have a home language other than English (the language of learning and teaching in most secondary schools). Many students struggle and some come to the conclusion that 'I'm just so dumb' or 'some people aren't that smart' (Secondary School Learner 10 and FET College Learner 2). Of those who take the NSC, around 30% fail. Of those who pass, more than half do not gain admittance to university.

Findings

This section shares some of the major findings associated with the research questions. In general I found learners and teachers to acknowledge multiple purposes, instrumental and existential, for secondary education. Instrumental purposes and practices were shaped by social and economic structures and dominant discourses and practices, while existential interests included learners' individual interests and values and educators' beliefs about learners' varied developmental needs. Main findings follow.

Finding 1: The Desire for, and the NSC as the Path to, a 'Bright Future'

Many learners describe the path to a bright future as involving passing the matric, entering university, obtaining a degree, and getting a job in the formal sector. This conceptualization of 'the path' is echoed in official policy documents which identify supporting entry into further education or the workforce as one of the main goals of secondary education (GDE, 2013). One learner notes that 'as a person that comes from the township I realize that employment is very scarce in our region and there are many social challenges such as drugs, teenage pregnancy, human trafficking ... maths and science I realize will open more opportunities for me' (SS Learner 11). Here a matric pass (and specializing in the sciences) is perceived as a ticket to further study and a desired job, as well as a means of escaping life in the township. Nearly all learners I interviewed saw no alternative to passing the matric. They would say things like, 'If you are sitting at home with a Grade 9 or Grade 10, what are you going to do? Where are you going to get a job?' (FETC Student 6) or, 'There is a common belief that if you do not go to university and study usually you are going to end up being unsuccessful so we are scared of breaking our future' (SS Learner 8). Many learners differentiated between the instrumental hurdles they faced (e.g. passing matric and getting a job) and their existential goals (e.g. doing something they loved, expressing values, having enough money). One learner made the distinction explicit: 'I'm going to school only to have a better life someday, not because I like it' (SS Learner 13). When pressed about what they meant by a bright future, learners often spoke of broad life goals: having financial security or material wealth, escaping poverty, becoming more independent, and/or having a job or career they found interesting or which resonated with their values.

Finding 2: The Preponderant Focus of Grade 10-12 Schooling is on Matric Preparation and Improving Matric Pass Rates

Nearly all participants identified the influence of DBE and GDE focus on the matric. One interviewee, based at the district-level education office, states:

> They are saying year after year, 'who is going to be number one as a province?' ... a lot of emphasis has been placed in saying for Gauteng no school can achieve less than [an] 85% [pass rate] ... it then comes down to our head office in Johannesburg to say 'districts: this is where you should perform' so certainly we are just running to meet that target. Running programmes to go into schools to say 'can we meet these targets?' (Interviewee A)

As noted in the introduction, school teachers and the principal appear to agree that 'the administration, the government and the Ministry of Education' focus on Grade 12 learners and NSC results' (SS Teacher 2). The secondary school in which I conducted research had added morning and afternoon classes focused on matric subjects, stretching the school day (classroom time) from 7 a.m. to 4 p.m. In addition, Grade 12 learners participated in SSIP, meaning they attended test-prep programs which meet on Saturdays and Sunday and during school holidays. Several learners I interviewed identified 'matric prep' as their *only* extracurricular activity. This phenomenon appears to be partly demand driven: nearly half of the secondary school learners I interviewed had migrated to Gauteng from other provinces, in part based on the belief that Gauteng schools were better than schools in other provinces.

Finding 3: The Influence of a Testing Culture on Learners' Classroom Experiences

Learners and teachers I interviewed spoke to four areas of matric 'backwash' – that is, the influence of the exam on classroom practices. The importance of the matric was argued to encourage teacher-centered education and banking education (e.g. emphasis on lower-level cognitive skills, lecturing and note-taking); to privilege a narrow domain of academic knowledge (i.e. knowledge needed to pass the test and in areas which increased competitiveness for university admissions); and to emphasize a particular purpose of schooling (i.e. passing the matric). Several teachers and learners shared banking education experiences. One teacher notes:

> It's really frustrating to *teach learners to pass* when they haven't been prepared [in earlier grades]. ... Every term we have reported speech and passive voice [topics in English] and we're going over it often, but when you look at the exam, there is only one question worth three marks on it. (SS Teacher 3, emphasis added)

Here the teacher, who focuses on teaching 'learners to pass', is frustrated because an area of the syllabus is insufficiently covered on the assessment. Several students distinguished between 'learning to pass' and 'learning to understand', as indicated in the exchange below:

> *Interviewee 12*: To pass is so easy because you can pass without understanding something ... there is this method we call it the CPF (Cram, Pass, Forget). That is what we mostly do. So we say tomorrow morning I'll be writing such test so I just have to cram and then I pass and I forget, without understanding. (SS Learner 12)
> *Interviewer*: Is the normal culture at this school learning to pass or understand?
> *Interviewee 11*: It's simple, it's learning to pass because there is this pressure that if you don't pass you is going to fail and you are going to end nowhere. (SS Learners 11 & 12)

The pervasive testing taking place in secondary school is evidenced in the exchange below between the researcher and two learners:

Interviewer: I heard from other students that next week it's [an] exam in math, Physics and Economics. Are you taking tests this week?
Interviewees 1 and 2: Yes.
Interviewer: OK.
Interviewee 1: We're writing one today ... Physics test.
Interviewer: When do you write it?
Interviewee 1: Early today.
Interviewer: And tomorrow, Economics?
Interviewees 1 and 2: Yes. After school.
Interviewer: And also you have exams next week, right?
Interviewee 1: And on Friday we're writing, Paper 2, Home Language and English.

All this testing and test focus comes with a cost: students expressed that they had no time for extra-curricular activities and teachers mainly appeared to be focused on activities related to test preparation. Learners I interviewed expressed interest in sports, the arts, learning about themselves, each other and their community, and reading – all of which appeared to be marginalized by matric preparation.

Two of the most frequent critiques expressed by learners were related to pedagogy: the amount of time spent copying notes, and the preponderant focus on 'theoretical' versus 'practical' instruction. 'It's ... why some people say school is boring,' says one learner, 'because we are just doing things [on paper instead of practically]' (SS Learner 12). One learner echoes this sentiment, saying that 'to sit in class for seven hours with different teachers coming and going out it's boring. It's boring. It would be easy ... if we could see an animal ... Like last year in Biology when we were doing a study of the heart. We got a real heart. A pig heart. Like you can dissect, feel it, touch' (SS Learner 8). The extent to which pressure to pass the matric and the design of the matric assessment influence these pedagogical practices is unclear. Alternative explanations include the severe lack of resources in many schools and the fact that in many schools teachers have not been trained in alternative pedagogies. Notably, several teachers I interviewed indicate that most learners entering Grade 10 were already 'behind' and that in grades 10-12 learners needed to focus on catching up. For many learners, this means taking three years of the same seven subjects in an effort to prepare for the end-of-cycle assessment. This also appears to mean a lot of lecturing and note-taking. One FET college lecturer, whose student population consists mainly of learners who dropped out of high school, notes that 'it's like where they [the students] come from before they were never given an opportunity to talk' (FETC Lecturer 3).

David Balwanz

Finding 4: The Relevance of Local Context and Experience

Students and teachers identified the following issues as destabilizing the learning environment: poor foundational education; poor knowledge of English; high levels of poverty; parental absence or lack of parental involvement; high levels of violence; sexual violence and child abuse in the community; lack of school safety; prevalence of drug, tobacco and alcohol use; service delivery protests (many of which are violent); and lack of basic services, such as access to water, electricity and transportation to schools. 'Improving school safety' was one of the top concerns expressed by learners I interviewed, and many students discussed problems with violence (e.g. a stabbing), bullying and theft, and intimidation. Several students spoke of the need to mend the school fence 'for security because we are not safe sir. Drug addicts can jump over the fence and steal our bags while we are at school' (SS Learner 7). Most teachers I interviewed said they acted '*in loco parentis*' – as counselors, role models, or simply as someone learners could talk to about their problems.

Some interviewees highlighted teenage pregnancy as an issue, though no one spoke of rape or other forms of sexual violence. While my research did not focus on gender-based violence, a study by Vetten et al (2008), which focused on rape and sexual violence in Gauteng province, indicated that more than a third of female participants reported having experienced sexual violence before the age of 18. For some young women I interviewed, changes associated with adolescent development can be highly disruptive. One female learner states, 'You know when you come to secondary everything changes. The way you feel about yourself changes. The way you look at yourself changes. You are growing up, you are a teenager, and a lot of things are changing. It happens all at once. ... If my parents didn't want me to come to school I would stay at home' (SS Learner 10). Another female learner indicates that she repeated Grade 11 in part because of issues with boys (SS Learner 9).

Drop-out among young men was associated with peer pressure and boredom, among other things. Of teenage boys, one learner notes that 'they love their friends and their friends will influence them into such things as drugs and smoking, if you are not smoking you are not cool so that makes people feel small' (SS Learner 11). Other learners may drop out of school 'to take care of their mother or somebody who is sick' (SS Learner 5). Each one of these issues highlights the lived experiences of a large number of secondary school learners in South Africa.

Finding 5: Learners and Teachers Identify Multiple Purposes for Secondary Education and Speak to the Existential Possibilities of Education

While the perspectives and experiences of teachers and learners evidenced the extent of a backwash effect, interviewees also shared alternative visions, which, if drawn on, could weaken the influence of the testing culture. One teacher, capturing a commonly expressed sentiment among educators I interviewed, argues that 'education should cover a person holistically: mentally, physically, emotional development in every aspect of their life. It's not just teaching and learning. Learners need to be kept physically active, they need to be emotionally intelligent, they need to know how to make decisions' (SS Teacher 4). Other teachers argue that secondary school 'concentrates way too much on studying to go to university. We need to think about employability. I am not saying that to offend them [the learners]. Some are not academic, some are not the type' (SS Teacher 3). Another teacher emphasized how exposure to new things can help learners learn about themselves. In the card sort which took place during individual interviews, twelve of fourteen secondary school learners prioritized 'learning about yourself'. Interviewees who had dropped out of secondary school and were attending a second-chance course (the NCV at an FET college) were more focused on 'getting a job'. Many NCV learners were five or six years older than the learners enrolled in secondary school – suggesting that existential exploration may be more likely to occur prior to a learner growing into adult responsibilities (such as providing income or caring for a family member).

Learners were often explicit in identifying instrumental purposes for secondary education: it is a 'stepping stone' to further education and a career path, and it can offer a second chance for learners who don't want to 'stay at home'. In the same way that learners articulate their vision of a bright future, so too do they identify existential purposes, such as discovering and doing what you love, becoming 'who you are', expressing values, or having a good future (e.g. independence, family, and escape from poverty). Combining the instrumental and the existential, one student says, 'After matric I would like to go to university and study nursing. ... I really like to take care of people and I think I can' (SS Learner 14). Another learner says that learning parenting skills is important and that to her, being successful is 'having a family, a happy one, having a great job, helping people out there' (SS Student 2). Even learners who had dropped out of secondary school or failed matric identified the critical importance of education and a matric-equivalent certification in helping them realize life goals. Echoing the sentiment of other learners enrolled in a second-chance program, one NCV learner states, 'I told myself I'm not gonna give up. I came here in 2011, registered for office admin, then I made it. ... I told myself I wanna pursue my dreams, I wanna be a person' (FETC Student 5). Another FET college student, who expressed his love of carpentry and working with his hands, notes, 'NCV helps students who don't have a matric so that they can pursue their dreams' (FETC Student 4). I want to emphasize these last two quotes: they come from students whom existing, not to mention higher, standards would identify as drop-outs and failures. Their quotes also represent values underrepresented in the global testing culture.

Discussion

This chapter draws on a review of literature and a small-scale qualitative study to identify the varied meanings and purposes attributed to the National Senior Certificate exam in South Africa; articulate some of the debates associated with NSC reform; provide discussion on the extent to which debate on secondary education has been reduced to discussion on the matric; and share grassroots perspectives on matric backwash and alternative visions for secondary education. This section considers the South Africa case in relation to the global testing culture framework; provides discussion on factors which may influence the persistence of the matric focus in South Africa; and closes by sharing alternative priorities identified by research participants.

In the introductory chapter to this volume, Smith (2016) states that one feature of the global testing culture is that its dominant norms, values and expectations come to be internalized by system stakeholders. This chapter argues that in South Africa, a large number of system stakeholders see passing the matric as the proximate goal of secondary education and equate high matric pass rates with quality education. Values associated with the global testing culture, including the privileging of academic intelligence, faith in science, and emphasis on neoliberal perspectives of test-based competition and accountability, are also seen in the South African system. This privileging of academic intelligence aligns with the existing construction of the labour market; the faith in science coheres with a desire for a 'fair' way to sort students; and the neoliberal tendencies speak to central-level quality assurance and control concerns in a decentralized system and goals of promoting economic growth and competitiveness. Given some of the critiques expressed in this chapter, why, we may ask, does a testing culture persist?

History and the desire for quality assurance mechanisms provide two explanations. For more than a century the matric has played a central quality assurance and differentiating role in the South African education system. Unlike in other countries, in South Africa there is no formal certification prior to Grade 12. While South Africa had effectively massified access to secondary education by 1995, the focus of the matric – certifying that secondary school leavers are prepared for university study – has not changed. Efforts to reduce the influence of the matric are met with two main critiques: weakening the matric would lower standards; and 'what is the alternative to the matric?' So far no one has put forth satisfactory responses to these critiques. When considered among available alternatives, the matric is still recognized as one of the best available indicators (of secondary quality) and signals (of youth readiness for further education and employment). As noted earlier, there are some signs pointing to a decreasing influence of the matric: employers and universities are increasingly using their own assessments to evaluate potential workers and students. Further, since education is also a positional good (Dore, 1976), as a greater proportion of the population attains a matric, its signal value will decline.

Another explanation for the discursive hold of the matric is that it fits well into dominant narratives which promote a particular understanding of the relationship between education, the economy and society. Human capital and productivist discourses argue that education raises productivity, which in turn grows the economy, creates jobs and enhances progress toward social justice. These same discourses explain the persistence of poverty, inequality and unemployment in South Africa as a failure of the education system: low matric pass rates, the low standard of the matric, poor teaching and unmotivated students. Government policy and popular discourse is largely shaped by this logic. This social narrative – of the matric as an indicator of 'development' and a just arbiter of who will succeed and who will fail in society – intersects with an urgent individual narrative: I need a matric pass to have a bright future. Here the gatekeeping role of the matric (i.e. that it is *the ticket* to tertiary education and, hopefully, highly sought-after formal-sector jobs) and the political economy of South Africa (e.g. high levels of poverty, inequality and unemployment) combine to increase the stakes of an already high-stakes exam. This is the pressure which leads youth to say, 'If you don't have matric, you are doomed.' For disadvantaged youth, and teachers who seek to help them, the surest path toward a bright future is a matric pass. This hurdle is straightforward, widely (if inaccurately) understood to be meritocratic, and points toward tangible, and highly sought-after, rewards. The majority of interviewees appeared to have internalized the narrative of the dominant discourse, saying things like, 'If you work hard, you will be rewarded with getting a job' (FETC Learner 7). However, many older youth and teachers identified de-industrialization, worker retrenchments and increasing numbers of unattached and unemployed youth (many with a matric or a higher certification) as evidence of the failure of the logic promoted by dominant narratives.[3]

It is worth emphasizing here that the above explanations evidence the tendency in popular discourse to value secondary education (and the matric) using criteria and measures over which educators and learners have little control: space available in universities, absorption of new workers into the labour market, and labour market composition. If, next year, all who took the matric passed (the ultimate measure of high quality in the current system), it is likely that historical patterns of absorption into higher education and the labor market would follow those of the previous year. This observation highlights a dilemma facing several countries in sub-Saharan Africa and elsewhere: the massification of secondary education and, with that, the corresponding growth of university-ready secondary graduates with nowhere to go. In 'The End of Middle Class Work: no more escapes', Collins (2013) foresees a bleak future marked by high structural unemployment and increasing inequality. We do not have to be as dystopian as Collins, however, to make the argument that the path to a sustainable future requires that we do better than create 'excellent sheep'.

Is there space for a new vision for secondary education in South Africa? Some argue that political economy analysis leads to an ideological cul-de-sac (McGrath, 2012). In my research, I see a solid political economy analysis as critical to keeping researchers from making false promises and to pointing toward more promising areas of inquiry. Many learners and teachers I interviewed offered a vision of secondary education which places a greater emphasis on *exposing* learners to a wider variety of knowledge, skills and experiences; supporting learners' holistic development, including their development of self-knowledge and exposure to sports, the arts and other activities; and, while supporting the development of 'college-ready' learners, taking care to cultivate and nurture the diverse potentials and talents of *all* learners. Interviewees spoke to what it was like to live in an insecure home and community environment, of the vagaries of adolescence, and, in some cases, of a role that schools should play in engaging with these issues. Each of these ideas can be drawn on to carve space away from test preparation and toward the development of an education which better nurtures the broad and more humanistic values and interests expressed by learners and educators involved in this research.

Notes

[1] Each interviewee was given nine cards, each of which identified a different type of learning. Types of learning were: learning in different subjects or occupational areas; learning skills to get a job; learning about community and other learners; learning thinking skills and how to solve problems; learning social skills; learning about yourself; learning through extracurricular activities; learning values; and learning to take initiative.

[2] Balwanz (2015) provides a full chapter on methods.

[3] Balwanz and Hlatshwayo (2015) draw on empirical research in South Africa to outline possibilities for developing grassroots counter-narratives to dominant discourses on the relationship between education and the economy.

References

Balwanz, D. (2015) Re-imagining Secondary Education: voices from South African academic and vocational secondary education program. PhD dissertation, University of Maryland-College Park.

Balwanz, D. & Hlatshwayo, M. (2015) Re-imagining Post-schooling in Sedibeng: community-based research and critical dialogue for social change, *Education as Change*, 19(2), 133-150. http://dx.doi.org/10.1080/16823206.2015.1085615

Biko, S. (2004) *I Write What I Like*. Johannesburg: Picador Africa.

Centre for Development Enterprise (CDE) (2012) Routes into Formal Employment: public and private assistance to young job seekers. Johannesburg: Centre for Development Enterprise.

Chisholm, L. (1999) Why We Don't Need Matric Exams, *Mail and Guardian*, 8 January. http://mg.co.za/article/1999-01-08-why-we-dont-need-matric-exams

Chisholm, L. (2012) Apartheid Education Legacies and New Directions in Post-apartheid South Africa, *Storia della donne*, 8(1), 81-103.

Christie, P., Butler, D. & Potterton, M. (2007) Schools that Work: report to the Minister of Education Ministerial Committee on schools that work. Pretoria: Department of Basic Education.

Coffey, A. & Atkinson, P. (1996) *Making Sense of Qualitative Data: complementary research strategies*. Thousand Oaks, CA: SAGE.

Collins, R. (2013) The End of Middle Class Work: no more escapes, in I. Wallerstein, R. Collins, M. Mann, G. Derluguian & C. Calhoun (Eds) *Does Capitalism Have a Future?* New York: Oxford University Press.

Crocker, D. (2008) *Ethics of Global Development: agency, capability, and deliberative democracy*. Cambridge: Cambridge University Press. http://dx.doi.org/10.1017/CBO9780511492594

Crouch, L. (2005) *Disappearing Schoolchildren or Data Misunderstandings? Dropout Phenomena in South Africa*. Research Triangle Park, NC: Research Triangle International.

Department of Basic Education (DBE) (2013) Annual Report 2012-2013. Pretoria: DBE.

Department of Basic Education (DBE) (2014a) The Ministerial Task Team Report on the National Senior Certificate. Pretoria: DBE.

Department of Basic Education (DBE) (2014b) NSC 2013: school performance report. Pretoria: DBE.

Dieltiens, V. & Meny-Gibert, S. (2008) Poverty, Equity and Access to Education. 2008 SACHES Annual Conference Paper, Maputo, Mozambique, 17-19 July.

Dore, R. (1976) *The Diploma Disease: education, qualification and development*. Berkeley: University of California Press.

Gauteng Department of Education (GDE) (2013) Annual Performance Plan 2013/14. Johannesburg: GDE.

Government of South Africa (1996) South African Schools Act. Pretoria: Government of South Africa.

Hesse-Biber, S.N. & Leavy, P. (2011) *The Practice of Qualitative Research*, 2nd edn. Thousand Oaks, CA: SAGE.

Jansen, J. (2012) Opinion on 2012 Grade 12 Matric Results. Bloemfontein, South Africa: University of the Free State (self-published as Vice-Chancellor and Rector).

Jansen, J. & Blank, M. (2014) *How to Fix South Africa's Schools*. Johannesburg: Bookstorm.

Jansen, J. & Taylor, N. (2003) *Educational Change in South Africa 1994-2003: case studies in large-scale education reform*. Washington, DC: World Bank.

Kanfer, S. (1993) *The Last Empire: DeBeers, diamonds, and the world*. New York: Farrar, Straus & Giroux.

Kincheloe, J., McLaren, P. & Steinberg, S. (2011) Critical Pedagogy and Qualitative Research: moving to the bricolage, in Y. Lincoln & N. Denzin (Eds) *The SAGE Handbook of Qualitative Research*, 4th edn, pp. 163-177. Thousand Oaks, CA: SAGE.

Lolwana, P. (2006) The History of Falling Matric Standards, in V. Reddy (Ed.) *Marking Matric. Colloquium Proceedings*, pp. 18-29. Cape Town: HSRC Press.

McGrath, S. (2012) Vocational Education and Training for Development: a policy in need of a theory?, *International Journal of Educational Development*, 32(5), 623-631. http://dx.doi.org/10.1016/j.ijedudev.2011.12.001

Motala, E. & Pampallis, J. (2002) *Education and Equity: the impact of state policies on South African education*. Aldershot: Ashgate.

Nel, C. & Kistner, L. (2009) The National Senior Certificate: implications for access to higher education, *South Africa Journal of Higher Education*, 23(5), 953-973. http://dx.doi.org/10.4314/sajhe.v23i5.48810

Sheppard, C. (2009) *The State of Youth in South Africa: trends in education attainment*. Pretoria: HSRC Press.

Smith, W.C. (2016) An Introduction to the Global Testing Culture, in W.C. Smith (Ed.) *The Global Testing Culture: shaping education policy, perceptions, and practice*. Oxford: Symposium Books.

Spaull, N. (2011) A Preliminary Analysis of SACMEQ III South Africa. Stellenbosch Economic Working Papers, 11/11. Stellenbosch: Stellenbosch University and the Bureau for Economic Research.

Spaull, N. (2012) Challenges in Education. Presentation at 2012 Equal Education National Congress, Johannesburg, 8-11 July.

Spreen, C.A. & Vally, S. (2010) Outcomes-based Education and its (Dis)contents: learner-centred pedagogy and the education crisis in South Africa, *Southern African Review of Education*, 16(1), 39-58.

Statistics South Africa (2014) Youth Employment, Unemployment, Skills and Economic Growth 1994-2014. Pretoria: Statistics South Africa.

Vetten, L., Jewkes, R., Sigsworth, R., et al (2008) Tracking Justice: the attrition of rape cases through the criminal justice system in Gauteng. Johannesburg: Tshwaranang Legal Advocacy Centre, the South African Medical Research Council and the Centre for the Study of Violence and Reconciliation.

Wedekind, V. (2013) NSC Pass Requirements. A Discussion Document for Umalusi on the NSC Pass Mark. Pretoria: Umalusi.

CHAPTER 16

Horizontal Accountability, Municipal Capacity and the Use of Data: a case study of Sweden[1]

TRACEY BURNS, PATRICK BLANCHENAY & FLORIAN KÖSTER

ABSTRACT The global testing culture is part of the accountability challenge faced by many countries. This chapter provides an in-depth look at Sweden, which undertook a radical decentralisation of its education system in the 1990s. This has proven to be challenging to implement, and student performance has deteriorated consistently since 2000. Many municipalities have fallen short on delivering on new responsibilities, in particular in the use of data aimed at increasing local accountability. Lacking strategic guidance and capacity building from the centre, the smaller municipalities in particular have tended to use truncated indicators or traditional methods of attributing funding rather than a comprehensive analysis and plan to improve education. In addition, parents have not filled the local accountability gap, despite wide availability of comprehensive data and the liberalisation of school choice. Sweden is now faced with a serious challenge and must find a way to improve school achievement and equity.

Introduction

There has long been a demand for tailoring education to local contexts. In many countries across the Organisation for Economic Co-operation and Development (OECD), systems have moved towards greater decentralisation and increasing school autonomy as a way to respond to local demands and build flexibility into the system. These shifts in governance have led to a greater number of powerful actors (local authorities and schools, as well as parents) and a push to increasing accountability and monitoring of performance, in order to ensure and protect the quality of education being delivered over (sometimes very) vast and diverse systems.

This push has led to the increased availability of comparable data on student achievement, gathered by numerous evaluations and assessments, including standardised tests. This volume is highly relevant to modern governance challenges for many countries across the world. This chapter provides an in-depth look at one specific country, Sweden.

The Swedish education system is particularly interesting as a broad decentralisation reform in the 1990s shifted a traditionally centralised education system rapidly towards a strongly decentralised one. The decentralisation reform delegated the responsibility for running public schools to the municipalities and created a system in which national goals would be set and monitored by the central administration. Intended to improve local education systems by increasing demand sensitivity, responsibility on how to reach central goals was delegated to municipalities. In a separate reform, far-reaching school choice was introduced, encouraging schools to compete for students. The reforms were accompanied by a comprehensive system of data collection and Internet-based portals to allow public access to achievement data (Carlgren, 2009; NAE, 2009). Sweden also began participating in international tests such as TIMSS (Trends in International Mathematics and Science Study) and PISA (Programme for International Student Assessment) early on – by the late 1990s and the first PISA round of 2000. Making the results of assessments publicly available at the school level was meant to stimulate competition among schools as the public could hold the municipalities accountable based on these data. The municipalities were meant to use the comprehensive data to inform decision-making and improve their educational practices, using the knowledge and expertise at the local level. The rapid pace and scale of the reforms meant that municipalities had to quickly adapt to new responsibilities and tasks.

However, the reforms did not yield the expected results. Early on, as early as the late 1990s, the central administration noticed difficulties in the local implementation of the reforms. The concerns that the reforms of decentralisation and local competition did not have the intended positive effect on education performance were subsequently confirmed by the results of international studies of student achievement. In particular, subsequent rounds of PISA revealed that the average student performance was deteriorating over time and that the gap between and top and bottom performers was increasing.

Against this background, this chapter focuses on two research questions:

1. How are national policy goals met by the municipalities, particularly in terms of data use as a tool for steering and governance of the system?
2. What are the major challenges observed in designing and implementing such a system, and does it work as intended?

Methods and Data

The analysis is based on material gathered for Report 362, 'Municipal Responsibility in Practice', of the Swedish National Agency for Education (NAE), published in 2011 (NAE, 2011). The purpose of that report was to increase the understanding of the responsibility and influence of the municipality as the responsible authority for schools on goal attainment in schools. The report's qualitative analysis used examples from different municipalities to illustrate the thoughts and actions of municipal leaders in terms of their municipality's responsibility and their reception and management of central government instructions. A total of 42 interviews were conducted in eight municipalities in late 2009. The interviewees comprised both elected municipal politicians and appointed administrative staff.

The selection of municipalities was made in order to yield as much breadth and variation as possible, while keeping the number of interviews manageable. The selection criteria [2] were based on municipal population, geographical location, political governance, proportion of pupils in Year 9 reaching the set goals for all subjects, size of children's groups in out-of-school centres and proportion of qualified teachers.

In addition, the OECD analysis complements this information with:

- PISA 2012 (OECD, 2014) analyses and statistics from OECD's Education at a Glance (EAG) 2013 (OECD, 2013) statistics;
- Findings from the Report 'Staten Får Inte Abdikera – Om Kommunaliseringen Av Den Svenska Skolan' [the State Must Not Abdicate – on the Municipalisation Reform of the Swedish School System] (Lewin Et Al, 2014);
- Interviews with officials from the Swedish National Agency for Education, a contributor to the 2011 NAE report, and a member of the research team of the Lewin et al (2014) report.

Governance of Education in Sweden

The decentralisation reforms from 1990 onwards shifted the Swedish education system towards being among the most highly decentralised systems in the OECD. As of 2011, close to half of the decisions in public lower secondary education are taken at school level (47.2%) and 35.3% are taken at the municipal level (e.g. allocation of funds). Only 17.5% of decisions are taken at the central level (Figure 1). The central level's main responsibilities are in setting the national curriculum and monitoring outcomes of the school system, and in the case of upper-secondary education, setting the objectives for the national programmes (OECD, 2013).

At the local level, education is generally governed by the municipal assembly as the municipality's highest decision-making body and a committee system concerned with the specific policy fields – among them education. This structure is defined by the Education Act as the basic legislation of the Swedish education (governance) system, although some exceptions exist. There is no regional level of governance in the Swedish education system.

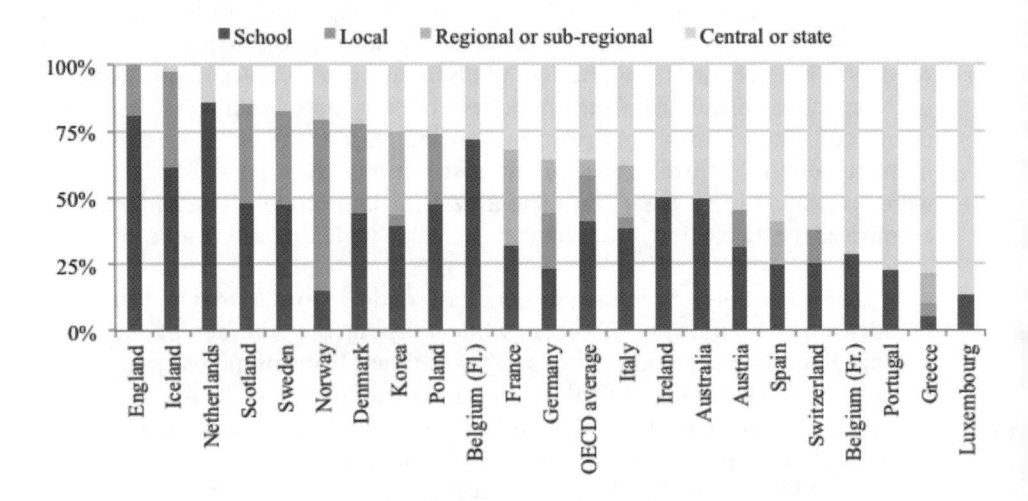

Figure 1. Levels of education decentralisation in OECD countries.
Source: OECD, 2013.

The Education Act establishes municipalities as the responsible authorities for schools, in charge of implementing educational activities, organising and operating school services, allocating resources and ensuring that the national goals for education are met. Municipalities are also in charge of other local matters, such as waste collection, public health, child and elderly care. Funding of school education is decided at the municipal level. The central government redistributes financing through state grants from wealthier to poorer municipalities via a structural equalisation system across municipalities. Since 1996, to decentralise responsibilities further, these grants have been untargeted and municipalities can allocate the funds as they see fit. Education is financed by municipal funds after redistribution.

Public schools are directly run by municipalities, with independent schools being allocated public funds according to the same principles. Financial backing of all schools is tied to their respective number of students enrolled and students' specific needs (e.g. special needs education). Comparable to the allocation of funds by the central level, the local level mainly reallocates funds towards schools usually on a lump-sum basis to provide for salaries, buildings, material and equipment. Budget administration is then performed by the school leader (OECD, 2011). Within municipalities, the general principles and objectives of schooling are decided at the Municipal Assembly level, while execution of duties is passed on to relevant committees. Figure 2 illustrates the general structure of education governance in Sweden.

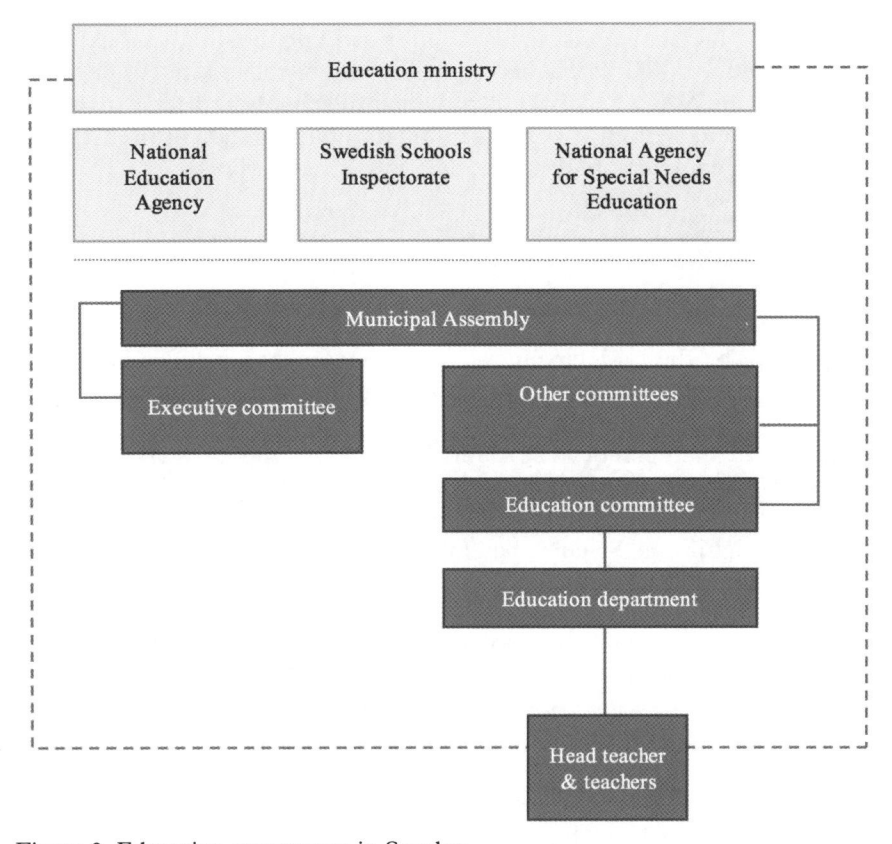

Figure 2. Education governance in Sweden.

The central government holds the overall responsibility for schooling and is in charge of developing the curriculum, national objectives and guidelines for the education system. As is typical in the Swedish public administration, tasks at the central level are shared between the respective ministry and a range of central agencies (OECD, 2011). Three agencies support the Ministry of Education and Research in the area of school education:

- The National Agency for Education (NAE) supports and evaluates the work of municipalities and schools.
- The Swedish Schools Inspectorate authorises new independent schools and ensures that municipalities, organisers of independent schools, and the schools themselves follow the centrally set laws and regulations.
- The National Agency of Special Needs Education coordinates the government's efforts regarding students with special educational needs.

These agencies are established by legislation and operate independently of the government (OECD, 2011).

The School Inspectorate, with its 290 inspectors (from a total staff of 360) and nine regional units, undertakes the actual school inspections across the country. Its activity is focused on providing qualitative feedback to schools based on site visits and specific school-related quantitative data provided by the NAE. Feedback is provided to schools and their maintainers through oral and written reports. The reports have a standardised structure that facilitates comparison over time and with other schools.

Testing and Availability of Data

The National Education Agency coordinates with the Ministry of Education and Research in setting the national goals and curriculum, which are then implemented by the municipalities. The agency manages collection, analysis and dissemination of quantitative data regarding the school system. Since 2011, national tests in the subjects of Swedish, Swedish as a second language, and mathematics are compulsory at the end of years 3, 6 and 9. Student assessments in compulsory school further take place through end-of-term reports at the conclusion of the autumn and spring terms of years 6, 7, 8 and 9. In addition, Sweden has taken part in PISA since 2000, TIMSS since 1995, and PIRLS since 2001. There is thus a wide variety of descriptive system-level data as well as testing data available to help govern the system.

All of these data are publicly available to educators, parents and communities. According to PISA 2012, over 80% of Swedish students are in schools whose principals report that achievement data are posted publicly, compared with an OECD average of 45%. Only the United States, the Netherlands and the United Kingdom have higher levels of publicly posted achievement data. Wide availability of achievement data increases transparency and allows for greater accountability of teaching practices. However, high degrees of transparency can be perceived by schools as intense scrutiny and pressure. Nevertheless, this depends strongly on how data are used and tied to formal accountability mechanisms. With Sweden being characterised by overall high levels of social trust, the decentralisation reform did not introduce sanctions for municipalities and schools that did not comply with achievement goals. In this, Sweden differs markedly from the United States and a number of other countries, where the posting of performance data is coupled with a system of sanctioning (Hooge et al, 2012; see also Smith, forthcoming).

These data and a comprehensive set of educational statistics are publicly available in two databases – SIRIS (Information System on Results and Quality) and SALSA (Local Relationship Analysis Tool) – presenting information on the characteristics and results of municipalities and schools. The Swedish Association of Local Authorities and Regions (SALAR), a consultative body designed to represent the views of local authorities, has additionally begun to publish its own analysis of National Education Agency data, developing success indicators and rankings of individual schools. The 'Open Comparisons' database presents 15 indicators on issues such as national test results, school costs and staffing. They are intended to (1) inform and stimulate the public debate about efficiency in public service; (2) support local and regional efforts to improve services; and (3) increase efficiency and control of activities (Cavalieri, 2010).

Horizontal Accountability and Capacity Building

Accountability can be differentiated into vertical and horizontal categories (Hooge et al, 2012). Vertical accountability is characterised by hierarchical relationships, with higher levels holding lower levels of governance accountable for compliance with laws and regulations as well as performance. As such, this encompasses likewise the quality of schools complying with education objectives. In a system of horizontal accountability, on the other hand, actors hold each other accountable outside of hierarchical structures. This can pertain to schools being held accountable by the wider community or teachers holding their peers accountable for their professional practice (Hooge et al, 2012).

Research has shown that vertical outcome-oriented accountability may lead to undesired effects when relying on market mechanisms, such as (adapted from Hooge et al, 2012) [3]:

- impoverishing the teaching and learning processes as a result of 'teaching to the test';
- narrowing the curriculum in order to focus on those elements that are tested;
- emphasising failure instead of learning or improvement if performance accountability lacks positive interventions designed to assist and support low-performing schools;
- reducing the quality of staff in schools serving low-performing students.

Public access to school performance data is often regarded as a mechanism of vertical accountability (Hooge et al, 2012). Importantly, there is a distinction between high and low stakes, describing whether rewards or sanctions are coupled with measured performance and 'for whom the stakes are high' – that is, whether students or educators face high stakes connected to student achievement (Hooge et al, 2012, p. 26). It has been argued that the higher the stakes are in formal accountability, the more likely the elements above are to occur (Resnik, 2006).

It should be noted that horizontal and vertical accountability are not mutually exclusive. Horizontal accountability has the potential advantage of complementing vertical accountability by broadening the input of information and offers a more well-rounded picture of education performance (Hooge at al, 2012). However, this depends crucially on capacity at the local level as the incorporation of heterogeneous inputs and reporting mechanisms requires much coordination.

In Sweden, the decentralisation of education took place rapidly and at the same time as a liberalisation of school choice. This was intended to improve education and local education systems by increasing demand sensitivity and competition among schools. Publicly posting achievement data was thus seen as necessary to provide transparency and enable parents and communities to select the schools they wanted for their children.

Decentralisation was carried out initially without much guidance from the central government to the municipalities. This was deliberate: at the onset, there was a ubiquitous concern that the central state should 'not step over the municipal boundary', warranting a non-interventionist approach. However, it became clear early on that municipalities were facing difficulties in assuming their new responsibilities. As early as 1993, the NAE reported on this and meetings between the NAE and municipal leaders were organised in 1997-98 to clarify municipal responsibilities and how municipal governance could be used to achieve national goals (NAE, 1996, 1997). Taking these steps did not signal a change in the NAE non-interventionist stance, as it was believed that these were just birth pangs of the reform and that municipalities would gradually be able to embrace their new responsibilities (Lewin et al, 2014).

The lack of intervention from the central government meant that municipalities would be, by design, left to their own initiative when it came to improving school performance. This expectation, however, has not always played out as planned. In particular, Lewin et al (2014) make very clear that some municipalities were insufficiently prepared. The municipalities did not necessarily have adequate governance structures or the internal culture to implement collaborative decision-making and widen input into decision-making processes. They did not receive or seek capacity building or training to make this possible. In many cases, local government was unclear about the changes in responsibilities the reforms entailed and did not provide adequate structures to facilitate the involvement of lower-hierarchy levels in the decision-making process. In turn, lower-hierarchy levels did not want to be held responsible for poor performance because of decisions taken at higher levels of local government.

Part of the challenge for municipalities is that the decentralisation reform was accompanied by deregulation and the introduction of school choice, thus giving parents and students more power at the same time that local authorities were handed individual responsibility for education. To some extent, this interaction has restricted what the municipalities could do, in the sense that they are also answerable to increasingly well-informed parents and in competition with a strong set of independent schools. This has given rise to the perception among some municipal actors that local government 'administrates the system rather than steers it' (Swedish researcher). Thus, in the Swedish case, being held accountable horizontally by parents and the broader community created a tension with the vertical (hierarchical) accountability of the municipalities to the central administration.

While in Sweden the stakes are relatively low (as the central level has only very limited levers to step in if national education objectives are not met), the interviews do indicate an over-emphasis on evaluated subjects (mathematics, Swedish, English) over non-evaluated ones. Whereas horizontal accountability can complement vertical accountability mechanisms, it relies crucially on enabling structures and processes and, as a prerequisite, adequate competence of the local authorities and, ultimately, the schools.

The capacity to use available data for thorough reflection and strategic decisions about education is fundamental to establishing accountability relationships across levels of the municipal administration and with community stakeholders. Yet, the interviews point to a lack of capacity for using assessment data to monitor and improve education systematically. Instead of carefully selecting and using indicators and research generated by the system, decision makers tended to prefer other sources of knowledge, such as traditional spending choices and simple comparative measures (instead of holistic assessment of cause and effect), and even followed pressure from the media and parents without due diligence. The following section explores this in more detail.

(Mis)use of Available Data

As mentioned above, the Swedish education system has relatively high levels of formal accountability mechanisms. Today, almost all students in Sweden (96%) are in schools that use assessment data to monitor the school's progress, above the OECD averages of 81%. Despite such high levels of formal accountability, the education system struggles to achieve national objectives and performance. In fact there is great concern about declining levels of performance in international comparisons. In PISA 2012, Sweden performed significantly below all other Nordic countries in mathematics. PISA trend data show that Sweden has declined from a position around or above the OECD average in 2000 to a position significantly below the average. No other PISA-participating country saw a steeper decline over the past decade than Sweden. These results, among other international comparisons, have provoked a national debate about governance, accountability and achievement.

These results coupled with a decentralised governance system that permits free school choice make it clear that that the availability of data per se to encourage stronger local accountability does not automatically lead to better performance. Although there are certainly elements of the evaluation and assessment system that could be improved, the challenge appears to be more related to how data are being used for accountability purposes rather than to their availability.

The decentralisation reform intended for municipalities to manage education based on regular assessment of their performance against nationally set goals and requirements. The interviews highlight that, in practice, municipalities rely heavily on such statistics as the Swedish Association of Local Authorities and Regions' (SALAR's) 'Open Comparisons' for assessment of their performance. Other diagnostic tools such as those mentioned above are taken into account comparatively rarely, despite their wide availability. Part of SALAR's appeal to municipal decision-makers is precisely its aforementioned simplicity. The higher political level appreciates the fact that SALAR's Open Comparisons provide an accessible overview of the situation and of the status in relation to other municipalities. 'I am an economist and not an expert on schools. I look at SALAR's summaries' (Chair of the Executive Committee, NAE, 2011, p. 40).

Municipalities also often prioritise particular forms of evidence (e.g. media-friendly rankings) that are deemed important politically but do not represent the depth and breadth of information necessary for making strategic choices for the long-term development of education. School rankings are indeed sometimes used by local politicians to exonerate themselves from responsibility. The Open Comparisons database reports calculations that take into account pupil composition in order to assess schools' actual performance against their expected performance given pupil composition. This is often used as an excuse for municipal leaders to argue that poor performance would be due to pupils' background rather than their own schooling strategies: 'We cannot do anything about the parents' background' (NAE, 2011, p. 42). The over-emphasis on external factors for achieving adequate performance (i.e. reaching national goals) is accompanied by a lack of analysis of potential causes of failure, which in turn leads to unchanged expectations of the municipal leaders regarding their schools' performances year to year.

Furthermore, the interviews point to a general lack of self-assessment. Rather, municipalities rely on the assessment by the inspectorate and on SALAR's results, and do not necessarily allocate enough resources to build their own monitoring system. At the time the interviews were conducted, quality reports were designed at the local level and were required to contain an assessment of the extent to which schools meet national goals; the objective was to provide a framework that allowed municipalities to remain in touch with the education situation in their jurisdiction. However, interviews show that quality reports were often discussed by the committee and were not passed on to the assembly. Instead, the assembly's role was limited to important decisions, such as decisions over school vouchers or school closure. This meant, in practice, that municipal assemblies did not build the appropriate expertise to discuss school performance with regard to national goals. The New Education Act, which took effect in 2011, removed the necessity for municipalities to draft such quality reports and instead stressed systematic school development work, and the move was complemented by a strengthening of the inspectorate's role in assessing schools' performance.

This analysis makes it clear that simply making achievement data available does not immediately translate into stronger accountability regimes or indeed better achievement. Too often, relevant knowledge is available but not rigorously used for strategic decision-making by higher levels of administration within municipalities. Instead, they rely on truncated indicators and do not sufficiently harness knowledge by stakeholders at grassroots level. Of the available knowledge and evidence, media-friendly rankings are clearly preferred, even though they are more useful for political purposes than for long-term strategic development of a culture of assessment in schooling. When a wide range of data becomes available, it becomes easier for individuals in charge to select the indicators that will paint a more favourable picture. Against this background, one interviewee stated, 'One cannot blame them [the municipal leaders] for being rational' (Swedish researcher).

Knowledge, Power and Capacity

By design, the education system in Sweden separates the role of the national government – steering – from the effective implementation of strategies at the local level. However, the interviews highlight a gap between perceived duties by local stakeholders and the corresponding definitions of formal powers.

Respondents indicated that municipalities veered away from national goals in several ways, and that there seemed to be very little enforcement of those goals from the national level. First, municipalities, facing budgetary constraints, often focused on a subset of the national goals, most often those that drew public and media attention. There was a strong tendency to make use of the indicators that enable comparison between municipalities and that appear in SALAR's Open Comparisons. Overall, the interviews gave a picture of the municipal priorities being cherry-picked, and when resources were not available to meet all goals and requirements, there was uncertainty among municipal leaders as to which of the national goals should be prioritised.

Second, when setting goals for their municipalities, local politicians often lowered requirements from the nationally set levels to levels more compatible with the municipalities' attainment expectations. In particular, interviews indicated that the national goals were seen as idealistic targets, rather than realistic ones. This mismatch between goal-setting and achievement, coupled with unclear lines of responsibility, has additionally resulted in pessimistic views of municipal actors' own efficacy, and a sense of not knowing how to tackle something as multifaceted as improving student achievement.

Crucially, there is no real enforcement mechanism for central authorities to ensure compliance with the goals, or at any rate, there seems among the interviewees to be little concern over the consequences of not meeting a particular goal. Given this, the government can only rely on emulation and competition between municipalities as mechanisms for encouraging compliance. Interviews clearly show concerns, particularly among elected officials, for comparison rankings between municipalities and statistics that receive media focus nationally, such as the SALAR's 'Open Comparisons' statistics. However, while interviews indicate that these rankings are very important for local politicians, their very existence seems to have distorted efforts away from other less specific national goals in favour of measurable (and comparable) goals. This also does not serve to reinforce the broader national agenda.

Finally, interviews show that the discrepancy between duties and actual powers generates frustration at the municipal level, as many interviewees expressed the view that they are doing more than they are officially assigned to do without necessarily having the official powers to do so, or without receiving due recognition. This is matched by frustration felt by a central level that finds itself responsible for slipping student achievement and yet with very few levers to effect change. Although there are talks at the national level to require more transparency from municipalities about their needs, resources and spending, it is not yet clear how the central government plans to use such data. This echoes a more general problem facing education as well as many other sectors: the tension between central steering and local autonomy. It is a careful act of balancing that the central government must do in order to steer the educational system and provide coordinated policies while preserving the autonomy of municipalities, an important element in the political culture of Sweden.

In addition to elements of power and responsibility, the municipalisation reform generated a gap between duties and capabilities. At all levels of the system, interviewees explained that their hands were often tied by decisions made elsewhere and that they had to do the best they could with what they had. They blamed poor performance on insufficient financial resources, and on political bargaining at the municipal level that does not lend enough weight to education.

From the interviews, it is clear that there is a lack of capacity for the efficient use of resources to enable the smooth functioning of the system. There may also be a lack of capacity, particularly in smaller municipalities, to ensure that education issues reach the top of the municipal agenda. In order to understand the needs of the system, municipal authorities must use different sources of knowledge, including the experiences of local actors in defining and solving problems in schools and classrooms. This is a nuanced skill and process, which requires connections to relevant stakeholders, the forums and capacities to gather and use achievement and assessment data, and the ability to formalise and make explicit what is often tacit or procedural knowledge.

Quality education provision requires both short-term planning and delivery and long-term strategic vision. A system characterised by high local variation will have to work extra hard to ensure comparability and alignment across the various governance arrangements and assessment and data structures. Currently municipal decision-making is too often done using poor or partial data, with an overemphasis on rankings and other media-friendly elements. This not only leads to a discrepancy between the real needs of the schools and system, it also prioritises short-termism over long-term strategic thinking. While this will be particularly an issue in smaller municipalities with less capacity for using data and strategic planning, it is also a weakness across the entire system, including at the central level.

Conclusion

This chapter provides an overview of twenty years of decentralisation reform in Sweden. By shifting decision-making to the local level, the reform was motivated by the assumption that education would be better managed as needed by local context. The shift in responsibility was accompanied by the expectation that the municipalities would assume responsibility for the performance of their schools. By doubling this devolution with a reform of school choice, it additionally made the bet that citizens would hold schools and municipalities accountable for education performance, either by voting directly or by voting with their feet.

However, municipalities have had difficulties embracing their new responsibilities. Although the use of comparative data on schools and media-friendly rankings is a powerful political and decision-making tool, without an appropriate culture of evaluation and a deep understanding of how to effect change in complex systems, municipal leaders may have the temptation to leave difficult issues unaddressed. At the same time, and somewhat puzzlingly, citizens do not exert sufficient power over Municipal Assemblies to make schools and teachers a priority, both in terms of a protected budget and in terms of holding schools accountable for substandard achievement. Whether this is an awareness issue (i.e. a belief that the system is more or less satisfactory) or a motivation issue (as long as your children are fine there is no need to intervene on the system level) remains unclear.

The reforms undertaken by the Swedish education ministry exemplify some of the challenges of standardised testing and accountability underlying this volume. The case study of Sweden makes it clear that despite the best intentions, increasing decentralisation and introducing free school choice have failed to ensure the quality and equity of the education system. This largely appears to be because the mechanisms for increasing local accountability – transparent and open access to data for local authorities and parents alike – have not been used in the manner intended. Lacking strategic guidance and capacity building from the centre, the smaller municipalities in particular appeared overwhelmed. This resulted in the use of truncated indicators or traditional methods of attributing funding rather than a comprehensive analysis and a strategic vision to improve education. Such a well-rounded picture requires the whole range of available knowledge, ranging from testing results to local stakeholder insights.

This work provides a look into the complexity of education governance from the perspective of the interplay between municipal capacity, horizontal accountability and data use. Complex systems are characterised by multi-dimensionality, non-linearity, interconnectedness and unpredictability. After a series of bold and innovative reforms, Sweden is experiencing first-hand the power and challenge of steering such multi-layered systems and the difficulty of changing course when reforms generate unexpected results. It is now clear that Sweden is facing a tipping point, and the time is right to harness the momentum for change.

One last comment: a note of caution is necessary regarding the findings of this chapter. This small sample of municipalities and interviews might not be representative of all Swedish municipalities, and thus these findings cannot be simply generalised to the entire country. In addition, this chapter does not include the voice of a major stakeholder: the teachers. Including their voices is essential when seeking solutions for the challenges laid out here. However, this analysis can still shed light on local dynamics at play regarding school responsibilities. As such, it offers crucial insights into the perceptions of municipal stakeholders and the way they have adapted to the deep reforms made since the early 1990s. It also sets out the scale of the challenge facing Swedish authorities as they seek to improve their system in the coming years.

Notes

[1] This chapter builds on a more comprehensive case study of Sweden's education reform (Blanchenay et al, 2014) conducted as part of the OECD's Governing Complex Education Systems (GCES) project (www.oecd.org/edu/ceri/gces).

[2] For a full description of municipalities and methodology, please see Blanchenay et al (2014).

[3] See also Ladd, 2001; Kane & Staiger, 2002; Ladd & Zelli, 2002; Resnick, 2006; Feng et al, 2010; Rosenkvist, 2010; Morris, 2011; Smith, forthcoming.

References

Blanchenay, P., Burns, T. & Köster, F. (2014) Shifting Responsibilities – 20 Years of Education Devolution in Sweden: a governing complex education systems case study. OECD Education Working Papers, no. 104. Paris: OECD Publishing. http://dx.doi.org/10.1787/5jz2jg1rqrd7-en

Carlgren, I. (2009) The Swedish Comprehensive School – Lost in Transition?, *Zeitschrift für Erziehungswissenschaft*, 12(4), 633-649. http://dx.doi.org/10.1007/s11618-009-0103-1

Cavalieri, P.A. (2010) Open Comparisons (OC) 'Focus on Quality, Improving and Evaluating What We Do'. Swedish Association of Local Authorities and Regions, PowerPoint Presentation.

Feng, L., Figlio, D. & Sass, T. (2010) School Accountability and Teacher Mobility. Working Paper 47. Calder Urban Institute.

Hooge, E., Burns, T. & Wilkoszewski, H. (2012) Looking beyond the Numbers: stakeholders and multiple school accountability. OECD Education Working Papers, no. 85. Paris: OECD Publishing. http://dx.doi.org/10.1787/5k91dl7ct6q6-en

Kane, J.K. & Staiger, D.O. (2002) The Promise and Pitfalls of Using Imprecise School Accountability Measures, *Journal of Economic Perspectives*, 16(4), 91-114. http://dx.doi.org/10.1257/089533002320950993

Ladd, H.F. (2001) School-based Educational Accountability Systems: the promise and the pitfalls, *National Tax Journal*, 54(2), 385-400. http://dx.doi.org/10.17310/ntj.2001.2.09

Ladd, H.F. & Zelli, A. (2002) School-based Accountability in North Carolina: the responses of school principals, *Educational Administration Quarterly*, 38(4), 494-529. http://dx.doi.org/10.1177/001316102237670

Lewin, L., Hammargren, L., Andersson, U & Erikson, J. (2014) Staten får inte abdikera – om kommunaliseringen av den svenska skolan [The State must not abdicate – on the municipalisation reform of the Swedish school system]. Statens Offentliga Utredningar SOU 2014:5, Stockholm.

Morris, A. (2011) Student Standardised Testing: current practices in OECD countries and a literature review. OECD Education Working Papers, no. 65. Paris: OECD Publishing.

National Agency for Education (NAE) (1996) Kommunernas styrning och egenkontroll [Muncipal steering and self-monitoring]. Stockholm: National Agency for Education (Skolverket).

National Agency for Education (NAE) (1997) Ansvaret för skolan en kommunal utmaning [The responsibility for schools – a challenge to municipalities]. Stockholm: National Agency for Education (Skolverket).

National Agency for Education (NAE) (2009) What Influences Educational Achievement in Swedish Schools? A Systematic Review and Summary Analysis. Stockholm: National Agency for Education (Skolverket).

National Agency for Education (NAE) (2011) Municipal Responsibility in Practice: a qualitative study. Report 362. Stockholm: National Agency for Education (Skolverket).

Organisation for Economic Co-operation and Development (OECD) (2011) OECD Reviews of Evaluation and Assessment in Education: Sweden 2011. Paris: OECD Publishing. http://dx.doi.org/10.1787/9789264116610-en

Organisation for Economic Co-operation and Development (OECD) (2013) Education at a Glance 2013: OECD indicators. Paris: OECD Publishing. http://dx.doi.org/10.1787/eag-2013-en

Organisation for Economic Co-operation and Development (OECD) (2014) PISA 2012 Resources: policies and practices in Sweden. Report prepared for the Swedish National Agency for Education.

Resnick, L.B. (2006) Making Accountability Really Count, *Educational Measurement: issues and practice*, 25(1), 33-37. http://dx.doi.org/10.1111/j.1745-3992.2006.00050.x

Rosenkvist, M.A. (2010) Using Student Test Results for Accountability and Improvement: a literature review. OECD Education Working Papers, no. 54. Paris: OECD Publishing.

Smith, W.C. (forthcoming) National Testing Policies, School Practices, and Student Outcomes: an analysis using data from PISA 2009. Education Working Papers. Paris: OECD Publishing.

Notes on Contributors

Brian Abery is a co-director of the Educational Assessment and Intervention core area at the Institute on Community Integration (ICI) and an adjunct faculty member within the Institute on Child Development and School Psychology Programs at the University of Minnesota. He has been principal investigator of numerous projects designed to enhance the educational outcomes, social inclusion and self-determination of persons with disabilities at both a national and an international level. His international work includes implementation of the Response to Intervention framework in India and the implementation of Inclusive Service Learning in Costa Rica. He holds a PhD in Educational Psychology/School Psychology and has an extensive background in research, assessment, program development and evaluation related to children, youth and adults with disabilities.

Sumera Ahsan is a doctoral student at the University of Massachusetts Amherst. She works as an assistant professor at the Department of Educational Evaluation and Research, Institute of Education and Research, University of Dhaka, Bangladesh. She also worked at the Institute of Educational Research, BRAC University, Bangladesh, as a lecturer. She is interested in educational assessment policies and practices in global context with a special emphasis on developing countries. She has also worked as consultant for the World Bank, Save the Children, UNESCO, UNICEF and Verulam Associates Ltd in areas such as quality of student assessment, project evaluation, technology in education, and teacher training & professional development. She has published several articles and books on educational assessment in Bangladesh. She was also involved in textbook writing and teacher training programs in Bangladesh.

Karen Egedal Andreasen holds a PhD in education and is Associate Professor in Education and Pedagogical Assessment at the Department of Learning and Philosophy, Aalborg University, Denmark. Her main interests concern questions of socialisation, social mobility and processes of inclusion and exclusion and marginalisation in different educational contexts.

Notes on Contributors

Hilla Aurén completed her MA in International Studies at the University of Denver's Josef Korbel School of International Studies, where she was a recipient of the PEO International Peace Scholarship, in 2014. A native of Finland, she has previously worked for the Finnish Ministry for Foreign Affairs and in international development in the Middle East and Central Asia. Her main research interests lie in the areas of development, education, good governance and peace-building.

David Balwanz is a postdoctoral research fellow at the Centre for Education Rights and Transformation at the University of Johannesburg, South Africa. His current research focuses on secondary education and youth development in low- and middle-income countries. David holds a PhD in International Education Policy/Political Economy from the University of Maryland-College Park.

Angeline M. Barrett is a senior lecturer in education at the University of Bristol, UK. For the last 15 years, she has conducted a range of research on the quality of basic education in sub-Saharan Africa. This includes work on teacher professionalism, pedagogic practices, social justice conceptualisations of quality and the development of innovative bilingual learning materials.

Patrick Blanchenay is an economist in the OECD's Directorate for Science, Technology, and Innovation. He holds a PhD in Economics at the London School of Economics, where he was also a Teaching Fellow. Prior to joining the OECD, his research revolved around skill accumulation in agglomerations. He also holds an MRes in Political Theory from Sciences Po Paris. and an MSc in Management from HEC Paris.

Sandra G. Bowman, EdD, is a senior researcher at the University of Arkansas working on the Math Science Partnership, Pre-K School Portal, Mathematics Portal, and other projects focused on improving educational outcomes for students. She is an expert on assessment and evaluation models designed to assess the effectiveness of educational programs.

Tracey Burns heads the Governing Complex Education Systems project in the OECD's Centre for Educational Research and Innovation (CERI). She also directs the Centre's work on Trends Shaping Education. She holds a Master of Arts and PhD in Psychology from Northeastern University, USA. Previous to her current work she worked on social determinants of health and on education and social inclusion issues both at the OECD and in Vancouver, Canada.

Hyeonwoo Chea is an elementary school teacher and a field researcher in Gyunggi Province, South Korea. She is a doctoral candidate at the Department of Education, Educational Administration, at Yonsei University in Seoul. Her research interests include accountability policy systems, social capital and school effectiveness for students with disadvantaged backgrounds, and comparative analysis of national education systems.

Pearl J. Chung is a PhD candidate in the Department of Education, Curriculum and Instruction, at Yonsei University in Seoul, South Korea, finishing her studies with funding from the Korean Global Scholarship Program (KGSP). Prior to this, she was a Global Apple Scholar and an elementary/middle school teacher at the Academy for Urban School Leadership in Chicago, Illinois. Her research interests include curriculum and instruction for students with disadvantaged backgrounds, accountability policy systems, and comparative analysis of national education systems.

D. Brent Edwards Jr. is currently an assistant clinical professor of educational administration and international education at Drexel University, Philadelphia, USA. His work focuses on the political economy of education reform and global education policies, with a focus on low-income countries. Previously, he has worked with the University of Tokyo; the University of California, Berkeley; the University of Amsterdam; the Autonomous University of Barcelona; the George Washington University; the Universidad Centroamericana; and the World Bank. In addition to his work appearing in such journals as *Comparative Education Review*, *Comparative Education*, *Journal of Education Policy*, *Prospects* and *Education Policy Analysis Archives*, among others, he has a forthcoming book, titled *International Education Policy and the Global Reform Agenda: education with community participation in El Salvador* (Palgrave MacMillan).

Bjørn Hamre has a PhD in History and Education (2012), and is currently assistant professor at Aarhus University. His work mainly concerns the sociology and history of diagnosing, special needs education and inclusion in an international perspective. He is engaged in developing the analytical use of Michel Foucault's concept of dispositive. He is chair of the Danish section of the Nordic Network on Disability Research (nndr.dk).

Devin K. Joshi is currently Associate Professor in the School of Social Sciences at Singapore Management University. Author of over two dozen academic journal articles and book chapters, his most recent co-authored book is *Strengthening Governance Globally: forecasting the next 50 years* (Paradigm/Oxford University Press, 2014). His research focuses on education policy, comparative politics and international relations.

Rie Kijima is a lecturer at the Stanford Graduate School of Education. Her research interests include education in developing countries, the politics of foreign aid, the impact of social policies on educational outcomes. With funding from Education International, she is completing her two-year postdoctoral research on why countries participate in cross-national assessments. Prior to starting her doctoral studies at Stanford University, she worked at the World Bank on education projects in the Middle East/North Africa and East Asia/Pacific regions.

Florian Köster is a consultant at the OECD's Centre for Educational Research and Innovation (CERI), on the Governing Complex Education Systems project. He holds a MA in Government (specializing in Public Policy and Comparative Politics) from the University of Konstanz, Germany, and a MRes in Political Science from Universitat Pompeu Fabra, Spain.

Kristine Kousholt has a MA in Danish Literature and Psychology (2004), a PhD (2009), and has been an associate professor since 2015. Her work primarily concerns assessment practice and teachers' and pupils' perspectives on and participation in educational standardised testing.

Jane Leer is a research specialist in the Department of Education and Child Protection at Save the Children, USA. She holds a Master's degree in International Education Policy Analysis from the Stanford Graduate School of Education and a Bachelor's degree in Development Studies from the University of California, Berkeley. Her research addresses the role of international aid in educational development, the links between education and socioeconomic development, and early childhood education.

Ji Liu is a PhD student in Comparative International Education and Economics at Teachers College, Columbia University. His research focuses on human capital theory in rural and development contexts, and pays particular attention to cross-national policy instruments, institutions and processes. He was born in Xian, China, and first arrived in the United States as a sponsored KU-IIE scholar through the Institute of International Education. He graduated with a Bachelor of Science degree in Education from the University of Kansas, and received his Master of Arts degree in International Education Development from Columbia University.

Sean W. Mulvenon, PhD, is Professor of Educational Statistics at the University of Arkansas and created the National Office for Measurement and Evaluation Systems (NORMES) in 1998. Since that time he has worked with numerous state educational agencies (SEAs) and spent 31 months as a senior adviser to the Deputy Secretary at the US Department of Education. He has developed large-scale data systems, growth models and policy associated with testing and assessment practices at both the SEA and national levels. He has served as a consultant on research projects in the United Arab Emirates, India and China.

NOTES ON CONTRIBUTORS

Mariam Orkodashvili has been affiliated with Peabody College of Education and Human Development, Vanderbilt University; UC Berkeley; Edinburgh University; Max Planck Institute for Social Anthropology; Tbilisi State University; Georgian American University; and the Parliament of Georgia. Her research interests include access to education; international large-scale data and comparative education; corruption in education; social cohesion and education; education and economic development; neural theory of metaphor; cognitive linguistics; language typology and universals. She has published articles in *European Education*, *Sociology of Education*; *Equity in Higher Education: theory, policy, and praxis*; *Journal of the European Higher Education Area*; *Comparative and International Education*; *International Perspectives on Education and Society, vol. 13: The Impact of International Achievement Studies on National Education Policymaking*; and *Peabody Journal of Education*.

William C. Smith is a senior associate with RESULTS Educational Fund, where he is developing the Right to Education Index (RTEI). Prior to this position he completed a dual-title PhD in Educational Theory and Policy and Comparative International Education at Pennsylvania State University and was a Thomas J. Alexander Fellow at the Organization for Economic Co-Operation and Development (OECD). His research addressing education's role in international development and educator-based testing for accountability has resulted in over 15 publications in high-impact journals such as *Social Science and Medicine*, *Education Policy Analysis Archives* and *Practical Assessment Research and Evaluation*.

Anthony Somerset is a Visiting Research Fellow at the Centre for International Education, University of Sussex. He has worked as an educational practitioner and research worker in developing countries since 1963, initially in Uganda, then in Kenya, where, as Head of Research at the newly established Kenya National Examinations Council, he was involved in a major examinations reform programme. More recently he has worked in a number of countries in South and South-East Asia, including Sri Lanka, Nepal, Indonesia and the Philippines.

Renáta Tichá received her PhD in Educational Psychology with emphasis on Special Education from the University of Minnesota, Minneapolis. She works as a Research Associate at the University of Minnesota's Institute on Community Integration. She has extensive experience in the development, implementation and evaluation of assessments and interventions for children, youth and adults with different types of disabilities on both a national and an international level. Her international work is focused on the development and validation of formative assessments for struggling learners in Indian elementary schools as well as on the development of a technology-based progress monitoring system for students with significant disabilities in the Russian Federation.

Christian Ydesen holds a PhD in history of education from the University of Aarhus, Denmark. He is currently an associate professor at the Department of Learning and Philosophy, Aalborg University, Denmark. His main interests are education policy, educational assessment, international organisations and education in multicultural contexts.

Oxford Studies in Comparative Education

Series Editor: David Phillips

Other volumes in this series....

Students, Markets and Social Justice: higher education fee and student support policies in Western Europe and beyond, eds. Hubert Ertl & Claire Dupuy, 2014

Transnational Policy Flows in European Education: the making and governing of knowledge in the education policy field, eds. Andreas Nordin & Daniel Sundberg, 2014

Internationalisation of Higher Education and Global Mobility, ed. Bernhard Streitwieser, 2014

PISA, Power and Policy: the emergence of global educational governance, eds. Heinz-Dieter Meyer & Aaron Benavot, 2013

Low-fee Private Schooling: aggravating equity or mitigating disadvantage? ed. Prachi Srivastava, 2013

Higher Education and the State: changing relationships in Europe and East Asia, eds. Robin Goodman, Takehiko Kariya & John Taylor, 2013

Education in South-East Asia, eds. Colin Brock & Lorraine Pe Symaco, 2011

Reimagining Japanese Education: borders, transfers, circulations, and the comparative, eds. David Blake Willis & Jeremy Rappleye, 2011

Education, Conflict and Development, ed. Julia Paulson, 2011

Politics, Modernisation and Education Reform in Russia: from past to present, ed. David Johnson, 2010

The Globalisation of School Choice? eds, Martin Forsey, Scott Davies & Geoffrey Walford, 2008

The Changing Landscape of Education in Africa, ed. David Johnson, 2007

Aspects of Education in the Middle East and North Africa, eds. Colin Brock & Lila Zia Levers, 2007

Exploring Cross-national Attraction in Education: some historical comparisons of American and Chinese attraction to Japanese education, ed. Jeremy Rappleye, 2007

Education's Abiding Moral Dilemma, Sheldon Rothblatt, 2007

Partnerships in Educational Development, eds. Iffat Farah & Barbara Jaworski, 2006

Political and Citizenship Education, Stephanie Wilde, 2005

The Challenges of Education in Brazil, eds. Colin Brock & Simon Schwartzman, 2004

Educational Policy Borrowing: historical perspectives, eds. David Phillips & Kimberly Ochs, 2004

Further details of the over 40 volumes in this series can be found at
www.symposium-books.co.uk
and can be ordered there, or from
Symposium Books, PO Box 204, Didcot, Oxford OX11 9ZQ, United Kingdom
orders@symposium-books.co.uk